James Stonehouse

Universal restitution a Scripture doctrine

James Stonehouse

Universal restitution a Scripture doctrine

ISBN/EAN: 9783337175269

Printed in Europe, USA, Canada, Australia, Japan

Cover: Foto ©Andreas Hilbeck / pixelio.de

More available books at **www.hansebooks.com**

Universal Restitution

a
Scripture Doctrine.

This prov'd in several LETTERS

WROTE ON THE

Nature and Extent of CHRIST's Kingdom:

WHEREIN

THE SCRIPTURE PASSAGES,

Falsly alleged in PROOF of

The Eternity of Hell Torments,

Are truly translated and explained.

Εἰ δὲ οἱ τοὺς ἀνθρωπίνους οἴκους διαφθείροντες, θανάτῳ καταδικάζονται· πόσῳ μᾶλλον οἱ τὴν Χριστοῦ διδασκαλίαν νοθεύειν ἐπιχειροῦντες, αἰωνίαν τίσουσι δίκην, ὑπὲρ ἧς σταυρὸν καὶ θάνατον ὑπέμεινεν ὁ Κύριος Ἰησοῦς, ὁ τοῦ Θεοῦ μονογενὴς υἱός· καὶ τὴν διδασκαλίαν ὁ ἀθετήσας, λιπανθεὶς καὶ παχυνθεὶς, εἰς γέενναν χωρήσει; ὉΜΟΊΩΣ ΔΕ καὶ πᾶς ἄνθρωπος, ὁ τὸ διακρίνειν παρὰ Θεοῦ εἰληφώς, κολασθήσεται, ἀπείρῳ ποιμένι ἐξακολουθήσας, καὶ ψευδῆ δόξαν ὡς ἀληθῆ δεξάμενος.

IGNATII Epist. ad *Ephes.*

Sold by R. DODSLEY, in *Pall-Mall*, LONDON;
and T. CADELL, in *Wine-Street*, BRISTOL.
MDCCLXI.

THE

Subject of each Letter respectively.

LETTER I.

THE English words eternal, everlasting, forever, &c. are unscriptural, and express not the true import of the original words æon, olem [αιων עלם] - - - - - - - - - - - - - 1

LETTER II.—*The kingdom of* Christ *which is call'd æonian* [αιωνιος] *is not eternal* - - - - - 23

LETTER III.—*Christ's kingdom what, and where it is, and when it began* - - - - - - - 34

LETTER IV.—*Christ's kingdom will consist of many successive parts or periods* - - - - - - - 64

LETTER V.—*The term* ÆONIAN [αιωνιος] *applied to the word* SPIRIT, *imports not that he is eternal* - 78

LETTER VI.—*Logos, the only begotten son of God, is the true æonian spirit* [αιωνιον πνευμα] *and distinct as such from the father* - - - - - - 105

LETTER VII.—*Farther remarks on* Christ's *æonian character, implying his personal distinction before insisted on.* - - - - - - - - - - - 118

As touching æonian restitution wrought by *Christ*,

LETTER VIII.—GOD *wills* EFFECTUALLY *that all men shall be restored* - - - - - - - - 135

LETTER IX.—*Of the explicit and implicit will of* GOD - - - - - - - - - - - - - 144

LETTER X.—Chrift *in his character of a reftorer* (æonian αιωνι⊙) *confidered at large* - - - 160

LETTER XI.—*The property of* Chrift *as redeemer may be doom'd to æonian fufferings* - - - - 208

LETTER XII.—*The doctrine of an univerfal reconcilement to* GOD *in* Chrift, *excludes not that of the damnation of the wicked* [εις τον αιωνα] *æonianly* - 229

LETTER XIII.—*The efficacy of* Chrift's *facrifice muft extend to all his creatures* - - - - - - - 244

LETTER XIV.—*The extent of the promife* (Rev. xxi. 4.) *that death fhall be no more* - - - - 270

LETTER XV.—*In* Chrift *the firft fruits, the whole creation is deem'd holy before* GOD - - - - 293

LETTER XVI.—*A paffage in the epiftle to the* Hebrews (viz. ch. ii. 8, 9.) *confider'd: and the fallen angels compared with fallen men* - - - - - 318

The fcripture paffages objected againft the doctrine of univerfal reftitution from

2 Cor. iv. 17.		XVII. - 337
1 Tim. i. 17.		XVIII. 345
Matt. xxv. 46.		XIX. 358
Eph. iii. 10.	confidered in LETTER	XX. - 367
Heb. xiii. 20.		XXI. 382
Matt. xxvi. 4.		XXII. 394
Heb. ii. 16.		XXIII. 411

☞ The QUOTATIONS in the learned languages, found in the notes, are all tranflated into Englifh at the end of the book, as are the other quotations in the text.

Universal Restitution, &c.

LETTER I.

That the English words eternal, everlasting, for ever and ever, &c. are unscriptural, and express not the true import of the original words (αιων עלם) æon olem.

TO ———

SIR,

WHAT I have to advance upon this great truth, the RESTITUTION of all things, will be drawn mostly from two considerations. 1st. From a consideration of the kingdom of GOD to be established by divine management in the person of the God-man *Christ Jesus*: And 2dly from a consideration of the present fallen nature and disposition of the creature; but more immediately of the human soul.

These two points will divide my enquiries into two parts, the first of which will respect the kingdom of GOD. But as preliminary hereto I must begin with what I take to be the true import of the words עלם olem and αιων æon, the foundation of the mistake I have so often complained of.

SECT. I.

The word עלם olem, its meaning and force.

THE word עלם olem (or עולם owlem) which the Septuagint translate (wherever it respects time) by the greek word αιων (and which translation seems to have been the occasion of the frequent use of that word αιων afterward among the greek christians) it is well known, is usually in our Old, as is also the word αιων in our New Testament, render'd by the english words eternal, everlasting, and without end; but how justly is the question in debate.

This word עלם olem among the *Hebrews* signified as a verb to hide, to conceal, to reserve in darkness and secrecy[a]; as a noun, uncertain, indefinite, undetermined, undeclared; and consequently

---

NOTES.

[a] *Thus* Job xxviii. 21. *it is hid* (λιληθε נעלמה *it hideth itself*) *from the eyes of all living, and kept close from the fowls of the air.* Eccl. xii. 14. GOD *shall bring every work to judgment with every secret thing,* (כל נעלם) *whether it be good or whether it be evil.* Pſ. x. 1. *Why ſtandeſt thou afar off, O* LORD, *why hideſt thou thyſelf* (תעלים) *in time of trouble?* So *Lev.* iv. 13; v. 2, 3, 4. *Num.* xv. 13. 2 *Kings* iv. 27. *Job* xlii. 3. *Lam.* iii. 56. *Nah.* iii. 11. 1 *Kings* x. 3. *Prov.* xxviii. 27. *Iſ.* i. 15. *Pſ.* xliv. 21.

ly, applied to a person it means an uncertain indeterminate person [b]; and applied to time (its only use which at present concerns us) an indefinite, undeclared, tho' very long, time. [c]

The word αιων among the *Greeks* signified in its genuine meaning **an age or so long as very old men live, a term of about an 100 years**; yet sometimes the *Greeks* applied it to a much longer term than an 100 years, and sometimes to a shorter term [d]: **So that the word** αιων **aion corresponds tolerably with**
the

NOTES.

[b] 1 Sam. xvii. 56. *And the king said enquire thou whose son this unknown person* (זה העלם i. e. הנער see v. 55.) *is.* Gen. xxiv. 43. *Behold I stand by the well of water, and it shall come to pass that when that unknown woman* (העלמה i. e. אשה see v. 40.) *cometh forth to draw water and I say unto her, &c.*

[c] Ex. xii. 14. *And you shall keep this day* **a feast by an ordinance** (עולם) *of long undetermined antiquity.* Is. lxi. 4. *And ye shall build up the desolations* (עולם owlem) *of long undetermined antiquity.* Jer. xxv. 9. *I will bring Nebuchadnezar against this land, and against the nations round about, and* **will destroy them utterly and make them deserts** (עולם owlem) *of long undetermined antiquity.* Mich. ii. 9. *The women of my people* (*of Judah*) *have ye* (*Israelites*) *cast out from their pleasant houses, from their children have ye taken away my glory* (לעולם) *for an age or long undetermined season.*

[d] αιων signifies the space of an 100 years, tho' the destruction of the *Jews* foretold *Mat.* xiii. 40. (η συντελεια τα αιωνος τετε) came to pass before 50 Years. See *Leigh*'s *Critica Sacra* upon the word αιων; and *Tully* it seems renders this greek word by the latin word *Annus* a year, and by *Sæculum* an age.

the word עלם olem in its use, tho' not in its natural import; for tho' αιων æon signifies, not as עלם olem hidden, cover'd, concealed, indefinite, unascertained, yet as applied to time it denotes, what is very like this, a long tho' undetermined portion or period of time.

SECT. II.

The word (αιων) means not eternity.

HOWEVER that the word αιων æon, even in the scripture acceptation of it, cannot signify, what we moderns mean by the word eternity, will appear for the following reasons.

First, Because such meaning of it is in many Instances repugnant to other parts of scripture; so 2 *Cor.* iv. 4. *In whom the* GOD τȣ αιωνος τȣτȣ *of this æon has blinded the minds of them that believe not, &c.* Now supposing the word æon to mean age and not eternity[e], *Satan* may here be aptly exhibited

---

NOTES.

[e] Since the words αιων αιωνος עלם עולם olem owlem have no word in the *English* language that will answer their use, I shall beg leave, as I shall have occasion, to make use of the words æon æonian to express them. Also as the word eternity in the modern notion of it (tho' not in its natural import) means a perpetuity endless and never ceasing, I shall henceforward mean thus much by the terms eternal and eternity.

exhibited to us in this grand and horrible description of him, the god of this age, or æon; but it were blasphemy to call him the god of eternity, besides the absurdity of stiling him the god of *this* eternity; for the word *this* so used must imply some other eternity besides the present, and two eternities are an inconsistency in terms.

Again, *Eph.* vi. 12. *We wrestle not against flesh and blood—but against the rulers of the darkness* τȣ αιωνος τȣτȣ *of this æon.* But translate the word æon here eternity, and this passage would be, *against the rulers of the darkness of this eternity;* so 1 *Cor.* i. 20. *Where is the wise, where is the scribe, where is the disputer* τȣ αιωνος τȣτȣ *of this æon,* and not of this eternity; 1 *Tim.* ii. 6. *Charge them that are rich* εν τω νυν αιωνι *in the now æon,* (not in the now eternity) *that they be not high-minded, &c.* so *Tim.* ii. 12. *That denying ungodliness and worldly lusts we should live soberly, righteously and godly* εν τω νυν αιωνι *in the now æon;* so *Mat.* xiii. 22. The seed among the thorns is, *he that heareth the word and the care* τȣ αιωνος τȣτȣ *of this æon* (not of this eternity) *and the deceitfulness of riches, choke the word and he becometh unfruitful, &c.* For what common sense can endure that the word αιων æon in these places should be thus render'd by the word eternity? [f] Secondly,

---

N O T E S.

The term αιων *in scripture no substitute for the term* κοσμυς.

[f] THE translators of our New Testament, sensible of this absurdity, have render'd the word αιων age in these places (as if a substitute or succedanum for

Secondly, That the word αιων does not signify eternity is also clear, because there was a time before

---

NOTES.

κοσμῶ) by the word world; viz. The rulers of this (αιων) world, the disputers of this (αιων) world, the rich in the present (αιων) world, &c. But without reaching the intention of the scripture, for it is the age and not the world which the scripture every where complains of. The worldly inhabitants of the present age are wicked, but the worldly inhabitants of a future age shall be righteous. The ruler of darkness in *(i. e.* the dark ruler of*)* this age is *Satan*, the ruler of a succeeding age, even upon this world of ours, will be *Jesus Christ*.

So that the cares of this æon are the cares of the people of this age; and a conformity to this æon is a conformity to the people of this age, &c. And so εις τον αιωνα, tho' it may be render'd phraseologically as long as the world stands, yet in its true force it means as long as the age (that is the great age of wickedness which comprehends many other lesser ages of the same kind) endures. This world will weather out many ages, and that not only the ages of rebellion, but also ages of godliness and peace. To suppose therefore the word αιων æon age, to be equivocal with the word κοσμος kosmos world, is without farther proof unreasonable: But besides this, and besides that we have no precedent for translating it so out of any of the *Greek* heathen authors whose works are transmitted down to our times, this way of translating the word will also make many scripture passages, more than absurd, even arrant nonsense, as the few following examples, which have very many like them, will demonstrate.

The term αιων then being translated world, the following texts will be translated as follows: *Mat.* vi. 13.

before (αιων) æon was, yea before the æons plural were; *e. g. Acts* xv. 18. *Known unto* GOD *are all his works* (απ' αιωνος) *since the æon (i. e.* the great comprehensive æon) *began. Acts* iii. 21. *Spoken by the mouth of his holy prophets* (απ' αιωνος) *since the æon began. John* ix. 32. (εκ τε αιωνος) *since the æon began, was it not heard that, &c.* And in the same
sense

NOTES.

Thine is the kingdom and the power and the glory (ις τες αιωνας) to the worlds. *John* vi. 15. *He that eateth of this bread shall live* (εις τον αιωνα) to the world. *ch.* xi. 20. *He shall not die* (εις τον αιωνα) to the world. *Heb.* xiii. 8. Jesus Christ *the same yesterday, to day* (και εις τες αιωνας) *and to the worlds. Rom.* xiv. 11. *The smoke of their torments ascendeth up* (εις αιωνα αιωνων) to a world of worlds. *Heb.* xiii. 20. *The* GOD *of peace who thro' the blood* (διαθηκης αιωνιου) of the worldly covenant. *Mat.* xix. 16. *The rich man says to our* LORD, *what shall I do to have* (ζωην αιωνιον) worldly life. 1 *Tim.* vi. 12. *Fight the good fight of faith, lay hold on* (αιωνιε ζωης) worldly life. *John* xii. 25. *He that hateth his life* (εν τω κοσμω τετω) *in this world, shall keep it* (εις ζωην αιωνιον) to worldly life. *Rom.* xvi. 26. *According to the commandment* (τε αιωνιε θεε) of the worldly God. *Heb.* ix. 14. Christ *who* (δια πνευματος αιωνιε) through the worldly *spirit offer'd himself to* GOD, *&c.*

But what common sense will admit of the strange impertinence of the above translations of the terms αιων, αιωνιος?

So that unless we claim a like use of the word æon as is related of a nose of wax, which its owner could convert and transform at pleasure, its vulgar translations (namely world, eternal, &c.) must be renounced.

sense are used æons, ages, in the plural number; *e.g.*
1 Cor. ii. 7. *The hidden mystery of* God *pre-ordain'd
unto his glory.* (προ των αιωνων) *before the æons began,
which none of the princes* (τε αιωνος τετε) *of this æon
knew.* Eph. iii. 9. *The mystery which has been hid
in* God (απο των αιωνων) *from the beginning of the æons.*
Col. i. 26. *The mystery that has been hid* (απο των
αιωνων ϗ απο των γενεων) *from the æons and the generations, but now is made manifest unto his saints.*

Thirdly, It is evident again, that the word æon
cannot signify eternity, because there are more
æons than one; whereas eternity, everlastingness,
and for ever, must be an individual, as implying
an unity of consistence, and simple continuance.
Luke xx. 34. *And* Jesus *said unto them, the children* (τε αιωνος τετε) *of this æon marry, and are given
in marriage, but they which shall be accounted worthy to obtain* (τε αιωνος εκεινε) *that other æon, and
the resurrection from the dead, neither marry, nor
are given in marriage, &c.*

Here we find *this* and *that*, and consequently
two æons, a distinction observable in many parts
of scripture; so 1 Cor. ii. 6. *Yet not the wisdom*
(τε αιωνος τετε) *of this æon which comes to nought.* Rom.
xii. 2. *Be not conform'd* (τω αιωνι τετω) *to this æon.*
And in a like distinguishing sense, we often find
mentioned the cares, the wisdom, the men, the
things, the children (τε αιωνος τετε) of this æon;
all which imply that there must be some other
æon beside the present, and consequently more
æons than one.

Fourthly, That the word æon cannot mean
eternity is evident yet farther, because there

are

are not only more æons than one, but these æons succeed one the other, as the links of a chain, the one beginning where the other ends; *e. g.* Mat. xii. 32. *But whosoever speaketh against the Holy Ghost it shall not be forgiven him, neither* (εν τετω τω αιωνι) *in this æon,* (ουτε εν τω μελλοντι) *nor in that to come.* Eph. i. 21. *And set him at his own right hand in heavenly places, far above all principality, and power, and might, and dominion, and every name that is named, not only* (εν τω αιωνι τετω) *in this æon, but also in that which is to come.* Gal. i. 4. *Who gave himself for our sins that he might seize us* (εκ τε ενεςῶτ͂ αιων͂τ πονηρε) *out of this present wicked æon.* Eph. ii. 7. *That* (εν τοις αιωσι τοις επερχομενοις) *in the æons to come, he might shew the exceeding riches of his grace*; so 2 Tim. iv. 10. *Demas is said to have forsaken* Paul *because of his love to the present æon.* Whereas Christians are described *Heb.* vi. 4, 5. *Such as have tasted of the heavenly gift, and have been made partakers of the Holy Ghost, and have tasted the good word of* God, '*and the power (or virtue)* ² *of the æon to come,* (ܛܒܐ, ' ܕܐܠܗܐ, ² ܘܚܝܠܐ ')

The present æon therefore, as it began, so will it also end; and in its end be succeeded by an æon to unfold itself in a most essential difference and dissimilitude from the past.

Fifthly, From hence also it appears again, That the word (αιων) æon cannot mean eternity because it must end, and be no more; of which we have further assurance, *Mat.* xxviii. 20. *And lo I am with you* (πασας τας ἡμερας) *all the days, even to the end* (τε αιωνος) *of the æon.* Mat. xiii. 29. *the harvest is the end* (τε αιωνος) *of the æon*; v. 40. *So shall it be in the end* (τȣ αιων⁃ τȣτȣ) *of this æon.* Mat. xxiv. 3. *What shall be the sign of thy coming, and of the end* (τȣ αιων⁃) *of the æon.*

Sixthly, And not only æon singly and indefinitely, but (οι αιωνες) the æons plural, shall also have an end. *Heb.* ix. 26. *But now once about (or towards) the conclusion (or closing up together) of the æons* (επι συντελεια των αιωνων) *he appear'd, to put away sin by the sacrifice of himself.* 1 Cor. x. 11. *And they were written for our admonition upon whom the ends* (των αιω.ων) *of the æons are come.*

※※※※※※※※※※※※※※※※※※

S E C T.   III.

Farther remarks upon the word (αιων) *æon.*

THO' the word (αιων) æon to a cursory reader may seem only a trite familiar term of no other import than vulgar use has given it; yet if one critically observes its variety, use, and acceptations in scripture; one may easily suspect that very mysterious truths may be couched in the diversity of its forms, and peculiarity of its applications. At least the æons, intelligently observed, must appear to be periods or portions of time, working together, by a divine mechanism, the will of GOD. For it is clear they have their beginning and end in what we call time, and are circumscribed by it, in the same manner as the several spherical systems that seem to mete out the universe,

verse, are altogether comprehended in space, are wholly circumscribed by it. And as the many systems of worlds promote and act their several appointed tasks in the boundless tracks and vast embrace of space: Thus the æons, operating in the capacity of time, have their several changes and revolutions to disclose, their several courses of mercies and judgments to exhibit, their several degrees of revelations and disciplines to unfold, with variety of strange and unsearchable parts and expedients and issues to produce, towards the successive reconciling, digesting, and ripening the many creatures subsisting in them, to the various purposes of GOD, and to their glorious ends and uses in eternity, or when time itself shall be no more.

Here many, convicted with these evidences of the temporal purport of the word æon, contend, that tho' in its proper signification and common use it may not denote eternity, yet that when applied to things of an eternal nature, its meaning is enhanced, and it acquires in scripture language, their force. That thus when we read of believers, *That* Luke xvii. 13. John xi. 26. *they shall live, or that they shall not die* (εις τον αιωνα) to the age. *That* John xiv. 16. *the comforter shall abide with them* (εις τον αιωνα) to the age. *That* 1 John ii. 2. *the truth shall dwell in them* (εις τον αιωνα) to the age. And of *Christ* John xii. 34. Heb. vii. 24. *that he abideth, continueth* (ܠܥܠܡ) to the age. *That* 2 Cor. ix. 9. Heb. i. 8. 1 Pet. i. 23. 1 John ii. 17. *his righteousness, his throne, his word, his will, remaineth, abideth, continueth* (εις τον αιωνα) to the

the age. *That* Heb. v. 6. vii. 28. Chrift *is a prieſt and conſecrated* (ܠܥܠܡ) *to the age. That* Heb. xiii. 8. *he is the ſame yeſterday, to day, and* (ܠܥܠܡ) *to the age*[g]. *And that glory be to him* (εις τας αιωνας των αιωνων) to the ages of the ages.
We

NOTES.

The true force of the jewiſh (ܠܥܠܡ) Lolm, *rendered in Greek by* εις τον αιωνα.

[g] IT is obſerved by ſome, and it ſeems very juſtly, that the word ܠܥܠܡ among the *Jews* rendered in Greek by εις τον αιωνα was a ſort of phraſe or idiomatical expreſſion of common uſe to ſignify at random a long doubtful time, as when we ſay in engliſh, while the world ſtands.

So we read 1 *John* iii. 8. *Peter ſaid thou ſhalt never* (εις τον αιωνα *to the age*) *waſh my feet.* Mat. xxi. 19. *Let no fruit grow on thee henceforth* (εις τον αιωνα) *to the age, or while the world ſtands.* John viii. 35. *The ſon abideth in the houſe* (viz. *of his father,* εις τον αιωνα) *to the age, or continually, or as long as he lives.* John vi. 51. *He that eateth this bread ſhall live* (εις τον αιωνα) *to the age, or continually.* 1 Cor. viii. 13. *If meat maketh my brother to offend, I will eat no fleſh,* (εις τον αιωνα) *to the age, or continually, or while the world ſtandeth, leaſt I make my brother to offend.* John xii. 34. *We have heard that* Chriſt *abideth* (εις τον αιωνα) *to the age, or continually, i. e.* without leaving the earth.

Now if this be ſo, the frequent application of the phraſe ܠܥܠܡ (or εις τον αιωνα) to things truly æonian is very accountable; for in the hebrew and other eaſtern languages we obſerve a familiar uſe of the figure meioſis, whereby, as ſay the rhetoricians, *Res extenuatur ultra verum*, or *minus dicitur quam intelligitur*; that is, whereby more is implied in an expreſſion than that expreſſion naturally imports.

We cannot understand by the word æon, so applied to these promises, declarations, and doxologies, any time short of eternity. But

---

NOTES.

So *Rom.* iv. 19. *And being not weak in Faith, &c.* Here the extenuating term not *weak*, the apostle explains in the following verse, as meaning (v. 20.) *being strong in faith.* Rev. xii. 11. *And they loved not their souls unto death*; i. e. John xii. 25. *And they hated their souls unto death.* Heb. xi. 16. *Wherefore* GOD *is not ashamed to be called their* GOD; by the expression not ashamed, we are here to understand, that, *Is.* lxii. 4. *He is delighted to be called their* GOD. So *Acts.* xvii. 28. *He* (GOD) *is not far from every one of us, for in him we live, and move, and have our being*; by the expression not far from, we are to understand most intimately present with every one of us: But to illustrate this the better, I will here present to your view a few instances of this vulgar jewish phrase (לעולם) lolm (that is, εις τον αιωνα) to the age, in contrast with a few other Instances of the figure Meiosis in scripture use.

| The figure Meiosis used in The phrase לעולם (or εις τον αιωνα) to the age. For in this phrase, tho' itself *expresses* only a less, intelligible, and decisive period; is *imported* yet a larger, unintelligible, and undetermined period.

לעולם.

John iv. 14. *He that drinketh of this water shall not thirst* לעולם (or εις τον | The figure Meiosis used in terms, which tho' *expressing* only moderate and diminutive particulars; yet *import* particulars of a far larger and sublimer nature.

Other Instances in contrast.

Is. xl. 28. *Hast thou not known that the æonian* GOD, *Jehovah, the creator* |

But is not this cavilling rather than arguing? If I was to say, that tho' the word smooth in its proper signification does not denote roundness, yet

---

NOTES.

αιωνα) to the age; that is to the utmost limits of this present secular state of our existence, hereby however is implied other succeeding periods, still far beyond.

John xiv. 16. *That he* (i. e. *the comforter*) *may abide with you* (εις τον αιωνα) to the age, *i. e.* and not only so, but to periods unknown and far beyond the age.

Luke i. 33. *And he shall reign over Jacob* (εις τον αιωνα) to the age, *i. e.* and not only so, but to periods far beyond this, even continually.

John x. 28. *And they shall not perish* (εις τον αιωνα) to the age, *i. e.* and not only so, but also for periods far beyond this, even to the utmost æon.

Mat. iii. 29. *He that blasphemeth against the Holy Ghost shall not be forgiven*, (εις τον αιωνα) to the age,

of the ends of the earth, fainteth not? The greatness of Jehovah is here express'd only in his being creator of the ends of the earth, yet in this diminishing particular, he is to be understood as God, the founder of all the universe.

Ps. lxxii. 11. *Kings shall fall down before him, all nations shall worship him.* (v. 17.) *His name shall be continued as long as the sun, and all nations shall call him blessed.* Here again, tho' the worship of kings and nations only are express'd, yet under them, all the powers of heaven, and all the realms of other worlds are implied, as also to become his worshipers. So again, tho' his reign is here express'd only by the continuance of the sun, yet thereby is imported the far exceeding extent of his dominion and autho-

yet that when applied to a bowl which is in its own nature round, this term smooth acquires one and

---

NOTES.

that is, and not only so, but also far beyond this.

Lam. v. 19. *Thou Jehovah shalt remain* (לְעוֹלָם) lowlem *to the age, and thy throne to generation and generation, i. e.* shall remain not only to the age, but also to a duration infinitely beyond human conception, even to eternity; for, as has been by many observed, the scriptures, which delight in types and analogy, do usually intend far more in their letter then the verbal scribe is aware of, or the critical infidel will venture to acknowledge, tho' to the seeing eye it be easily discernible.

rity even to the end of the æons.

Ps. cxxi. 6. *The sun shall not smite thee by day nor the moon by night; Jehovah shall preserve thee from all evil.* Tho' the particulars from which Jehovah's people shall be preserved, are here express'd by the heat of the sun and moon, yet therein is intended all the evils of fallen nature, both in our present, and in our every other state of life.

Ps. xc. 2. *Before the mountains were brought forth, and thou hadst formed the earth and world, and from age to age thou art* God. And so again in this passage, by the terms *before the mountains were brought forth*, there is no doubt but we must understand far more then the words themselves do naturally import.

So then in the scantiness of scripture terms we have often to expect a meaning of the greatest latitude, and yet that latitude discovered will not prove any natural and adequate comprehensiveness in the terms implying it.

and the same import with the word round; and that therefore when I say a smooth bowl I must mean a round bowl; would you not laugh?

If it be a just inference that because the word æon is often applied in scripture to eternal things, therefore it must mean eternal; it may be as fairly pronounced that the word smooth is often applied to round things, therefore it must denote roundness.

Again, if the word æon is to signify eternity only when adjunct to objects of a suppos'd eternity, this its comprehensive import being no more than its object gives it, one needs only deny the eternity of the object, and the comprehensiveness (*i. e.* the eternal import) of the adjunct fails with it.

In other words, if the term smooth is to denote roundness only when adjunct to objects of a supposed roundness, one need only to deny that an object is round, and then the word smooth ceases to denote its roundness.

Again, if the word (αιωνιος) æonian is not to prove the eternity of the noun substantive to which it is adjunct, but the said noun substantive the eternal import of its adjunct (αιωνιος) æonian, then is the term (αιωνιος) æonian become as useless towards any proof of a thing's eternity as if it had never been applied to it at all.

Or in other words; if the term smooth is not to ascertain the roundness of a bowl, but the bowl (which is called smooth) is to ascertain a globular import in the term smooth, then does the term smooth become as useless towards any proof of an object's being a bowl, as if it had never been applied to it at all. In

In short, as the word smooth does not import a globular form, neither does the word æonian import an eternal duration; and therefore **as** one may call a bowl a smooth body without denoting thereby that it is globular, so one may call an eternal object æonian, without denoting thereby that it is eternal.

However, not to be tedious upon this absurdity, I shall prove lastly as follows:

SECT. IV.

PROPOSITION.

*To things of an eternal nature (or supposed by our adversaries to be so) terms of a finite limited intention may be applied, without having such their natural limited import changed, without becoming thereby characters of **eternity**.*

PSALM lxxxix. 36. *His seed* (יהוה לעולם) *shall be æonian and his throne as the sun before me; it shall be established* (עלם) *æonianly, as the moon, and as the rainbow* (or faithful witness in heaven) v. 29. *His seed also* (ישבתי לעד) *I establish secularly* (or to a seculum, age) *and his throne as the days of heaven.* Pf. lxxii. 5. *They* (i. e. the church) *shall revere thee as long as the sun and moon endureth, throughout all generations.* V. 17. *His name shall be* (לעולם) *to the æons, his name shall be continued as long as the sun.*

Now since these passages, and many others of like expression, apply the establishment of the sun, the duration of the moon, of the rainbow, of the days of heaven, of an age, and of the generations of men, in order to illustrate the continuance of the church of GOD, and of the seed of CHRIST and of his throne, and kingdom, and name, and glory, without supposing any alteration in nature, without supposing any unnatural continuance of such sun, moon, rainbow, age or days of heaven; why must these things, *viz.* the throne, the kingdom, the name, the glory of CHRIST, because of their eternal nature, have a different effect upon the words (עלם αιω) olm æon, when applied to them?

The duration of the sun, moon, and rainbow, is allowed to be only temporal, notwithstanding things of an eternal nature are compared to their continuance; why then may not the words עלם and αιων retain the temporal import which is natural to them, notwithstanding they may therein be applied to eternal things?

Yea, and unless the terms olm and æon import a duration as far short of the word eternity, in our modern notion of it, as is the duration of the sun, moon, rainbow and generations, which must all pass away and reach their end; the holy writers mislead us in blending the expressions (לעלם ܠܥܠܡ) lolm (i. e. εις τον αιωνα to the age) with the duration of the sun, moon, rainbow and generations, in one and the same sentence, and as if terms of equal force; since by such application they teach and unteach, averring the same

things

things to be of finite duration and of infinite duration in one and the same line; for if it be needful to believe that our Saviour's throne and his church and his name as head of such shall endure to all eternity, then is that a misleading comparison which shall date its perpetuity by the enduring of the sun, moon, rainbow and generations, which all must pass away.

And on the other hand, if it be not a point needful to be believed that the LORD's throne and church shall continue to all eternity; then may we without scruple declare aloud that the word (αιων) æon means not eternity, and that the idea of eternity can never be prov'd by the word æon in any form of it; and that whatever part of speech we may shift it into, it can no more pronounce the eternity of any thing by becoming its adjunct, than the duration of the sun, moon, rainbow, or foundations of the world can pronounce the eternity of the subject with which they, or any of them, may stand in comparison.

Yea a man might with a more tolerable assurance suppose the sun and moon to be eternal, than that the word æonian means eternal; because the scripture no where says, in express terms, that the sun and moon shall pass away, whereas it declares in express terms that the earth shall pass away, and that on that earth so to pass away the seed of *Abraham* shall have the land of *Canaan* for an æonian possession. So *Gen.* xvii. 8. *And I will give unto thee and thy seed after thee all the land of Canaan for an æonian* (עולם) *possession,* Gen. xiii. 15. (עד עולם) *even to an æon* (Ex. xxxii.

13. *and they shall inherit it æonianly* (לעלם) *to an æon.* Is. lx. 21. *They shall inherit the land* (לעולם) *to an æon,* Ezek. xxxvii. 25. *and they shall dwell therein, even they and their children, and their childrens children* (עד עולם) *even to an æon, and my servant David shall be their Prince* (לעולם) *even to an æon.*

But if after certain æons are pass'd away, 2 Pet. iii. 10. *The heavens shall pass away with a great noise, and the elements shall melt with fervent heat; the earth also and all the works that are therein shall be burnt up;* what must then become of the æonian land of *Canaan?* From the face of our Saviour, *Rev.* xx. 11. *The earth and heaven shall fly away;* and will not the land of *Canaan* fly away with it? How then will it be, or have been, an æonian possession to the seed of *Abraham* supposing æonian to mean eternal? When at the last day, the stars shall fall from heaven, and all the worlds we see, starting from their spheres, shall crush together in one vast ruin, our little world will be lost in the immence combustion; and then must the land of *Canaan* also be no more.

And if the land of *Canaan* will not be an eternal possession to the seed of *Abraham,* then neither is it promised to be so, and consequently the term (עלם) olm cannot mean eternal, but still it must mean an æonian possession: and as we have already shewn that there are many æons, and that these æons will succeed one the other, and at last will all of them have an end, we must search for the meaning of the word (αιωνιος) æonios in time and not in eternity.

LET-

LETTER II.

That the Kingdom of CHRIST *which is called æonian, is not eternal.*

TO ——

SIR,

THE vulgar fenfe of the Greek words αιων αιωνι⊙, &c. and as they are rendered in our englifh bibles eternal, everlafting, for ever and ever, affording the moft prevailing arguments againft that beautiful truth, the Reftitution of all things, it was the bufinefs of my former letter to prove that thofe words are miftranflated.

My next labour ought to be the afcertaining the true meaning of thefe words; but this cannot well be done otherwife than by a previous account of the kingdom of *Chrift*; becaufe, as the diftinguifhing **character of** this kingdom is that it is æonian, the word æon, in its feveral applications throughout the fcriptures, will always allude

to,

to, and bear such alliance and affinity with the kingdom of *Christ*, as that its notion and latitude will be determined by it.

Thus indeed our task considerably enlarges, yet, since my work requires it, I will undertake it chearfully. And to obviate the error of *Christ*'s kingdom being eternal, my first point to prove must be as follows:

LETTER II.

SECT I.

Christ's æonian kingdom will not be eternal.

IT has been the usual method with divines to prove the eternity of *Christ*'s kingdom from the words æon and æonian (αιων αιωνι☉) being so often applied to it: and yet at other times, and on other occasions, they argue that the words æon and æonian (αιων αιωνι☉) must signify eternal, because spoken of *Christ*'s kingdom which, say they, is eternal.

Now if it can be proved that *Christ*'s kingdom is not eternal, it will follow that the words æon and æonian (αιων αιωνι☉) not only cannot be thus converted to these purposes, but that the words themselves must import some limited duration, for that *Christ*'s kingdom is and will be æonian is beyond dispute.

The word eternal is used by divines to import a twofold duration, and must therefore be considered in its different acceptations. Eter-

Eternity then 1st and in its strictest sense and propriety, imports duration abstracted from quantity and mutability; or existence altogether, without any flux or succession of parts prior or posterior to each other: and this the schools call *perpetuum nunc*, perpetual now; others, unsuccessive duration or absolute immutability.

But since eternal in this notion of the word cannot be applied either to the kingdom of *Christ*, or to the land of *Canaan*, or to any other creature; we will consider, 2dly, the word eternal as meaning duration in succession, or as a series of times infinitely protracted; an infinitely perpetuated chain of distinct NOWS.

Now in this account of the word eternal, the difficulty is that at the same time that *Christ* is declared the æonian GOD, and his kingdom the æonian kingdom, his gospel also is stiled the æonian gospel, *Rev.* xiv. 6. and the land of *Canaan* is promised to the *Jews* for an æonian possession, *Gen.* xvii. 8. which applications quite confuse the meaning of the term, since we know not what to understand determinately by this term so differently applied.

If we are to understand by the term æonian when applied to *Christ* the æonian GOD, that he is of immutable duration; we must not understand by the same term, when applied to *Christ*'s kingdom, that this is not of immutable duration, but of infinitely progressive duration.

However, to connive at this, what are we farther to understand by this term eternal when applied to the gospel, or to the *Jews* æonian inheritance in the land of *Canaan*?

LETTER II.   [26]   SECT. I.

To the *Jews* is promised the land of *Canaan* for an æonian possession, and yet this land can neither be of duration immutable, nor of duration infinitely progressive; for it must have an end when this world shall be destroyed. And the same may be objected to the æonian gospel, since the gospel also, when its testimony shall be superseded by our immediate vision of *Christ*, (καταργηθησεται) 1 *Cor.* xiii. 8, 12. shall be invalidated, or rendered useless, and so will not be eternal in either of these acceptations.

But if the kingdom of GOD, and his gospel, and the inheritance of the *Jews* in the land of *Canaan* be all æonian; if all and each of them have the word æonian equally and respectively applied to them, then have they all that which the word æonian imports in common; and consequently as the word æonian applied to the jewish inheritance of the land of *Canaan* is no proof that *Canaan* will be a land of eternal duration; neither is the same word applied to the kingdom of GOD, a proof that the kingdom of GOD will be of eternal duration in either senses of the word eternal.

However, for our better security of this consequence, and as a more certain evidence that the kingdom of GOD will not be eternal, we have the words of St. *Paul*, 1 *Cor.* xv. 24,—27. *Then cometh the end when he shall deliver up the kingdom to God even the father; when he shall have* (καταργηση) invalidated *all principality and authority and power, for he must reign 'till he has put all enemies under his feet. The last enemy that shall be* invalidated (καταργηται) *is death* (or, Heb. ii. 14. *He who has the*

power

power of death, that is the devil) for he has subordinated (ὑπεταξεν) *all things under his feet.* But when he says that all is subordinated (ὑποτετακται) to him, it is manifest that he is excepted who did subordinate all things unto him; and when the all shall be subordinated unto him, then shall also the son himself be subordinated (ὑποταγησεται) unto him who subordinated all things unto him, *that* GOD *may be the all in all.*

In which words we find comprised the following Points, viz.

1st. That our saviour's kingdom shall have an end.

2dly. That its end shall be after a previous subordination of all things to himself.

3dly, That its end shall be by a surrender of the kingdom unto GOD the father.

4thly. And shall be attended with a subordination of the son to the father: And

5thly. That this final subordination of *Christ*, being the ultimate end and point in view of all his wishes, must be the uttermost completion (or πληρωμα) of the joy that was set before him.

The kingdom of *Christ* is that which he rules and conducts as mediator. But when all things shall be subordinated unto him, and shall with one breath say unto him " my LORD, my GOD, " my ALL," then will *Christ*'s mediatorial office cease, as having attained its purpose; and so ceasing, that great comprehensive æon of his mediatorial kingdom will be accomplished, and will be succeeded by a purely divine œconomy, wherein

Christ will no longer reign as mediator, but as GOD, and one with his father.

And thus we understand our LORD's words, *Luke* xxii. 37. *For the things concerning me have an end*; by the word ME he means himself as mediator, and by the end which the things concerning him should have, he means a final conclusion of his mediatorial office: for a mediator is, *Col.* i. 20. *A peace maker*, Rom. v. 10, 11. *A reconciler*, 1 John ii. 1. *An advocate:* so that finity and determination are implied in the very term; when therefore the creature's subordination is accomplished, and in consequence thereof every creature is become perfectly at peace with, and perfectly reconciled to GOD, then is also our LORD's business as a mediatorial advocate accomplished, and at an end.

SECT. II.

Four points requisite.

WE find in scripture frequent mention of four points destined to be necessary to this great end. Two of these are fulfilled; namely,

First, Our LORD's sacrifice and satisfaction by virtue of which *Heb.* vii. 3. *He abideth a priest continually* (or ܠܥܠܡ æonianly or through all the æonian life, and not as other priests ceasingly. See *Heb.* x. 1.)

Secondly, His instalment into his father's throne of which we read, *Heb.* x. 12. *He is set down at the*

the right hand of God (ܠܝܡܝܢܐ) æonianly, that is, he is to continue head and king over his church, and with a view to this over all the creatures, till the end of his government is answered.

But the two following points are still in expectation and unaccomplished, viz.

Thirdly, That GOD shall make the enemies of *Christ* his footstool; of which we read *Mat.* xxii. 44. Jehovah *said unto* Adni *sit thou on my right hand till I make thy foes thy footstool*; as likewise in the 24th verse above quoted; *he* (*i. e.* GOD) *hath put all enemies under his feet*: for it is remarkable that our mediator waits for his possession from the immediate donation of his father: so *John* vi. 37. *All that the father giveth me shall come unto me*; and the like as to his exaltation, of which we read, *Eph.* i. 20. *He* (GOD) *raised him from the dead, and set him* (or caused him to sit) *at his own right hand in the heavens, far above all principality, and power, and might, and dominion, and every name that is named*, not only in *this* æon, *but also in the* future; so that being already made the powerful sovereign of all the obedient children of GOD of whatever kind and degree, he shall also be made so over all the rebellious part of the creation, for that these in due time shall also be made his footstool: and this effected, the fourth point shall ensue, namely,

Fourthly, These the enemies of *Christ* shall by *Christ* be reconciled to their GOD, who is already reconciled to them; of which we read, 2 *Cor.* v. 19. *God was in Christ reconciling the world unto himself*. And again, *Col.* i. 20. *And by him to*
reconcile

reconcile all things unto him (having made peace by the blood of his cross, by him I say) *whether they be things on earth, or things in heaven.* And again, *Phil.* ii. 10, 11. *In the name of Jesus every knee shall bow of things in heaven, and things on earth, and things under the earth, and every tongue shall confess that Jesus Christ is Lord to the glory of God the father.*

So then we have to expect that after *Christ's* kingdom shall have lasted thro' several generations and æons, even to the utmost æon very far beyond the end of this world, and probably long after the new heaven and the new earth; when (by a management most divinely wise, and merciful, and righteous, and within compass of *Christ's* æonian kingdom) GOD shall have put down all unchristian power, dominion and authority, and shall have put under the feet of *Christ* every enemy, even lastly satan himself who is the prince, or has the power, of death; and when *Christ* shall have effected the general Restitution, by the reconciling of all things to GOD, and by the making all things new; and in consequence hereof shall have extinguished all pain and sorrow and death; *Rev.* 21. Then shall 1 *Cor.* xv. 28. (καὶ αυτος ὁ ὑος,) even the son himself, *Col.* i. 15. (πρωτοτοκος πασης κτισεως,) the first begotten of every creature, now his father's substitute and lieutenant, deliver up his vicarial and æonian, or temporary power, together with all the subjects of it, to GOD, even the father; and become thenceforward, together with all the subjects of his now harmonizing kingdom, subordinate, that is voluntarily,

luntarily, as the complement of his desires and end of his ministry, unto God; that so God may be himself immediately *the all in all*, communicating himself in fullness to all his saints, and admitting them to an union with the Deity without farther intercession of the mediator.

SECT. III.

Christ's *kingdom how without end.*

NOW to this doctrine is very reasonably objected the passage in *Luke* i. 33. *And of his kingdom there shall be no end.*

And to this we answer, that the end of the Messiah's reign as Messiah, or anointed one, will be the beginning of his reign as God.

As the spirit covenanting with God, as the sent of God, the anointed one, his priest, and mediatorial agent with his creatures; as his æonian vice-gerent whom he has set at his own right hand, in his own throne, and entrusted solely with the concerns of the creation; himself the Messiah will be subordinated to the father, and all creatures with him.

But when the father's purpose in his son's vicarial government is answered, this very Messiah as equal with the father, the splendor of his glory, his express character, whom *Heb.* i. 2. *He has constituted heir of all things*, will inherit the then restored creatures in some immutable, and

perhaps

perhaps purely divine manner, transcending all that we can conceive of it infinitely; and at a much farther distance from reality, than the beauty of light and colours exceeded the blind man's description of them, when he supposed them to be somewhat like the sound of a drum.

This doctrine of a final conclusion of our saviour's kingdom, suits with all scripture accounts of the nature of this kingdom: for this kingdom is there represented as a state preparatory to some great design, the concern and employment of the whole triune GOD; a state of drawing, reproving, condemning, cleansing, regenerating, creating anew, reconciling, chastising, and comforting.

A state wherein *Christ* the LORD of it is represented as a purifier or a refiner's fire, as a fountain opened for sin and for uncleanness, as a pastor or bishop, as a priest, propitiator and ransom, as a mediator, as the power of GOD to salvation, and as the door and open entrance into him.

A state which has in view the creature's piety, love, and humility towards GOD; and his compassion, innocence, uprightness, and communion with all his brethren and fellow-creatures. A state in short where every creature (ὑποταγήσεται) shall be reduced to its natural subordination.

But then what means (the ὑπόταξις and ὑποταγή) this subordination? The word is plainly applied to both the creature and to *Christ* himself: the creature shall be subordinated to GOD; and the son of GOD shall be subordinated to the father.

Is

Is then *Chriſt* now in some inconceivable manner (and for the creature's sake) distinct from his holy father? And if *Chriſt* shall in the end be what he now is not, surely this must imply some change which at the end of things shall be wrought on him, as with regard to his human, so no less with regard to his angelic nature, and thro' him on his now holy family, who in, with, and by means of their most intimate oneship with him, *As* John x. 9.—xiv. 6. *the door or paſſage opened, ſhall then,* Eph. ii. 18. *have an acceſs unto the father.* And Heb. x. 19. ܠܟܐܘܬ ܐܦܐ ܒܟܕܕܠ, ܐܦ,ܐܝ, ܐܠ ܣܘܠܩܐ, ܢܘܣܐ, [1] *an openneſs of countenance* (the mark of confidence) [2] *to an enterance* [3] *of the houſe* [4] *of holineſs* [5] *thro' the blood* [6] *of Jeſus*; and thereby the honor of becoming 2 Pet. i. 4. *partakers of the divine nature*, even of being so united to God as that God may be the all in all; and ourselves Eph. iii. 19. *filled with all the fullneſs of* God.

And here then is that end in view which the whole creation drives at; the labour of the æonian life. And, in defiance of all cavilling, this end, place it where you please, must prove at last the limit closing, and the determining of this æonian life. But Mark xiii. 32. *of that day and hour knoweth no one* (ȣδεις) *neither the angels which are in heaven, neither the ſon, but the father only.* Of so high a valuation is the creature with his God!

LETTER III.

CHRIST's *kingdom what, and where it is; and when it began.*

SECT. I.

Of the power of Satan.

TO ———

SIR,

THERE are various conjectures concerning the power of satan over degenerate nature, but among the most probable are the two following.

Some have thought this his power to be connatural to him, an original ascendency given him at his creation over certain principalities, dominions, and orders of creatures, of which part fell with him and so continued his subjects, and part revolted from him, and so continued heavenly inhabitants in their respective habitations.

This his authority *these* suppose to be founded upon virtues and endowments lodged personally in him, and communicable from him to his dependents, as light and heat are communicated from the sun to all sublunary beings; or as many animals receive their life and vivid efficacy from the rays and nourishing warmth of its effluence.

Others again have supposed this power of satan over fallen creatures as neither originally designed by GOD, nor the effects of any natural ascendency given him over others; but to be meer usurpation, the work of satanic art and sagacity.

That as by dint of our human endowments, man, having arts and sciences which brutes can form no conception at all of, not only becomes superior to the brute creation, but, by the exercise of these arts, the master also and tyrant over the brutes: so satan, by means of his superior contrivance, subtlety and penetration, is become the prince and tyrant over other fallen creatures, domineering in them with an authority which they can no more escape or resist, than a blind man can escape the malice of his adversary, or an horse in harness the drudgery of his driver.

But whichever of these conjectures be true, and by whatever means, in fact it is certain that satan is possessed of a vast sovereignty, wherein he controls with a force and despotism, of which the oppression and cruelty of the most mighty tyrant over his brethren upon earth, is but a faint and unequal figure or resemblance.

In the scriptures therefore he is described as a powerful potentate. Eph. ii. 2. *The prince of the power of the air, the spirit that now worketh in the children of disobedience.* That in our christian warfare we have him for our enemy, that as such he exceeds in ability of mischief every thing that flesh and blood can work against us; or to give it in the apostle's own words, *Eph.* vi. 12. *We wrestle not against flesh and blood, but against principalities, and powers, against the rulers of the darkness* (τυ αιωνῷ τυτυ) *of this age, against wicked spirits in heavenly places.* Yea satan is declared to be even 2 *Cor.* iv. 4. (θεος τυ αιωνος τυτυ) *the God of this* (not world, but æon, or) *age; and to have* Luke xi. 18. *his kingdom,* Rev. ii. 13. *his seat and throne,* 1 Cor. viii. 10. *his temple,* Rev. iii. 9. *his synagogue,* Rev. xii. 7. *his angels,* 2 Pet. ii. 1. 2 Cor. xi. 13. Rev. ii. 2. *his prophets,* 2 Kings xi. 18. *his priests,* Ps. cvi. 37. Rev. ix. 20, 21. *his sacrifices and worshipers,* 2 Thes. ii. 2. 1 John iv. 1. Rev. xiii. 4. *his revelations,* Matt. iv. 9. *his promises; and even,* 2 Thes. ii. 3, 8, 9. Rev. xiii. 2. *a chief son, to be hereafter revealed in the person and character of the antichrist, after the working of satan, with all powers, and signs, and lying wonders.*

SECT. II.

Our LORD's *descent into hades.*

BUT this dreadful authority of satan king of terrors, and *John* viii. 44. first murderer, God in his compassion determined (καταργειν) to defeat or invalidate in the person of his son, now the man *Christ Jesus:* and for this purpose the

soul

foul of *Jesus* was to descend into hades, where is the principal seat of satan's empire.

Accordingly after his death upon the cross, his flesh being deposited like that of other dead men in the grave, his soul like theirs went into hades, as St. *Paul* tells us, *Eph.* iv. 9. *Now that he ascended, what is it but that he descended first* (εις τα κατωτερα μερη της γης) *into the lower parts of the earth*. That by the expression lower parts of the earth is meant hades, appears not only from the general opinion of the primitive people to whom the scriptures were addressed, but from the very context of the above quoted scripture passage; for herein our LORD's descent into the parts below the earth, stands in opposition to his assent into the parts above the earth; and implies that his ascending was in consequence of his prior descending; that he ascended far above all heavens that he might fill all things, as the natural process of his work, having first descended into the parts below, and there dispensed of his fulness.

And agreeably with this notion, was this his descent into hades also prophesied of him, *Psalm* xvi. 9, 10. *Therefore my heart is glad, and my glory rejoiceth; my flesh also shall rest in hope,* ¹*because* ²*thou wilt not leave* ³*my soul* ⁴*in* saul, *or* hades,ʰ

F

NOTES.

ʰ THE greek word (ἀδης) hades, which answers to the hebrew word (שאול) saul, does by no means denote a place of misery, neither does it a place of happiness. But as, *First,* the word (קבר) qbr de-

(כִּי ²לֹא תַעֲזֹב ¹) (תַעֲזֹב i. e.) ³נַפְשִׁי ⁴לִשְׁאוֹל) *neither wilt thou give thy compassionate one* (חֲסִידְךָ ⁵) *to see corruption* (שַׁחַת ⁶). For this prophesy is applied to him

---

NOTES.

notes the grave or repository of dead bodies; so does, *Secondly*, the word (שאול) saul the repository of souls departed; also, *Thirdly*, that in hades (or saul) there is a place of residence for happy souls, what follows will evince.

First, The word (קבר) qbr used as a verb, signifies to bury, and as such is rendered in the septuagint by (θαπτω) *sepelio* to bury; and as a noun it is there rendered by the word (ταφος) *sepulcrum*, a grave. Let the following instances suffice in proof of this, *Gen*. xxiii. 6. 1 *Kings* xiii. 22, 31. xiv. 13. 2 *Kings* xiii. 20. xxiii. 16. *Jer*. viii. 1. *Ez*. xxxvii. 13, 14. *Ps*. v. 9.

Secondly, That by the word (שאול) saul or hades, is meant a repository for departed souls, appears from *Ps*. lxxxix. 48. *Job*. vii. 9. xxi. 13. xxvi. 6. And because the dead were supposed, upon their bodies being deposited in (קבר) qbr, the grave, to find this their soul's reconditory in the lower parts of the earth; the word saul or hades is used for the depths below, in opposition to the heights above: so *Ps*. cxxxix. 8. *Deut*. xxxii. 22. *Amos* ix. 2.

At least that by the word saul is not meant a grave, is evident from *Job* xi. 7, 8. *Canst thou find out the Almighty to perfection? It* (i. e. Providence) *is high as heaven, what canst thou do? deeper than* (saul or) *hades, what canst thou know?* Here the depths of saul or hades, are set in opposition to the heights of heaven, importing that as nothing is higher than the heavens, nothing is deeper than saul or hades. Now supposing saul or hades here to mean (קבר) qbr, the grave (which all know is seldom more than five feet under ground;

him by St. *Peter*, Acts ii. 25, 27. *For David spake concerning him—because thou wilt not leave my soul* (εις ᾅδε) *in hades, neither wilt thou suffer thine holy one to see* (διαφθοραν) *corruption.* And

---

NOTES.

however, suppose if you please, the ancient burying-places to have been five yards under the surface of the earth) how idle a comparison were these shallow vaults to the heights of heaven? Again, *Matt.* xvi. 18. *Upon this rock have I built my church, and the gates of hades shall not prevail against it.* By gates in scriptures it is well known are meant the council-rooms, or courts of judicature, which in all cities were anciently kept over their gates; see *Deut.* xxi. 19. *Ruth* iv. 1. 2 *Sam.* xviii. 33. xix. 8. *Ps.* xcvi. 12. cxxvii. 5. *Dan.* ii. 49. *Jer.* xxxviii. 7. xxxix. 3. *Amos* v. 10. *Zech.* viii. 16. &c. But what can be meant by the door or gate of a sepulchre prevailing against any thing? And what harm is the church of GOD to expect from the gate or trap-door of a vault under ground? Whereas one may well suppose, that courts of council are held in the regions of the dead, where is the domain and empire of satan; and supposing so, our scripture expressions speak good sense. Again it is said of *Christ*, Acts ii. 27. *Thou wilt not leave my soul* (εις ᾅδε) *in hades*, among the disembodied souls. Again, *Luke* xvi. 23. *The rich man being in torments in hades, lift up his eyes*, *i. e.* not the eyes of his dead body, but of the body called, 1 *Cor.* xv. 40. (σωμα επουρανιον) *heavenly body*; because of its heavenly nature and original.

Thirdly, That in saul or hades there is a place of residence for happy souls, is again evident from *Gen.* xxxvii. 35. *I shall descend unto my son mourning into seol*, or *saul*, or *hades*; it is plain that *Jacob* expected to meet his son after death, since he says, *I shall go*

And from hence we infer as follows: The soul of *Jesus* was *not left in hades, or saul*; therefore his soul had been in saul, or hades: but his soul

---

NOTES.

down to my son; but he expected not that his body should go down to his son's body, because his son's body, having been in his belief devoured of beasts, was not supposed by him to be in the grave: therefore this expectation in *Jacob* of going to his son after death, argues that he supposed a place where the departed souls of men resided; where his son's soul then was, and where his own, when dead, should find him.

Again, since it cannot be thought that *Jacob* expected, either that himself after death should go into a state of torment, or that his son's soul was then in such a state of torment, he must have understood by the word saul or hades some happy region, the residence of blessed souls after their bodies are deposited in (קבר) qbr the grave; and this opinion concerning departed souls we find also in *Plato, Sophocles, Diodorus Siculus, Virgil, Plutarch*, and other heathen philosophers.

The paradise in hades, whither *Lazarus* was translated, consisted of mansions of delight and consolation, where also *Abraham* before the resurrection of our saviour, presided as the head of the family of all the faithful; and as it seems in patriarchal honours, a representative of *Christ*: for under his patronage it may be presumed these blessed souls had a hopeful expectation of the time of our saviour's resurrection, when his heavenly sanctuary should be opened, and themselves received into the presence of the divine humanity. Of this we therefore read, *Luke* xvi. 22, 23. That *Lazarus* was seen in it by the rich man, enjoying the comforts of the faithful *Abraham*.

soul was not left in hades *at his resurrection;* therefore his soul must have been in hades before his resurrection: but his soul was not in hades
during

николай O T E S.

As to the expressions εις τον κολπον and εν τοις κολποις some suppose them to denote the same as the latin phrase *(in sinu esse)* to be under the umbrage, care, or protection of any one; as the complaint of *Moses* seems to import, *Numb.* xi. 12. *O Jehovah, wherefore layest thou the burden of this people upon me, that thou shouldst say unto me, carry them in thy bosom:* in which use of it, a wife is in scripture familiarly paraphrased by, *she who rests in thy bosom; she who lies in thy bosom:* but others again, insisting upon the remarkable variation of number in the word κολπος, conjecture that εν κολποις ειναι must have been a Greek phrase (since St. *Luke* wrote in greek) denoting what the *Latins* express by *in deliciis esse,* according to which it is to be presumed, that tho' *Lazarus* was carried by the angels directly (v. 22. εις τον κολπον) into the embrace of *Abraham,* yet that *Dives* did afterwards see *Lazarus,* not (εν τω κολπω) in the bosom, but (εν τοις κολποις, *in deliciis*) in the enjoyments of *Abraham.*

But be this remark good or bad, the antiquity of the doctrine among the *Jews* is certain; they believed that the souls of all men when they died went to hades, and that they there divided into two different societies, viz. the souls of the just went into the comforts of *Abraham,* and the souls of the wicked into the torments of the damned. And from them this opinion was adopted by the *Gentiles:* therefore in *Virgil* we read,

Hic locus est partes ubi se via findit in ambas;
Dextera quæ Ditis magni sub mænia tendit;
Hàc iter elysium nobis: at læva malorum
Exercet pœnas, & ad impia tartara mittit.

during his bodily life; therefore the time of his soul's being in hades must have been the interval between his death and his resurrection.

SECT.

NOTES.

which passage corresponds likewise with that of *Sophocles*,

Και γαρ καθ' ἀδην δυο τριϐους νομιζομεν,
Μ.αν δικαιων, χἀτιραν αδικων ὁδον——
Καπειτα σωσει πχυθ' ἀ προσθ' απωλισεν.

From which words I beg leave also to remark, that the verb σωζω among the *Greeks* was quite consistent with their verb απολλυμι; and that a soul may be (σωθηναι) restored which also (απολλυται) is destroy'd; and consequently that the verb σωζω does not properly signify to save (viz. from wrath to come) but to restore, (viz. from evil which has befallen us.)

For the truth of the above account of hades, the curious are referred to *Justin Martyr, Origin, Tertullian, Chrysostom, Josephus* and *Jerom*; in which last author we read as follows:

Ante adventum Christi (i. e. before the heavenly paradise was opened, of which season he says, *Necdum paradisi januam Christus effregerat, necdum flammeam illam rompheam & vertiginem præsidentium cherubin sanguis ejus extinxerat) omnia ad inferos pariter ducebantur; unde & Jacob ad inferos pariter decensurum se dicit; & Job pios & impios in inferno queritur retentari: & evangelium chaos magnum interpositum apud inferos; & Abraham cum Lazaro, & divitem in suppliciis esse testatur.*

But now, the heavenly paradise being opened by *Christ* ascended, all true believers go thither, *John* xii. 26.—xvii. 24. 2 *Cor.* v. 8. *Phil.* i. 23. where the patriarchs also now are, in the enjoyments of the glory of *Jesus; Matt.* viii. 11, 12. *Mark* xvi. 19. *Heb.* x. 12. 13.—xii. 22—24.

The reason of our LORD's *descent into hades.*

OUR LORD's business in hades was to loose the bands or ties of hades (or seul, or siul, or siol, or sheol, or saul) this we learn from *Acts* ii. 24. *Whom God hath raised up having loosed* (ܚܒܠܐ‎² ܣܘܠܐ‎¹) '*the ties or cordages* ²*of siul*,¹ *because it was not possible* (ܟܕ‎² ܢܬܚܒܫ‎¹ ܒܣܘܠ‎³) '*that he should be detained* ²*in the* ³*siul (or saul.)* Our LORD's breaking thro' the bands hereof, became the deliverance of all others its inhabitants, who then incorporated themselves into *Christ*, and became his members by believing in him. Here

---

NOTES.

¹ IT is true we read this passage in the greek (λυσας τας ωδινας τȣ θανατȣ) *having loosed the pains of death*; but it is possible that the word (ωδιν) pain was used by the *Greeks* to signify band, cord, fetter, ligament as well as pain, since the syriac (ܚܒܠܐ) hbla does certainly mean both; that it does so, appears from *Acts* xxvii. 32. *Then the soldiers cut* (ܣܘܠܐ) *the ropes, or cords, of the boat and let her fall off*; as also from the hebrew word (חבל) hbl a rope, from whence the syriac word hbla is indisputably taken. 'And as hbla must necessarily signify a rope in this passage, how reasonable is it that we should render (ܚܒܠܐ‎² ܣܘܠܐ‎¹ ܘܫܪܐ‎¹) '*and he loosed* ²*the bands* (or fetters) ¹*of hades.* As to the place of hades

LETTER III. [48] SECT. III.

Here therefore was the theatre of our LORD's triumph, of which we read, *Col.* ii. 15. *Having spoiled* (or devested) *the principalities and powers, he made a shew of them openly triumphing over them* (εν αυτω *i. e.* εν εαυτω)[k] *in himself*; viz. in the victorious efficacy of his presence, in the authoritative ascendency of his own personage.

The

NOTES.

we need only say, that there is space enough between us and the sun for all the several apartments which the scriptures seem to suppose in it. That hades is out of this our world we think, with *Grotius*, very probable: who speaking of the abyss in his comment on *Luke* viii. 31. Says, *Si quis tamen modestæ conjecturæ est locus, malim extra hunc mundum aspectabilem, eum (i. e. abyssi locum) ponere, ut & regionem beatorum spirituum, quam cum quibusdam in centro terræ. Ipsa certe vox* αβυσσα *vastitatem quandam præ se fert; & videri potest* το σκοτ{Θ} το εξωτερον *ideo dici quod extra hunc orbem sit qui in usus nostros est conditus. Nec male forte huc referas quod apud Johannem est cap.* xii. 31. *Princeps hujus mundi ejicietur foras.* Which opinion the ancient author of the book of wisdom seems also to favour; see Wisd. i. 13, 14. And that hades is within the earth's orbit, and so, according to the copernican system, under the earth, or farther retired from the heavens than we are, seems to be reasonably conjectured, from the scripture expressions concerning it, as well as from other considerations too long, and perhaps impertinent, to deserve inserting in this place.

[k] IT is well known that the greek pronoun αυτος signifies either him or himself; and that in this place the latter is intended appears from the syriac, viz.

The events here presumed correspond also with our LORD's own account of things, *Luke* xi. 21. *When a strong man arm'd keeps his palace, his goods are in peace; but when* a *stronger than he shall come upon him, and overcome him, he taketh from him all his armour wherein he trusted, and divideth his prey* (ܒܙܬܐ bztha, that which he has, ܒܙܐ bza, plunder'd, or possess'd himself of by robbery)

However, to pursue my point more distinctly, I shall prove the three following articles.

First, That the kingdom of *Christ* is already begun.

Second, That the kingdoms of this world will all at last be comprehended in it.

Third, That the kingdom of *Christ* is under his particular conduct as son of GOD and man.

SECT. IV.

CHRIST'S *kingdom began.*

OF the three points proposed we have to prove, Ist.

That the kingdom of *Christ* is already begun.

For this we have our LORD's express words, *Luke* xi. 20. *If I by the finger of God cast out devils, no doubt the kingdom of God is come upon you,*

NOTES.

Col. ii. 15. ܘܐܒܗܬ⁴ ܐܢܘܢ¹ ܓܠܝܐܝܬ³ ܒܩܢܘܡܗ² ¹*et erubescere fecit* ²*eos* ³*palam* ⁴*in semetipso*, and put them to an open shame in himself.

or (as in the syriac testament ܥܠ ܠܘܢ ܗܐ ܩܪܒܬ݂ ܡܠܟܘܬܐ ܕܐܠܗܐ) *The kingdom of God draweth near unto you.* Again, Mark ix. 1. *There be some of the standers here, who shall not taste death, till they shall see the kingdom of God come in power.* Again, Col. i. 13. *Who has delivered us from the power of darkness, and has translated us into the kingdom of his dear son.*

Not that the kingdom of GOD prevails as yet visibly in this world, but it is nevertheless begun, and has therefore many of its people and denizens living in it, having its triumphant country and œconomy elsewhere, in as much reality, as any earthly nation has an œconomy upon the earth.

St. *Paul* has given us a most majestic account of our LORD's entry into his kingdom in *Eph.* iv. 8, 9, 10. *Wherefore, he saith, when he ascended up on high, he led captivity captive, and gave gifts unto men; now that he ascended, what is it but that he also descended first into the lower parts of the earth? He that descended, is the same that also ascended far above all heavens, that he might fill all things.*

Which may be paraphrased as follows: He, the Jehovah *Christ*, when he ascended up into the heavens, having rescued as his own rightful property, those who had hitherto been the captives of other potentates, out of the hands of their oppressors; he took them in triumph as his own captives, and made them a part of that magnificent retinue which attended him: but in saying that he ascended it is necessarily implied, that he also descended first into the lower parts of the earth,

LETTER III.   [51]   SECT. IV.

earth, where are the regions of hades: he that descended is the same also that ascended far above all heavens, that being there seated in the fullest power and dignity, he might fill all things. And hence it is that we his members (and meerly because we are his members) receive of him gifts and graces, becoming thereby *some apostles, some evangelists, some pastors and teachers, for the perfecting of the saints, for the work of the ministry, for the edifying of the body of Christ; till we all come in the unity of the faith, and of the knowledge of the son of God, unto a perfect man, unto the measure of the stature of the fulness of Christ.*

But because the meaning of the word captivity in this text is disputed, before we go farther, we should give our *reasons* for what we here presume upon as the true import of this passage.

Verse 8th, *He led captivity captive* (in greek ηχμαλωτευσεν αιχμαλωτιαν.)

We understand what it is to lead a captive in triumph after a conquest made; somewhat like this was done by our LORD when he ascended up on high; and on this account we have the great events of his passion expressed in this resemblance: Is it not strange then that it should remain a question what we are to understand by the term captivity?

However, let us first observe of this term captivity, that it is an abstract noun-substantive, and as it is known that the syriac language, which was native to our saviour and his apostles, does mostly express its adjective by an abstract noun-substantive, we may conclude this expression to be a syriacism, with which the greek testament abounds.

Like it both in term and construction is that in *Rev.* xiii. 10. (ει τις αιχμαλωσιαν συναγει, εις αιχμαλωσιαν υπαγει) *If any one lead captivity, he shall go into captivity.* Here the abstract noun (αιχμαλωσια) captivity is used for the adjective (αιχμαλωτον) captive, *i. e.* a captive person or prisoner.

In confirmation of this remark, I here give in the notes[m] a few of numberless other Instances obvious in the greek testament; and must confess that these several instances are of themselves sufficient evidence, that by the apostle's word captivity

---

NOTES.

Syriacisms why so frequent in the New Testament.

[m] NOUNS adjective in the greek testament are in syriac express'd by abstract nouns: Thus,

Instead of,	We read
An iron rod,	A rod of iron.
A glorious throne,	A throne of glory.
The highest power,	The power of the highest.
His glorious power,	His power of glory.
Unjust works,	Works of injustice.
Our vile body,	The body of our vileness, (το σωμα της ταπεινωσεως ημων.)
His glorious body,	The body of his glory, (τω σωματι της δοξης αυτα)
A contrite spirit,	A spirit of contrition.
Impious works,	Works of impiety.
Shameful affections,	Affections of shame.
A forgetful hearer,	A hearer of forgetfulness.

captivity is to be meant, those who are in a state of captivity, or the captives; and that therefore by our LORD's leading captivity captive must be meant, that he seized himself of those who were captives,

---

NOTES.

The unjust steward,	The steward of injustice. (οικονομον της αδικιας)
The elect have obtain'd it,	The election has obtained it.
The fleshly mind is dead, φρονημα σαρκικον θνησιμαιον; ſo φρονημα πνευματικον ζωον,	The mind of the flesh is death, (φρονημα σαρκος θανατος; ſo φρονημα πνευμα[τος] ζωη)

Whatever may be the reason, certain it is that St. *Paul* usually prefers the hebrew, that is the syriac manner of expression to the greek idiom. Altho' he surely must have understood the greek in its purity and elegance, yet he writes all his epistles as a native of *Judea*, that is in the syriac phrase and diction; so that tho' they consist of greek words, they are in form and construction mostly syriac.

This indeed often renders his greek obscure to the polite reader, upon which account St. *Jerom* censures him pretty freely, not considering that, to the learned in the holy languages, such style is of all others the most apposite, significant and intelligible.

Notwithstanding the *Jews* must have used the chaldee tongue during their captivity, yet they still retain'd the phrase and idiom of the hebrew; and from hence it came to pass that the syriac, which results from the union of the two, retains the force and liberty of the latter: of which therefore says our learned *Fuller*, " *It is so near akin to the hebrew as deservedly to be called its daughter; and is the only language which can with*

captives, and so delivered them from their state of captivity, to their becoming his own freemen.

This was also foretold of him, *Is.* xlii. 6, 7, 8. *I Jehovah have called thee in righteousness, and will hold thee by thy hand, and will keep thee, and will give*

NOTES.

propriety, and true emphasis, render the hebrew word for word."

Beza seems to have believed that the hebrew only can with propriety express the mind of God to man; if this be so, the syriacisms frequent in the New Testament bespeak propriety instead of inelegance, the syriac dialect being as well adapted to the divine manner of expression as the hebrew.

This remarkable opinion of *Beza's* we find in his notes upon *Acts* the 10th as follows, " *Ut autem hebraismos permiscerent, non modo hæc causa fuit quia hebræi erant (potuisset enim spiritus sanctus hoc quicquid erat in ipsis emendare, si displicuisset) Sed quia cum de iis rebus differerent quæ Hebraicis literis erant traditæ, necesse fuit multa retinere, ne doctrinam quampiam novam afferre viderentur. Et certe tam multos hæbraismos ab illis servatos fuisse minime miror, quum plerique sunt ejusmodi ut nullo alio idiomate tam feliciter exprimi possint, imo interdum ne exprimi quidem: ut nisi illas formulas retinuissent, nova illis interdum vocabula & nova dicendi genera comminiscenda fuerint, quæ nemo plane intellexisset. Postremo (ut tandem dicendi finem faciam) quum hos unos delegerit Deus, per quos scribi vellet quæcunq; ad nostram salutem necessaria sunt, illud quoq; nobis est constituendum, eundem illum Deum ita esse ipsorum linguis moderatum, ut ne verbum quidem temere ipsis exciderit, imo vero cuncta sic plane, apte & apposite dixerint, ut plenius ac melius a quopiam de his dici nunquam potuerit.*

give thee for a covenant of the people, for a light of the nations, to open the blind eyes, to bring out the prisoners from the prison, and them that sit in darkness out of the prison house; I Jehovah this is my name, and my glory will I not give to another.

So then the expression (ηχμαλωτευσεν αιχμαλωσιαν) he captivated captivity, together with that passage in *Rev.* iii. 10. (ει τις αιχμαλωσιαν συναγει, εις αιχμαλωσιαν υπαγει) *If any one lead captivity, he shall go into captivity,* may be justly translated, the former text, he led away in triumph those that had been captive; the latter, if any one lead away any other for his captive, himself shall become a captive.

This presumed meaning will also appear from that original prophesy from whence St. *Paul* quotes this passage, for he gives us this prophesy, not as his own, but as the words of the *Psalmist, Pf.* lxviii. 18. *Thou hast ascended* into heaven (the exceeding height, שבית שבי) *hast* captivated 'the captives, hast received gifts for men.* But to captivate captives is to take for ones captives those who were before captives, or in a state of captivity; as *Isaiah* explains this expression, *If.* xiv. 2. *And they shall take them captives, whose captives they were* (והיו ²שבים ³לשביהם *'et erunt ²captivantes ¹captivantes eos*) *and shall rule over their oppressors.*

This same expression we likewise find in *Ezek.* xvi. 53. (¹ושבתי ²את ³שביתהן ⁴את ⁵שבית סדם) *¹And I captivate* (or will captivate) ²*their ¹captives ³even the ⁴captives ⁵of Sodom, and their daughters, and the captives of Samaria, and their daughters, ¹and the captives (that are) ²thy captives*

captives (ושביח' ¹) *in the midst of them* (viz. *Sodom* and *Samaria*.)

And again, in *Judges* v. 12. *Arise Barak,* '*and captivate* (or lead captive) ² *thy captives* (ושבה שביך ²) that is lead home out of that part of *Canaan* which is the kingdom of *Jabin*, those *Jews*, thy brethren, which he, the said king *Jabin*, there detain'd in captivity."

Whether therefore we compare the term captivity in the place contested with that other place in the *Revelations*, where alone we find the word (αιχμαλωσιαν) repeated in our greek testament; or whether with the original passage in the *Psalms*, from whence the apostle quotes it; or whether with the several like passages in the old testament; or whether, lastly, we compare it as an abstract noun substantive with other such in the new testament; still we find this term every where speaking, that our LORD at his ascension carried with him as captives, not satan lord of death, but of those who had been the captives of satan, and other infernal powers before that time, and consequently that his kingdom was at that time began authoritatively.

SECT.

NOTES.

" The words (ישבה שבין) captivate thy captivity, in this place cannot be understood of *Sisera*'s army, since it is expressly said of these (chap. iv. 16) that *they all to a man fell by the edge of the sword:* so that the captives which *Barak* was invited in this song to lead captive, must have been his brethren, who had been before the captives of *Jabin*.

Christ's kingdom shall prevail under his government, as God-man universally.

II^{dly}.

THE thing we have to prove, is that the time will come when the kingdom and œconomy of GOD shall possess itself of, and prevail over all the world.

To this purpose we have only to produce a few texts.

Isa. xlix. 5, 6, 7. *And now said Jehovah, forming me from the womb to be his servant, to reduce Jacob to himself; Tho' Israel be not gathered yet shall I* (namely אדני the my LORD the future man *Christ Jesus*) *be glorious in the eyes of Jehovah, and my God has been my strength. And again he said, it is a light thing that thou* (the Adni or Lord, *i. e.* the future man *Christ Jesus*) *shouldst be my servant to raise up the tribes of Jacob, and convert the preserved of Israel: I have also given thee to be a light of the Gentiles, to be my salvation even to the end of the earth. Thus said Jehovah the redeemer of Israel his holy one; to the despised soul, to the abominated nation, to the servant of masters, kings shall see, and arise; princes shall bow themselves, because of Jehovah; for he is faithful, the holy one of Israel; and he hath chosen thee.* Pf. lxxii. 8. *He shall have dominion also from sea to sea, and from the river unto the ends of the earth.* Pf. ii. 7, 8. *Jehovah said to me* (אדני adni, for that these words were spoken typically of, and relate properly to *Jesus* we are assured, *Heb.* i. 5.

chap. v. 5. *Acts* xiii. 23. *Thou art my son, to-day have I begotten thee; ask of me and I will give thee the Gentiles for thy inheritance, and the ends of the earth for thy possession.* Zech. xiv. 9. *And Jehovah shall be king over all the earth; in that day Jehovah shall be one and his name one.*

Promises like this are to be found in so many other places, that this point will, I suppose, be easily granted me.

III^{dly}.

This kingdom of *Christ* is under his particular conduct as son of GOD, both Logos and man.

First. This kingdom of *Christ* is his as a man the son of GOD.

John xiii. 3. *Jesus knowing that the father had given all things into his hands, &c.* Matt. xxviii. 18. *And Jesus came and spake unto them saying all power is given unto me in heaven and on earth.* Ep. i. 19.—*According to the energy of his mighty power which he wrought in Christ, raising him from the dead; and he hath set him* (namely the son of man) *at his own right hand in heavenly places, far above all principality and power and might and dominion, and every name that is named not only in this æon, but also in that which is to come, and he hath put all things under his feet.* 1. Cor. xv. 27. *But when he saith all things are put under him, it is manifest that he, who did put all things under him, is excepted.*

The kingdom of *Christ* may again be called his as man, in regard also to its being conducted singly and solely by himself without deputies or representatives.

This is a most invaluable privilege, since we have reason to believe that the government of all
those

those regions and systems of worlds in the immense depth of space, excepting only where the paradise or kingdom of GOD is extended, is carried on by the administration of the angelic powers; and that from such delegated authority these potentates have their titles of thrones, dominions, principalities, lordships, virtues, &c. But in the regions of paradise the case is otherwise, for, *Heb.* ii. 5. *Unto the angels he has not put in subjection the future age* (ܠܥܠܡܐ, ܥܬܝܕܐ) *whereof we speak,* *i. e.* the christian kingdom or paradisaical age, which is began only among the blessed.

So that what unchristian, (*i.e.* strange) subjection a christian has ever to experience, will be in this short worldly age only, since, not only no enemy or injurious being shall, after our LORD's resurrection, have been suffered to approach his paradisaical domains, as he says *John* xii. 31. *Now shall the prince of this world* (τε κοσμε τέτε) *be cast out*; but neither will any celestial dignity however great or holy have any sort of authority therein.

And it is to be presumed that on account of this especial prerogative of the people of Jehovah, was the *Israelites* desire of a king so particularly signalized by the expressions of his resentment, as we read 1 *Sam.* chap. viii.

Secondly, This kingdom of our LORD's is his also as Logos son of GOD, *i. e.* as Jehovah Adni.

Heb. i. 2,—10. *And in these last days has he spoken with us by his own son, whom he hath ordained the heir of all things, by whom also he constituted the ages; who is himself the splendor of his glory, and the image of his essence, and upholds all things by the virtue of his word, and he by himself purged* our sins, and sat at the right hand of the majesty in the highest; 'and (for) he was ²altogether ³more excellent than ⁴the angels (ܘܠܘ ܗܟܢܐ ܡܢ ܡܠܐܟܐ⁴) as he inherited a more exalted (ܡܝܬܪܐ) name than they; for unto which of the angels did God ever say (ܡܠܐܟܐ ܓܝܪ ܠܐܝܢܐ) thou art my son —and let all the angels of God worship him—of the angels he saith, who maketh his angels spirits and his ministers an ardent fire: but to the son he saith, thy throne, O God (ܟܘܪܣܝܟ ²ܐܠܗܐ¹) is ¹to the age of ²ages, a scepter of equity is the scepter of thy kingdom, thou hast loved righteousness and hated iniquity, therefore God, even thy God, hath anointed thee with the oil of gladness above thy fellows. And again, Thou from the beginning hast laid the foundations of the earth, and the heavens are the work of thy hands; Again, *Heb.* ii. 5—8. He hath not subjected to angels the future age of which we speak, (i. e. that age which is quite a new scene of being, opened only in the paradise of GOD, where the new creation in *Christ* is began) *but—thou hast humbled him a little lower than the angels, and put upon his head glory and honour, and given him power over the work of thy hands; and hast subjected all things under his feet; but in that he subjected all things unto him, he left not any thing not subjected unto him; but now hitherto we by no means see all things subjected unto him.* And this He is, *Isa.* ix. 6. *The child born, the mighty God,* (אב עד) *the æonian father, the prince of peace.*

    This first general exercise of our LORD's æonian power, seems likewise to be the thing meant, when he says *John* xii. 31, 32. *Now shall the prince of this world be cast out;* ¹*and I,* ²*when* ³*that I am lifted up* ⁴*from* ⁵*the earth* (ܘܐܢܐ¹ ܡܐ² ܕܐܬܬܪܝܡܬ³ ܡܢ⁴ ܐܪܥܐ⁵) *shall draw all men unto me.* And

And thus, I suppose, this point also to be sufficiently proved.

But least what I have advanced in my present letter may appear to you as wild and fantastical, I shall endeavour to justify myself, by subjoining a few quotations from most of the christian writers of the two first centuries, which too will, I dare say, yield you an agreeable entertainment.

The testimonies of the most primitive christian writers, touching our LORD's descent into hades.

ORIGEN.

SOLUS enim (Christus) *fuit inter mortuos liber. Et quia liber inter mortuos fuit, idcirco devicto eo qui habuit mortis imperium, abstraxit captivitatem quæ tenebatur in mortem; et non solum semetipsum resuscitavit à mortuis, sed et eos qui tenebantur in morte, simul excitavit, simulq; sedere in cælestibus fecit. Ascendens in altum captivam duxit captivitatem; non solum animas educens, sed et corpora eorum resuscitans, sicut testatur evangelium, quod multa sanctorum corpora resuscitata sunt, et apparuerunt multis et introierunt in sanctam civitatem Dei viventis, Hierusalem. In canticum canticorum,* Homilia tertia.

IRENÆUS.

EA propter dominum in ea quæ sunt sub terra descendisse, evangelizantem et illis adventum suum, remissam peccatorum existentem his qui credunt in eum. Crediderunt autem in eum omnes justi & prophetæ & patriarchæ: quibus similiter ut nobis remisit peccata. Omnes enim homines egent gloria Dei; justificantur autem non a semetipsis, sed a domini adventu, qui intendunt lumen ejus. Lib. iv. Cap. xlv.

JUSTIN

Letter III.   [62]   Sect. V.

Justin Martyr.

ΕΜΝΗΣΘΗ δὲ Κυριος ὁ Θεος των απο Ισραηλ νεκρων αυτα των κεκοιμημενων εις γην χωματος, κ᾽ τα τι εθη προς αυτας ευαγγελισασθαι αυτοις το σωτηριον αυτα. *Dialogus cum Tryphone Judæo.*

Justin Martyr.

QUUM dicit; excitata sunt multa eorum qui obdormierunt sanctorum corpora: perfectam denotat resurrectionem. Præstita autem est sanctorum istorum resurrectio, ut demonstratio esset, mortificationem esse mortis omnium nostrum Christi mortem, quam pro salute et vitâ *mortalium omnium pertulit. Is certe quidem* vivificam *potentiam suam, mortuis excitandis mirifice exhibuit in præsenti rerum statu, et animis piis defunctorum apud inferos omnibus liberandis.* Δι᾽ ἣν αιτιαν ουδὲ ετελευτησαν παλιν, αλλα μενουσιν εν αθανασια; καθαπερ ὁ Ενωχ κ᾽ ὁ Ηλιας, κ᾽ εισι συν αυτοις εν τω παραδεισω αναμενοντες, την ηδη αιωνιαν της τα Χρ.σου ανασασεως γινομενην κατα εναλλαγην, καθ᾽ ἣν, ὡς φησ.ν ὁ θειος απος᾽ολος, παντες αλλαγησομεθα· εις γαρ αθανατον τε κ᾽ αφθαρτον ζωην ουπω γεγονε τινος ἡ ανας᾽ασις, πλην τα σωτηρος Χρισα. διο κ᾽ πρωτοτοκος των νεκρων, κ᾽ απαρχη των κεκοιμημενων ανηγορευται. *Responf. ad orthodoxos.*

But *Clemens Alexandrinus* even exceeds this, for, says he,

Ο ΚΥΡΙΟΣ ευηγγελισατο κ᾽ τοις εν ἁδου—οἱ εν ἁδα καταγινοντες, κ᾽ εις απωλειαν ἑαυτας εκδεδωκοτες, καθαπερ εκ τινος νεως εις θαλασσαν ἑκοντες απορρι᾽ψαντες· αυτοι τοινυν εισιν οἱ επακουσαντες της θειας δυναμεως τε κ᾽ φωνης. *Clementis Alexandrini stromatum.*   Liber sextus.

As also Tertullian.

INFERNUM petit hic animas pro crimine vinctas, *Quæ sine præsidio,* conclusæ *pondere legis,*

Olim

Olim promissa, & sperata, & tarda rogabant,
Sanctorum in requiem dedit, & cum luce retraxit.
Tertia namq; die subiens cum corpore victor,
Immani virtute **patris,** *via facta salutis,*
Inq; creatura portans hominemq; deumq;
Conscendit cælos, captivas ille reducens
Primitias, munus domino caramq; figuram.
Conseditq; patri lucis virtute recepta,
Gloria qua munitus erat, dum vinceret hostem,
Spiritu conjunctus, de nobis carne ligatus.
Hunc pater, & dominum & **Christum,** *regemq; deumq;*
Judicio **regnoq;** *dato, missurus* **in orbem** *est.*

Adversus Marcionem, Liber quintus.

I beg leave to trouble you with only one more short quotation, which shall be from

IGNATIUS.

ΑΛΗΘΩΣ δὲ, κỳ ȣ δοκησει, ϛαυρωθη, κỳ απεθανε, βλεποντων ȣρανιων, κỳ επιγειων, κỳ καταχθονιων. ȣρανιων μεν, ὡς των ασωματων φυσεων; επιγειων δε Ιȣδαιων κỳ Ρωμαιων, κỳ των παροντων κατ' εκεινο καιρα ανθρωπων, ϛαυρωμενα· τα Κυριε; καταχθονιων δε, ὡς τα πληθους τε συναναϛαντος τῳ Κυριῳ; πολλα γαρ, φησι, σωματα των κεκοιμημενων ἁγιων ηγερθη, των μνημειων ανεωχθεντων; κỳ κατηλθεν εις ἁδην μονος, ανηλθε δε κατα πληθους.   *Epist. ad Trall.*

LETTER IV.

CHRIST's *kingdom will consist of many successive parts or periods.*

SECT. I.

TO ——

SIR,

MY third point as to the kingdom of *Christ*, was, that as it will be secular, it will also, like other secular things, consist of many successive parts or periods of time.

And this you will admit of as evident from the letters I sent you upon future events foretold in scripture; wherein I argued that our LORD's next coming to judgment, and the resurrection of the saints which shall attend it, will be a season very far short of the end of this world; that it will be the end only (τȢ αιων ΤȢΤȢ) of this present age or period of time, this present untheocratical state of things.

That

LETTER IV. [65] SECT. 1.

That when the unbelieving part of *Israel*, which hitherto have been and shall be enemies to the gospel, shall all have had their effectual æonian sufferings (namely the dead in *Gehenna*, the living under the antichristian persecution); and when after the fulness of the *Gentiles* is come in, the *Jews* shall, all of them, even the whole family of *Israel*, be saved from the wrath that shall then come upon this world: that then such *Jews* as shall be dead shall rise again into life, and shall with their then persecuted brethren be securely gathered into their own land in *Judea*, and become a nation and people of GOD, according to the promise made to their father *Abraham*, which is circumstantially described *Gen.* xxviii. 4. *By the land wherein thou art a stranger*, that is, of which thou art not as yet owner but a sojourner by faith, as in a foreign country, *the land thou seest, even the land whereon thou liest,* (v. 13) *to thee ° will I give it, and to thy seed.*

I For

NOTES.

° THE inheritance of the land of *Canaan*, is promised not only to the descendants of the patriarchs, but to the patriarchs themselves; therefore the patriarchs must personally possess this land; and this their possession must be after their resurrection from the dead, for whilst they were living in this world, *Acts* vii. 5. *God gave them none inheritance in this land, no not so much as to set their foot on:* so then the patriarchs shall hereafter be members of both the paradise above, and the paradise below, and probably hold a free, mutual intercourse with both at the same time, residing sometimes in heaven and sometimes on earth.

LETTER IV. [66] SECT. I.

For the *Jews* being now cleanfed from all their wickednefs, fhall live a devout earthly life, in the millenium, on this earth, fee *Jer*. chap. xxx, and xxxi. *If*. xl. *Ez*. xxxvii. while the chriftian church, even all the firft fruits, fhall form the millenium which is above in heaven, fee *Luke* xxii. 28, 29. *Rev*. xix. 1—7.

You there find it proved that all this fhall happen upon our LORD's very next coming to judgment, when the antichrift and falfe prophet fhall be caft into the lake of fire, but fatan fhall be imprifoned for 1000 years in the abyfs.

And that during this period the heathen (probably a remnant who fhall efcape in this vifitation of the lamb's wrath, and fhall not be killed by his next appearance) fhall be converted by the *Jews* now chriftian inhabitants in the land of *Canaan*, and that fo the world for a feafon (fhort indeed, yet typical of what in fome after age will be produced in a more eminent manner) fhall become the kingdom of GOD and his *Chrift*. For the kingdom of the faints fhall prevail over all the kingdoms of the earth, and fucceed in their place, and confequently fhall be an earthly kingdom, or kingdom below, anfwerable to the heavenly kingdom, which fhall alfo be at the fame time in the paradife above.

That towards the end of the jewifh millenium, and in this fair ftate of things, fatan fhall be releafed out of prifon, but with a fpirit not much altered by his confinement; for he will deceive the nations (tho' not the *Jews*) who by his artifices fhall decline in heart from bad to worfe, being
firft

first lukewarm, then careless, then infidel, and at last devilish; in which wicked zeal they will become the army of *Gog* and *Magog*, and be gathered by satan to battle against *Jerusalem*, where they will be destroyed, and satan cast to the beast and prophet in the lake of fire, by our LORD himself, 2 *Thes.* ii. 8. *Rev.* xx. 10. appearing now again to vindicate his people's honour, and judge the rest of the dead, spoken of in *Rev.* xx. 5. who shall live again, when the 1000 years are finished.

That these events shall be followed by yet another period of happiness; for, *Ez.* xxxviii. they who dwell in the cities of *Israel* shall burn the weapons of *Gog Magog*'s Army, as being enough for seven years fuel for them; so that they shall take no wood out of the field, neither cut down any out of the forests; and seven months shall the house of *Israel* be burying of the multitude of *Gog*, and all the heathen shall see the LORD's judgment: and *Zec.* xiv. 16—26. *Every one left of all the nations which came against Jerusalem, shall go up from year to year to worship at Jerusalem; and in that day the bells upon the horses shall be holiness unto the Lord.* If. xi. 6. *The wolf also shall dwell with the lamb, and the leopard shall lie down with the kid; and the calf, and the young lion, and the fatling together, and a little child shall lead them; for the lion shall eat straw like the ox, and they shall not hurt nor destroy in all the mountain of my holiness,* (i. e. in *Jerusalem*) *the holy city, the city of the living God, the place which he hath chosen, the joy of the whole earth, which shall be then called,* Jer. iii. 17. *Jerusalem the throne of the Lord, and all nations shall be gathered into it; for the earth shall*

shall be full of the knowledge of the Lord as the waters cover the sea.

And these events shall succeed one another in a regular process and time-like series, even to the end of the world, when 2 *Peter* iii. 10. *the heavens shall pass away with a great noise, and the elements shall be melted with fervent heat, the earth also and all that are therein shall be burnt up*; and, If. xxxiv. 4. *all the host of heaven shall be dissolved, and the heavens shall be rolled together as a scroll, and all their host shall fall down* (whither their centripetal force shall hurry them) *as a leaf falleth off from the vine.*ᵖ

And

NOTES.

ᵖ This universal catastrophe was also the expectation of the *Gentiles,* as we read in *Ovid.*

    Esse quoque in fatis reminiscitur affore tempus,
    Quo mare, quo tellus, quo rectaq; regia cœli
    Ardeat, & mundi moles operosa laboret.

Which words say near as much as the sybil oracles, supposed to be the forgery of (tho' probably only collected by) some christian.

    Tunc ardens fluvius cœlo manabit ab alto
    Igneus, atq; locos consumet funditus omnes,
    Terramq; oceanumq; ingentem, & cærula ponti
    Stagna, lacus, fluvios, fontes, Ditemq; severum,
    Cœlestemq; polum; cœli quoq; lumina in unum
    Fluxa fluent, formâ deletâ prorsus eorum:
    Astra cadent etenim de cœlo cuncta revulsa.

So again *Sophocles,*

    Εϛαι γαρ εϛαι κεινος αιωνων χρονος,
    Οταν πυρος γεμοντα θησαυρον σχαση
    Χρυσωπος α θηρ; η δε βοσκηθεισα φλοξ,
    Απαντα τα πηγεια κỳ μεταρσια
    Φλοξ μανεισ'

And since thus far, and in all the changes and periods revealed, and which reach to and beyond the end of this world, we so evidently see all things to move in a regular series and gradual process from event to event; we cannot well suppose otherwise of what is yet farther forward in the depths of time, and which will occupy the immense interval between the end of this world and our LORD's delivering up the kingdom into his father's hands, when GOD shall be all in all; especially since this kingdom is every where in scripture described as successive, as having successive work to be performed in it, and in many parts emphatically declared to subsist from time to time, from age to age, from generation to generation.

So *Lam.* v. 19. *Thou, O Jehovah, shalt remain* (לעולם) *to the age, and thy throne* (לדור ודור) *from generation to generation*. Dan. iv. 3. *His kingdom is an æonian kingdom, and his power with generation and generation* (עם דר ודר) and verse 34. *whose power is an æonian power, and his kingdom with generation and generation* (עם דר ודר) i. e. in a succession of ages and generations even to the time when, *Dan.* vii. 27. (מלכותא ושלטנא ורבותא the (די מלכות תחות כל שמיא יהיבת לעם קדישי עליונין) *kingdom and empire and greatness of dominion under all heavens, shall be given to the people of the saints of the most high one*.

Doubtless there are innumerable alterations in the womb of destiny, which surmount the scanty capacities of human conception and intelligence: but yet that these will be, in like manner with what has been, temporal and successive, thro' all the
variety

variety of stages, issues, and astonishing revolutions in the creature life, may as reasonably be presumed, as that the course of nature, which has been for ages and years and months and days, will still be continued 'till the objects of nature become themselves different and fit for immutability.

Says our LORD, *John* v. 17. *My father worketh hitherto, and I work:* and here stands the foundation and reason of *Christ*'s kingdom, the propriety and convenience of the created æonian life; all the dread conduct of divine love during this his æonian government, thro' all its unfolding scenes, towards those that love and those that hate him, those who know him and those who know him not, whether in heaven or earth or hell or wherever else, rests upon this truth, that GOD hath a work to finish, a work for which his inviolable word is engaged, a work upon a creature already produced, a creature born and existing in time and in variety.

SECT. II.

IV^{thly}.

WE have to prove that the kingdom of *Christ* will be a season of a vast continuance.

WE look upon it as an exceeding length of time since our father *Adam* and his wife rejoiced together over their first-born son *Cain* in their mistaken hopes of him as the promis'd restorer. See *Gen.* iv. 1. *And she conceived and bare Cain, and said,* (קניתי אישׁ את יהוה) which should be rendered
'*I have*

¹*I have gotten* ²*a man* ³*the* ⁴*Jehovah.* For the series of years passed since *Adam* lived in this world, a fruitful season of so great a variety of events, seems very great indeed when compared with the few uncertain years which each of us expects as his residue in life; and yet all this length of years is far less than so many minutes compared with the duration of the æonian life.

I remember to have heard you speak very highly in favour of *Bengelius*'s *Gnomon*, but as you have no other of his writings, let me here give you the opinion of this sagacious author upon the word æon: the ideas which it excites will at least dilate your thoughts agreeably.

By dividing the number of the beast 666 by 42 the months of the beast, he has exhibited a sett

of

NOTES.

⁴ When אֵת stands between two nouns, it joins them together by apposition, and always denotes an accusative case; but it then only signifies (עִם) *cum* when joined with a verb transitive or verb in hithphael; in the Lutheran bible this passage therefore is translated *Ich habe den mann den Herrn*, I have gotten the man the Jehovah: according to which is also the syriac version (ܩܢܝܬ ¹ ܓܒܪܐ ² ܠܡܪܝܐ ³)
¹*I have gotten* ²*a man* ³*the Jehovah.*

Eve supposed that she had now brought forth the promised seed Jehovah, who, she believed, would become a man by being born of her, the offspring of her husband: for the doctrine of the preincarnate existence of souls is as old as the human race; our first parents presumed not that by *begetting* they *created* men, but only that beings already created, were thro' them formed into human existences.

of products which he thinks correspond so fortunately, as to bid fair for opening some of the most important truths of the revelations.[r]

In this work an (αιων) æon proves to be a term of 2222½ years, which squared yields the (αιων αιωνων, age of ages, i. e. the) æonian æon, or the term of 4938271,605 years.[s]

This is a very short time compared with what the plural æons import, and yet supposing our world

---

NOTES.

[r] See *Bengelius*'s introduction to his exposition of the apocalypse, translated by Dr. *Robertson*.

[s] *Ævi quadratum (ne de cubo dicamus) est* ævum ævorum, *annorum* 4938271$\frac{17}{81}$ *longissime ultra ætatem mundi excurrens: quadrati duplum, æva (duo) ævorum, annorum* 9876543$\frac{17}{81}$. *Hoc ideo tantum notamus, quia apertius figuratum habet numerum; in ævo ævorum notabiles sunt saltus a* 9 *ad* 8, *ad* 7. & *a* 4 *ad* 3, *ad* 2, *ad* 1. & *in fracto, si eadem proportione resolvatur, numerator supplet* 6. 5. *In ævis ævorum notabiles sunt gradus a* 9 *ad* 3. & *sic in fracto, si eadem proportione resolvatur, numerator supplet* 2, 1. &*c. vividius rem subjecerint occulis numeri expansi:*

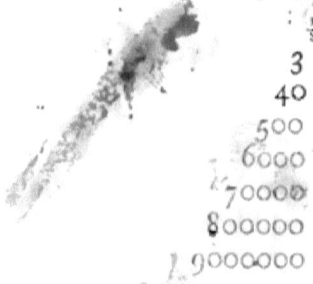

$$\begin{array}{c}\frac{17}{81}\\3\\40\\500\\6000\\70000\\800000\\9000000\end{array}$$

In illo, fractura $\frac{17}{81}$ *accedit ad* $\frac{6}{10}$ + $\frac{1}{100}$ &*c. in his fractura* $\frac{17}{81}$ *accedit ad* $\frac{2}{10}$ + $\frac{1}{100}$ &*c. in utraq; fractura numeratores* 6, 5, & 2, 1. *seriem ab* 1 *ad* 9 *explent.*

world to be 6000 years old, this simple square will amount to above 823 times our world's age.

But how prodigiously is this simple square exceeded by only the (αιωνες αιωνων or) ages (dual) of ages, a term still so very short of the vast excess involved in the (αιωνες αιωνων) the æons of æons three, 4, 100, 1000 times augmented, that human thought baffled in the conception must cry out, *O profundum!*¹

K And

NOTES.

Quid porro erunt æva ævorum tria, quatuor, centum, mille? &c. O profundum! & tamen hoc ne vadum quidem est de mari Æternitatis absolutæ, quam denotant OI αιωνες TΩN αιωνων. *Ingentia momenta interdum scriptura per subtiles stricturas obiter innuit. Qui capit, capiat.*

Caveant sibi, qui apocatastasin *post hanc vitam docent, ne rem jubilæo in millennium ducto exhauriri putent; multo amplior est mensura æonum; quæ hic attigimus, non ad curiositatem irritandam, sed ad pectus dilatandum, ut canditati æternitatis, accipiamus. In tempore sumus.*

See Bengelii ordo temporum, p. 325. *Stut.* 1741.

¹ THE COMPUTATION.

Αιων, an æon or age = $2222\frac{2}{9}$ years.

Αιων αιωνων, an æon of æons $2222\frac{2}{9} \times 2222\frac{2}{9} = 4938271, 605$ years.

OI αιωνες TΩN αιωνων, the æons of the æons $4938271, 605 \times 4938271, 605 = 24386526444749, 276025$ years. So that

Supposing the world's age to be 6000 years, the above last product being divided by them, you have the number of times this world's age is contained in the said last product, viz. 4064 millions 421 thousand, &c.

6000) 24386526444749, 276025 (4064421074, 124879.

So that our LORD's kingdom by the shortest calculation will continue 4064 millions 421 thousand and 74 times the age of this world, when this world shall have arrived to 6000 years of age.

And yet even all this, says *Bengelius*, is still scarcely a ford of that ocean of perpetuity denoted in the still higher terms ΟΙ αιωνες ΤΩΝ αιωνων, &c. found in certain parts of scripture; so *Rev.* iv. 9, 10. *The living creatures give glory to him that sitteth on the throne, and liveth to the æons of the æons* (εις τας αιωνας των αιωνων) in syriac (ܠܥܠܡ ܥܠܡܝܢ;) lolma dolmin 'to the secula ²of the secula; and again, *Rev.* xi. 15. *The kingdom of this world is become the kingdom of our Lord and of his Christ, and he shall reign to the æons of the æons* (εις τας αιωνας των αιωνων) *Rev.* xxii. 5. *And his servants shall see his face, and his name shall be in their forehead, and there shall be no night, for the Lord shall give them light, and they shall reign* (εις τας αιωνας των αιωνων) *to the æons of the æons.*

But these conceptions you say favour too violently of the astonishing and marvellous, and that they have too much of wonder in them to be true. Shall then the term marvellous render the promises of God ridiculous? His dispensations are all marvellous and full of wonder; and that they appear otherwise to the infidel, is owing to his blindness, and brutal stupidity.

" For that a branch cut off, a wither'd rod
Shou'd at a word pronounc'd, revive and bud;
Is this more strange, than that the mountain's brow,
Strip'd with december's frost, & white with snow,
Should push in spring ten thousand thousand buds,
And boast returning leaves, and blooming woods?

That each successive night from op'ning heav'n,
The food of angels shou'd to man be given,

Is this more strange than that with common bread
Our fainting bodies every day are fed;
Than that each grain and seed consum'd in earth,
Raises it's store, and multiplies its birth;
And from the handful, which the tiller sows,
The labour'd fields rejoice, and future harvest
[flows?"

But as to *Bengelius*'s calculation whether this may have been right or wrong, yet that the length of our LORD's æonian kingdom must needs be prodigious, the very nature of such an œconomy might perswade the unprejudic'd; especially when we observe the singular structure of the expressions teaching this doctrine in the original, and the remarkable suggestions they contain.

So *Exod.* xv. 18. *Jehovah shall reign to the æon and beyond.* (לעלם ועד) Dan. xii. 3. *They shall shine as the brightness of the firmament, and they that turn many to righteousness, as the stars to the æon and beyond* (לעלם ועד). Mich. iv. 5. *We shall walk in the name of Jehovah our God to the æon and beyond* (לעלם ועד). Dan. ii. 44. *And in the days of these* (clay-iron) *kings, shall the God of heaven set up a kingdom which to* (plural) *æons* (לעלמי) *shall not be destroyed,—and shall stand to* (plural) *æons* (לעלמיא). Dan. vii. 18. *And the saints of the most high shall take the kingdom, and shall possess the kingdom to the æon, even to the æon of the æons* (עד עלמא ועד עלם עלמיא)

The adding od to olem, and the shifting the terminations from hebrew to chaldee, from singular to plural, and from simple to emphatic, and that too in the same verse, as tho' the expression

preſſion was not to be found which might reach the prophet's purpoſe;" and the labour'd periphraſis of the laſt text, are all indications ſtrong enough that in the prophets then ſublime idea, the

---

NOTES.

Why the word æon in ſcripture imports otherwiſe than in the heathen greek authors.

"IT is on account of the ſingular uſe of the word (עלם) olm in the old teſtament, that the word (αιων) æon in the new is uſed in forms ſo unlike what occurs in our heathen greek authors. I ſuppoſe that among theſe the following expreſſions will not very readily be found, *viz.* εις τας αιωνας· εις αιωνα αιωνος. εις αιωνα αιωνων. εως της συντελειας τα αιωνος. εις ους τα τελη των αιωνων κατηντησεν. εις τας αιωνας των αιωνων. εις πασας τας γενεας τα αιωνος των αιωνων.

And the reaſon is becauſe inſpired writers only had ſuch notions of the ages as theſe expreſſions import.

Theſe ſons of light reading in the old teſtament עד עולם. עד לעלמי עד. לעלמין. לעלמיא ועד. עלמא. עלמה *&c.* at once underſtood that there was a plurality of ages; and that a certain number of theſe conſtituted a general or incluſive age, as a number of days conſtitute a week, or as ſeven years conſtitute a week of years; and theſe again ſeven times repeated, compoſe the great week of all which is reckoned from one jubilee to another, terminating in a great ſabbath, to the general delivery of every bondſman and priſoner.

I ſay our ſacred writers underſtood that the ceremonies of their law, *Heb.* viii. 5. *were ſhadows of heavenly things,* or, *Heb.* ix. 23. *patterns of things in the heavens,* and this occaſioned their uncommon critical uſe of the word æon. So when they intended a du-

the words olem and od, in whatever form, would denote but very inadequately, the boundlefs fpace of the æonian life.

LET-

NOTES.

ration of many ages, they wrote (εις τὰς αιωνας) to the æons, when they had in view a comprehenfive æon including in it many other fubordinate æons they wrote (εις αιωνα αιωνων) to the age of ages: when they intended the comprehenfive æon alone without regard to its conftituent particulars they wrote (εις αιωνα αιωνος) to an æonian æon (for this being a fyriacifm, means in greek the fame as εις αιωνα αιωνιον) to the æonian æon: and when they intended the feveral general or comprehenfive æons altogether, collectively, they wrote (εις τὰς αιωνας των αιωνων) to the (plural unafcertained) æons of the (plural unafcertained) æons.

LETTER V.

The term æonian applied to the word Spirit, imports not that He is eternal.

TO ———

SIR,

HAVING proved that the terms æon and olm are frequently used in scripture to denote a temporal duration, the conclusions built upon them as importing eternity, are at once defeated. Notwithstanding, I dare maintain (tho' my present argument does not require it) even what you challenge me to maintain, viz. that the words æon and olm do no where in scripture signify eternity; and that in whatever passages we find them, they relate to time, and the periods of time, either before, during, or after the continuance of this world.

It is easily granted that the æonian life will in effect be an eternity to them that are saved; for when time arrived to its end vanishes away, and

is

is no more; then that life, which was before temporal, will commence somewhat else, which those who like the term may call eternal.

This, however, in the course of our correspondence will appear upon examination of the usual texts urged against us; and among the chief of them will be that in *Heb.* ix. 14. which as you declare in your last to be your strongest proof that the idea of eternity is scriptural, shall be my next business.

I foresee indeed that it will require a good deal of time, and the length of several letters, to explicate this text to your satisfaction, and to the purposes I have in view; it being necessary that I clear my way by discussing another point in which I know we greatly differ: however, all I will demand for my trouble in writing them is, that you read them once over considerately, before you proceed to censure.

SECT. I.

Heb. ix. 14.

IF *the blood of bulls and goats sanctify to the purifying of the flesh; how much more shall the blood of Christ, who thro'* the æonian *spirit* (δ ὰ πνευματος αιωνι or as in the syriac we read it 'who by the spirit ' (olem) æonian 'offered up 'his soul 'without 'blemish 'unto God, *purify our conscience from dead works, to serve the living God.*

The

The character here given us of the æonian spirit is, that thro' it *Chrift* offered up himfelf to God irreprehenfible or without fault.

Now tho' we feem fufficiently acquainted with the term *Chrift*, yet before we can judge fairly of this text, we ought alfo to know, 1ft, who the fpirit is, thro' whom *Chrift* offered up himfelf to God; 2dly, upon what account it is faid that thro' him *Chrift* offered up himfelf to God; and 3dly, why he is called the æonian (or the olem) fpirit.

For effecting this to our purpofe, we beg leave to clear our way by the following pofitions, viz.

I. That the name Spirit does belong to the Logos or Meffiah, or that the only fon of God is a fpirit.

II. That this Logos, Meffiah, or Filial Spirit, exifts perfonally diftinct from God the father.

III. That this Logos or Filial Spirit has a will diftinct from God his father, in the freedom of which will he offered himfelf to the father to be a facrifice for man in the future man *Chrift Jefus*.

IV. That this Logos or Filial Spirit muft have been that fpirit who moved or influenced the man *Chrift Jefus* to become (i. e. is He thro' whom He became) a facrificial offering for us.

And having proved thus much (fince we have already proved that *Jefus Chrift* is the æonian God) we fhall have confirmed our point, viz. that the æonian fpirit, thro' whom *Chrift* offered up himfelf to God for us, was the Logos, or Filial Spirit, ufually called Adn, Lord, or rather Adni, my Lord, in the old teftament, and who is the only fon of God, perfonally diftinct from his father.

I. The

LETTER V. [81] SECT. I.

I. The name Spirit belongs to the Logos[w] or Messiah; in other words, the only begotten son of GOD is a spirit.

1 *Cor.* xv. 45. *The first Adam became a living soul* (i. e. became an animal or soul life) *the last Adam* (became) *a quickening spirit*; that is, being

in

NOTES.

[w] The term (λογος) Word, in greek, is intended to answer the term (ממרא) mmra, or (מימרא) mimra, which signifies just the same in the chaldee language, and very frequently occurs in the ancient jewish writings, and was well known to the *Jews* of our saviour and his apostles times.

Now by the term (מימרא) mimra, *i. e.* Logos or word, they understood that personal presence who in the old testament is called Jehovah Adni, and which St. *Paul* calls (πρωτοτοκος) the first begotten, who talked face to face to *Moses, Adam, Noah, Abraham, Isaac, Jacob*; and is every where stiled the creator of all things.

This appears from the jewish targums, or chaldee paraphrases on the books of *Moses*, which being written before our LORD's time, and being still in high repute among the *Jews*, are an unexceptionable witness of their opinion concerning the Messiah. Also it appears from them that they believed him to be an angelic personage in whom the divine nature resided; and they ascribe to him all the attributes of GOD.

So then by the terms Logos, Jehovah, Adni, and first-begotten, we must mean what the apostles and their cotemporaries thereby meant, namely, one and the same person express'd only by different titles; the (אדני Adni or) my lord of the *Jews*, the (κυριος or) LORD of the *Christians*, i. e. *Luke* ii. 11. *Christ the Lord, who* (Acts x. 36) *is Lord of all.*

in himself a spirit, even a quickening spirit, he became a quickening principle to the sons of Adam; for *John* iii. 6. *That which is born* (or begotten) *of the flesh, is flesh; and that which is born* (or begotten) *of the spirit, is spirit.*

And this begetting, and so quickening spirit is the very son of GOD, who is the LORD, the Logos, or word of GOD. *John* v. 21. *As the father raiseth up the dead, and quickeneth them; even so the son quickeneth whom he will.* 2 Cor. iii. 16. *Who also hath made us able ministers of the new testament, not of the letter, but of the spirit; for the letter killeth, but the spirit giveth life.* V. 17. *Now the Lord* (i. e. the Logos or Adn) *is that spirit.* As he is again stiled, 2 *Cor.* iii. 18. *The Lord the spirit.* (απο κυριε πνευματος)

But the Logos, or Adn, or son of GOD, is also called the father of spirits, which is again a proof that the appellation spirit is most justly his.

Heb. xii. 6, 9. *Whom the Lord loveth he chasteneth*; v. 9. and *shall we not be in subjection to the father of spirits, and live?* But the same who chasteneth is also the father of spirits; therefore the LORD called (Adni) my Lord in the old testament, even the first and only begotten son of GOD, who is now become the man *Christ Jesus,* he is the father of spirits.

To conclude then. Since it appears that *Christ* is a quickening spirit, the spirit of the resurrection, the accomplishing spirit of the law, the true son of GOD who is a spirit, and the father of spirits; characters all which are no where applied as belonging to any other person than *Christ Jesus*;

our

our first article is evinced; namely, that the Messiah must be a spirit, and therefore may, at least for any thing contained to the contrary in the term spirit, be aptly called the æonian spirit.[x]

SECT. II.

II. *He this only begotten son of* God *or* Logos, *exists personally distinct from* GOD *the father*.

THIS appears from *Ps.* cx. 1. *Jehovah* (יהוה) *said unto* (אדני Adni) *my Lord, sit thou on my right hand 'till I make thy foes thy footstool;* this passage we also find *Mat.* xxii. 44. *Mark* xii. 36.

Now Jehovah is GOD, and Adni is the spirit covenanting with GOD, who said, *Heb.* x. 7. *Lo I come to do thy will, O God,* i. e. He is the Messiah: GOD therefore and the Messiah are personally distinct from each other, or are two contracting parties, the one propounding, the other accept-

NOTES.

[x] Possibly you may expect that I here speak more distinctly concerning the scripture doctrine of the spirit of the father, and the spirit of the son, observable in many parts of the new testament. So *Mat.* xii. 28. *Luke* iv. 1. *Acts* x. 38. *John* xv 26. *Gal.* iv. 6. 1 *Pet.* i. 11. 1 *John* iv. 13. 1 *Cor.* vi. 11. *Rom.* viii. 9, 15. But as this point belongs especially to the second part, which I intend, if it please GOD to give me life and ability, to write to you upon the human soul, as I promised you, I shall decline it in this place.

accepting proposals of treaty: but without further urging this passage at present, I shall proceed to prove my point from the visibility and other properties of the Logos, which cannot be applied to the invisible father.

1. That GOD the father of the only begotten son of GOD, is not visible, appears from many places of the bible; let the following suffice *John* i. 18. *No one* (ἀδεὶς) *hath seen God at any time; the only begotton son* (ὁ ὢν) *who is in the bosom of the father, he* (*i.e.* he only, having seen him) *hath declared him.* John vi. 46. *Not that* (τὶς) *any one hath seen the father, except he who is of God, he hath seen the father.* 1 John iv. 12, 20. *No one* (ἀδεὶς) *hath seen God at any time.—He who loves not his brother, whom he has seen, how can he love God whom he has not seen?* 1 Tim. vi. 16. *whom no man hath seen, nor can see.* So 1 *Tim.* i. 17.[y]

2. That the Logos or only begotten son of GOD is visible, appears from numberless passages in scripture, of which we shall produce a few.

Gen.

N O T E S.

[y] *Non enim (ut quidam putant) natura Dei invisibilis est alicui & aliis visibilis est; non enim dixit apostolus imago invisibilis Dei hominibus, aut invisibilis peccatoribus; sed valde constanter pronunciat de ipsa natura Dei dicens; imago invisibilis Dei. Sed & Johannes in evangelio dicens, Deum nemo vidit unquam, manifeste declarat omnibus qui intelligere possunt, quod nulla natura est cui visibilis sit Deus: non quasi qui visibilis quidem sit per naturam, & velut fragilioris creaturæ evadat atq; excedat aspectum, sed quoniam naturaliter videri impossibile est.*

Origen de principiis, lib. i. cap. i.

Gen. iii. 8. *And he heard the voice of Jehovah God walking in the garden in the cool of the day; and Adam and his wife hid themselves from the presence of Jehovah God,* (יהוה אלהים) *among the trees of the garden.*

Jehovah God is here declared visible, so visible as to be the object of human eyes, and so the object of them, that *Adam* in his nakedness, would have avoided seeing him, by hiding himself among the trees.

Now that no objection may be here started from that great term (יהוה אלהים) Jehovah God (or Gods) it should be observed that God both father and only begotten son are distinctly and separately called by names denoting in common the divine being. So *Gen.* xix. 24. *And Jehovah* (יהוה) *caused to rain upon Sodom and Gomorrah, brimstone and fire from the Jehovah* (מאת יהוה) *out of the heavens, i. e.* Jehovah the son, personally distinct from Jehovah the father, caused this rain from his father, who was in heaven.

Gen. xvii. 1. *And when Abraham was* 99 *years old, Jehovah appeared to Abraham, and said unto him, I am* (אל שדי) *the almighty God,* (or rather GOD that produceth or poureth forth all things) *walk before me, and be thou perfect.*

Here again is certainly a person seen of *Abraham:* but *Abraham* could not see the father GOD invisible: Whom saw he then? he saw him who is GOD visible, who is. *Col.* i. 15. *the image of the invisible God, the first-begotten of every creature,* and in seeing him he in effect saw the father, as says our LORD, *John* xiv. 9. *He that hath seen me, hath
seen*

LETTER V. [86] SECT. II.

seen the father also; because (ver. 10.) *I am in the father, and the father in me.* The like again we read *Gen.* xxxv. 9, 11, 13. *And God appeared unto Jacob again when he came out of Padanaram, and blessed him, and said I am God Almighty, be fruitful and multiply,* &c. *and God went up from him in the place where he talked with him.* Exod. xxxiii. 11. *And Jehovah spake unto Moses face to face, as a man speaks unto his friend.* Numb. xii. 5, 8. *And the Lord said, if there be a prophet among you, I the Lord will make myself known to him in vision, and will speak unto him in a dream; my servant Moses is not so; with whom I will speak mouth to mouth, and in vision, and not in similitudes; and* (in so much that) *he shall contemplate* (ותמנת יהוה יביט) *the image* (or figure, or personage) *of Jehovah* [z]. This

---

NOTES.

[z] יביט Is the third person singular of the future tense of the conjugation hiph of the verb נבט, which signifies to speculate upon, look into, revolve in mind, contemplate. See in *Isaiah* viii. 22. xxii. 11. li. 1, 2, 6. The antithesis here is remarkable; says the LORD, *To a prophet I will reveal myself only in dreams and visions, but to Moses* more apparently and as a friend familiarly And may we not hence infer that the LORD revealed himself to *Moses* neither by phantasm, nor by proxy, but in a way more evident and apparent than these, yea than vision itself? And what could this way be less than (what the words we insist upon mean in their critical acceptation and truth) a familiar converse with Jehovah in his personal circumscribed presence, called in the old testament (פני יהוה) the face of Jehovah? These words can in no wise be

LETTER V.   [87]   SECT. II.

This personage *Moses* first saw at the bush; *Exod.* iii. 2, 15. who there declared himself to be *the God of his fathers, the Jehovah, the* (אהיה אשר אהיה or which is the same, אהיה אשר אהוה) *I will be who will be*; from whence his name (יהוה) Jeve, or Jehovah, He will be.   Jehovah

---

NOTES.

said of that divinity which no one has seen or can see, nor can they be understood of an airy phantastic body, because to contemplate such is so far from seeing GOD face to face apparently, that it is not to see him at all, so that this appearance can have been no other than that real angelic preincarnate personage, which was the (πρωτοτοκος or) first-begotten son in which the divine nature dwells.

Christ in his invisible, inscrutable, eternal nature, is, 1 *John* v. 20. (ὁ ἀληθινος Θεος) *The true God.* Tit. ii. 13. (ὁ μεγας Θεος) *The great God.* Rom. ix. 5. (ὁ ἐπι παντων Θεος) *The God over all, blessed for ever.*

In his preincarnate manifestation, he is (πρωτοτοκος) the first-begotten, (μονογενης υἱος) the only generated son of GOD; *Mat.* xvi. 16.(ὁ υἱος τε Θεε τε ζωντος) *The son of the living God*; Rom. viii. 32. (ἰδιος υἱος) *his own proper son*; whom *Melchisedeck* is made to typify by being represented as having, *Heb.* vii. 3. (μητε αρχην ἡμερων μητε ζωης τελος) *neither beginning of days, nor end of life*; the same who appeared to the patriarchs in form angelic, and who performed the work of creation; *Col.* i. 16, 17. *For by him were all things created that are in heaven, and that are in earth, visible and invisible, whether they be thrones, or dominions, or principalities, or powers; all things were created by him and for him. And he is before all things, and by him all things consist.*

And as he was the angelic son of GOD before the fall; so afterwards and by occasion of the fall, he became the man-son of GOD, *i. e.* like one of us, our

Jehovah therefore has an image, or figure, or personage; and this image *Moses* having seen with his eyes, could ideally contemplate; and agreeably with this account of him St. *Paul* calls him, 2 *Cor.* iv. 4. *The image of God* (εικων τȣ Θεȣ) Heb. i. 3. *The shining forth of his glory, the express image of his substance,* (απαυγασμα της δοξης κ᾽ χαρακτηρ της ὑποςασεως αυτȣ) and hence it is that our saviour says, *John* xii. 45. *He that hath seen me, hath seen him that sent me.*[a]

Jos. v. 13. *And Joshua looked and behold there stood a man over-against him, with his sword drawn in*

NOTES.

brother; in which form the father proclaims him his *Christ*, and *Mat.* iii. 17. *His beloved son, in whom he is well pleased;* and in which he atchieves the work of restitution, *becoming* (*Col.* i. 18.) *the head of the body, the church: who is the beginning, the first-begotten from the dead, that in all things he might be the foremost.*

By the word son we here understand, a reality of relation, aptly and analogously signified in that of sonship known among men: since we have reason to believe, that the human relation of father and son was at first ordained on earth, to exhibit to us what the word of GOD is to his invisible father.

Thus is our LORD at all times and in every view of him (ἡ αληθεια αποφαινομενη) the truth manifested, or reality displayed; and his essential character is perpetually preserved.

[a] Some have thought that GOD in these places describing his presence, must have spoken in the person of some angel, that is of a creature; but when we consider his authority who appeared, who spoke, who moved, was seen, and heard, we cannot reconcile our-

in his hand, and Joshuah went unto him and said unto him, art thou for us, or for our adversaries? and he said, nay but (¹אני ²שר ³צבא ⁴יהוה ⁵עתה ⁶באתי) ¹*ego* ²*princeps* ³*in ordine militari stans* ⁵*nunc* ⁶*veni* (vel, nunc in venire me) ¹I ⁴Jehovah ⁵am now ⁶come ²a prince ³in military attitude, &c. *and Joshuah fell upon his face and worshiped:* ¹*then answered* ⁴*Jehovah* ¹*standing* ²*a chief* (or prince) ³*in military attitude,* ⁵*unto* ⁶*Joshua* (¹ויאמר ²שר ³צבא ⁴יהוה ⁵אל ⁶יהושע) *loose thy shoes from off thy feet, for the place whereon thou standest is holy; and Jehovah said I have given into thy hands Jerico.*ᵇ

Isaiah vi. 1.—*And in the year that king Uzziah died I saw* (את אדני) *the Adni sitting upon a throne high and lifted up, and his train filled the temple; above it stood the seraphim—and one cried unto another and said, holy, holy, holy is Jehovah of hosts.— Then said I wo is me for mine eyes have seen the king Jehovah of hosts.*

M   That

NOTES.

selves to this opinion; especially as this presence stiles himself (what no angel would dare) absolutely, directly and without restriction, *Ex.* xxxiv. 6. *Jehovah, Jehovah God,* (אל יהוה יהוה) *merciful and gracious, long-suffering and abundant in goodness and truth;* and distinguishes himself (as sending) from an angel (his messenger) *Exod.* xxxiii. 2, 3. *And I will send an angel before thee, and will drive out the Canaanite,* &c. *for I will not go up in the midst of thee, for thou art a stiff-necked people.*

ᵇ No being by appearing can evidence his presence more sensibly, than the sublime object here seen of *Joshua,* the real preincarnate personage of our saviour.

As his form was visible, so was his voice audible; and his manner and gesture were altogether human, the mien and carriage of a man.

That this glorious object seen here of *Isaiah* was Jehovah, we are assured both from the apostle *John*, who says of this appearance, chap. xii. 41. *These things said Isaiah when he saw his glory and spake of him*; and likewise from the words of *Isaiah* himself, who says, ver. 5. *Mine eyes have seen the Lord of hosts.*

And yet it is likewise as evident that the object here seen was a substantial appearance of human shape, of personage circumscribed, distinguish'd by features, lineaments and other personal accidents and properties, specifically expressive of himself, and in like manner as one man is by such distinguished from another; insomuch that the individual substantial personage now seen by *Isaiah*,^c was in strictest truth there, where this his presence was obvious to the sight.   For

---

NOTES.

We have in short as good reason to doubt whether our fellow creatures whom we daily see and hear, are real beings, as *Joshua* had to doubt of the real personal presence of Jehovah Adni now before him.

Yea these appearances of the Logos were so sensible, that the *Jews* even thought the eternal GOD to have a material personage; *Justin Martyr* therefore reproaches them as follows,

ὥσπερ ὑμῶν οἱ διδασκαλοι ἀξιουσιν, οἰομενοι χειρας κ᾽ ποδας κ᾽ δακτυλ.ους, κ᾽ ψυχην εχειν, ὡς συνθετον ζωον, τον πατερα των ὁλων, κ᾽ ἀγεννητον θεον; οἱ τινες κ᾽ δια τουτο ωφθαι τω Αβρααμ κ᾽ τω Ιακωβ αυτον τον πατερα διδασκουσι.

Justin Martyris dialog. cum Tryphone judæo.

^c And in like personal characters of distinction was our LORD frequently seen of the *Israelites*; as of *Gideon*, see *Judges* vi. 11.—24. where the posture, the action, the name as well as the express words of the

For as a man, tho' he cannot behold either the spirit or the soul of his father, friend or fellow creature, yet beholding the personal presence of these, may in strict truth be said to behold even them; so the patriarchs seeing the angelic presence of Jehovah, were said, even by GOD himself, to behold Jehovah.

Says Jehovah, *If.* xlv. 22. *I* (that is I whom thy eyes behold) *am God, and there is none else.* The object here visible was only the angelic personage of Jehovah, i.e. of the son of GOD; and yet this seen, Jehovah, the only GOD, is declared to be himself seen, in that he was so seen as a man is seen when he says of himself, I whom thou seest am thy father, friend or brother; altho' he distinguishes not between his external and internal existence; between the temple visible, and its inhabitant the inward man invisible. And in this

---

NOTES.

history, do all attest the LORD visible to him, and the same to *Manoah*, see *Judges* xiii. 3.—22. and to *Amos, Zechariah, Ezekiel, Daniel* and *Elias,* and *Simeon,* and even most of the prophets. But not only the *Israelites,* for even *Nebuchadnezar* saw him in the furnace of fire walking with *Shadrack, Mesak* and *Abednego*; and says of him, *the form of the fourth is like the son of God:* by which it seems that the appearance of *Christ* was no uncommon thing in those days; for since it is the usual manner of speech to describe strange, new, unknown things, by comparing them to things better known, and of which one has a clearer notion; *Nebuchadnezar*'s words imply, that he knew the son of GOD by the description of him heard from others, who had seen the real presence he exhibits.

this regard of them are the following scripture passages to be understood by us.

Isaiah xliv. 6. *I am the first and I am the last, and besides me there is no God.* Verse 8. *Is there a God besides me? yea there is no* (other) *rock, I know not any.* Deut. iv. 35. *Jehovah he is God, there is none else besides him.* Deut. xxxii. 39. *I even I am he and there is no God with me.* If. xliii. 10. *Believe and understand that I am he; before me there was no God formed, and after me there shall be none.* Isa. xlv. 5. *I am Jehovah, there is none else, there is no God except me* (אלהי) ver. 6. (בלעדי) *besides me.*

That the person speaking in the above passages may be the son of GOD cannot be doubted, since we find the son of GOD expressly called (*John* i. 1. Matt. i. 23.) *God.* John xx. 28. *My Lord and my God.* 2 Pet. i. 1. *Our God.* 1 John v. 20. *True God.* Psalm lxxviii. 56. 1 Cor. x. 9. *The most high God.* Rom. ix. 5. *God over all.* Rev. xv. 3, 4. *Lord God Almighty, who only art holy:* and in numberless places Jehovah, names intelligible only in our LORD's own account of himself, *John* x. 30. *I and my father* (not εἰς ἐσμεν are the same in person or manner of subsistence; but ἐν ἐσμεν) *are the same thing, or one in nature*; and for this reason also the son is called GOD even by his father himself. Heb. i. 8. *But unto the son he* (the father) *saith, Thy throne, O God, is to the æon of æons, a scepter of equity is the scepter of thy kingdom.*

This visible GOD of glory before the incarnation is called (אדני יהוה) Adni Ieve or) *My Lord Jehovah.* If. lix. 20. *Job* xix. 25. (גאלי or גיאל) *My redeemer.* Mal. iii. 1. *The angel of the covenant.* Zech. iii. 1. *The angel Jehovah.* If. lxiii. 9.

The

The angel of his presence; but most usually Jehovah or God: and when his distinction from the father is intended, himself is called singly God, and his father is called his God; so *Psalm* xlv. 6, 7. *Thy throne, O God, is æonian and beyond* (אלהים עולם ועד)—*God even thy God* (אלהים אלהיך) *hath anointed thee with oil of gladness above thy fellows. i. e.* Thou who art God, art anointed by thy God above the angels, who, tho' created by thee, are notwithstanding thy fellows, in that they bear thy likeness, and are **the varying images of thee the one God-begotten uncreated angel**; for such thou art in thy visible nature, at the same time that in thy unsearchable nature, thou art unknown to, being beyond the conception of all but thy father only.

And with like import and insinuation speak our Lord's own words, *John* xx. 17. *I ascend unto my father, and your father, and to my God, and your God.*

But after the incarnation our visible God is called, *Matt.* xvi. 16. *Christ the son of the living God.* 1 Cor. xv. 47. *The Lord from heaven.* Acts x. 36. *The Lord of all.* Acts vii. 2. *The God of glory.* Phil. ii. 6, 7. *Who being* before his incarnation (εν μορφη Θευ) *in the form of God,* did, after his incarnation, assume *the form of a servant* (μορφην δουλου) becoming *the likeness of man*, and is distinguished from the father by the term son.[d] Of

---

NOTES.

[d] Some of the primitive christian writers speak very clearly of both these natures of the son of God. So Ερεις εν μοι, συ φης τον θεον εν τοπω μη δειν χωρεισθαι, η πως νυν λεγεις αυτον εν τω παραδεισω περιπατειν? ακουε ὁ φημι,

LETTER V. [94] SECT. II.

Of these his two distinct states, viz. that before his incarnation, and that after it, our LORD often speaks in the gospel.

Thus when our LORD prays, *John* xvii. 5. iii. 13. *And now, O father, glorify me with the glory which*

NOTES.

ὁ μεν θεος κ̃ πατηρ των ὁλων αχωρητος ετι, κ̃ εν τοπω ουχ ευρισκεται; ου γαρ ετι τοπος της καταπαυσεως αυτȣ; ὁ δε λογος αυτȣ, δι ȣ τα παντα πεποιηκε, δυναμις ων κ̃ σοφια αυτȣ, (for the antient *Jews* and primitive Christians describe the Logos, as having in him, for his characteristic attribute, a principle of divine wisdom and efficacy; and on account of this they frequently call him the wisdom of GOD and the virtue of GOD) αναλαμβανων το προσωπον τȣ πατρος κ̃ κυριȣ των ὁλων, αυτος παρεγινετο εις τον παραδεισον εν προσωπω τȣ θεȣ (for *Christ*'s angelic form is here meant by το προσωπον τȣ πατρος and τȣ Θεȣ, *i. e.* the personage of *Christ* is here also called the personage of the Father and the personage of GOD) κ̃ ὡμιλει τω Αδαμ.—Theophilus ad Autol. lib. ii.

Ουτε ουν Αβρααμ ουτε αλλος ανθρωπων ειδε τον πατερα κ̃ αρρητον κυριον των παντων ἁπλως, κ̃ αυτȣ τȣ Χριςȣ; αλλ' εκεινον τον κατα βȣλην την εκεινȣ κ̃ θεον οντα υιον αυτȣ, κ̃ Αγ̃ελον εκ τȣ ὑπηρετειν τη γνωμη αυτȣ; ον κ̃ ανθρωπον γεννηθεναι δια της παρθενου βεβουληῖαι; ὁς κ̃ πυρ ποτε γεγονε τη προς Μωσεα ὁμιλια τη απο της βατȣ. Επει εαν μη ουτω νοησωμεν τας γραφας, συμβησεῖαι τον πατερα κ̃ κυριον των ὁλων μη γεγενησθαι τοτε εν τοις ȣρανοις, ὁτε δια Μωσεως λελεκῖαι, κ̃ κυριος εβρεξεν επι Σοδομα πυρ κ̃ θειον παρα κυριȣ εκ τȣ ουρανȣ. κ̃ παλιν δια Δαβιδ ὁτε λελεκῖαι ουτως, αρατε πυλας οἱ αρχοντες ὑμων, κ̃ επαρθητε πυλαι αιωνιοι, κ̃ εισελευσεῖαι ὁ βασιλευς της δοξης.—κ̃ ὁτι ὁ χριςος κ̃ θεος θεου υιος ὑπαρχων, κ̃ δυναμει φαινομενος προτερον ὡς ανηρ, κ̃ αγ̃ελ☉, κ̃ εν πυρος δοξη ὡς εν τη βαῖω περανῖαι, κ̃ ετι της κρισεως της γεγενημενης επι Σοδομα, αποδεδεικῖαι εν πολλοις τοις ειρημενοις, &c. &c.

Justin Martyr, dialog. cum Tryphone judæo.

which I had with thee before the world was; how can this be understood but of his preincarnate angelic nature which we maintain? Can *Christ* in his divine nature suffer any diminution of his glory? Must not the son of GOD in his divine essence be immutable, without variation or shadow of changing?

But in his angelic nature, as the first begotten of the creation, or as the begotten before all creatures, all this may be, consistent with all revealed accounts of him. As we read *John* i. 1. *In the beginning* (that is before the creation began) *was* (i. e. existed) *the word* (Logos; but how did he exist, by Creation? No;) he was Col. i. 15. (πρωτοτοκος) *The first-begotten* (and so begotten as to be) *the image of God* (and so compleatly his image as) *that in him should dwell all the plenitude of the Godhead.* In him, in his angelic state, dwelt the plenitude of the Godhead; and because all fulness (i. e. creaturely as well as divine) must dwell in him, he also became man; in which capacity being now the bodily temple of GOD, we read of him, that Col. ii. 9. *In him dwelleth all the plenitude of the Godhead bodily.*

It is therefore this the preincarnate personage or filial spirit, Logos or *Christ*, which enjoy'd a glory with GOD before the worlds were; which laid aside his glory at his incarnation, and resumed it after his resurrection; of which himself speaks, *John* vi. 62. *What if you shall see the son of man ascend up where he* (i. e. who now inhabits my body) *was before*; i. e. Rom. vi. 4. *into the glory of his father*, which *John* xvii. 5. *He had with the father before the world was.*

In

In this personage *Job* both saw him and heard him, when he says, *Job.* xlii. 5. *I heard of thee with my ears, but now mine eye hath seen thee*; i. e. I have seen thee as evidently with my eyes, as I had heard of thee with my ears: and again, *Job.* xix. 26, 27. *Yet in my flesh shall I see God, whom I shall see for myself* (י insuper porro as well as, and i. e.) *Yea mine eyes have seen thee, and not a stranger.*

And of this again our LORD speaks, when he tells us *John* iii. 13. *No man hath ascended up to heaven, but he that came down from heaven, even the son of man, who is in heaven.*

So that, as there is a personal distinction between GOD the father and the man *Christ Jesus*, and yet the man *Christ Jesus* is the son of GOD; so there is also a personal distinction between GOD the father and the filial spirit call'd Jehovah Adni, and yet Jehovah Adni was the son of GOD.

And as the man *Christ Jesus* is not created, but the begotten son of GOD; so Jehovah Adn was not created, but the begotten son of GOD:
only

N O T E S.

¹ ומבשרי ² אחזה ³ אלוה ⁴ אשר ⁵ אני ⁶ אחזה ⁷ לי ⁸ ועיני ⁹ ראו ¹⁰ ולא ¹¹ זר

¹*et de carne mea* ²*videbo Deum* ⁴*quem* ⁵*ego* ⁶*visurus sum* (i. e. *videbo*) ⁷*mihi*, ⁸*et* (i. e. *porro*) *oculi mei* ⁹*viderunt* ¹⁰*et non* ¹¹*alienum.*

The original speaking first in the future tense (אחזה) *videbo*, and then in the preter tense (ראו) *viderunt*, imports that *Job* comforts himself in the hopes of seeing our LORD in another state of being; and grounds his hopes on a confidence of his redeemer's living, because his own eyes had now seen him in his true, and not in a strange or borrowed appearance.

only the man *Chriſt Jeſus* was begotten after the creation, whereas Jehovah Adn, or the Logos, was begotten before created nature began.

Again, as Jehovah Adn, being begotten of the father, became the (ἡ ἀρχὴ τῆς κτίσεως τῦ Θεῦ) the original of the creation of GOD; ſo the man *Chriſt Jeſus*, being begotten of the Holy Ghoſt, becomes the original of the new creation which is to be effected by him, *Rev.* xxi. 5.

Again, as after the incarnation, the individual perſon *Chriſt Jeſus* was GOD and man; ſo before the creation, the individual perſon Logos was the GOD afterwards known by the title Jehovah Adn, or GOD and angel the LORD.

Again, as *Jeſus Chriſt* after his incarnation was viſible as to his manhood, and not as to his divinity; ſo Jehovah Adn before the incarnation was viſible as to his angelical perſonage, and not as to his divine nature.

Again, as it is the eſpecial privilege of chriſtians to know that *Jeſus Chriſt* is the ſon of GOD; ſo it was propounded to the *Jews* as their eſpecial privilege, to know that their gracious Adni was true Jehovah.

And here I cannot forbear remarking, that in this idea of the divine Logos, that text which the *Mennoniſts* ſo tenaciouſly and commendably inſiſt upon, and with which they ſo much perplex their learned oppoſers, namely, *John* i. 14. (ὁ λόγος σὰρξ ἐγένετο) *The word was made fleſh*, becomes quite intelligible and without exception. For theſe words ſay not that the divine nature was converted into humanity; but that the viſible Logos, who was the angelic (ἀποστόλους or) first-begotten of GOD, the original or beginning of the creation of GOD, (σαρξ εγενετο) was made flesh or man, or became om-anu-al, i. e. עם with אנו us אל GOD, or GOD visible and knowable; for the divine essence is *itself* ever with us, as being every where present; but then whereas this presence yields us neither knowledge nor view of GOD, because we are utterly incapable of seeing it; the Logos by being man not only becomes himself a natural object of our sight, and knowledge; but in him, that is in his human presence, his holy ones shall be enabled also to behold the glory of the divine nature.

SECT. III.

The man Jesus *a true son of* GOD.

THE comfortableness of these reflections again increase upon us, when we consider that even the manhood of *Jesus Christ* is of divine generation; *Mat.* i. 18. *Mary* (ευρεθη εν γαςρι εχεσα εκ πνευματος αγιε, or as in the syriac, in which this gospel was written, ܐܫܬܟܚܬ¹ ܒܛܢܐ² ܗܘ³ ܡܢ⁵ ܪܘܚܐ⁴) ¹*was found* ²*pregnant* ³*by* (of or from) *the* ⁵*holy* ⁴*ghost*. So verse 20. (ܗܘ¹ ²ܒܗ ܕܐܬܝܠܕ⁴ ܒܗ³) ²*For* ¹*that* ³*which is begotten* ⁴*in her is by* (of or from) *the holy ghost*. Again, *Luke* i. 35. (πνευμα αγιον επελευσεται επι σε, ϗ δυναμις υψιςε επισκιασει σοι ᶠ διο ϗ το γεννωμενον αγιον κληθησεται υιος θεε)

the

NOTES.

ᶠ Επισκιασει σοι, shall over-shadow thee, that is, (says *Lightfoot* in his harmony) *supplebit defectum maris, est*

the holy ghoſt ſhall come upon thee, even the higheſt power ſhall overſhadow thee, wherefore alſo that holy begotten one ſhall be called the ſon of God. That is, that ſame perſon who ſhall be called (*i. e.* ſhall be) the ſon of man as conceived in thee, ſhall be alſo called ſon of God, being an offspring from the holy ghoſt.

Theophilat gloſſes thus on theſe words; *Virtus altiſſimi filius Dei eſt, Chriſtus enim eſt Dei virtus: obumbrabit tibi, hoc eſt conteget te, hoc eſt undique te circumdabit, ſicut avis obumbrat pullos ſuos.——— Illud quod naſcebatur in utero fuit filius Dei, et non alius*

NOTES.

enim hæc modeſta phraſis quâ amplexus conjugalis exprimitur, ut Ruth iii. 9. and ſo (as ſays *Vetablus*) *Illud ſanctum non humanâ ſed divinâ vi gignitur.*

t *Theophilact* in confining the term (δυναμις ὑψιςυ) the power (or efficacy) of the higheſt to the Logos, ſeems to miſtake the true force of theſe words.

In the ſyriac tongue, in which theſe words were ſpoken (δυναμις ὑψιςυ) the power of the higheſt is equivalent to (δυναμις ὑψιςη) the higheſt power (ſee Letter III. note ᵉ) and ſo the terms (δυναμις ὑψιςυ) the power of the higheſt, are appoſite to (πνευμα ἁγιον) the holy ghoſt, according to which conſtruction this paſſage ſhould be tranſlated, *the holy ghoſt ſhall come upon thee, even he who is the higheſt power* (or efficacy) *ſhall overſhadow thee*, the event of which ſhall be, that holy conception, which ſhall therefore be called the ſon of God. For the holy ghoſt may as aptly be call'd (δυναμις ὑψιςυ) the higheſt efficacy, as the Logos. And ſince St. *Mathew* expreſsly tells us that the holy conception was of the holy ghoſt, we muſt believe that the holy ghoſt is diſtinctly the agent in this holy conception.

alius quidem fœtus est uteri, alius autem filius Dei (id est, non unus sit Dei alter vero Mariæ filius) sed unus et idem fuit filius virginis & filius Dei. " That is, the virtue of the highest is the son of " GOD, but *Christ* is the virtue of GOD (see the " note foregoing) shall overshadow thee, i. e. shall " cover thee, i. e. shall surround thee on every " side, as a bird overshadows her young—That " which was conceived in the womb was the " son of GOD: also the fruit of the womb " was not one object, and the son of GOD ano- " ther (that is, the son of GOD and the son of
" Mary

N O T E S.

The very words of the angel were probably as follows, (ܐܠܐܠ¹ ܐܡܪ² ܠܗ³) the ²spirit ⁴of holiness (*i. e.* the holy spirit) ⁵shall come (ܘܢܚܘ¹ ܥܠܝܟܝ² ܘܚܝܠܗ³ ܕܡܪܝܡܐ⁴ ܢܓܢ⁵ ܥܠܝܟܝ⁶ ܘܡܛܠ⁷ ܗܢܐ⁸ ܕܡܬܝܠܕ⁹ ܡܢܟܝ¹⁰ ܩܕܝܫܐ¹¹ ܘܢܬܩܪܐ¹² ܒܪܗ¹³ ܕܐܠܗܐ,¹⁴) ¹even the ²supreme ³efficacy ³shall cover ⁴over thee, ⁵for this reason, ⁶he ⁷who is begotten ⁸of thee ⁹ is holy, ¹⁰and ¹²shall be called ¹⁰the son ¹¹ of GOD.

And thus this text is quite consistent with that in St. *Mathew*, which tells us expressly that the virgin was pregnant from or by the holy ghost, and that her conception was of the holy ghost.

In this view of our redemption, is also that dark passage found in *Ignatius*'s epistle to the *Ephesians*, very intelligible. Ειθεν εμωρχινετο σοφια κοσμικη, αγνοιας ζοφ⊕ διεσκεδαννυτο, κ᾽ τυραννικη αρχη καθηρειτο, θεου ως ανθρωπου φαινομενα, κ᾽ ανθρωπου ως θεκ ενεργουντος. αλλα ουτε το προτερον δοξα, ουτε το δευτερον ψιλοτης. αλλα το μεν αληθεια, το δε οικονομια.

" *Mary* were not different) but identically one
" and the same, the son of the virgin and the
" son of God."

Agreeably hereto we also read in *Justin Martyr*.
—Μελχισεδεκ. Ου σημαινει ημιν ετι ανωθεν, ϗ δια γαςρὸς ανθρωπειας, ὁ θεος ϗ πατηρ των ὁλων γενασθαι αυτον εμελλε?
" That is,—*Melchisedec*. Does not this signify to
" us that from above and in an human womb (see
" *Mat.* i. 20. το εν αυτη γεννηθεν) the God and father
" of all would have that he (the Logos) should
" be begotten (ανωθεν, i. e. by the holy ghost.)—
" See *Dialog. cum Tryphone judæo.*

So also *Tertullian*. *Non competebat ex femine humano Dei filium nasci, ne si totus esset filius hominis, Non esset et Dei filius, nihilq; haberet amplius Solomone. Ergo jam Dei filius ex patris Dei femine* [h] *ut esset hominis filius. Caro ei sola erat ex hominis carne sumenda sine viri femine. Vacabat enim viri Semen, apud habentem Dei femen.* Tertullian de Carne Christe, cap. 18.

" It suited not that the son of God should be
" born of human seed, least if he were altogether
" the son of man, he would not be also the son
" of

NOTES.

[h] By *patris Dei femine*, *Tertullian* means the divine spirit, and supposes its distinction from his flesh to be the ground of our Lord's words, which he cites as follows, *Quod ex carne natum est caro est, quia ex carne natum est; & quod de spiritu natum est spiritus est, quia Deus spiritus est, & de Deo natus est.* And this palliates his otherwise strange expression, the seed of God.

" of GOD, having nothing more than *Solomon*.
" He is then the son of GOD by a seed of GOD
" the father, that so he might be the son of man.
" His flesh only was to be derived from human
" flesh without the male seed; for the male seed,
" in that she had the seed of GOD, was spared."

But without appealing to the authority of antiquity, our own judgment must teach us, that if the body of *Christ* had been radically the offspring of the virgin, it must have been, like its source, unclean; since, *Job* xiv. 4. *John* iii. 6. *a clean thing cannot come out of an unclean*; and since the virgin mother must have been, *Eph.* ii. 3. *by nature the child of wrath, even as others.*

Also if the sacrifice of an impure thing is odious to GOD, our LORD's body, had it been primarily the offspring of the virgin, must have been so far from a sufficient attonement for sin and uncleanness, as to have been in itself an offensive and rejected offering.

As we learn therefore, *Gal.* iv. 4. *Rom.* i. 3. *that he was born of, or conceived out of a woman,* (ἐκ γυναικὸς γενομενον) *of the seed of David, according to the flesh*; and from thence infer that, with respect to our LORD's maternally augmented substance, he was the true son of the woman; so we learn that that very conception of the woman was begotten of the holy ghost, and thence infer that with respect to our LORD's being a human subsistence or man begotten, he was the the true son of GOD, that is, he was his son-man, called in the jewish language (ܒܪ ܐܢܫܐ) son-man; or which is the same (ܐܢܫܐ, ܒܪ) *filius qui Homo (scilicet est)*

est) son who (is) man; or as in other places (ܐܢܫܐ, ܒܪܗ *filius ejus qui homo*) his son that is a man: for by some one of these appellations does our Lord usually call himself.[1]

And for this reason also, is the human person of *Jesus* called in scripture *the son of God*, and his blood *the blood of God*, and his congregation of the faithful *the church of God*; so *Rom.* viii. 32. *If God spared not his own son* (ܒܪܗ *filio ejus*, namely the man *Christ Jesus*) *but delivered him up for us all*, &c. *Rom.* v. 10. *We were reconciled to God by the death of his son*. *Acts* xx. 28. *The church of God which he has purchased with his own blood*, &c. For the man, or human person, *Jesus Christ* is singly and individually that son of God, 1 *John* i. 7. *whose blood was spilt for us, who* (Heb. vi. 6.) *was crucified, and* (Acts iii. 26) *was raised up from the dead; after having indeed suffered* (Rom. vi. 10) *death, even the death of the cross.*

There can be no doubt but God is able to effect out of his own fulness a bodily substance, verily indued with all the properties of an human body; and such substance we believe did result

from

NOTES.

[1] I would not here be understood to say that (ִ) d affixed to the latter of two substantives in the syriac language, may not answer to the latter of two substantives of a genitive case in the greek or latin tongue; for it is certain it does. But I say that the import of these two forms are different; and that (ִ) d in the syriac tongue affixed to the latter of two substantives signifies the same as *qui est*, who is; and will therefore bare a construction and force which the latter of two substantives in the greek will not.

from GOD as a father, to the effecting the human nature of our LORD; but with respect to that substance which as the son of a woman accrued to this his divinely generated substance, this we doubt not was from the virgin.

The man *Jesus Christ* was therefore the son of GOD, raised out of the fruit of *David*, conceived of (by being implanted into) *Mary*, who was of the seed of *David*; and hence that distinction, 1 *Cor.* xv. 47. *The first man is of the earth earthy, the second man is the Lord from heaven*, i. e. is the Jehovah Adn, who (σαρξ εγενετο) is become flesh, or man, in a conception divinely derived, tho' earthlily augmented.

Having then sufficiently proved that there must be a personal distinction between the first-begotten son of GOD and his holy father,[k] we will proceed to our third point proposed.

LET-

NOTES.

[k] In the present state of nature, no creature probably can think as he ought of the veiled or hidden nature of the son of GOD. *Mat.* xi. 7. (ουδεις) *No one knoweth the son but the father.* But we hope this will not be always the case with us, for that we shall hereafter see him, whose we all are, and by whom we all subsist, not as now, only in his personal distinction, but as he is, i. e. in his as yet invisible nature; yea, and this sight of him may then be natural to us that are his, because we shall ourselves bare his likeness. 1 *John* iii. 2. *We know that when he shall appear, we shall be like him, for we shall see him as he is*; and 2 *Cor.* iii. 18. *with face unveiled* (ανακεκαλυμμενω προσωπω) *beholding as in a glass the glory of the Lord, shall be changed into the same image, from glory to glory, even as by the Lord, the spirit* (απο κυριου πνευματος.)

LETTER VI.

Logos the only begotten son of God is the true æonian spirit, and distinct as such from his father.

TO ──────

SIR,

HAVING in my last letter proved two of the points proposed, namely, 1st. That the term spirit belongs to the only begotten son of GOD; and 2dly. That the only begotten son of GOD has a personal distinction from GOD his father; the 3d and 4th points will be the business of my present; and first the 3d point, or that

III. The Logos or only begotten son of GOD, as he exists personally distinct from GOD his father, so has he a will distinct from GOD his father, in the freedom of which will he offered himself

himself to the father, to be a sacrifice for man in the future man *Christ Jesus.*

John vi. 38. *I came down from heaven, not to do my own will, but the will of him that sent me.*

They who believe *Jesus Christ* to be the Lord God, revealed in the old testament by the name of Jehovah Adni, believe that he was with the father in heaven before he became incarnate, or man reveal'd in the flesh; and therefore that when he became man, he came down from heaven: and in this view of him these words of his will be duly paraphrased as follows; *I, who came down from heaven, came down not to do my* own will, *but the will of him that sent me.* For the terms own will belong to the person *I*, and by the person *I*, being meant he who came down from heaven, the single question arising is who this *I* that came down from heaven must be, and this will appear from other texts. So *John* xvi. 28. *I came forth from the father and am in the world;* but who is the I who came forth from the father? The answer we shall find in *John* xvii. 5. *And now, O father, glorify me with thy own self, with that glory I had with thee before the world was.*

The person therefore who came forth from the father is he who was with the father, and who had a glory with the father before the world was; but the man *Jesus*, who was born of the virgin *Mary*, was not with the father, neither had a glory with the father, before the world was; therefore neither is the man *Jesus* the person here meant by the terms, *I that came forth from the father, I who came down from heaven.*

This

This exposition of the above text is indeed forced upon us by St. *Paul's* way of reasoning, *Eph.* iv. 9, 10. *Now that he ascended, what is it but that he also descended first into the lower parts of the earth? He that descended, is the same that also ascended, &c.* That is to say, That which never was beneath the heavens, cannot be said to ascend into the heavens; by a parity of which reasoning we insist also, that if the man *Jesus Christ* never was in heaven, neither could he have descended from thence, or came down from heaven; and that therefore the man *Christ Jesus* came not down from heaven: who then did come down from heaven? The omnipresent divinity, the GOD who filleth heaven and earth? No man in his senses will suppose so much; it must then be the sacred Adni of the *Jews*, the Logos, or filial spirit, who came down from heaven to be a sacrifice for man in the future man *Christ Jesus*.

And this is again declared in *Heb.* x. 5. *Wherefore entering* (or being about to enter διο εισερχομενος) into

---

NOTES.

[1] That εισερχομεν☉ has here a future import, appears from *Heb.* i. 6. ὅταν δὲ πάλιν εἰσαγάγῃ τὸν πρωτότοκον εἰς τὴν οἰκουμένην; *and again, when he is about to introduce his son into the world*; for the word εισαγαγη, which here answers to the word εισερχομ☉, being the 2d aorist subjunctive, has a future import, and therefore also must εισερχομεν☉ have the same; and the like force of expression is no less visible in the syriac ܟܕ ܡܥܠ ܠܒܘܟܪܗ [1] 'when [2] that introducing [3] his first-begotten.

into the world, he faith, a body haft thou prepared me, that is me the Adn, or Jehovah, who am about to come down from heaven, having been there with the father, and having had a glory with the father from the beginning.

For Adn or Jehovah is alone the perfon, who *Phil.* ii. 6, 7. *Being in the form of God,* before the creation was, did in due time become a man, or emptied himfelf, *and took upon him the form of a fervant, and was made in the likenefs of man.*

But moreover this text, thus underftood, argues alfo that the Jehovah, who came down from heaven, having been from the beginning with the father, had a will of his own, a will diftinct from his father's who fent him; and the which will he entered this world not to do, but to deny; by doing, what was diftinct from it, his father's will, tho' this might oppofe his own.

For if Adn came from heaven not to do his own will, but the will of his father, then muft he have had an *own will,* diftinct from the will of his father; as we alfo read, *Heb.* x. 7. *Then faid I,* (that is I who was about to enter this world) *lo, I come to do thy will, O God.*

The apoftle defcribes the fon here as difcourfing with his father concerning our redemption, the conditions of which fhould be a body prepared for him. The fon's reply to this propofal was, *Lo I come to do thy will, O God.* So that his affuming a body was the confequence of this his voluntary compliance with the will of GOD, the event of his furrendering himfelf up to the will of his father; and it is in purfuance hereto (namely to

Chrift's

LETTER VI. [109] SECT. I.

Christ's assuming the body) that we are a sanctified people, as it follows, ver. 10. *by the which will we are sanctified, thro' the offering of the body of Jesus once for all.*

And of this contract, and will renounced, our LORD may be presumed to speak, *John* xvii. 2, 4. *I have glorified thee on earth, I have finished the work thou hast given me to do.* John v. 30. *I seek not my own will, but the will of my father who hath sent me.* Mat. xxvi. 39. *Nevertheless not as I will, but as thou wilt.* John iv. 34. *My meat is to do the will of him that sent me.* But in the psalmist, speaking of the divine covenant before the incarnation, we find the passage above insisted upon in terms strongly expressive of this personal distinction: *Pf.* xl. 7. *Then said I, lo I come, in the volume of the book it is written of me.* Ver. 8. *I delight to do thy will O my God, yea thy law is within my secret recesses,* (בתוך מעי *in interno interiorum meorum,* or sing. *interioris mei*) *i. e.* in the central faculties of the Logos (Adn or filial spirit) who afterwards became the man *Christ Jesus.*

We conclude therefore that the Logos or Jehovah Adn, being a person distinct from his father before he came into the world, was our LORD spoken of, 1 *Cor.* viii. 6. *To us there is one God the father, of whom are all things, and* (who in his image or visible character, the first-begotten, is after the incarnation distinctly called) *one Lord Christ Jesus by whom are all things, and we by him.* So 1 *Cor.* xv. 47 *The second man is the Lord from heaven:* and again, 1 *Tim.* ii. 5. *For there is one God and one Mediator between God and men* (namely the Adni or Logos or first-begotten, who afterwards became)

became) *the man Christ Jesus.* He being in his single person, *Acts* ii. 36. *Both Lord and Christ*; or, *Luke* ii. 11. *Christ the Lord, or Jehovah.*[m]

Again, we conclude that being personally distinct from, he had also a will distinct from his father's; that in the freedom of this will he offered himself to be a sacrifice for man in the future man *Christ Jesus;* in whose person he also conducted himself as a devotee to the covenanted purpose of his father's will, in the manner described thro' all the gospels: and as we read of him in *Heb.* v. 7, 8. *Who in the days of his flesh, when he had offered up prayers and supplications with strong cryings and tears, unto him who was able to save him from death, and was heard* (so as to be delivered by an angel sent to strengthen him) *from his horrors; tho' he were a son, yet learned he obedience by the things which he suffered, and being perfected, he became the author of æonian salvation to all them that obey him.*

SECT. II.

IV. THE Logos (offering himself in the freedom of his will to be a sacrifice for man in the future man *Christ Jesus)* must have been

---

NOTES.

[m] The visible Adn, address'd every where throughout the old testament as God, was not the father, therefore he was the son of the father, therefore the same whom St. *John* calls the Logos, *Rev.* xix. 13. 1 *John* v. 7. *John* i. 1. St. *Paul* the (πρωτοτοκος or) first-begotten, *Col.* i. 15. *Heb.* i. 6.

been that spirit who moved or influenced the man *Chrift Jefus* to become (i. e. is that spirit through whom he became) a sacrificial offering for us.

This proposition follows from the foregoing already proved; for if the Logos or Adni had been other than that spirit who was to move or influence the future man *Chrift Jefus* to become an offering; he could not have covenanted with the father that the future man should become that offering.

So that his covenanting with his father in the words, *lo, I come to do thy will*, argues him to be that spirit who was to move or influence the future man *Chrift Jefus* to become, in the body prepared, a sacrifice for sin.

Moreover as the person covenanting is denoted to us in the first person I, viz. *I come to do thy will*, and the body prepared was to be the body of him who so covenanted, the personal property of the I covenanting, express'd in the term *me* (namely a body haft thou prepared *me*); it appears from the very text itself, that the body and the person covenanting were to be one and the same individual: and so it follows, that this prepared body was both the future body of that pre-incarnate person who covenanted with the father, and was also the very body of the incarnate man whom we call *Jefus Chrift*.

That is, the Adn or Logos, who was the covenanting spirit before the incarnation, was the man *Chrift Jefus*, to whom the prepared body belong'd, after the creation.

And whereas the will of GOD, we are now speaking of, was to be done by him the Adn or Logos;

Logos; the offering made of the prepared body must have been performed by him the Adn or Logos.

But this offering was performed by the man *Chrift Jefus*; therefore the Logos and the man *Chrift Jefus* were both of them the offerers or priefts offering the prepared facrifice.

Now how fhall we adjuft this account of thefe divine matters but by conceiving that *Jefus Chrift*, who was the incarnate prieft or offerer, was the Logos himfelf, in his preincarnate ftate, and before he became man?

Again, whereas we know that the man *Jefus Chrift*, being compleatly man, had a fpirit, a foul and a body, (for every perfect man confifts of fuch, fee 1 *Thef.* v. 23. *Gal.* vi. 18.) we may eafily conceive that the fpirit by whom the man *Jefus Chrift* offered himfelf may have been his own fpirit; that is, that *Jefus Chrift*, moved by his own fpirit, who is a fpirit of compaffion and zeal, covenanted with his father to perform our redemption in a body, to be prepared and by him affumed for that purpofe.

Thus, *Heb.* i. 3. *Being the brightnefs of his father's glory, and the exprefs image of his perfon, and upholding all things by the word of his own power, he by himfelf* (δι ἑαυτου) *purged our fins, to the fulfilling the will of the father.*

This furvey of our redemption is anfwered by a variety of fcripture paffages, of which I fhall produce a few.

The bufinefs of a prieft is, *Heb.* viii. 3.—v. 1, 2. *to offer facrifice for fin; and Chrift was to be a prieft after the order of Melchifedec;* that is, *Heb.* vii. 3.
without

without father, without mother,[n] *without pedigree, having neither beginning of days, nor end of life:* But the man *Chrift Jefus* had a known mother,

P and

NOTES.

Jefus Chrift *is that God with whom the creatures are immediately concerned.*

[n] The invifible GOD, the father of the Logos, being utterly undifcoverable to us but by the fpirit of *Jefus Chrift*, who is the light of man, living in us; we cannot poffibly know any thing of him, till we are what the apoftle calls, *Eph.* v. 8. (Φως εν τω Κυριω) *Light in the Lord.* Says he, *Ye were indeed a while ago darknefs, but now are ye light in the Lord.* So that to man void of the chriftian light, the father is as tho' he had no being at all, as tho' he were not; that is, the Logos, or the fon, is to us as the original GOD, or fole παντοκρατωρ. Yea probably the creatures (at leaft man) would not know that a father was, but by being informed hereof by him who only has feen the father, namely the LOGOS or GOD of nature.

Therefore, fay the fcriptures, *John* i. 18. *No one hath feen* (that is known, fee 3 *John* 11. *John* xiv. 7.) *God at any time, the only begotten fon, who is in the bofom of the father, he hath declared him*; i. e. revealed him fo as to render him the object of our knowledge, tho' not of our fight. See alfo *John* xiv. 8, 9.

And thus *Irenæus* teaches us, *Edocuit autem Dominus quoniam Deum fcire nemo poffit, nifi Deo docente, hoc eft fine Deo non cognofci Deum. Hoc ipfum autem cognofci eum, voluntatem effe patris; cognofcunt enim eum quibufcumq; revelaverit filius, & ad hoc filius revelavit patrem ut per eum omnibus manifeftetur, & eos quidem qui credunt ei, jufti in incorruptelam & æternum refrigerium recipiat. Credere eft facere ejus voluntatem, eos autem qui non credunt, & propter hoc fugiunt lumen ejus, in tenebris quas ipfi fibi elegerunt jufte recludet.*⸺ *& ideo juftam*

and a reputed father; a known lineal descent from *David,* by his mother's side; and a known beginning of days and end of life; therefore unless

---

NOTES.

judicium Dei super eos qui similiter quidem viderunt, non autem similiter crediderunt———& per ipsum verbum visibilem & palpabilem factum, pater ostendatur, etiamsi non omnes similiter credebant ei; sed omnes viderunt in filio patrem; invisibile etenim filii pater, visibile autem patris filius.——— Irenæus, lib. iv. cap. 14.

That collective knowledge we have of GOD from his creation, as a being endued with all power, wisdom, justice, as good to the obedient, terrible to the wicked, and controlling the universe, belongs to the Logos, who is, and is beheld personally as being, all this, and whose spirit pervades the whole creation.

But such our knowledge affords us no conception of that eternity, infinity, and immutability which belongs not negatively but positively, to the simple essence GOD.

In his essence GOD is, *Heb.* xiii. 8. *The same yesterday, to day, and for ever,* James i. 17. *with whom is no variableness, or shadow of altering (* *, changing like the weather or seasons of the year);* and this account of him so baffles all our notions of an active omnipotent agent, creating, governing, altering, pleased and angry with his creatures, as to leave us quite in the dark, and without sentiment concerning him.

And as our knowledge and experience drawn from things sensible, can only teach us what the Logos must be; the Logos is that only GOD whom the creature can know; yea, he is so the utmost limit of our intelligence, as if he were without father and without ulterior source or origin.

Christ therefore is described as one whose original no man knows, *Isaiah* liii. 8. *And who shall declare his*

less we will consider *Jesus Christ* as more than a son of *Mary*, he proves not to be the true melchisedecal priest promised us for our redeemer.

Who

NOTES.

generation; as says *Irenæus, Quis prolationem sive generationem ejus inenarrabilem novit ? neq; angeli neque archangeli, nisi solus qui generavit pater & qui natus est filius.* See p. 134.—So *Justin Martyr,* Οταν γαρ ὡς υἱον ανθρωπου λεγη Δανιηλ τον παραλαμβανοντα την αιωνιον Βασιλειαν, ουχ αυτο τουτο αινισσεται? (*scilicet* that *Christ* the Jehovah of the old testament was to be born a man) το γαρ ὡς υἱον ανθρωπου ειπειν, φαινομενον μεν και γενομενον ανθρωπον μηνυει, ουχ εξ ανθρωπινου δε σπερματος υπαρχοντα δηλοι: και το λιθον τουτον ειπειν ανευ χειρων τμηθεντα, εν μυστηριω το αυτο κεκραγε; το γαρ ανευ χειρων ειπειν αυτον εκτετμησθαι, ὁτι ουκ εστιν ανθρωπινον εργον, αλλα της βουλης του προβαλλοντος αυτον πατρος των ὁλων Θεου. και το Ησαιαν φαναι, την γενεαν αυτου τις διηγησεται? ανεκδιηγητον εχοντα το γενος αυτου εδηλου. ουδεις γαρ ανθρωπος ων εξ ανθρωπων, ανεκδιηγητον εχει το γενος.——*Justini Martyris Dialog. cum Tryphone Judæo.*

And as the generation of the Logos is (like *Melchisedec*'s) unknown, and as his father is likewise utterly unknowable, till the son (who is our known GOD, who gives us life and breath and all things, and made heaven and earth) reveals him, so are our addresses to the father to be considered as a matter of christian privilege, indulged us purely as members of his son. *John* xvi. 25, 26, 27. *But I shall shew you* (namely that are mine) *plainly of the father. At that day ye shall ask in my name, and I say not unto you, that I will pray the father for you; for the father himself loveth you, because ye have loved me, and have believed that I came forth from God.* And (v. 23.) *whatsoever ye shall ask the father in my name, he will give it you.*

Who then was this melchisedecal priest without known father, mother, pedigree, and without beginning of days or end of life?

The answer is, the person whom *Melchisedec* represents, namely the only begotten son of GOD; for *Melchisedec* was *Heb.* vii. 3. (αφωμοιωμεν⊕ τω υιω τε θεου) made a type° of or proposed to represent in the prementioned particulars the son of GOD. The motherless son of GOD then is our true melchisedecal priest, and the same of whom our LORD says, *John* viii. 42, (εκ τε θεε εξηλθον κὶ ἡκω) *I* (the Adn or LORD the son of GOD) *came forth from God, and am here* (a bodily man.) i. e. *I*, John i. 18. (ὁ μονογενης υιος ὁ ων εις τον κολπον τε πατρος) *the only begotten son, who was in the bosom of the father,* am now become a palpable man; *Heb.* ix. 11. *Rev.* xiii. 6. *Jehovah tabernacled in the flesh*; a body prepared, altho' of precious, yet of corruptible materials (even as the sanctuary called, *Heb.* ix. 1. ἁγιον κοσμικον the wordly sanctuary was made of corruptible

---

N O T E S.

° The greek word αφωμοιωμενος being rare and unknown, has been misrepresented by some of our most able commentators to the confusion of the text. But the syriac testament helps us here, by ascertaining its meaning in the word ܕܡܘܬܐ, which signifies type, pattern, image, &c. and frequently occurs in the new testament. So in *Heb.* viii. 5. ix. 23. ix. 24. *Rom.* i. 23. viii. 29. 1 *Cor.* xi. 7. xv. 49. 2 *Cor.* iii. 18. *Phil.* ii. 6. iii. 17. *Col.* i. 15. iii. 10. 1 *Thes.* i. 7. 1 *Tim.* iv. 12. *Tit.* ii. 7. *&c.* Insomuch that we can have no longer any doubt that ܒܕܡܘܬܐ ܕܒܪܗ ܕܐܠܗܐ means *In the pattern of the son of God.*

ruptible materials) and which I am entered, the æonian prieſt, to make atonement by performing a ſacrifice, according to a covenant which I made with my father, before I became the ſon-man.

Beſides all this, that the Adn or Logos in the freedom of his will offered himſelf up to GOD a ſacrifice for us, without being moved thereto by any other influence than that of his own bounty and benevolence, and which was the offspring of his innate love, appears farther from his own words.

John x. 18. *No one* (ϑδεις) *taketh it* (my life) *from me, but I lay it down of my own ſelf* (απ' ἐμαυτȣ) *of my own free will: I have* (εξȣσιαν) *authority to lay it down, and I have authority to take it again: this* (εντολην commiſſion or) *inſtruction have I received of my father (who impoſes no neceſſity upon me his boſom love.)*

But if *Chriſt* enterpriſed his redeeming office as a matter precarious, and dependant upon his own will, as a voluntary atchievement, to which he was incited purely by his own native commiſeration; then is *Chriſt*'s ſpirit that only ſpirit by whom the man *Jeſus*, the *Chriſt*, devoted his body a ſacrifice for ſin; or in other words, then is that Logos, Adn or filial covenanting ſpirit that æonian prieſtly ſpirit, thro' which the man *Jeſus*, the *Chriſt*, offered up his prepared body for the ſin of the world. For

That ſpirit who moved the man *Jeſus Chriſt* to become a ſacrifice for ſin is the true æonian ſpirit;

But the Logos (or which is the ſame his ſpirit) is that ſpirit who moved the man *Jeſus Chriſt* to become a ſacrifice for ſin;

Therefore the Logos (or which is the ſame his ſpirit) is the true æonian ſpirit.

LETTER VII.

Farther remarks on CHRIST's *æonian character, implying his personal distinction, and insisted on in the two foregoing letters.*

TO ——

SIR,

YOUR interpretation of the word (πρωτοτοκος or) first-begotten appears to me to be unwarranted by scripture; neither see I how this word infers created existence in the ordinary acceptation of it.[p] But that in my acceptation of it, it imports distinction I readily

---

NOTES.

[p] That the Messiah was the begotten of GOD before the creation began is certain, because all the creatures were made by the first-begotten: but it does not thence follow that we are to understand otherwise by

LETTER VII.   SECT. I.

I readily acknowledge, have been in my two laſt letters contending for, and ſhall in my preſent inforce with farther arguments; as judging that the ſcripture accounts of our redemption cannot be underſtood without ſuch diſtinction ſuppoſed.

We are taught to conceive of our redemption as a contrivance between two parties, who tho' of divine exiſtence, are the one a father, the other a ſon; and of the agreement itſelf, as depending upon reciprocal covenants binding each party.   SECT.

NOTES.

the word (πρωτοτοκ⊙) firſt-begotten than is its natural import, and known uſe in ſcripture. We read *Matt.* i. 25. *That Jeſus was the* (πρωτοτοκ⊙) *firſt-begotten of Mary*; *that* (Heb. xi. 28.) *the* (τὰ πρωτοτοκα) *firſt-begotten of Egypt were deſtroyed* (Heb. xii. 23.) *that the church conſiſts of the* (πρωτοτοκων) *firſt-begotten of our Lord*, or ſuch as *Chriſt* has regenerated or rebegotten, i. e. whom *Chriſt* has made his children by (παλιγγενεσια) a begetting again, *Matt.* xix. 28; or by (αναγενεσια) a regeneration, viz. 1 *Pet.* i. 3, 23. (ουκ εκ σπορας φθαρτης, αλλα αφθαρτου) *not of corruptible ſeed, but of incorruptible*. And ſince the ſame word is ſingly applied to the Meſſiah as the ſon of the father, we are at liberty to underſtand this word thus uſed, in the ſame ſimple meaning of it, as in other applications.

It behoves us alſo to obſerve here that our erroneous deductions concerning the ſon of GOD ariſe chiefly from our miſtaking the force of the word *beget*, in which his relation to the father is revealed to us.

The word *beget* by no means implies creation or a ſtate of not-being antecedent to that of being begotten. For altho' a man is begotten by his father, yet he is not created by his father; and altho' he becomes a

I. ON the part of the son it was covenanted
1st. That he should become man made of a woman, made in the likeness of man.

2dly. That being so incarnate, *Emanuel*, the word made flesh, *If.* liii. 10. *He should make his soul an offering for sin*, his body an atoning sacrifice.

And this appears from the text so much urged in my last letter, *Heb.* x. 5. *Sacrifice and offering thou* (my GOD) *wouldst not, but a body hast thou prepared me; then said I* (viz. this spirit, the Messiah) *lo, I come to do thy will, O God*. That is, as has been already argued, to do the will of the father: with relation to which will our LORD
speaks;

N O T E S.

man by being begotten, yet he becomes not a possessor of life or being, thro' his father's begetting him.

Yea our LORD himself, who was the only begotten of GOD before he became man, did likewise become man by being again begotten of GOD; and farther, when afterward he became the first son of the resurrection, he became a third time the begotten of GOD; as the Apostle assures us, *Acts* xiii. 33. *This day* (i. e. the day of his resurrection) *have I begotten thee*, i. e. regenerated (or re-begotten) thee; for the resurrection is called the regeneration, and *Christ* is called *the first-begotten of* (or from among ܡܢ ܒܝܬ) *the dead*. *Col.* i. 18. *Rev.* i. 5. and being so, he is after his resurrection, address'd in these words by his father, *This day have I* (ἀναστήσας having raised, γεγέννηκα) *begotten thee*.

speaks, *John* vi. 38. *I came down from heaven, not to do my own will, but the will of him that sent me.* And as this is that part in the divine covenant which it became the son to perform, so by his performance of it, *Heb.* x. 10. *We his children are sanctified;* or have his holiness imparted to us.

This contract is given us in like form in *Isaiah*, where Jehovah is represented as saying, *If.* liii. 10. *If he shall make his soul an offering for sin, he shall see his seed, and prolong his days, and the pleasure of Jehovah shall prosper in his hands.*

And as the terms of this treaty between the father and his son do manifest their personal distinction, so does also St. *Paul* confirm the same, *Gal.* iii. 20. *Now a mediator is not a mediator of one, but God is one*; and who then must the mediator be, but he whom I have been describing; and of whom says good old *Justin* the martyr, τȣτο το τω οντι (or ονϊως) απο τȣ πατρος προβληϑεν γεννημα, προ παντων των ποιηματων συνην τω πατρι, και τȣτω ὁ πατηρ προσομιλει. "This is that offspring truly produced "from the father; before all creatures he was "with the father, and with him the father holds "conversation."—*Dialog. cum Tryphone Judæo.*

So then the Messiah (being before he became flesh a spirit, namely, the first-begotten of GOD; and existing filially distinct from his father; and having as such a will distinct from his father) was capable of entering into a conditional agreement with his father; wherein his father accepts a profered service of the son, who undertakes to execute it, according to that sublime account of him in *Isaiah.*

Isaiah

Isaiah lxiii. 1, 2, 3. Q. *Who is he that cometh from Edom* (the *Edomites* being the most inveterate enemies of the *Jews*, do represent all the church's enemies) *with dyed garments, travelling in the greatness of his strength* (or as a victorious general)? A. *I who speak in righteousness, mighty to save.* Q. *Wherefore art thou red in thy apparel, and thy garments like one that treadeth the wine-fat?* A. *I have trodden the wine-press* (trampled down the enemies of the church) *alone, and of the people there was none with me.*

And as this Messiah, this first and only begotten son of GOD, made a compact, and concerted its covenants, before his taking upon him our fleshly nature; so he provided for the full performance of them, in that nature; and being indeed, from first to last, the life, and source, and root of all its workings, he faithfully accomplished the utmost requisites, both as son Logos and son man, with the utmost zeal, industry, and success.

As he is in himself, and throughout his whole nature, the true copy ($\alpha\pi\alpha\upsilon\gamma\alpha\sigma\mu\alpha$ and $\chi\alpha\rho\alpha\kappa\tau\eta\rho$) the shining forth and express image of the father; so is his will also as absolutely the express copy of his father's will.

And tho' filially distinct from his father, nevertheless he coincides compleatly with him both in nature, and in will. Therefore as in nature he is described to be, *John* xiv. 10. *In the father, and the father in him*; and *John* i. 18. *In the bosom of the father*; so speaking of his will he tells us, that *John* v. 19. *The son can do nothing of himself,*

but

but what he seeth the father do; for whatsoever things the father doth, these also doth the son likewise.

SECT. II.

II. WE have to speak of the divine covenant, as to its articles on the father's part, whereby it was stipulated,

1st. That the son should have the power of the resurrection given him.

Not that he had no native power in him to raise the dead, but that this event should be effected by a new kind of life, first to be produced and manifested in *Christ* as mediator; by a life hitherto unknown in the creation; and whereby the dead in him should likewise be quickened into his likeness, when risen; and become that new creature which St. *Paul* calls, *Eph.* ii. 10. *Created in Christ, his workmanship.*

Moreover this power of raising the dead was to belong to *Christ* in the capacity of a mediator, as his own property by covenant, and in his own right; or as that to which he was equitably intitled by dint of his own personal merit.

John v. 20, 21. *The father loveth the son, and sheweth him all things that himself doth, and he will shew him greater works than these, that ye may marvel; for as the father raiseth up the dead and quickeneth them, even so the son quickeneth whom he will.* Verse 26. *For as the father hath life in himself, so hath he given to the son to have life in himself.*

Christ's mediatorial prerogatives being his (v. 27.) *becaufe he fubmitted to be, or becaufe he is the fon of man.*�q

Again, *Phil.* ii. 6.—*Who being in the form of God, deemed it no act of robbery to be equal with God; yet emptied himfelf, and took upon him the form of a fervant, and was made in the likenefs of men, and being*

N O T E S.

q Ver. 27. καὶ ἐξυσιαν εδωκεν αυτω καὶ κρισιν ποιειν, οτι υιος ανθρωπυ εςι. *Beza* tranflates οτι in this paffage by *quatenus*, viz. *quatenus filius hominis eft*; and tells us that οτι is put for καθοτι or καθως; and fo καὶ *etiam* he refers, not to κρισιν ποιειν, but to οτι υιος ανθρωπυ εςι, by which means the fenfe, he fays, will be " and he gave him " authority to execute judgment not only as God, " but alfo as fon of man."

But I cannot interpret this paffage fo; 1ft. Becaufe οτι for καθως appears to me unnatural. 2dly. Becaufe καὶ becomes thus awkwardly mifplaced; for certainly as it ftands immediately before, it naturally refers to κρισιν ποιειν. 3dly. Becaufe the fyriac interprets οτι by ? *quod* ــــ ? *vero, quidem, etenim*, viz. ܕܝܢ ?¹ ܒܪܗ,³ ܗܘ² 'becaufe ²he was ¹the fon ³of man.' 4thly. Becaufe it is not true that *Chrift* will judge the world as man, but as God in the man *Chrift Jefus*. So *Acts* xvii. 30, 31. *God hath appointed a day wherein he will judge the world in righteoufnefs* (εν ανδρι ω ωρισε) *in the man whom he has appointed, Rom.* ii. 16. *In the day when God will judge the fecrets of men* (δια) *by Jefus Chrift*; i. e. by the Logos or firft-begotten called, *Dan.* vii. 9, 10, 11. *The ancient of days*; and *Zech.* xiv. 5. exprefsly *Jehovah*. So that not the man, but Jehovah, in the man *Jefus Chrift*, will be judge of quick and dead. See alfo *John* xii. 47.

being found in fashion as a man, he humbled himself and became obedient unto death, even the death of the cross; wherefore *God also hath highly exalted him, and given him a name which is above every name; that in the name of Jesus every knee should bow, &c,* Pf. xcviii. 1. *Sing unto the Lord a new song for he hath done marvellous things, his right hand and his holy arm hath gotten him the victory.*

That mighty power therefore which wrought upon our LORD, and raised him from the sepulchre, *Acts* ii. 24. *Loosing the* (ܒܚܒܠܐ hblie) *bands of death,* a power resulting from his becoming again begotten, even the first begotten from the dead; was the wages of his sufferings, his by purchase from his father, a property derived from his own meritorious obedience, the earnest (τῆς περιποιήσεως) of that *purchased possession* spoken of, *Eph.* i. 14.

It is also by virtue of this mediatorial title that our LORD prays in such confidence, *John* xvii. 24. *Father* (θελω ἱνα) *I will that they also whom thou hast given me, be with me where I am; that they may behold the glory which thou hast given me.*

But had there been no distinction of will in the Messiah or first-begotten spirit; *Christ* could not have performed his mediatorial office agreeably to the scripture account of it: and without a mediator, and (what such supposes) the agreement or contract between the son and the father; there had been no debt or demand commenced, no merit contracted, no sacrifice made, no ransom given; and, as far as we can see, no restoration or redemption contrived for man.

For

For since it is upon a distinction of will that the contract between God and the æonian spirit, his only begotten son, rests for its foundation and validity; without this distinction, all that solemn account, which the scriptures give us of a divine treaty, must be meer farce and falsehood, too weak to amuse silly men, much less those great intelligent spectators of the other world, who long so earnestly (1 *Pet.* i. 12.) to pry into (παρακυψαι) this mystery; and to whose capacities it is so full of miracle and astonishment.

2dly. A second article of the divine treaty was, That the Messiah should have given him a kingdom, and a people.

Luke xxii. 29. *My father hath covenanted to me a kingdom* (διεθετο μοι ὁ πατηρ μȣ βασιλειαν).

Dan. ii. 44. *In the days of these kings shall the God of heaven set up a kingdom, which shall never be destroyed; and the kingdom shall not be left to another people.*

Luke i. 31—33. *And thou shalt call his name Jesus, he shall be great, and shall be called the son of the highest; and the Lord God shall give unto him the throne of his father David, and he shall reign over the house of Jacob forever, and of his kingdom there shall be no end.*

Isaiah xlii. 1. *Behold my servant whom I uphold, my elect in whom my soul delighteth; I have put my spirit upon him, and he shall bring forth judgment unto the Gentiles;* (v. 4.) *and the isles shall wait for his law.* Isaiah xix. 25. *Jehovah of hosts shall bless, saying, blessed be Egypt my people, and Syria the work of my hands, and Israel my inheritance.*

And

And these are said to be given him for a retribution, and recompence, and reward; yea, and as his absolute right, so 1 *Tim.* ii. 6. *Who gave himself a ransom for all.* 1 Cor. vi. 20. *Who hath bought us with a Price.* Acts xx. 28. *Who has **purchased us with his own blood.***

And from hence it is likewise evident that the æonian spirit must be distinct from the father; for he to whom this kingdom is promised as a recompence, retribution, and purchase, is that spirit who afterwards became the *Christ*; and by force of whose will and determination *Christ* suffered, or offered himself without spot to GOD; he is therefore the æonian spirit: and since that spirit who afterwards became *Christ*, did himself earn his kingdom, and receive it from the father, not as his native right, but as his acquired right; he must also be in his redeeming mediatorial character distinct from the father.

3dly. By a third article in the divine treaty, The kingdom of the Messiah was to be enjoyed by him as a son, **distinct from his father.**

This indeed may also be rationally infer'd from the nature of *Christ*'s right to his kingdom, *viz.* the having earned or purchased it of the father; for to possess as earned or purchased of, is to possess as distinct from the father, therefore not as the father, but as the only begotten of the father, become a mediator.

And so *Christ* as king in his kingdom appears by necessary consequence, as to be the æonian spirit, so also to be the son of GOD distinct, or become distinct from his father.

Of this we are farther assured from *Daniel*; Dan. vii. 13, 14. *I saw in the night visions, and behold one like a son a man came with the clouds of heaven; and he came to the ancient of days, and they brought him near before him, and there was given him* (this human personage) *a dominion, and glory and kingdom, that all people and nations and languages should serve him. His dominion is an æonian dominion which shall not* (עדה) *be taken away* (or of which he shall not be spoiled) *and his kingdom what shall not be dissolved* (or ruined לא תתחבל) all which answers to what we are taught in the passage already quoted, viz. *John* v. 27. *The father hath given the son authority to execute judgment, because he is the man-son.*

And from hence we argue as follows;

The son covenanting with God his father is he who enjoys the kingdom of God;

Therefore is he who bought or purchased the kingdom of God;

Therefore is he who offered up the body of *Jesus* for it;

Therefore is he by power of whose will and influence the man *Jesus* became a sacrifice;

Therefore is he to whom the term æonian spirit belongs.

The kingdom of God was, not only by covenant, the property of the son of God long before the man *Jesus* was born; but the birth and being of the man *Jesus* or son-man was in pursuance of this covenant; and this in order that the son of God might, in the man *Jesus*, have a body to offer up unto his father for the fulfilling the terms of such covenant with him made. Neither

Neither was the son of GOD meerly to offer up a body, but a body which should be his own, himself. And therefore is the body of *Jesus* the body of the son of GOD, and the person of *Jesus* the person of the son of GOD, as is evident from the scripture accounts of this sublime matter, which tells us, *Rom.* viii. 32. *That God delivered up his son for us all:* Rom. v. 10. *That we are reconciled to him by the death of his son:* And (Acts xx. 28.) *that we are the purchase of his* (viz. GOD's) *own blood; for that he offered up his body for us, and shed his blood for us upon the cross.*

4thly. A fourth article in the divine treaty was, That the kingdom which should reward the son's mediatorial services should become an universal dominion, wherein the whole creation should be his subjects.

Isaiah iv. 5. *The glory of Jehovah shall be revealed, and all flesh shall see it together.* Is. xxvii. 6. *Israel shall blossom and bud, and fill the face of the world with fruit.* Is. xlii. 6, 7. *I the Lord have called thee in righteousness, and I will hold thy hands, and will keep thee, and give thee for*—**a light of the Gentiles,** *to open the blind eyes, to bring out the prisoners from the prison, and them that sit in darkness out of the prison-house.* Is. xlix. 18. **Lift up thine eyes round about,** *and* **behold** *all these gather themselves together and come to me: as I live, saith the Lord, thou shalt surely* **cloathe** *thee with them all, as with an ornament, and bind them on thee as doth a bride.* Is. liii. 11. *He* (viz. my holy one, whom v. 10. It pleased Jehovah to bruise) *shall see the travail of his soul, and be satisfied; by his knowledge shall my righteous servant justify the many* (הל

R   the

the multitude, *i. e.* all the members of *Christ's* fulness) *for he shall bear their iniquities.* If. xlix. 6. *And he Jehovah said, It is a light thing that thou shouldst restore the remnant of Israel—I will also give thee—that thou mayest be my servant unto the ends of the earth.* Eph. i. 8, 9, 10. *He has abounded towards us in all wisdom and prudence, having made known unto us the mystery of his own will, according to his own good pleasure which he has purposed in himself* (ܒܚܟܡܬܐ ⁺ ܥܠ ¹ ,ܙܒܢܐ ²ܠܡܫܠܡ ¹) *even* ¹*that* (or namely that, *in the dispensation of the fulness of times*) ²*he should gather together in one* ¹*all things (anew or)* ³*from* ⁴*the beginning* ¹ *in Christ, both which are in the heavens, and which are on earth, even in him.*

The extent therefore of *Christ's* acquisitions is no less than this his purposed recollection of all things into himself, the work of his æonian government; and the knowledge of this his purpose, is the especial privilege of his church.

❖❖❖❖❖❖❖❖❖❖❖❖❖❖❖❖❖❖❖❖❖❖❖❖❖❖❖

SECT. III.

Of the æonian spirit.

NOW every use of the word æonian in scripture will vouch for the consistency of the account

---

NOTES.

¹ ܡܢ ܪܝܫܝܬ *ab initio, capite, principio* in this place must import like *ab integro* in Latin, so in *Virgil* we read

Magnus ab integro seclorum nascitur ordo.

the harmonious unity of the creation, being dissolved in its revolt from God, is to be constituted anew, repeatedly, over again, afresh in *Christ*.

account here given, at the same time that, after the vulgar acceptation of it, this word becomes in many places absurd, vain, yea ridiculous and unintelligible. Suppose only the word æon to signify an age or seculum, and that the æonian life is a life constituted secularly; with what propriety and strictness may that spirit, who now is *Christ Jesus*, be called the true æonian spirit, being in the fullest sense the GOD and soul of the æonian life, in the person of the man *Jesus?* In which person also he becomes seated in the throne of divine majesty, has all things put under him, rules all as the head of all, *Heb.* i. 3. *Upholding all things by his power*, consuming all things that oppose him, and is likewise to continue thus, in pursuance of his agreement made before the world was, the ruling GOD; till the æons and time itself shall be no more, till all be subordinated to GOD in the man *Jesus Christ*, and till even the man *Jesus Christ* becomes the omega, or concluding of all the creation.

And thus again we have propounded to our faith things not repugnant to our human notions of fitness when we read, *Matt.* xxviii. 18. *All power is given unto me in heaven and earth.* 1 Pet. iii. 22. *He is gone into heaven, and is on the right hand of God, angels, authorities and powers being made subject unto him* Eph. i. 22. *God hath put all things under his feet, and gave him to be head over all things to the church.* Heb. ii. 8. *Thou hast put all things in subjection under him;—he hath left nothing that is not put under him.*

So that the distinction of the Logos (whose is the æonian spirit) from the father is a doctrine, much more than supported by the words of a single text; it is the voice of the grand principles of our redemption.

It is true the manner of this distinction must be to us inconceivable; but if it might therefore be denied, we may also deny for the same reason that *Christ* is at once both GOD and man; which yet is an unquestionable article of our faith.

Yea the visible, intelligible, æonian nature of *Christ* is not only distinct from the father, but can also act uninformed by his invisible incomprehensible nature; and from hence we observe that admirable variety in the motions of his soul, now become human, thro' all the gospels; where sometimes we see him affected with so sublime a sentiment as scarcely to remember that he is a man, engaged among earthly creatures; at other times again, so depress'd and humble, as scarcely to advert to his being Jehovah from heaven.

And his speech being always the language of his heart, we hear him talk sometimes as transported with the sensibility of his native glory and fellowship with his holy father; at other times again, when immersed in the mortifying sensations of his human infirmities, as meer man.

Nor is this difference less conspicuous in him even before his state of manhood; insomuch that, tho' the old testament speaking of him as the Jehovah GOD, calls him the only GOD, the almighty GOD, besides whom there is no one, no other, none else; yet when it speaks of him singly as Jehovah Logos, it tells us, *Gen.* vi. 6. וינחם¹ יהוה² כי³ עשה⁴ תא⁵ האדם⁶ בארץ⁷ ויתעצב⁸ אל⁹ לבו¹⁰ ¹*and it repented* ²*Jehovah*
³*that*

¹*that* ⁴*he had made* ⁵*the* ⁶*man* ⁷*on the earth* (i. e. that he had undertaken his terrestrial œconomy with us); ⁸*yea, he grieved himself* ⁹*to* ¹⁰*his heart.*

So that as the human son of GOD was forsaken of him, to his agonizing, even to the sweating of blood in the garden, and to his suffering for our redemption; in like manner had the angelic son of GOD been before forsaken of him, to a state of sorrowful repentance over us. For it was Jehovah in his angelic nature only that grieved; and he was forsaken to this state of grief provisionally to his future incarnate sufferings: so amazingly is the son of man the concern of the almighty GOD!

Yet then we may suppose that this state of our LORD's grief could have been only critical; for when his internal ungenerated nature (which had suspended its sensible influences for a while) again exerted itself within him, he must have seen also with joy, what St. *Paul* afterwards learnt of him, viz. *Rom.* xi. 29. *That the gifts and callings of God are* (αμεταμελητα) *without repentance*; or as we read it in the syriac testament, that (ܠܐ¹ ܗܘܐ² ܡܗܦܟ³ ܕܢܘܗܒ̈ܬܗ⁴ ܘܩܪ̈ܝܢܘܗܝ⁵) ³*God* ²*alters* ¹*not* ⁴*in his gifts,* ⁵*and in his callings.*

But what can mortal (that is sinful) thought presume upon these sublime matters? We can only say, that they are reasonably inconceivable? As says the poet:

" How GOD exists, and what he is,
" His own omniscience only sees."

Agreeably to what our LORD himself says, *Matt.* xi. 27. *No one* (ουδεις) *knoweth the son but the father; neither knoweth any one the father, but the son, and he to whom the son will reveal him.*   Not

Nor is this to be wondered at, since the creature knows not how himself is at one and the same time both distinct from, and subsisting in him, who is *Rev.* iii. 14. (ἡ αρχη της κτισεως τȣ θεȣ) *The beginning of the creation of God.*

Irenæus therefore writes very discreetly upon this head:—*Si quis autem nobis dixerit* quomodo *ergo* filius prolatus a patre? Dicimus *ei* quia prolationem istam, *sive generationem, sive nuncupationem sive adapertionem, aut quomodolibet quis nomine vocaverit,* generationem ejus inenarrabilem *existentem* nemo novit, *non Valentinus, non Marcion, neq; Saturninus, neq; Basilides, neq; angeli neq; archangeli, neq; principes, neq; potestates,* nisi solus qui generavit pater, et qui natus est filius. *Inenarrabilis itaq; generatio ejus cum sit,* quicumque *generationes et prolationes,* enarrare nituntur, non sunt sui compotes, *ea quæ inenarrabilia sunt narrare promittentes.*

' Should any one ask us, how then is the son
' produced from his father? We answer that the
' production, or generation, or pronouncing, or,
' by whatever other term one calls it, his ineffa-
' ble generation, no one knows; neither *Valen-*
' *tinus,* nor *Marcion,* nor *Saturninus,* nor *Basi-*
' *lides,* nor angels, nor arch-angels, nor principa-
' lities, nor powers, but the father alone who
' begat, and the son who was begotten. And
' since his generation is ineffable, they whoever
' attempt to declare it, are *to be reputed* not in
' their right senses, pretending to speak things
' unspeakable.'———Irenæus lib. 2. chap. 48.

But I have now said on this subject all which I think needful to my present purpose.

LETTER VIII.

God *wills effectually that all men shall be restored.*

TO ———

SIR,

SECT. I.

SCEPTICKS and Deists suppose themselves to have advanced an invincible argument against the scriptures, when they tell us that these describe the God of the christians as either cruel, implacable, unjust; or else, which is no less absurd, impotent and unfortunate in his labours; being found unable to effect his purposes in his own creation.

For say they, its abettors divide themselves into two parties, both of which maintain as a certain truth the eternity of hell torments: only the one party presumptuously avows, that God has made

made a vaſt number of his creatures ſenſible and patible, with a predetermined purpoſe that they ſhall endure in the flames of hell, which ſhall never be quenched, an endleſs and exquiſite pain and wretchedneſs; while the other party, ſay they, being a better natur'd people, will have it that theſe poor ſufferers are damned to their eternal miſery, not by the poſitive decree of their creator, for that God is benevolent and merciful, but becauſe, tho' he would fain have obviated their fate, and prevented their torments, this could not juſtly be effected; in defiance of all his wiſdom, love and power, not only the bulk of mankind, but, among theſe, many alſo of his darling people, even thoſe he once called the ſheep of his paſture, muſt become doom'd to tortures that ſhall laſt, like himſelf, to all eternity.

The poet deſcribes the loſt ſheep expoſtulating in flames as follows: [bliſs,
" And canſt thou then look down from perfect
" And ſee me plunging in the deep abyſs?
" Calling thee father, in a ſea of fire;
" Or, pouring blaſphemies, at thy deſire?
" With mortal anguiſh, wilt thou raiſe thy name,
" And by my pangs, omnipotence proclaim?"
So that, tho' the end (ſay they) which the God of the chriſtians might have in creating were, according to the latter, worthy this his infinite bounty and benevolence; yet as his wiſdom and power were not adequate to his love and goodneſs, he could not ſucceed in his attempts, conſiſtent with his creatures native liberty; and upon this account he muſt, as a patient, hear their

rage

rage and blasphemies, and be witness of their fruitless distress and agonies, thro' all eternity.[s]

This their argument the Scepticks also deem justified by the following scripture passage, viz. 1 *Tim.* ii. 4. *God will have all men to be saved*; for say they, if GOD wills this which will not be, he wills impotently and in vain, and not as a GOD omnipotent, and from whom all defects must be removed.

Let us then examine this scripture passage in the original languages, 1 *Tim.* ii. 1—4. *I exhort therefore, that first of all, supplications, prayers, intercessions, and thanksgiving be made for all men; for kings, and all that are in authority, that we may lead a quiet and peaceable life in all godliness and honesty; for this is good and acceptable before God our* (syr. ܡܚܝܢܐ) *life-giver, or* (gr. τυ σωτηρος ημων) *our restorer*; *who wills that all men* (according to the vulgar translation) *be saved*; (but according to the greek σωθηναι) *be recovered or restored* (and according

S

NOTES.

[s] GOD is to be called good only in so far as he wills and does good to his creatures; but he is good to all, or universally; therefore he must will and do good to all, or universally; *i. e.* he must work or decree the good or happiness of all, in general, and every one, individually, of all his creatures. We must however consider well here, what deserves to be called doing good; because that which may seem a good to us at present, may in its issue prove an evil, at least may introduce what is so.

ing to the syriac ܢܚܐ ') *shall live, revive, or recover* (syr. ܘܢܬܦܢܐ) *and be converted to the acknowledgement of the truth.*

But from this passage thus translated either by the greek or syriac, all the absurdity vanishes: it only

---

NOTES.

The words to save, saviour, salvation, &c. so much used in our new testament, convey not the true force of the greek, σωζω, σωτηρ, σωτηρια, *&c.*

† In the greek testament this passage runs thus: ὁς παντας ανθρωπους θελει σωθηναι.————In the syriac, ܗܘ' ܕܨܒܐ,² ܕܟܠܗܘܢ,³ ܒܢܝ̈ܢܫܐ,⁴ ܢܚܐ'
¹ *ipse* ² *qui vult* ³ *ut omnes* ⁴ *filii hominum* ⁵ *vivant.*

But *first* we affirm that the word saved can by no means be a fit translation of the greek σωθηναι in this passage, because what it imports is so contrary to the sentiments of an apostle who so well knew that all men would not be saved from the wrath of GOD, *Col.* iii. 6. *Which should come upon the children of disobedience.* St. *John* in a like case speaks thus, 1 *John* v. 16. *If any man see his brother sin a sin which is not unto death, he shall ask, and he will give him life for him that sinneth not unto death: there is a sin unto death, I say, that he shall not pray for it*; for GOD willeth not that his people should pray in vain. *Deut.* iii. 26. *Jer.* vii. 16. xv. 1.——

But can it be believed otherwise than that St. *Paul* must have thought too like St. *John*, to have advis'd *Timothy* to pray for what he well knew could never be? Whereas on the other hand, supposing St. *Paul*'s directions to *Timothy* to have been only to recommend all men in his prayers to the mercy of *Jesus Christ*, this was acceptable to GOD, and a praying after the mind of GOD; since his will is that all men shall be restored, or recover their original spiritual life; and so be delivered from a state of misery.

only assures us that GOD wills (what at present is not, but by the efficacy of his will we doubt not shall in its due time be accomplished, viz.) that all men shall live, or (as in the greek σωθηναι) be recovered,

---

NOTES.

It is also a praying to some purpose, not only because GOD knows how to shew mercy to those that perish, as well as to those that are saved; but also because he has in his eye the real, tho' distant, restitution, delivery, and quickening of all his creatures, having 1 *Tim.* ii. 6. *Given himself a ransom for all, to be testified in due time* (το μαρτυριον καιροις ιδιοις).

But, 2dly. It being evident that St. *Paul* could not order *Timothy* to pray that all men might be saved; we will examine what he must have advised *Timothy* to in the word σωθηναι; and this will appear in the following texts, where the words σωζω σωζομαι must evidently intend, what is very different from the meaning of our english words TO SAVE, TO BE SAVED, as that word is usually understood by us.

Matt. ix. 21, 22. *And the woman* (with the issue of blood) *said within herself, If I may but touch his garment* (σωθησομαι) *I shall be* (not saved, but) *restored to health; and the woman* (ισωθη) *was* (not saved, but) *restored to health from that hour.* Mark v. 21, 22, 23. *And Jairus besought him greatly, saying, I pray thee lay thy hands upon her* (οπως σωθη) *that she (his daughter) might* (not be saved, but) *be restored to health.* Mark vi. 56. *And as many as touched him* (εσωζοντο) *were recovered to health.* John xi. 12. *And his disciples said, Lord, if he* (Lazarus) *sleep* (σωθησεται) *he shall be* (not saved, but) *restored to health.* Acts xiv. 9. *And Paul perceiving that he had faith* (σωθηναι) *to be restored to health, said,* ———— See also, *Luke* viii. 36. xviii. 42. *Acts* iv. 9.

recovered, or restored, and come to the acknowledgement of the truth. It is not said he wills that all men (τηρηθηναι) should be saved, viz. from the wrath appointed to fall upon this world, or on

NOTES.

James v. 15. and page 46 in the notes, where a like remark is made on a quotation out of *Sophocles*.

Hence then let us take our notion of the words σωζω σωζομαι when applied to the following texts: 1 *Tim.* ii. 4. *Who wills that all men* (σωθηναι) *should be* (not saved from the wrath prepared, but) *restored to health, and come to the acknowledgment of the truth.* John iii. 17. *God sent his Son into the world, that the world thro' him might be* (not saved from hell, but) *restored to health* (ινα σωθη ὁ κοσμος δι αυτου). 1 *Tim.* iv. 10. *Who is the* (σωτηρ) *restorer of all men, especially of the faithful*; (because he saves them even from the wrath prepared.) 1 *John* iv. 14. *We do testify that the father sent the son to be* (σωτηρα τȣ κοσμȣ) *the restorer of the world*, notwithstanding its previous doom to the æonian fire. So again, *John* iv. 42. *This is indeed the restorer of the world, the Christ*, (αληθως σωτηρ τȣ κοσμȣ, ὁ χρισος) i. e. because the world's recovery, or restoration, will be its last resource in *Christ*, therefore is our Lord thus called, its restorer.

A critical observer will, I think, find the words σωζω σωζομαι, when spoken with reference to a state of evil or danger into which a man is fallen, to signify to deliver, to rescue: so *Mat.* xxvii. 42. *He delivered* (εσωσεν) *others, can he not deliver* (σωσαι) *himself.*

But when spoken in reference to a state of happiness or blessing lost, or from which man is fallen, it signifies to restore, or recover: so *Luke* xix. 10. *The son of man is come to seek and* (σωσαι το απολωλος) *to recover that which is lost.*

on the wicked in general; scripture speaks nothing of, is quite silent as to any such will in GOD; it says only that it is the will of GOD that all shall live, or be restituted, or restored.

SECT. II.

Of damnation and restoration.

ALL men as sons of *Adam* are under doom of æonian death, all men as heirs in *Christ* are destined to an æonian life: but then this life, being

---

NOTES.

So that tho' in english we say a man is *delivered* out of a state of danger or misery, and that he is *restored* into a state of security or happiness, yet in greek the same word serves both purposes.

But I no where find that the verb σωζω imports the same with the verb τηρεω; when the *Greeks* would signify to save, preserve, or keep from mischief they used the verb τηρεω; so *John* xvii. 15. *I pray not that thou shouldst take them out of the world, but that thou shouldst save, preserve, or secure them* (ἱνα τηρησῃς αυτȣς) *from the evil one.* Rev. iii. 10. *I will preserve, secure, or save thee* (τηρησω σε) *from the hour of temptation which shall come upon all the world to try them.* Jude 1. *Jude the servant of Jesus Christ to the sanctified by God the father, preserved, secured, saved* (τετηρημενοις) *in Jesus Christ, &c.* 1 Thes. v. 23. *I pray God your whole spirit, soul and body be preserved, secured, saved* (τηρηθειη) *blameless, unto the coming of our Lord.* And thus it is also said of wordly treasures; as *John* ii. 10. *But thou hast preserved, secured, or saved* (τετηρηκας) *the good wine until now.*

being in *Chrift* only as the root, muft firft be by him quickened in a man, before that man can live; and this quickening is his reftoration; when we are begotten of GOD, then only are we reftored, by having a new fpiritual life begotten in us, by being quickened in *Chrift*'s æonian life, *i. e.* by being new begotten of our fecond *Adam* as really as we were before of our natural parent.

But then where this regenerating does not happen before the day of the divine wrath is difclofed, there is damnation; or the being condemned to the fuffering of that wrath; as the reverfe of this is falvation, or the being faved from the power of that wrath: and thus you arrive at the difference between the terms reftored and faved.

Neither life nor falvation belong to us as men; as men we are all obnoxious to divine wrath, and doom'd to the terrors of the æonian death; wrath is our natural element, and death our natural tendency. Yet then when *Chrift*'s feed of immortality is within us; that which in the loft may feem to be the wrath of GOD reveal'd, will prove in us a kindling of life inftead of death, and heaven inftead of hell.

And now let us put our queftion, it being the will of GOD that all men fhall be reftored, or become quick in fpiritual life, when ever this happens, viz. that all men do fo live, is not the will of GOD in this refpect accomplifhed? And may he not then have reached an end in creating man worthy his love and benevolence? If GOD created man for the enjoyment of the divine life, the purpofe of GOD is effected when

the

the divine life, is generated in a man; also the works of satan, which *Christ* came *to dissolve*, 1 *John* iii. 8. (ἵνα λυση τα εργα τȣ διαβολȣ) are then in that degree dissolved.

Or to apply the term deliver in this case; GOD expressly willeth that all men shall be delivered from their misery; this their deliverance must therefore certainly be in its due time: but GOD willeth not expressly that all men shall be kept, preserved, or saved from falling into misery; misery therefore may happen to many; there is no decree of GOD against it; it stands among the possibilities of nature.

Tho' what has been already said may prove a sufficient answer to the above-mentioned Objections of the Deists and Scepticks; I shall however proceed to give you briefly my present sentiments concerning what we call will in GOD. But this I must reserve for the subject of my next to you.

LETTER IX.

Of the explicit and implicit will of GOD.

TO ———

SIR,

SECT. I.

IN treating on the will of GOD, I shall consider it in two respects.

I. As existing in its original freedom in the divine mind unexpressed, unproduced, unformed, having only an essence in GOD; tho' discoverable to us by analogy and resemblance with what we find in the only begotten son our creator, his true type or pattern."

II. As

NOTES.

Our relation to the Logos as our GOD.

" We are taught of the Logos or (πρωτοτοκ⊙") first-begotten, *Col.* i. 17. *That he is before all things, and*

II. As expofed, given forth, produced; **as we behold it in active exiftence, exhibited in, and exprefs'd by the fon of his love, in whom we call it his decree, or will declared.** For diftinction fake, and that we may fpeak the more clearly of fcripture reprefentations, **the firft of thefe we will call the implicit will of God, the fecond the explicit will of God.**

By the implicit will of God I therefore mean, that fimple velleity in the divine mind which lives there eternally, even while as yet undecreed, unproduced, unexhibited.

T   This

NOTES.

by him all things (συνεστηκε) *confift*; or that there is, 1 Cor. viii. 6. *One Lord Jefus Chrift, by whom are all things, and we by him.* Acts xvii. 24, 25, 28. *Who made the world and all things that are therein;—who giveth to all life, and breath, and all things;—in whom we live, and move, and have our being;—for we are all his offspring.*

The Logos or firft-begotten is alone the offspring of the father: but we are the offspring of the Logos. As fays *Clemens Alexandrinus* (ἡ μεν γαρ τυ Θευ εικων ὁ Λογος αυτα; εικων δε τυ Λογυ ὁ ανθρωπος) ' the image of ' God is his Logos or word, the image of the Logos is ' man.' *Admon ad Gentes.*

It is true the Logos is to moft men, as worfhipped by the *Athenians,* the unknown God; yet this is fo becaufe, *Rom.* i. 28. *As they approved not to retain God in their knowledge, he gave them up to a mind* (αδοκιμον) *void of judgment*; even that judgment which all men might otherwife make concerning him; for *Acts* xiv. 17. *He left not himfelf without a witnefs, in that he did*

This being implied in the nature of God, we will here, for conveniency of conception, ascribe to the father as his especial character; and it is discoverable to the creature in the harmony of those excellencies which we attribute to the Logos our creator, whose likeness we bare, and therefore whose good pleasure we conceive: Seeing the will of the Logos, we can conceive of his father's will, by presuming its harmony therewith.

In contrast hereto we set the explicit will of God; whereby we mean what exists, as produced

---

NOTES.

good, and gave us rain from heaven, and fruitful seasons, filling our hearts with food and gladness.

But the father of the Logos, by whom the Logos doth all these things, is unknown to all besides the Logos only; unknown thro' his essential distinction from the creature; 1 *Tim.* vi. 16. *Dwelling in the light which no man can approach unto, whom no man hath seen, nor can see.*

The personal distinction between the Logos and his father seems conceivable to us in the following respect, viz. that the father is the essential source of all possibility, ungenerated, and so concealed in the divine invisible fulness; whereas the Logos is this essential source of all possibility, generated, and so revealed, and exposed to those who are created into a likeness of his nature; and this production seems to be the ground of their distinction of wills; and yet this is a distinction consistent with a fundamental sameness.

But that will which we vulgarly call the will of God, and which to us is intelligible, is properly the will of

duced or exhibited out of the father, in his word or Logos, his æonianly or temporally form'd will.

This we afcribe to the Logos or only begotten fon of GOD, as remarkably belonging to his office and character; and it is cognifable to man, and poffibly to all other creatures, thro' him only, and that by revelation.

By revelation we here mean not meerly the written word of GOD, but every other way of difcovering the mind of GOD with certainty.

So then, when we fpeak of the implicit will of GOD, we here mean that which is fuppofed to fubfift in GOD, as the original and father of

T 2   the

NOTES.

the Logos our creator, whofe offspring we are; and his will is intelligible to us becaufe we are his offspring.

By being his offspring we perceive the propriety of goodnefs, juftice, truth, and virtue; and the deformity of malice, unrighteoufnefs, falfhood, and vice; i. e. the Logos is intelligible to us by what we learn of him in our ownfelves. And therefore St. *Paul* tells us *Rom*. xii. 2. that in order to a true teft of his will, we muft have our minds *renewed and transformed*; *for that* (Eph. v. 8, 10.) *we are to prove what is acceptable unto the Lord, by becoming light in the Lord*.

Our perception of virtue or fitnefs, is not the refult of reafoning, or juxta-pofition; but of our fpiritual feeling and inward light; *John* i. 9. *He is that true light, which lighteth every man that cometh into the world*. This, however, may in fome wicked people be much obfcured, and in others as it were loft.

So then we know the divine will by the Logos; but the Logos, exifting in an immediate fenfation, and uninterrupted vifion of the will of his father, frames all whatever he does by this as his meafure and archetype.

the Logos; and when we speak of the explicit will of GOD we mean the copy and likeness of the former, and as subsisting in the Logos or only begotten son of GOD: for as the son of GOD is the express image of the father, yet distinct from the father; so is the will of the son of GOD the express image of the father's will, yet distinct from it.

SECT. II.

The implicit and explicit will of GOD *contrasted.*

THE *implicit will of* GOD, above consider'd, we may conceive as exerting no active force or power upon the creature, otherwise than thro' the son: we may also conceive of it as temporally resistable; yea, as violently resisted by the creature. For all the works of satan which *Christ* came to loosen or dissolve, all the distresses and miseries of human life, all the defects, confusions and deformities in the natural world, all that which the scripture forbids or complains of as odious and repugnant to the divine nature, is also odious and repugnant to this implicit will of GOD; for GOD forbids only what he dislikes, and complains only of what is hateful to him.

But that *explicit will of* GOD which subsists in *Christ* as first-begotten, seems to be irresistable;* and to

---

NOTES.

* This is thus described in many parts of scripture. See *Gen.* xviii. 4. l. 19. *Is.* xlvi. 10. *Rom.* ix. 19. but

to have in it an effectuating energy which no creature can withstand; this is excellently described by *Moses*, Gen. i. 3. *And God said, let there be light, and there was light*; (v. 6--) *and God said, let there be a firmament in the midst of the waters, and let it divide the waters from the waters; and it was so. And God said, let there be lights in the firmament of the heavens; and it was so.*

The *implicit will of* GOD seems to have, as the object of its concern, singly his only begotten son; however for him, and that he may *see the travail of his soul and be satisfied*; it likewise seems to concern itself with the essences of all things, and with contingents of all kinds, even all that may not as well as that may exist.

Any of the possibilities of futurity surveyable in the divine mind, one should think, might become matter of divine favour and complacency, without having actual existence decreed them; without being pronounced creatures. And it seems as tho' GOD had thus, in his implicit will, approved of the creation long before it was created

---

NOTES.

the passage in *Job* is very expressive. *Job.* xlii 2. *I have known that thou canst do all things, and that no thought conceivable in thy divine mind shall be cut off from thee* (בצר *decisa erit, prohibetur*; *id est, non prohibetur a te quicquam eorum quae tibi venerint in mentem*) or be impracticable to thee; and so *Christ* himself says, *Luke* i. 37. *With God nothing shall be impossible*, i. e. with GOD as he is pleased to operate in his first-begotten the Logos.

ated: and this his approbation, we call his velleity or unactive will, since his will, thus regarded, expresses some approbation of what it forbears to produce.

The *explicit will of* GOD has for the objects of its concern the whole creation external to, and distinct from GOD: It regards the several creatures as related both to himself, and to one another, naturally or accidentally; and to the several ends and purposes he has in them. It regards them, not only as what they were when they came pure and simple out of his forming hands, but as they now are deformed, and different, creatures by their sin and rebellion.[x]

The

NOTES.

The expediency of a mediatorial GOD *to the happiness of the creature.*

[x] LET us here consider that upon the existence of the creature, GOD became otherwise related than whilst himself was THE ALL; that he became in some manner so concerned with his dependants, as that his being influenced and affected by them should be absolutely necessary for the creature's good; and then the idea of a mediator at once appears quite reasonable.

But when the creatures are farther considered as both variable and to vary; as liable to unnatural contingencies, yea as actually fallen, divided into differencies, and deformed with strange contrarieties and repugnancies; a mediator, partaking of both the divine and the created nature, by being inconceivably connected with the latter, and so invested with a vicarial office; appears, much more than reasonable, a sentiment of most delightful propriety.

LETTER IX. [151] SECT. II.

The *implicit will of* GOD is immutable, because it is implied in his immutable nature, and has its foundation in that central principle, whence we suppose his excellencies radically to result.

Thus an immutable benevolence is one of the attributes of what we call GOD's implicit will, because it is implied in his nature love; has its foundation in his very essence. And as GOD cannot

---

NOTES.

We may suppose in such an one, what cannot well be presumed in the divine essence, a sensation or feeling of the creatures evils and casualties. Tho' nothing can move GOD in his original nature, tho' no creature can have any necessary connection with this, yet certainly the case is far otherwise with our LORD the son of GOD; we find in him one (Heb. iv. 15) *that cannot but be touched with a feeling of our infirmities*; for having our real genuine nature in his own self, in and thro' that nature there lives in him such a susceptibility of relative impressions from our necessities, and so of solicitude in behalf of us, and of sympathetical attachments to us, that he cannot but love us. Yea and does not the scripture give us to understand that our mediator ('tho' not in himself, and as the son of the father, yet as the head of his body the church, and as the resource, or uniting point, of the creation, *i. e.* as now related to his creatures) is even imperfect, or short of what he is intended to be, without us? Col. i. 19. *It pleased God that in him should all fulness* (*i. e.* both eternal and created) *dwell.* Ep. iv. 10. *He is ascended far above all heavens, that he might fill all things.* The Logos then is not only necessary for our creation, he is forever needfull for us.

not diminish his benevolent will, because emergent from his nature love; neither can he diminish his implicit will, because that same lovely nature is also its source.

The *explicit will of* God is mutable and conditional; and it exists thus in *Christ* with a view to his concern with mutable creatures, and their complicated circumstances; and this seems to be the foundation of our blessed Lord's wonderful prayer to his father,[y] *that this cup* (whatever he thereby meant) *might pass away from him, Mat.* xxvi. 39; and of his no less mysterious lamentation over *Jerusalem*, (*Mat.* xxiii. 37.) and of all his conditional dispensations, (*Rev.* iii. 20. *Ez.* xviii. 23.) and of the astonishing efficacy of prayer. So *James* v. 16, 17, 18. *Jonah* iii. 5—10.

The *implicit will of* God affects not immediately any creature, but leaves the whole creation both to will and act in its full liberty; so that all the efforts and transactions of evil creatures are one continued opposition to it. *Acts* vii. 51. *You do always resist* (ἀντιπίπτετε bare against) *the Holy Ghost, as your fathers did so do you.*

The *explicit will of* God is the power of every creature; without it no creature can be or act, and no event can happen; both good and evil exist, continue, and have their effect by this.

Isaiah

NOTES.

[y] We may easily suppose our Lord to have known that his father's will was at liberty to decree or pronounce, and so to produce explicitly, as he pleased. See *John* viii. 28, 29. *John* v. 19, 20. *And without his will,* himself he tells us, *can do nothing.*

Isaiah xlv. 7. *I form light and create darkness, I make peace and create evil; I Jehovah do all these things.*[z]

The *implicit will of* GOD regards nothing as lovely but (what is so) his only son;[a] those who are in the image and likeness of his son (*i. e.* to whom his holiness is imparted); and those who are dear to him upon his son's account. The last in scripture terms are called *accepted in the beloved*, and mentioned in the following manner; *John* xvi. 26.—*And I say not unto you that I will pray the father for you, for the father himself loveth you, because you have loved me, and have believed that I came out from God.* Gal. iv. 7. *Now after that ye have known God, or rather are known of God, how,* &c. 1 Cor. viii. 3. *If any man love God, the same is known of him.*

By this his implicit will, GOD seems to renounce all concern with what is wicked, and to repel every evil creature from his presence. *Hab.* i. 13. *He is of purer eyes than to behold evil, and cannot look upon iniquity.* James i. 13. *God cannot be tempted with evil, neither tempteth he any man.* For the contrariety between GOD and sin is as that

U   be-

NOTES.

[z] *Amos* iii. 6. *Shall there be evil in a city, and I Jehovah have not done it?*

[a] The father loveth no one necessarily besides his son; and he being his own true image and perfect self, is adequate, and singly so, to all the divine capacities of love and enjoyment; the one sufficient object for the whole exertion and display of infinite benevolence.

between light and darkness; 1 *John* i. 5. *God is light and in him is no darkness at all.*

The explicit will of GOD permits providently the wicked in all kinds of evil and wickedness; makes use of both good and bad to subserve his end;[b] engages both men, devils,[c] and all the perversest powers that are or will be, in its service:[d] and exerting itself in the midst of all confusion and mischief, guides the malice of his creatures

---

NOTES.

[b] Ps. lxxviii. 49. *He cast upon them the fierceness of his anger, wrath, indignation and trouble, by sending evil angels among them.* Ez. xiv. 9. *And if the prophet be deceived when he hath spoken a thing, I the Lord* (i. e. Jehovah) *have deceived that prophet.* Rom. i. 24. *Wherefore God gave them up in the lusts of their own hearts to uncleanness;* (ver. 29.) *being filled with all wickedness.* —Jer. vi. 21. *Therefore I will lay stumbling blocks before this people, and the fathers and the sons together shall fall upon them.* If. lxiii. 17. *O Lord, why hast thou made us to err from thy ways, and harden'd our heart from thy fear? Return* ———

[c] 1 Kings xxii. 23. *The Lord hath put a lying spirit into the mouth of all these thy prophets; and the Lord hath spoken evil concerning thee.* Judges ix. 23. *And God sent an evil spirit between Abimelech and the men of Sichem, &c.*

[d] 2 Thes. ii. 11.—*For this cause God will send them a strong delusion that they should believe a lie, that they all might be damned who believed not the truth, but had pleasure in unrighteousness.* 1 Tim. iv. 1. *Now the spirit speaketh expressly that in the latter times some shall depart from the faith, giving heed to seducing spirits and doctrines of devils.*

tures and regulates the profoundest of their evil productions, to more profound and more solid, tho' secret good.[e] Insomuch that satan himself knows not how to resist the implicit will of GOD, without serving the purposes of his explicit will. Yea satan becomes in all he contrives a most important instrument in the sublimest plan of created good.[f]

SECT. III.

Reflections on the above distinguished will of GOD.

WE may reasonably presume that all our philosophical inquiries, and researches into nature would at once be answered in a competent knowledge of the Logos. Because since

---

NOTES.

[e] The good thus contrived is hitherto revealed only as touching the first fruits; so *Rom.* viii. 28. *And we know that all things* **work** *for good to them that love* **God,** *to them who are called according to his purpose.*

[f] Rom. ix. 17. *The scripture saith unto Pharoah,* (who was a type of satan) *even for this very purpose have I appointed thee, that I might shew my power in thee.* Ver. 18. *Therefore he has mercy on whom he will have mercy, and whom he will he hardeneth.* Ver. 22. *And willing to shew his wrath and to make known* (το δυνατον αυτȣ) *the capability of his power,* or what effects it was able to produce (i. e. was potential of) *he endureth with* **much** *long-suffering the vessels of wrath fitted* **for** *destruction.*

nature results from the God of it, who is the Logos; the knowledge of him seems to imply the knowledge of his productions.

And if we could see the Logos as he is, the knowledge thence resulting, would in all likelihood give us also a view of that distinction which arose between himself and his father, by his becoming the first-begotten; and so of consequence we might discover how the will of the Logos, altho' ever regulated by, yet becomes distinct from his father's will; as also how the creation sprung from hence; that is, as we imagine it, a finite from an infinite. But all this is at present altogether inconceivable to us.

At present, the implicit will of God, as visible to the creature by semblance and in parts, is, like the members of a machine not understood, mysterious, and unaccountable: yea, we cannot penetrate the reasons and proprieties even of its dispensations; who can explain how wrath, and pain, and misery should be allowed of in the creation of God; should prove a contrivance of his love, and infinite benevolence; or in anywise subserve or tend towards consummate happiness? And yet, this our darkness notwithstanding, that so it does, we cannot doubt, when we behold our Lord himself drinking of his bitter cup, bound to the pillar, trembling under the tormenting lash of the Scorpio, and nailed to his cross; of whom says the Poet:

" ———— That *healing hand*—
" The skies it form'd; and now it bleeds for me—
" But bleeds the balm I want—yet still it *bleeds*;
" Draw

" Draw the dire steel—ah no!—the dreadful
      blessing
" What heart, or can sustain, or dares forego?
" There hangs all human hope: that nail supports
" Our falling universe: that gone, we drop;
" Horror receives us, and the dismal wish
" Creation had been smother'd in her birth.—
" Darkness his curtain, and his bed the dust;
" When stars and sun are dust beneath his throne!
" In heaven itself can such indulgence dwell?
" O what a groan was there? A groan *not his:*
" He seiz'd our dreadful right, the load sustain'd;
" And heav'd the mountain from a guilty world.
" A thousand worlds, *so* bought, were bought too
      dear."

When we view this amazing object, we cannot but acknowledge it a most convincing evidence that infinite love is indeed capable of beholding the miseries of what it loves, with a view to its happiness: Yea, and not of beholding only, but of enduring itself the utmost extremities in prospect of future good.

For it was the bands of our LORD's love that bound him to the pillar; and the nails of his compassion that fastened him to the cross: No other bands, and no other nails could have held him; no material cords could have confined him, whom the sepulchre could not hold; no iron nails could have detained him; who *Acts* i. 9. *While they beheld was taken up, and a cloud received him out of their sight.*

If any one will dispute what we here advance concerning the explicit will of GOD, as especially
                                                            visible

visible in the Logos, *him with whom we have to do,* and as the exact pattern of that implicit will of GOD which we call his immutable will, and of which we can have no adequate idea or conception; let him first teach us better, and we will hear him: but at present we both see no absurdity in this opinion, and think it reasonable: for as the son is the express image of the father, so must his will be the express image of the father's will; and in proof that it is so, we think we have many scripture testimonies.

Thus says our LORD, accommodating this great truth to our human conceptions. *John* viii. 28, 29. *I do nothing of myself, but as the father has taught me, so I speak; and he that sent me is with me: the father has not left me alone, for I do always those things that please him.* Again, *John* v. 19, 20. *The son can do nothing of himself, but what he seeth the father do; for whatsoever thing he doth, these also doth the son likewise; for the father loveth the son, and sheweth him all things that himself doth:* and (ver. 30.) *I seek not my own will, but the will of the father who hath sent me.*[g]

And

NOTES.

[g] We above observed that our LORD, knowing the will of GOD in its inmost centre, governs his creatures, and conducts himself in exact conformity to it. But notwithstanding this, *Christ*'s conduct as it appears to the creature, may seem repugnant to the will of his father, and such seeming repugnancy is owing to the narrowness of our apprehensions, and weakness of our judgments; for tho' our LORD sees in the bosom of

. And as man by an innate propensity wills always what he thinks his own good; so our LORD being the GOD of nature, seeks indefatigably the good of his creatures: *Is.* lxiii. 15. *The sounding of his bowels and of his mercies is towards us,* and all the workings of his will tend incessantly to our ultimate, and highest happiness: *Carior est illi homo quam sibi*; man is dearer to him than to his very self.

LET-

NOTES.

his father a pure disinterested invincible love of the creature generated there upon his account; yet our LORD sees also how the creatures temporal miseries and afflictions suit and consist with this love: He sees that the benevolence of his father towards the wicked is answered in their damnation and death, yea in all that will or can be suffered 'till to the end of suffering in his æonian kingdom. No wonder therefore that there should be an imaginary difference between the implicit and explicit will of GOD, between the wrath of the Lamb, the terrors of the LORD, the fiery indignation of the Lion of the tribe of *Judah*, of whom we read, *vengeance is mine, and I will repay it, saith the Lord*; and that will which is pure immutable love, which is good to all, which breathes with a tenderness of mercy over all his works, which *maketh his sun to rise on the evil and the good*; *and sendeth rain on the just and the unjust*.

LETTER X.

CHRIST *in his character of a restorer consider'd at large.*

1 TIM. iv. 10.
We trust in the living God, who is (σωτηρ) *the restorer or deliverer of all men, especially of the believers.*

TO ―――

SIR,

I HAVE already shewn that the words σωτηρ, σωτηρια, σωζω, &c. which we render saviour, salvation, to save, &c. are improperly so render'd; and that they would be more justly render'd restorer, restoration, to restore, implying thereby some misery or misfortune already incurred, some distressed circumstances befallen the person so to be restored or delivered out of them.

In this notion of it, the term (σωτηρ) soter in our present text, is to be understood; and by so understanding it, the passage becomes intelligible and unexceptionable, and yields us three points of consideration; namely, that *Christ* is (σωτηρ i. e.)

i. e.) the restorer or deliverer; 2dly. that he is the (σωτηρ) restorer of all men; 3dly. that he is in an especial manner the (σωτηρ) restorer of believers, or them that believe.

Adam in that he was appointed to be the father of all mankind, had a general character, becoming the representative of all mankind by their appointment to be his seed or children; insomuch that all those souls who were destined to become *Adam*'s seed (*i. e.* who were appointed thro' him to the privileges of humanity) were to share the fate of him their common parent; and this is an act of grace indulged them out of the bounty of their great creator.

But because in treating here on our restitution, I cannot well speak intelligibly, without betraying my belief that the human soul was a fallen creature before the creation of this world; and that *Adam* was appointed to be our father with a view to our recovery; I shall first declare my opinion on this subject.

SECT. I.

The sons of Adam *were sinners before they became the sons of* Adam.

ALTHO' *Adam* be the father of all men, yet the creator of all men is GOD.[h] So says the

---

NOTES.

[h] It has been indeed the opinion of some that both the souls and bodies of men are formed out of the sub-

the Pfalmift, *Pf.* c. 3. *Know that Jehovah himself is God, he himself hath made us, and not we ourselves*; reflecting hereby upon fuch infidels as vainly imagined that men by being begotten of their fathers do derive their exiftence from him. So again fays *Malachi* ii. 10. *Have we not all one father; hath not one God created us?* So *Eph.* iv. 6. *There is one God and father of us all; who is above all, and thro' all, and in you all.*

And fince creation and generation muft be the effects of powers fo different, there muft be between thefe two kinds of productions fome difference as incomparable as their caufes are incomparable.

Hence we obferve of the creatures that they have all of them a power to generate, yet that they have no power at all to create, no nor even *to make one hair black or white*; and why is this

fo,

NOTES.

ftance of their parents, as a branch grows out of the. fubftance of a tree, and this they therefore call traduction.

But this notion few will now infift upon, becaufe of the abfurdities attending the fuppofition of fuch a partial and progreffive production.

Very like this, altho' in name different, and no lefs irrational is the opinion of others that the foul is produced by propagation, and that out of the body, and by the agency of bodily organs. For to fuppofe that a foul fhould be propagated by a body, and become thereby of a nature different from that body whence it fprung; is to fuppofe in the body a creative power (for to produce what onefelf is not is to create) and of fuch

so, but becaufe creation refults from nothing fhort of omnipotence itfelf?

So then begetting being only a manner of producing or exhibiting what is already created, into a new ftate of exiftence (a power common to man with the meaneft infect whofe life is but for a day) muft always imply creation as antecedent to it, or that the fons of *Adam*, altho' not as fuch, had fome real exiftence antecedent to their becoming by generation his children.

Thus was our LORD himfelf the firft-begotten (and prior to all creation, the Logos) before he became the human fon of GOD, invefted in the flefh of *Mary*. This has been already urged in letter 5th, and appears alfo from the words taken notice of letter 4th, fect. 2. note (°) on *Gen.* iv. 1. *I have gotten the man the Jehovah*; for certainly when *Eve* fpake thefe words, fhe muft have believed

NOTES.

fort as to yield forth a nature, not only diftinct from, but even fuperior to itfelf, and even with faculties which itfelf has not.

And befides all this (and which is ftill harder to be conceived) this production muft refult, a moft accomplifhed and artificial fyftem, by the operation of a body which knows not what it does, which acts not with defign of (but without either thought, or purpofe, or confcioufnefs of) the thing produced.

Thefe two perfuafions were therefore condemned as one in the Lateran council, held in the 15th century, who determined it as a point of orthodoxy, that every fingle foul, in every fingle man, was created and infufed by GOD.

lieved that Jehovah should become a man by being born of her; and that men are not (as is the vulgar notion) created and begotten at one and the same time; but that they are first created of GOD, and afterwards begotten of men; that they have their first existence from their heavenly father, and afterwards their production from their earthly father; and hence it is that the scripture so often speaks of people as in being for ages before they are born; our LORD says of himself, *John* iii. 13. *No one has ascended up to heaven, except the son-man who came down from heaven, where he was before*, vi. 62. And again we read of *Cyrus*, *Is*. xliv. 28. *I am Jehovah that saith to Cyrus who is my shepherd, and shall perform all my pleasure, &c.* but this *Cyrus* here spoken of by name, lived not on earth 'till above 100 years after this prophecy of him. And so we read of the anti-christ, that *man of sin and son of perdition, that* (Rev. xvii. 8.) *he shall ascend out of the bottomless pit, or abyss*; but he must have been in the abyss, before he can ascend from thence, and be born a man upon earth; and at his death he shall not return to the abyss, but (*Rev*. xx. 10.) *be thrown into the lake (*εις αιωνα αιωνος, or ܠܥܠܡ ܥܠܡܝܢ,) *for an æonian æon.*

Now this our antecedent state of existence supposed, we must have existed in it either fallen creatures, or else creatures pure and innocent.

Had we been innocent, we could not have forfeited our favour and access to GOD by the personal sin of *Adam*; for the injustice of such forfeiture GOD renounces; *Ez*. xviii. 19. *And yet say ye, why? Doth not the son bear the iniquity of the father?*

LETTER X. [165] SECT. I.

father? (ver. 20.) *The son shall not bear the iniquity of the father, neither shall the father bear the iniquity of the son, but the righteousness of the righteous shall be upon him; and the wickedness of the wicked shall be upon him.*[i] Therefore we must have been creatures

---

NOTES.

[i] GOD can consistent with justice, confer good upon his creature, without proposing his intention to that creature, for the concurrence of his choice therein.

Wherefore, we being fallen creatures, GOD can appoint us to become the begotten sons of fallen *Adam* for our good, without having our consent to such appointment.

Also, by such his appointment, GOD may entitle us to all that his acceptance, and pardon, and grace, and other blessings which he has caused to belong to *Adam*'s nature, or endowed it with.

Also, these Blessings to which we are entitled as sons of *Adam*, GOD can charge with limitations, granting them only on certain terms and provisos; and one of these provisos may be, that we shall inherit the miseries and evils together with the good and benefits of that nature, and which thro' our father may contingently affect us.

Again, we may aver with certainty that, if the condition of the most unhappy man upon earth, be preferable to the former condition of the least miserable of those souls that are begotten men; every soul becoming a gainer by his being begotten, has reason to be thankful to GOD for his humanity.

According to this view of manhood, a man becoming a looser in his father's loss, or a sufferer in his father's nature; ought not to be called a sufferer for his father's sin, but a sufferer by implicit contract; because his sufferings, being a part of the terms where-

-tures fallen from GOD before we were begotten of fallen *Adam*.[k]   Again

---

NOTES.

by he enjoys the rights, immunities and other blessings of his paternal nature, are to be regarded as only circumstances accidentally connected with an advantageous inheritance; as casual, unfortunate incidents attending a beneficial compact made for him in his parent.

For it may by no means be supposed that the judgments of GOD upon the guiltless sons of a wicked father, can bespeak his anger against those guiltless sons as sinners personally; because to affirm such anger to be in GOD, is to affirm that GOD can be angry at people as being what they are not, and for crimes which they have not committed.

Lastly then, hereditary right, or a right by geniture being thus considered; I suppose no instance can be found in scripture to contradict the passage above quoted out of *Ezekiel* xviii. 20. viz. *The son shall not bear the iniquity of the father; neither shall the father bear the iniquity of the son, &c.* for the evils which we inherit from our father, are in consideration of blessings which we also derive from our father by assuming his nature, and which abundantly more than recompense such evils: even as the shame and persecutions which fail upon men for being Christians, call'd *bearing the reproach of Christ*, our second father, Heb. xiii. 13. xi. 26. are infinitely exceeded by the privileges and honours that shall reward them, so bearing his shame.

[k] If we suppose the souls of men (for I here concern myself not with their bodies) to have been creatures of GOD before they were begotten on earth, we must either suppose them to have been fallen from GOD before that time; or else we must say that GOD forces his holy creatures into a state of existence, wherein, by passing thro' a vile abominable parent,

Again this notion of the pre-incarnate delinquency of man seems to be no less clearly implied in the contract and covenant between the father and the Logos touching our redemption: because to suppose the Logos offering himself to the father as a victim for sinners who as yet had no existence, for a people who were first to be made by the Logos, and afterwards to become a guilty sinful race, is not only unnatural; but even imports that sin results originally from the approbation and choice, and so operative will of GOD: whereas we learn from scripture that sin results not from the will of GOD, but merely from the creature's choice; that sin is altogether the event of the creature's choice in his liberty to will and do, and that no other in GOD than his permissive will only, was concerned in the production of sin and misery. Every

---

NOTES.

they must infallibly become a race, like that parent, (*Job.* xxv. 4. *Pf.* cxliii. 2.) wicked, corrupt, malicious, the object of GOD's disgust, yea more, of his afflictive wrath and indignation. But we cannot say thus without a violent impeachment of his justice and love towards a creature pure and holy like himself, and so deserving good and not evil from his bounty and benevolence.

This conjecture is also repugnant to all our ideas of the divine regard for fitness, truth, and mercy.

Yea and since it supposes that the vile passions found in man arise from his soul's union with flesh, a fabrick of inert and harmless matter: we demand how such a depravity can be supposed to arise from such an union? And on what experience we are to ground this supposition?

Every creature has his emanations or flowings forth or issues, answering to his inward nature; and a sinful course of living is the emanation of a creature cut off, alienated from, or in a state of enmity against GOD.

But it appears to me extravagant to affirm that the son of GOD should suffer, from the hands of his holy father, for creatures not as yet existing in such state of malice and sin-production; for creatures that were first to be made by him pure (since nothing can exist impure immediately from his forming hands) and then to be cut off from, or made sinful enemies to GOD, by being begotten or born of a sin-producing and infectious human creature, his future father.

For this not only implies our LORD's sufferings for crimes not committed, and that need not to be so; but it also implies either 1st an absolute predestination of GOD that the souls which he should hereafter make pure, should become impure, and haters of GOD and goodness; or else 2dly. that *Christ* should suffer, and that for sin, whether such sin might be ever committed or not.

That is, either that *Christ* must suffer by the decree of GOD for sins not decreed to be committed; or else that the innocent creatures of GOD (to be created) must be predestinated (before they were made or had being) to become (*i. e.* must unavoidably become) wicked: they become unavoidably wicked, and yet must so forfeit the favour of GOD by being wicked, as to need the blood of *Jesus* to restore them.

How much more reasonable is it to believe that all the creatures were already made of GOD, and

fallen

fallen from GOD, before the covenant between the Logos and his father existed: and that by virtue of this covenant the creatures, being so already fallen from GOD, were destined to become men, together with the Logos; that so, thro' the manhood of the Logos, they might be restored.

And thus also it is easy to conceive that all creature guilt, both in its root and in its outflowings, being already so recompensed and atoned for by *Christ*, as that himself should now be our only creditor; he our redeemer or purchaser, can pardon or punish his own (*John* i. 11.) when, where, and how he pleases.

That *Christ* by his act of ransoming from a doom voluntarily and previously incurred, being most equitably possessed of the thing ransomed, in all its circumstances of debt, and obnoxiousness, and with all its rights and forfeitures; enjoys even all that arbitrary dominion over all who have sinned, whether before or since their human form of life, which is in any wise transferable from his father to himself.

Christ being personally the plenitude of his father, and containing in his single person greater worth than exists in all the creatures put together; is in himself a sacrifice equivalent to all the creation: wherefore, supposing only that this doctrine of atonement is not unnatural, the practicability of it in the dignity of *Christ*'s person may be presumed without difficulty; which done, it ceases to be incredible that all creatures as they are, with all their past, present and future guilt, may be the purchased possession of *Christ*, and as such the devoted subjects of his will and pleasure.

In this case, whatever right satan might originally have had to sinners by the permission of GOD, this is now all done away and superseded in the sacrifice of *Christ*, become in his æonian character the absolute LORD and uncontrollable despot of every sinful subject, yea and even of satan himself.

Again, In this notion of our original condition are the words of Jehovah to the prophet *Jeremiah* very apposite and intelligible. *Jer.* i. 4, 5. *Then the word of Jehovah came unto me, saying, before I formed thee in the belly, I knew thee; and before thou camest out of the womb, I sanctified thee, and ordained thee* (to be) *a prophet unto the nations.*

And from these words we learn three things;
1st. That GOD respects those creatures whom he has chosen to be a part of human race, with favour and acceptance, and as a people he is already reconciled to. Thus much is implied in the words, *I knew thee, I sanctified thee.*

2dly. That the guilt of our fall in our state of existence prior to our state of manhood, must have been deem'd as aton'd for in some destined expiation by *Christ*, before our birth into this world.

3dly. That upon our becoming men we were esteemed pure and innocent, as to all other guilt than that only which belongs to us by generation, and that federal relation to GOD in which we stood by being the appointed sons of *Adam*.

So that being now regarded (by virtue of *Christ*'s covenant with his father for us) as redeem'd in *Christ*, and so guilty to him only; it was his pleasure that we should become men, the sons of fallen man, and change our personal, for a guilt by birth; our guilt contracted before our human life, for a guilt assumptive with our father's nature.

To this doctrine refers also that remarkable question proposed by the apostles to our LORD at his healing a blind man. *John* ix. 2. *Master, who did sin, this man, or his parents, that he was born blind.*

They conceived that this man had enjoyed life in some state of existence antecedent to this of his fleshly; and that he might have been born or begotten a blind man in punishment for his sins perpetrated in his pre-existent life.

That such was the opinion of the *Jews* in our saviour's time, we have unquestionable testimony from *Josephus* and *Philo Judeus*; who tell us, that they believed the souls of men to be of one nature with angels and demons; that they were created together with them; and that they lived with them in the regions above, from whence they descended into the bodies they animate upon earth.

Also *Menasse Ben Israel*, so famous for his jewish learning, tells us, *Communis est opinio omnium Hebræorum animas humanas præcessisse corpora.*— Lib. de creat. prob. 15. p. 61.—" It is the com-
" mon opinion of all *Jews* that human souls were
" before their bodies." See also *Wisd.* viii. 19, 20.

Many of our modern divines, who protest against this doctrine as erroneous, presume that it is rejected as false in our LORD's reply to his disciples upon this occasion: but if it were so, one would think that our LORD, having so fair an opportunity, would have been more explicit on this occasion, would have now reproved

proved this error so universal among the *Jews*, and regulated his disciples notions of human nature[1] by truth; which yet his answer is so far from doing, that it manifestly imports the truth of the opinion; for silence in the face of such a doctrine cannot but authorize it.

Jesus answered (John ix. 3) *neither hath this man sinned nor his parents; but that the works of God should be manifest in him:* our LORD could not here mean, that neither this man nor his parents had ever committed any sin, his objection therefore must evidently have respected *the application* only; and not *the matter itself* of his disciples opinion: that is he denied that the sin of this man or of his parents was the very reason of his being born blind; but he denied not that they had sinn'd; they still might both have sinn'd; as the father before he begat his son, so the son before he was begotten of his father. For since our

LORD's

NOTES.

[1] This too is the more probable because our LORD tells his disciples, *Luke* viii. 10. *Unto you it is given to know the mysteries of the kingdom of God.* And again, *John* xv. 15. *Henceforth I call you not servants but friends, for the servant knoweth not what his Lord doth; but I have called you friends, for all things that I have heard of my father, I have made known unto you.* Our LORD often declares to his apostles that, and what himself was before he became incarnate: and since he knew that his apostles, with all other *Jews*, supposed that all mankind also existed before they became incarnate; he could not but be conscious that his account of his own pre-incarnate state, would confirm them in this opinion: but he who was truth itself would not confirm his apostles in any error.

Lord's answer on this occasion cannot be understood of the father, *i. e.* as saying that the father had never sinn'd, why should it be so understood of the son? It equally relates to both; and if it argues not but that the father had sinn'd in this life before he begat his son; neither does it argue but that the son also had sinn'd in a former life before he was begotten.

And in this view of it, our Lord's answer proves a tacit acknowledgment of the justness of this jewish maxim; disowning only the conclusion his apostles would draw from it: for our Lord's objecting nothing to the supposition itself, of a man's sinning before he was begotten, must certainly have confirm'd his disciples in their notion of the soul's pre-existing; at the same time that it dilated their minds with other and greater conceptions as to the dispensations of divine providence.

So that if this opinion be false, our Lord's answer to his apostles thus believing, would have amused and deceived them with a notion repugnant to the reality of things, *i. e.* would never have been given by so wise and gracious a teacher, to his first and most beloved church; and if not, then that the soul pre-exists the body, deserves our assent, not merely for being a received maxim among the *Jews*, but for being a doctrine countenanced, and assented to by our Lord himself; and as we may judge, to indicate thereby to his apostles this point as the key for opening the mystery of our defection in our father *Adam*, and recovery by means of him.

We have an instance of our saviour's conduct on an occasion very like this in *Acts* i. 6. where his

his apostles ask him, *Lord wilt thou at this time restore the kingdom of Israel.*

The temporal kingdom on this earth, it is well known was expected by all the *Jews* as one day to be restored to them. And as this belief of the *Jews* was founded upon indisputable promises; we here observe our LORD acquiescing in it, and approving of it, in like manner as in the instance above, by his silence; tho' at the same time he corrects his apostles curiosity, as to the time of this expected event; ver. 7. *It is not for you to know the times or the seasons, which the father has put into* (not mine but) *his own power.*

They are reproved only for inquisiting the times, because as to the event itself they were not reprovable, the kingdom of *Israel* must be restored, and that temporally.

So in the foregoing instance, the apostles were reproved only in the conclusions they would draw from their knowledge of the soul's pre-existence; because as to the pre-existence itself, they thought right; it was a found truth.

Things thus considered we may presume 1st. that if *Adam* had not fallen, *i. e.* had not forfeited his spiritual life or quickening grace; altho' we should have been, in his likeness, upright; [for *Eccles.* vii 29. *God made the man Adam* (את האדם *Adam's* self, so אתך thyself, ישר) *upright*] yet since uprightness does not import purity or holiness inherent in a man's own person; how easily might numbers of us have fallen, as did *Adam*, after our becoming men.

Again, altho' if *Adam* had not forfeited the terms of his paradisaical happiness, we should have

have been happier in this life than we now are, yet it seems not that we should have been thereby happier in an after life; or that we should have been securer or less liable to damnation from our conduct in this; or that either the restored or lost among men would have been gainers upon the whole.   But

2dly. If our condition as the begotten sons of *Adam* fallen, be in itself preferable to our preincarnate condition, our condition before we became men; it is our interest to have been begotten, even tho' begotten into the likeness of a fallen parent. Yea and who knows how hopeless our circumstances might have been if we had never been begotten men?

SECT. II.

Christ *the second* Adam.

IN regard to his general character, and as representative of all who were to be born of him, the first man *Adam* was the figure of *Jesus Christ*, typifying *Christ* as a future representative or head of all mankind, in some general parental character, like that of *Adam*'s: in that as all mankind was to share the fate of their common parent *Adam*, so might they afterwards share the fate of him who, in some other respect, might also become their common parent, *Jesus Christ*.

Upon this foundation is grounded the apostle's reasoning: *Rom.* v. 12. *As by one man sin entered into the world, and death by sin, and so death pass'd upon all men, for all have sinned.* (Verse 15.) *If thro'*

thro' the offence of one, the many (or multitude οἱ πολ-λοι) *are dead, much more the grace of God, and the gift by grace, which is by one man Jesus Christ, hath abounded unto the many* (or multitude τὰς πολλοὺς) *: wherefore* (ver. 18, 19.) *as by the offence of one, judgment came upon all men to condemnation; so by the righteousness of one, the free gift came upon all men unto justification of life. For as by one man's disobedience the many* (or multitude) *were made sinners;* (because, having now forfeited in their father's fall that spiritual life which by his fall their father lost, and which had been sufficient to have supported them upright, had they inherited it, as was intended, from him by bearing his likeness,) *so by the obedience of one, shall the many* (or multitude) *be made righteous.* 1 Cor. xv. 21, 22. *Since by man came death, by man came also the resurrection of the dead; for as in Adam all die, even so in Christ shall all be quickened.*

Adam by sin became a subject of satan's power; and all mankind in *Adam* are also become the subjects of satan's power.

This power (as resulting only from the fall of *Adam*) is at present indeed much contracted and restrained, rendering us only partially the subjects of that great fallen chief; insomuch that, tho' lord of corrupted nature, he is forced upon shifts and expedients to rule and manage us.

But this notwithstanding, so formidable a hold has he in us, that by dint hereof, he can exasperate and provoke that which is akin to him in our nature, to the producing in us all kinds of lusts and fears and baneful passions, *inworking* as St. *Paul* terms it *in the children of unbelief* (ἐνεργοῦν-τος

τος εν τοις υιοις της απειθειας): and as he sees occasion, or has permission, he can send his angels, or infernal messengers to possess us, even (*Luke* xi. 26.) *to enter into* us by legions *and* **dwell** *there*.

Partial therefore **as this power of the evil** one is over us, it is still **great**, forcible, full of horror, and **by** those **who understood it best, is called** our state of bondage or slavery: *John* viii. 34. *Jesus answered, verily, verily, I say unto you, he that committeth sin is* (δαλ☉) *the bond-servant of sin* (i. e. of the sinner, or of satan.ᵐ Again, *Rom*. vi. 16.) *Know ye not, that to whom ye yield yourselves* (δαλοι) *bond-servants to obey, his bond-servants ye are to whom ye obey, whether of sin* (ητοι αμαρτιας, *i. e.* whether of the grand sinner satan) *unto death, or of obedience* (*i. e.* the obedient one, or *Christ*) *unto righteousness*: so **2** *Pet*. ii. 19. *While they promise*

Y *them*

NOTES.

ᵐ Satan in this, the following, and such like places is called αμαρτια and φθορα by a syriacism. The *Jews*, as has already been shewn page 52, use the abstract noun instead of the adjective, so that (δυλοι της αμαρτιας, or της φθορας) the servants of sin, of corruption, are to be understood as if it had been written (δυλοι τυ αμαρτωλυ) slaves of the sinful one, i. e. of satan prince of sinners; and (δουλοι τυ φθορευς) *slaves of the corrupter*, i. e. of satan, the lord of corruption. See also the like expressions in *Heb.* xi. 25. 2 *Thes.* ii. 3. *Rom.* viii. 7, 14, 17, 23. *Gal.* iii. 13.

For when St. *Paul* wrote in greek, he thought in the oriental tongues. The above expression is however not altogether oriental, but partially so, a mixture of both greek and oriental; for the *Orientals* instead of the genitive case, the latter of two substan-

them liberty, they themselves are the (δουλοι) bondf-
men of corruption (της φθορας) i. e. of the corrupter.

Now from what has been advanced we at once
arrive at the true meaning of the term (σωτηρ)
deliverer, or restorer.

The son of GOD is called so from his relation
to human nature fallen into a state of slavery to
satan, the great sinner and corrupter.

'Till exhibited unto us in this last character,
our LORD's title is Jehovah Adni, my LORD Jehovah; and he reveals himself to us in this last
character before his incarnation, because he had
already undertaken to redeem us.

Out of the numberless passages of the old testament, prophesying of him under the character of
a deliverer, let the following suffice. *Jer.* XV. 21.
Saith Jehovah '*I pluck (or will pluck) thee* ²*out of
the*

NOTES.

tives, use two apposite substantives; and before the
latter, the *Syrians* mostly set ، *qui,* so Heb. צבא השמים
the host, the heavens. Syr. ܫܡܝܐ, ܚܝܠܘܬܐ *the
powers which heaven.* Heb. עבד אלהא חיא *servant God
living.* Syr. ܚܝܐ ܐܠܗܐ, ܥܒܕܐ *servant who God
living.*

By this idiom the oriental expression becomes much
more equivocal and indeterminate than the greek: so
מלאך אלהים may be rendered either *angel God,* or
angel of God; מלאך יהוה *angel Jehovah,* or *angel of
Jehovah*; ܐܠܗܐ, ܡܠܐܟܐ *angel who God,* or *angel
of God*; ܡܪܝܐ, ܡܠܐܟܐ *angel who the Lord,* or *angel of the Lord.* So Chald. אלה שמיא and Heb.
אל השמים *God heavens* mean *the God of heaven*; and

the hands of ⁵the wicked ones ⁴and deliver thee ⁵from the palm of ⁶the terrible ones. (עָרִיצִים ⁶טַף ⁵מִיַד ³וְיַצִלְתִּיךָ) Is. xliii. 1. O Israel, I have purchased thee (גְאַלְתִּיךָ) I have called thee by my name, thou (belongest to me or) art mine; Is. xli. 14. Fear not thou *worm Jacob, I will heal thee, saith Jehovah, and thy deliverer* (or purchaser גֹאֲלֵךְ) *the holy one of Israel*.

All these expressions are intended as allusive to the condition of bondage and misery which is ours by the fall of *Adam*, and wherein the wicked ones and terrible ones, even in this life, control us with a mighty sway and influence.

In terms similar hereto we likewise find our LORD described in the new testament; *Mat*. i. 21. *And thou shalt call his name Jesus, for he shall deliver his people from their sins*, (in which they are by nature) Again, *Luke* iv. 18. *He hath anointed me to preach the gospel to the poor, he hath sent me to heal the broken-hearted, to preach deliverance to the*

Y 2 *captives*,

N O T E S.

in the Syriac ܐܠܗܐ ܕܒܫܡܝܐ, *God who in heaven*, means *God of* (or *who is in*) *heaven*. So *Col.* i. 5. ܒܡܠܬܐ ܕܫܪܪܐ ܕܐܘܢܓܠܝܘܢ, *in the word of the truth of the gospel*, may be rendered, *in the word which* (is) *the truth, which* (is) *the gospel*. Again, *Mat.* xvi. 23. thou savourest not (the things) ܕܐܠܗܐ, *which* (are) *of God*, but (the things) ܕܒܢܝܢܫܐ, *which* (are) *of the sons of men*. Again in the 'LORD's prayer, ܐܒܘܢ ܕܒܫܡܝܐ, *our father who in heaven*, means *our father who art in heaven*. This note may serve to illustrate what has been already observed, page 103. note ⁱ.

captives, and recovering of fight to the blind, and to set at liberty them that are bruised (under the yoke of their servitude); *to preach the* (year of jubilee, the) *acceptable year of the Lord.* Again *Luke* xiii. 16. *And ought not this woman being a daughter of Abraham, whom satan has bound, lo these eighteen years, be loosed from this bond on the sabbath day?* For that which our LORD performed visibly, on the bodies of the distress'd, during his ministry in this world; was only to represent his invisible work upon the souls of them who in their distress should cry unto him: his true character is, *Luke* i. 71. (σωτηρια εξ εχθρων ημων, ϰ εκ χειρος παντων των μισαντων ημας) *A deliverer from our enemies, and from the hands of all them that hate us*; and in healing the bodies of the afflicted, (*Acts* vii. 25.) *He supposed his brethren would have understood how that God by his hand would give them* (σωτηριαν) *deliverance*; and that in him the grace of GOD was intended as *Tit.* ii. 11. (η χαρις η σωτηριος πασιν ανθρωποις) *a restoring (recovering, or delivering) grace to all men*; since (*Luke* xix. 10.) *the son of man is come to seek and to restore or deliver the ruined* (σωσαι το απολωλος) *i. e.* such whose desperate and undone circumstances St. *Paul* personates, *Rom.* vii. 24. *O wretched man that I am, who shall deliver me from the body of this death!*

And because this our delivery was to be effected by means of a sacrifice expiatory and equivalent to our guilt, we also have our LORD charactered to us in the term λυτρον a ransom, or price given to redeem a captive out of his slavery; for the word (λυτρον) lutron, contains the notion of loosening, from the verb (λυω) luo, to loosen,

viz.

viz. the chains and fetters that bind the prisoner; we being all considered as naturally (at least by inheritance) the slaves or bondsmen of the wicked one.[n]

Agreeably hereto we are told, *Mat.* xx. 28. *the son of man came* not *to be ministered unto, but to minister; and to give* (την ψυχην αυτυ λυτρον αντι πολλων) *his* (single) *soul a ransom for many.* Tit. ii. 14. *Who gave himself for us that he might ransom us* (ινα λυτρωσηται ημας) *from all iniquity.* Upon which account he is said, *Heb.* ix. 12. *to have obtained* (λυτρωσιν αιωνιαν) *an æonian ransom for us.* And this acceptation we find again confirmed by the like term (εξαγοραζω) which signifies to recover or redeem again a mortgaged land: *Gal.* iii. 13. *Christ has redeemed us* (ημας εξηγορασεν) *from the curse of the law, being made a curse* (καταρα for καταρατος accursed) *for us.*

This our redemption from the tyranny of satan was moreover prefigured by the *Jews* delivery from their cruel bondage in the land of *Egypt*, of which *Jehovah* boasts to his people; *Mich.* vi. 4. *I brought thee up out of the land of Egypt, and from the house of slaves have I redeemed thee:* I say Jehovah boasts of this with a view to an after-work,

---

NOTES.

[n] It is observable, in evidence that this idea may be depended upon, that the *Jews* were likewise taught to conceive of their redemption by a word of like import, viz. ܦܪܩ that which breaks off or forces asunder, namely ones bonds or fetters, and so sets a man free from slavery.

LETTER X. [182] SECT. II.

work, of like kind, tho' of a far higher nature, and more worthy for him to boast of, the redemption of their souls; concerning which St. *Stephen* so keenly insinuates in his speech to the sanhedrim, *Acts* vii. 25. *For he supposed his brethren would have understood that God by his hand would give them* (σωτηριαν) *a deliverance* (or restoration to their lost liberty) *but they understood not.*

It is also observable that this our delivery from the tyranny of satan being our LORD's proper work, we find that they only who feel the want of such delivery, are called upon to accept of him for their lord and master. So *Mat.* ix. 13. *Go ye and learn what this means, I will have mercy and not sacrifice, for I am not come to call the righteous but sinners.*° *Mat.* xi. 28, 29. *Come unto me all ye that labour and are heavy laden, and I will give you rest; take my yoke upon you—and ye shall find rest unto your souls.* And because the unbelieving *Jews* were insensible of their slavery, says our LORD to them, *John* viii. 34. *Whosoever committeth sin is the servant of sin;* ver. 36. *If the son shall make you free you shall be free indeed.* But seeing you will not believe, ver. 44. *you are of your father the devil, and the lusts of your father ye will do.* That is, since ye seek not me for your deliverer, you will and must continue in your slavery to him who is of old your father, and into whose power you are relapsed by the fall of your father *Adam*. And

---

NOTES.

° The words to repentance are not read in the most antient MS. nor in the syriac testament, and may therefore be deemed as an interpolation.

And thus I suppose it proved that the english word saviour does not answer the import of the word (σωτηρ) soter in the new testament; and that by this word we are to understand a retriever or deliverer out of lamentable, distressful circumstances.

Permit me farther to observe that our delivery as men out of the tyranny of satan, may presume and refer to a delivery far exceeding this, altho' at present we have no remembrance of it; namely a delivery from an oppression and tyranny by means of our becoming invested in our human state of life, a delivery consequent upon our being begotten sons of *Adam*; and concerning which, since revelation affords us too little light to speak with confidence, we shall be silent.

Wherefore we content ourselves with saying, that altho' our lapse into and under the power of satan by the fall of *Adam*, was our misfortune and not our fault; yet that we may well think of it with satisfaction, seeing it is a misfortune belonging to our most advantageous covenant in our earthly father; a misfortune too whose ill effects we may easily escape, whose real evils are tolerable, and of very short duration, and whose bondage we may shake off without difficulty, and render vain and harmless; if only we provide for this in time, and use the opportunity put into our power; before the stroke of our natural death shall seal and ratify our slavery; confirm us the æonian property of our enemy, inevitably; and at the same time aggravate our wretchedness, with the guilt of having neglected the gracious call of GOD to liberty.

SECT.

SECT. III.

II. CHRIST *the* (σωτηρ) *restorer, or deliverer of all men.*

THIS truth is pronounced and establish'd by so many corresponding texts in scripture, and in such variety of expression, that the unprejudiced mind must readily assent to it. So *Luke* iii. 6. *All flesh shall see the restoration of God.* 1 John ii. 2. *He is a propitiation for our sins, and not for ours only, but also for the sins of the whole world.* John iv. 42. *We know that this is indeed the Christ the restorer of the world.* 1 Tim. ii. 4. *Who wills that all men should be restored, and come to the acknowledgment of the truth.* Tit. ii. 11. *The grace of God which bringeth restoration to all men hath appeared.* In the syriac this passage is read thus: ܐܠܗܐ ܕܝܢ ܛܝܒܘܬܗ ܕܡܚܝܐ ܟܠ ܐܬܓܠܝܬ ܠܟܠܗܘܢ ܒܢܝܢܫܐ *The grace of God restoring* (or quickening) *all has appeared unto all the sons of men.* 1 John iv. 14. *We do testify that the father hath sent the son to be the restorer of the world.* 2 Pet. iii. 9. *The Lord is long-suffering for your sake, being not willing* (μη βυλομεν⊛ i. e. not counselling) *that any one should perish, but that all should come to repentance.*

Neither is this great event revealed to us merely as what shall be; but as an event resting upon and having its root in the very nature of things: as a purpose in GOD not arbitrary; but grounding its basis upon the greatest of all other occurrences which heaven or earth has yet been witness of,

namely

namely redemption finish'd for us. For *Christ* has indeed exhausted the whole venom of sin in his own body, and is in himself singly both the cause and power of our recovery.

And hence again we read *John* i. 29. *Behold the lamb of God which beareth away* (την αμαρτιαν) *the sin* (in the singular number) *of the world*; 2 Cor. v. 19. *God was in Christ reconciling the world unto himself, not imputing their trespasses*; ver. 21. *for he hath made him to be sin for us* (υπερ ημων αμαρτιαν εποιησεν) *that we might be made the righteousness of God in him*. Is. xxxviii. 17 *Thou hast cast all my sins behind thy back*. 1 John i. 7. *If we walk in the light, &c.*—*The blood of Jesus Christ his son cleanseth us from all sin*; insomuch that Is. i. 18. *tho' your sins be as scarlet they shall be white as snow; tho' they be red like crimson they shall be as wool*. And this merely because **Christ** is singly and in his own person the propitiation for the sins of all; so *Heb.* i. 3. *who being the brightness of his glory and the express image of his person, and upholding all things by the word of his power, when he had by himself* (δι εαυτε) *purged our sins, sat down on the right hand of the majesty on high*. Col. ii. 13. *Having forgiven all trespasses* **blotting out the** *hand-writing of ordinances that was against us, which was contrary to us, and he took it out of the way nailing it to his cross*. Heb. ix. 26. *But now once* (επι συντελεια των αιωνων) *about the meeting of the extremities of the æons*[p] *hath he appeared to put away sin by the sacrifice of himself*.

NOTES.

[p] In speaking of the two extremes of a thing, we say the two ends; so end is the nomen generis, as is

Our redemption being now perfected in *Christ*, the sins of man no longer respect GOD distinct from *Christ*, but GOD in *Christ*; and all our guilt is that of ingratitude to him our common LORD and GOD.

As we were originally GOD's by creation, even so are we now *Christ*'s by purchase; and his purchase of us has given him a title to us so absolute, that we are now guilty to no one besides him, indebted to no other but him, obnoxious to no other punishment than his, being with all we are or have, his slaves, his prisoners, his forfeiture; and, when freed by him, his freemen.

And since his father is satisfied with us in him, earth and hell cannot be otherwise; so that we are altogether compleat in him, innocent in him. Can satan then accuse us? Yes, but not upon his own account. Can man condemn us? Yes, but not

---

NOTES.

τελος finis. When we speak of two species separately, we call the one αρχη initium the beginning, the other retains the nomen generis the end. A common practice in divisions, as a man in genere is in specie a man or woman.

Τα τελη των αιωνων are the contiguous extremities of the two æons of figure and reality, shadow and body, law and gospel; which are also (considered as one boundary) συντελεια confinium the confines; and that common boundary (whether you end the æon of the law [the old testament קץ] at the death or resurrection of *Christ*, at the destruction of the temple, or between both, with the ends of both æons, or end of one and beginning of the other) came in St. *Paul*'s time or his cotemporaries.

not as his own debtors. Our debts are all amply discharged to all in *Christ*.[q] *Rom.* viii. 33, 34.

Again, becaufe all, both men and angels, are debtors to our LORD infinitely more than they can be to one another; all equity, foreign to this of *Chrift*'s, finks and terminates in the perfon of *Chrift*. And hence it is that his righteoufnefs fets afide and fuperfedes all other righteoufnefs, fpreading as far and as wide as the univerfe itfelf; for being of one compafs and comprehenfion with his paffion, it grafps the concerns of all his creatures put together. *Rom.* iv. 5, 6, 7—13, 16—22. x. 4.

This is again the reafon that nor men nor devils can touch an hair of our heads but by his leave.

NOTES.

[q] It is upon this account, and to obviate any perverfe reafonings that might arife in the view of this truth, that we have it fo often and eminently related of *Chrift*, that he is a righteous and impartial king, that (*Heb.* i. 8) *a fcepter of equity is the fcepter of his kingdom*; fo 1 *Cor.* iv. 5. *Acts* xvii. 31. *&c.* For hereby we are cautioned to take no falfe umbrage in an imputed righteoufnefs, which belongs only to the ingrafted and living members of the vine; whom his imparted nature has cleanfed; *in whom he is the hope of glory*; who are *Heb.* xii. 10. *The partakers of his holinefs*. Our LORD can with all equity act abfolutely in his æonian kingdom, as being in himfelf the folution of all debt, and recompence of all merit; yet he will moft furely punifh and reward every one perfonally, according to his works; infomuch that injured innocence and injurious power fhall in no inftance efcape his notice; neither fhall the unholy fee him. *Heb.* xii. 14.

leave. Being creatures devoted to his purposes, as absolutely his property as a man's goods (earned by his labour) are the creatures of his sovereign will and pleasure; our well or ill-being are by all the rights and terms of justice at his sole disposal. No hell can torment us, no fire can burn us but as he consigns us to such torment, and gives such flames their commission to consume us. neither is this any exclusive privilege for the elect only; all the veriest bondsmen and slaves of satan are his property as truly as are the saved; and must also be restored, like ourselves, by being begotten anew of him. Upon this ground says St. *Paul*, 1 *Cor*. xi. 3. *He is the head of every man*; and not of man only; for (*Rom*. xiv. 9.) *to this end Christ died, and rose again, and revived, that he might be the Lord both of the dead and of the living* (or quickened), as it is written, *Every knee shall bow to me*.' But

---

NOTES.

CHRIST *truly tasted death for all.*

' OUR LORD had not a mere human body capable of suffering, as some have imagined; but his very soul, by means of his body, was rendered obnoxious to, and sufferable from the wrath of man. And herein lay the efficacy of our redemption; for this soul of *Christ* was the true atoning son of GOD, and is that of which he speaks *Mat*. xxvi. 38. *My soul is exceeding sorrowful even unto death.* And *John* xii. 27. *Now is my soul troubled.*

But the most astonishing account that revelation ever gave us, is of that divine dereliction of the soul of *Christ*, which was his experience at his entrance into his state of death.

But if all this be true how idle the supposition that satan shall be the lord of corrupted nature so long as is *Christ* of restored nature: or that sinners shall be sinners in hell eternally irrecoverably? Does the scripture teach us so? 1 *John* iii. 8. *For this purpose the son of God was manifested, that he might dissolve* (λυσῃ) *the works of the devil.* He will therefore most surely dissolve them or reduce

---

NOTES.

When a christian man is said to die, thereby is only meant that his body, being so separated from his soul (which is the quickening principle of his bodily life) as that its vital union therewith is dissolved, ceases to partake of the soul's quickness, and other faculties, and so becomes a lifeless mass: but then the soul, retaining the communion with GOD which is natural to it, still continues to partake vitally of the divine fulness (*John* i. 16.) is in GOD alive and immortal. Therefore says our LORD of the believers, *John* viii. 52. *He that believeth in me shall* (ου μη) *by no means taste death*; that is, shall never have the experience of a soul vitally separated from GOD.

But with *Christ* the case was otherwise; it is said of him, *Heb.* ii. 9. *He tasted death* (ὑπερ παντος) *for all*: that is, not that either his body or his soul corrupted (for he saw no corruption) but that both his body and his soul were in a state of vital distinction and separation from their true quickening source; were even vitally disunited from GOD. Even as his body was vitally relinquished of his soul, so was his soul vitally relinquished of his holy father; and it was our LORD's sensibility of this condition that made him cry out, *Mat.* xxvii. 46. *My God, my God, why hast thou forsaken me?*

duce them to nothing; and how? In a few instances only? But his work will be a perfect and accomplished work, extending universally to every individual. Yea, if he should fail in any single instance, his work in that degree must fall short of the purposes of his will, *seeing he will have all men to be restored, and come to the acknowledgment of the truth*; which is only saying in other terms, that he

---

NOTES.

Christ the (אדנ) Lord, or (πρωτότοκος) first-begotten, had emptied himself before he came down from heaven; for *Phil.* ii. 7. (ἑαυτὸν ἐκένωσε) *He emptied himself when he took upon him the form of a servant, and was made in the likeness of men.* Yet still, so emptied, he enjoy'd the fulness of his father by a free and full communication and influence from him; for *John* i. 14. *He was full of grace and truth*; and *Col.* ii. 3. 9. *The fulness of God* (the Godhead) *dwelt in him bodily.*

But in his last extremities the divine influences seem to have ceased, and our Lord seems to have been quite deserted, forsaken, cut off from all vital union with his God, an event now only seen; and which we find expressed (*Dan.* ix. 26.) by the verb כרת cut off or severed, as a branch is severed from its trunk; for says the angel *Gabriel* to *Daniel*, *And after 62 weeks shall Messiah be cut off* (יכרת משיח) *but not for himself.*

Death consists in a separation from our true life, as its life support; and the father is the true life or vital support of the son; what then must have been our Lord's sensibilities in this strange separation? He was left as forlorn and naked as ever soul was or shall be left. And at the same time he knew that all guilt must exhaust and consume itself in his person. In these excesses of distress, resignation was his resource,

he will have all the mischievous works of satan in every man, to be utterly defeated and invalidated; he will have all to be restored to life in him.

But besides these considerations, are not lost souls declared *expressly* to be our saviour's? Are we not assured that the lost are those very souls which he *came to seek and to restore*; so far are these from being unsusceptible of restoration, that they are the very *destined* subjects of his restoring power, the reason that he now is God-man. 1 *Tim.* i. 15. *This is a faithful saying, and worthy of all acceptation, that Christ Jesus came into the world to restore* (or deliver) *sinners.* Our

NOTES.

Luke xxiii. 46. *Father, into thy hands I deposit my spirit.*

Had there been now in the soul of *Christ* any principle of guilt or mortality, corruption would have seized upon it; so then that corruption could not touch him, was an evidence both of his purity, and of his having life in his own self. *John* v. 26. *As the father hath life in himself, so hath he given* (εδωκε) *the son to have life in himself.*

Our LORD's inviolable condition in this his state of death, was also as mighty an evidence that all that guilt which lay upon him as the atonement, must have been fully abolish'd on his cross.

Think only what an object of astonishment must our LORD now have been among the inhabitants in Hades! This point, however, I shall not farther expose; I should rather say upon it, *Procul este profani!*

But the reason of our LORD's dying, and so of his rising and reviving, the apostle tells us (*Rom.* xiv. 9.) was, *that he might be the Lord of both the dead and living*; i. e. both of them, who should hereafter be abandoned and in a like condition of death; as well as of those, who should be his living members, quick in him.

Our LORD accordingly styles himself, *The friend of publicans and sinners*; tells us, that he died for sinners while they were sinners; *that he was manifested to take away their sins*; that this taking away their sins, is that favourite business which first brought him down from the bosom of his father; which moved him *to empty himself, to take upon him the form of a servant, to become a man of no account, a man of sorrows, acquainted with grief.*

Moreover when a man, it was not any natural insensibility or hardiness, for he had a weak and delicate frame of body, but it was the expectation of seeing the travail of his soul in the restoration of sinners, that encouraged him thro' all his sufferings; that made his thorny crown tolerable; that allay'd the violence of his stripes; and that supported his resolution upon the cross, 'till he could cry out with a loud voice, *It is finished.*

Luke xii. 50. *I have a baptism*, says he, *to be baptised with, and how am I straitened 'till it be accomplish'd!* and can we believe that this his straitening labour, his restoring office, is now no longer his dear concern; that it now ceases to be his urgent employment, his joy, his glory? can we believe that *Christ*'s love is abated by his dying? or is his power lessened since his ascension? is he now no longer able to restore lost souls from hades, or seize his redeem'd from out of the grasp of the wicked one? The thought *either way* is very unworthy of him, a base impeachment of so much love, of so efficacious a sacrifice, and of so great an authority.

Wickedness shall have its due punishment, yet shall not defeat our LORD's *purposed restoration.*

I HAVE often wondered at the weakness of people's reasoning for an eternal damnation from the observed prevailing power of sin, from its abounding as it were in defiance of GOD, and because, say they, such numbers of the dying must be daily lost among the damned.

For what can be argued from hence against the universal efficacy of our LORD's atonement hereafter to prevail, as now in the first fruits, so, finally in all? Does it follow that because the effects of our LORD's sacrifice do not immediately display themselves universally, that therefore they never will?

Were not the *Jews* declared to be a redeemed people long before that redemption was dispens'd to them? For ages before its accomplishment, or even his incarnation, does our LORD pronounce himself the restorer or redeemer of his people. So *Is.* xliv. 22. *I have blotted out as a cloud thine iniquities, and as a thick cloud thy sins, return unto me for I have redeemed thee: sing O heavens for Jehovah has done it.* A promise not even yet formally accomplished, *Rom.* xi. 25, 26. so *Is.* liv. 4. 5. *Thou shalt forget the shame of thy youth, for thy maker is thy husband, Jehovah of hosts is his name, and thy redeemer the holy one of* Israel, *the God of the whole earth.* Again, *Jehovah is king of* Israel, his re-

A 2 *deemer*

deemer *Jehovah of hosts*. Again, *I will gather them for I have redeemed them*. Again, *Their redeemer is strong, Jehovah of hosts is his name*. Again, *Hof.* vii. 13. *Wo unto them for they have strayed from me, destruction unto them because they have transgressed against me. Tho' I have redeemed them, yet have they spoken lies against me.*ˢ

The whole therefore we can conclude from the threatnings against the wicked is, not that the blood of *Jesus* shall never be applied to them, but that (*Rev.* xiv. 10, 11.) *they shall drink of the wine of the wrath of God* (τȣ κεκερασμενȣ ακρατȣ *quod infusum est non mixtum*, that is prepared without gust of hope or mercy, or) *poured without mixture into the cup of his indignation; and shall be tormented with fire and brimstone in the presence of the holy angels, and in the presence of the lamb* (*i. e.* with their fullest approbation of that dreadful scene); *and the smoke of their torments ascendeth up* (εις αιωνα αιωνων¹) *to an age*

NOTES.

ˢ Here we see destruction and redemption expressly declared of the same individuals; and that they on whom woes and destruction are denounced are nevertheless the redeemed of GOD.

¹ We find this remarkable expression in three places of the *Revelations*, viz. in ch. xix. 3. denounced upon the great whore; in ch. xx. 10. denounced upon satan the beast and the false prophet; and in the quoted text, denounced upon the wicked. In the common editions of the greek testament the reading in these places is εις τȣς αιωνας των αιωνων, to the æons of the æons. But the authority of such reading is disputed, because they are found in *Andreas* arch-bishop of *Cæsarea* (who wrote

age of ages, or the æonian age; whilst they who are restored shall rejoice, because *(Luke* i. 77*) he giveth them the knowledge of their restoration in the remission of their sins:* the foretastes of which even in this life amounts so high that (1 *Pet.* i. 8.) *whom having not seen we love, in whom tho' now we see him not, yet believing we rejoice with joy unspeakable and full of glory.*

We cannot doubt but that it is by the permissive will of *Christ* that the principles of fallen nature are not as yet abolished; and that, tho' the malice of satan has no natural tendency towards the will of God, has nothing in itself that can produce his kingdom, yet eventually, and under the conduct of our Lord's wisdom, this malice of our arch enemy may greatly promote his end. Tho' heat in a piece of iron will by no means of itself constitute it an instrument useful to mankind; yet

---

NOTES.

upon the *Revelations* in the year 500 or about the latter end of the fourth century, and doubtless both had and used the best copies of it, as follows, viz. the former passages εις αιωνα αιωνων, to an æon of æons, the latter εις αιωνα αιωνος, to the æonian æon, which are equivalent according to *Bengelius*'s computation of the word æon.

For this and other reasons (see *Bengelius*) the collectors of the various readings of the new testament freely prefer the reading found in *Andreas*'s copy to that of the usual editions of our greek testament, where doubtless we find in many places the wrong reading.

According to this reading the punishment of the wicked is not threatened to the æons of the æons; but

yet that heat, by the malliable effects it gives, will render that iron, under the shapening hand of a skilful artificer, susceptible of all kinds of useful forms.

Compassion in GOD proceeds not, like compassion in man, from a weakness of nature; it is the efforts of his pure, genuine benevolence.

We men are urged to relieve a suffering fellow creature from the uneasy impressions which his sensations make upon ourselves. These impressions, as GOD immutible cannot have, so neither can our LORD (whose conduct is the copy of, and altogether regulated by, his holy father's mind) be determined by them; as the father's compassion must be the same with his goodness, so must the son's also attend upon it, and be regulated by those great ends he has in view for his creatures real interest, to the abolishing and removing the very root of our disease. There-

---

NOTES.

εις αιωνα αιωνων, and, which amounts to the same, εις αιωνα αιωνος, to the æonian æon.

But the promises to the blessed are express'd in far higher terms. *We* (the blessed) 1 *Thes.* iv. 17. *shall meet the Lord in the air, and so shall we* (παντοτε συν Κυριω εσομεθα) *ever afterward be with the Lord;* that is our existence with the LORD in glory shall be cœval with his glory. But his glory shall be, not (as the punishment of the damn'd εις αιωνα αιωνων) to the æonian æon; but, what infinitely exceeds this in duration, viz. *Eph.* iii. 21. (εις πασας τας γενεας τε αιωνος των αιωνων) or which seems at least to be the same (εις τας αιωνας των αιωνων) to all the generations of the æon of the æons, or to the æons of the æons.

Therefore as GOD could see his own beloved child in agonies sweating great drops of blood, and not spare him in all the miseries of his sufferings, even 'till he bowed his head and gave up the ghost: so also are the terrors of our redeemer Christ. *Heb.* x. 31. *It is a fearful thing to fall into the hands of the living God; a God* (Deut. x. 17.) *great, mighty, and terrible.* And yet are our sufferings permitted in his tender love of us: they result from a beneficence veiled, that it may be the more effectual, in the forms of severity.

" Good when he gives, extremely good;
" Nor less when he denies:
" Even curses, from his bounteous hand,
" Are blessings in disguise."

But for vain and useless miseries, or which have no good event in view, we can find neither ground of existence, nor place in nature, nor author to produce them; they contradict all our ideas of power, goodness, mercy and wisdom in the divine dignity; and have nothing to recommend them besides texts mis-rendered, and an authority which it is the profession of protestants to renounce.

Tho' GOD may not have decreed one half of the events that occur, yet since he has provided that every course of willing within the possibility of the creature's choice, shall terminate ultimately in real good; the free will of any creature can ultimately do him no harm.

Temporal sufferings, however exquisite or lasting, necessarily suppose an end suitable to the nature of him by whose authority they are contingently constituted; and of consequence an end
salutary;

falutary; i. e. one way or other, according to the creature's choice, for the creature's benefit. But what is permitted by GOD as falutary, muſt be big with falutary effects.

In purſuance of this reflection then we may well ſuppoſe the moſt violent infernal anguiſh (altho' merely the event of the creature's own will) to be occaſionally a production of love concealed, having joy and glory, with all the bleſſings of a divine bounty, in its iſſue: and this too infallibly, ſince no reſiſtance in the creature can finally defeat the gracious ends of *Chriſt*'s ſacrifice for all.

Moreover the workings of our æonian GOD, or the GOD of nature, towards this gracious direction of all occurrences, are already, even at this very time, obvious in all men; as we gather from the apoſtle's words, *Rom.* viii. 19—23. *The earneſt expectation of the creation waiteth for the revelation of the ſons of God. For the creation was made ſubject to vanity (not willingly, but by him who ſubjected it) in hope that the creation itſelf ſhould be delivered from the bondage of corruption, into the glorious liberty of the children of God. For we know that the whole creation groaneth together, and travelleth together until now: and not only they, but even we ourſelves who have the firſt fruits of the ſpirit, even we ourſelves groan within ourſelves, waiting for the adoption, the redemption of the body.*

A late good author whom we will call B. remarks with a generous frankneſs upon this paſſage as follows:

" Verſe 19. 𝕮𝖍𝖊 𝖊𝖆𝖗𝖓𝖊𝖘𝖙 𝖊𝖝𝖕𝖊𝖈𝖙𝖆𝖙𝖎𝖔𝖓. The
" words denote a lively hope of ſomething draw-
" ing

LETTER X.   [199]   SECT. IV.

"ing near, and a vehement longing after it.
"**Of the creation**—of all visible creatures (be-
"lievers excepted, who are spoken of apart) each
"kind according as it is capable. All these have
"been sufferers thro' sin, and to all these shall
"refreshment redound from the glory of the
"children of GOD. Upright heathens are by no
"means excluded: no, nor the vainest of men,
"who (altho' in the hurry of life, they mistake
"vanity for liberty, and partly stifle, partly dis-
"semble their groans, yet) in their sober, quiet,
"sleepless, afflicted hours pour forth many sighs
"in the ear of GOD. Verse 21. **Shall be de-
"livered.**—Destruction is not deliverance."

Mr. B. here by the whole creation, mentioned of the apostle in this passage as subject to vanity, and groaning together for deliverance, understands "all visible creatures who are unbelievers;" for, says he, "the believers are excepted, and spoken of apart:" and whereas the whole creation so groaning, according to the apostle's words, verse 21. *Shall be delivered.* Mr. B. must mean that " all the visible creatures who are unbelievers shall be delivered, even the vainest of men."

We make no doubt but Mr. B. will likewise acknowledge that all unbelievers shall die, perish, be destroyed; because we can no otherwise believe the scriptures. But he says farther, that "destruction is not deliverance;" therefore according to him the whole creation of unbelievers must be both destroyed and delivered.

And because Mr. B. cannot suppose that the whole creation of unbelievers shall first be delivered,

vered, and afterward destroyed; he must mean that the whole creation of unbelievers shall first be destroyed, and after that delivered; as has been already observed on a passage of Sophocles, see page 46, the wicked soul (σωθησεται) shall be recovered, after that (απωλέιο) it has been destroyed.

According to Mr. B. therefore, destruction and delivery infallibly awaiting all the unbelieving visible creation, the one, namely, destruction, shall be the doom, the other, namely, deliverance, the recovery of all visible creatures who are unbelievers.

Now a type of this our destruction and deliverance we have daily before our eyes in the bodies of our fellow creatures, which all die and corrupt in order to revive again into an higher kind of life.

Let us then satisfy ourselves that as *Christ*, is the restorer of the world, the world must finally be restored; that as he draws all men unto him, all men must finally come unto him; that as he enlightens every man that cometh into the world, every man that cometh into the world must be finally a child of the light; (for this light so given must have an end worthy the kind giver;) and that as he died for the sins of the whole world, and in so dying tasted death for every man, the sins of the whole world are atoned for; and the benefit of his tasted death must finally reach every man.

But before I leave this head, permit me to advance only one consideration more, which is, that since mankind cannot judge of things but by the sensations which those things excite in us;
and

and since these excited sensations bare no real resemblance with the objects that excite them; Our conceptions of GOD, founded upon those sensations which we call the perceptions of his wrath or anger, may also have nothing in them resembling any reality in the divine essence: In like manner as those sensations which we call pain, sickness, pleasure, smells, colours, tastes, sounds, have nothing resembling them in the objects themselves that raise them in us, have no correspondent reality existing in the bodies felt, heard, or seen.

By this way of thinking the sensations of GOD's wrath, revenge and anger (excited in the minds of reprobates by the light of their reason and remonstrances of a dissatisfied conscience) are like the yellowness of objects to a jaundiced eye; which exists not in the objects of its vision, corresponds not at all with any reality in the things seen; but is the mere effects of inward distemper, vitiated juices, and a ruinous constitution.

And to this idea of things answer all the scripture accounts of the darkness of lost souls; that *They who believe not, walk in darkness, that darkness has blinded their eyes:* whilst of believers it is said, that they are *called out of darkness into the marvellous light;* and that *God hath shined in their hearts to give the light of the knowledge of the glorious God, in the face of Jesus Christ.* 2 Cor. iv. 6.

And from hence also we may presume it happens, that even the holy angels, and most benevolent and reasonable of all creatures, will behold the miseries of the damned with all approbation and praife: *Rev.* xiv. 10. xix. 1—7. xv. 3. *Exod.* xv. 1, 6, 13. even as GOD beheld the fufferings of his only begotten, in view of the glorious energies and iffues which he had decreed to produce out of them.

SECT. V.

III. *Especially of thofe that believe.*

HAVING infifted upon the former claufe of this text as declaring *Chrift* to be the reftorer of all men, it will be incumbent upon me to account for the word *especially* in the latter claufe of it; and this is done by fhewing how thofe who believe are diftinguifhed from the reft of mankind by an *especial* reftoration; fo that the illuftrating this difference will be our bufinefs under the prefent head: and this will be fufficiently done in the acknowledgment that the unbelieving part of mankind fhall die in their fins; and fo be left to tafte what death means; or what it means to exift without him, who is the fupport of all life, in a ftate of feparation from GOD, in the violence and fiercenefs of their own nature, in a wrath not allay'd by the blood of that man who alone was begotten of GOD, and who alone is in all his natures the true offspring of the Deity, and principle of life.

He who can engage (if I may ufe the expreffion) the good will of *Chrift*, acquires in him all that his foul can wifh for: therefore fays *David,*
Pfalm

Pſalm ii. 12. *Kiſs the ſon leſt he be angry, and ye periſh from the right way; when his wrath is kindled yea but a little, bleſſed are all they that put their truſt in him:* becauſe he only can deliver from the jaws of ſin and death; and his authority to deliver is ſure, and what we may rely upon ſafely, as ſays the prophet *Iſaiah*, xxviii. 16. *Behold I lay in Zion for a foundation, a ſtone, **a tried ſtone, a precious corner ſtone, a ſure foundation*** (Jer. xxiii. 6.) *the Lord our righteouſneſs.*

But what then is the *eſpecial* reſtoration of them that believe? And to anſwer this, we refer you to *John* v. 24. *Verily, verily, I ſay unto you, he that heareth my word, and believeth on him that ſent me* (εχει ζωην αιωνιον) *hath æonian life, and ſhall not come into condemnation, but is paſſed* (μεταβεβηκεν) *from death into* (εις) *life.* 1 John iii. 2. *Beloved, now are we* (νυν εσμεν) *the ſons of God.* (verſe 14.) *We know that we have paſſed* (μεταβεβηκαμεν) *from death into life.* Heb. x. 14. *By one offering he hath perfected æonianly* (ܠܥܠܡ) *them that **are ſanctified**.* Eph. ii. 5. *He hath quickened us together* (συνεζωοποιησε) *with Chriſt.* 1 John v. 12. *He that hath* (ὁ εχων) *the ſon of God, hath life; and he that hath not the ſon of God, hath not life.*

So that the eſpecial reſtoration of believers conſiſts in that they are now, even in this life, without any acceſſary ſufferings, without any damnation to be inflicted upon them, reſtored to life; having their ſins obliterated, and their perſons accepted, merely for their believing; they believe and are reſtored, at once reſtored, and ſo reſtored as that they paſs from death into life, never taste what death means, and are in short without any previous merit the children of GOD, compleat in *Christ*, by dint of free gift and a superinduced nature.

In this view of free-grace are described to us the conversions of many in the acts of the apostles and elsewhere; thus the LORD no sooner opened the heart of *Lydia*, but she believed and was baptized: the jaylor at *Philippi* was no sooner touched in his heart, so as to cry out to his prisoners, *Paul* and *Silas, What shall I do to be saved,* but *he was also baptized and rejoiced, believing in God with all his house.* The thief upon the cross, crying out to our LORD, *Remember me when thou comest into thy kingdom,* was immediately answer'd by our LORD himself, *This day shalt thou be with me in paradise.* The eunuch pointing out the water to *Philip,* (saying, *See here is water, what should hinder me to be baptized*) *was immediately baptized, and went his way rejoicing.* And the like may also be said of *Crispus,* and *Justus,* and *Sergius Paulus,* and *Dionysius,* and *Damaris,* and *Eneas,* and *Cornelius,* and the 5000 to whom *Peter* opened the gospel at the day of pentecost.

All these without any conditional virtues, probationary works, or initial services, received the word and were restored; they became with all readiness of acceptance and freedom of access, of heathens christians, of the bondsmen of satan, a quicken'd people, alive in *Christ:* they pass'd from death into life, even into the glorious liberty of the children of GOD, and were renew'd at once, by the all-powerful gift of grace. So great is the efficacy of the believing spirit! Now

Now when one considers the vast difference between being thus received in the favour of GOD for believing only, and the passing thro' the horrors of hell-fire; one has abundant reason to apply the word *especial* to the salvation of those that believe.

Indeed, a man's restoration being so easily attainable in this life, the guilt of those that perish will be aggravated hereby, and their damnation render'd the more severely afflictive in their after state of being; therefore says the apostle, *Heb.* xii. 25. *See that ye refuse not him that speaketh; for if they escaped not, who refused him that spake on earth, much more shall not we escape, if we turn away from him that speaketh from heaven; for* (verse 29.) *our God is a consuming fire*: and again, *John* iii. 18, 19, 20. *He that believeth not, is condemned already, because he hath not believed in the name of the only begotten son of God. And this is the condemnation, that light is come into the world, and men loved darkness rather than light, because their deeds were evil; for every one that doth evil, hateth the light, neither cometh to the light, lest his deeds should be reproved*; and he must therefore experience the condition of *Esau*, who, having slighted his birthright, found no place of repentance; but spent his tears and earnest suit in vain. *Heb.* xii. 17.

So then the difference between the *especial* restoration, and the *universal* restoration, is still the difference, which, for the present æon, subsists between heaven and hell, between *Adam* in his state of innocence, and a lost soul in the realms of darkness.

Where the spirit of GOD is there is beauty and uprightness; and herein consisted the beauty and uprightness of *Adam* before he fell. So long as he continued the temple of the living GOD, the beauty and fruits of the Holy Ghost display'd themselves in him; and he was both the wonder and envy of satan.

But having neither uprightness nor beauty, but by donation and grace; the spirit of GOD had no sooner departed from him, than he found himself naked: *Gen.* iii. 10. *And Adam said, I heard thy voice in the garden, and I was afraid, because I was naked, and I hid myself.* He was now stripp'd at once of all his excellencies, and stood detected in his shame. Having forfeited the free-gift, his investment of immortality, he appeared, as he truly was, a poor, contemptible, apostate wretch, a source of misery and uncleanness.

Says our LORD to him, (verse 11.) *Who told thee that thou wast naked?* How didst thou discover this thy condition? *Hast thou eaten of the tree?* Here therefore was the means of this discovery. And this distressing shame of *Adam* will be ours also, if we die in our fallen nature; unrenew'd, unquicken'd, not cloathed upon by the spiritual nature of *Jesus Christ.*

The christian nature is that new man which we are bid (*Eph.* iv. 24. *Col.* iii. 10.) *To put on, and which after God is created in righteousness and true holiness.* This is (*Rev.* xix. 8.) *That fine linen clean and white, the righteousness of the saints;* in which (2 *Cor.* v. 3.) *Being cloathed we shall not be found naked;* but shall be secured and saved when

that

that fire passeth over us, which (1 *Cor.* iii. 13—15.) *Shall try every one's works of what sort it is*; for this test-fire will reach every one; as says our LORD (*Mark* ix. 49.) *Every one shall be salted with fire, and every sacrifice* (viz. whoever has devoted himself *to God a living sacrifice*, as St. *Paul* persuades, *Rom.* xii. 1. *Phil.* ii. 17. 2 *Tim.* iv. 6. 1 *Pet.* ii. 5.) *shall be salted with salt* (Lev. ii. 13); which, being a symbol of incorruptibility (*Numb.* xviii. 19.) relates to incorruptible (or, as it is mostly called, eternal) life. 1 *Cor.* xv. 50—54. 2 *Cor.* v. 4.

This our new nature is called a cloathing, or a put-on incorruptibility, because it is our's assumptively only, and by free gift; a nature possess'd by a new birth, or rather by being re-begotten. And because it is our only title to paradise, and to an access into the presence of the LORD; it is represented as a royal caftan, a *wedding garment* (Mat. xxii. 11—14.) without which we cannot be admitted into that immediate rest which will be the portion of the blessed: and whose difference from their brethren, as yet unrestored, is as the difference of that glory to be revealed in the first fruits; and the wish'd for drop of water to cool one's tongue amidst the torments of the æonian burnings.

And yet notwithstanding all this, against the endless damnation of the damned, our text is still a sufficient witness: because the LORD *Jesus* cannot be the restorer or deliverer of all those that will be eternally damned; i. e. who will never have any restoration or deliverance at all.

LETTER XI.

The property of CHRIST *as redeemer may be doom'd to æonian sufferings.*

TO ——

SIR,

1 TIM. ii. 6.

Who gave himself a ransom for all to be testified in due time.

A Very ingenious writer argues for his favourite point of partial redemption as follows:

PROP. 1. All men who are of the ransom'd of *Christ* will be saved;
    2. But all men will not be saved;
    3. All men therefore are not of the ransom'd of *Christ*.

His mistake here lies in the word *saved*, if instead of *saved* he had used the word *restored*, his second

second proposition would have been false: but as his argument is now worded, his first proposition is false, since all the ransomed of *Christ* will not be *saved*, altho' they will be restored. For I shall endeavour to shew that a man may be damned, condemned or accursed, and yet at the same time be a person ransomed of *Christ*; and as such that his restoration or delivery from that damnation may be determined in the decree of GOD.

So that my argument will be as follows. *Christ* is a ransom for all men; but many of that all so ransomed will be damned; therefore *Christ* is a ransom for many that will be damned.

And thus my business will be to prove the following proposition.

SECT. I.

The beloved property of Christ *may, for good reasons, be damned or accursed to certain pains and penalties due to a damned and accursed creature.*

MY first argument shall be drawn from a sameness of nature in GOD and his *Christ*. Our LORD CHRIST and his father are one, so that speaking after the manner of men, we may say that *Christ* and his father have one heart and one mind; that whatsoever the father is capable of doing consistent with the genuine goodness of his nature, *Christ* is likewise capable of doing consistent with the genuine goodness of the same nature.

Now the especial and most beloved property of God is the man *Christ Jesus*; and yet for good reasons God surrenders up him, his only son to be as an accursed man, banished his presence (tho' that was his natural right) to be confined in a body subject to all the calamities, distresses, and hardships of a fallen, accursed nature; and imprisoned in an afflictive mortifying world, the abode of wicked men and wicked angels, and where satan his greatest and most inveterate enemy was permitted to rule as a god. Yea lastly this great object of paternal love omnipotent, thus confined and invested in a vehicle whereby he became accessible and obnoxious to diabolical wrath, and forlorn in a wicked world which hated him, was also delivered up a sacrifice to the malice and cruelty of its inhabitants, by his beloved father, and only comfort, the God of all; who all this time beheld and acknowledged him notwithstanding as the joy and glory of his nature, his bosom delight, his only offspring, his ownself.

The father therefore of our Lord *Jesus Christ* is capable of yielding up, for good reasons, his most beloved property to be condemned or accursed to the pains and penalties due to a condemned or accursed creature.

But as the father is capable to deliver up, for good reasons, the dearest object of his love to curse and condemnation; our Lord *Jesus Christ* is also capable to do the like.

So we read (*Heb.* xi.) that in old times, he delivered up his dearest people among the Jews, (of whom he tells us, *The world was not worthy)*
into

into the **hands** of wicked men to be stoned, and mocked, and scourged, and tempted, and sawn asunder; to wander about in sheepskins and goatskins, thro' desarts and mountains and dens and caves of the earth; being destitute, afflicted, tormented.

And it has been the constant observation of all ages, that (as says *Justin Martyr*, see his *apologia prima*) κατα την των φαυλων δαιμονων ενεργιιαν, τας σπουδαιας, οιον Σωκρατην και τας ὁμοιους, διωκισθαι, ἡ ἐν δεσμοις ειναι; Σαρδαναπαλον δε, ἡ Ἐπικουρον, ἡ τους ὁμοιους, ἐν αφθονια ἡ δοξη, δοκειν, ευδαιμονειν. "Thro' the work-
"ings of evil spirits, the well-meaning, such as
"*Socrates*, and those like him, were persecuted
"and imprisoned; while *Sardanapalus*, *Epicurus*,
"and those like them, lived in affluence, and
"honour; were **well** treated, **and** fortunate."

And a like argument **may be drawn** from the *Jews* themselves; our LORD declares that his love of this people is indefesible; *Rom.* xi. 28. *That they are his beloved for their fathers sake*; (Rom. iii. 3.) *that their unbelief shall not make his faithfulness invalid*; for that (*Rom.* xi. 29.) *his gifts and callings are without repentance*. And yet this **very** people (that is all who believe not on him, and notwithstanding that (*Rom.* ix. 4.) *They are Israelites, to whom appertaineth the adoption, and the glory, **and** the covenants, and the giving of the law, and the service of God, and the promises, and whose are the fathers*) are by him consigned to the damnation and curse of hell-fire.

Christ therefore, as well as his father, is capable of yielding up for good reasons, his beloved property to the curse and damnation of hell; to pains and penalties due to damn'd and accursed creatures.

But because a proof may be called for to establish this last argument taken from the unbelieving *Jews*, I shall proceed to shew, 1st. that the *Jews* not believing in *Christ* are in the damnation of gehenna. And 2dly. that those very *Jews* who are delivered up to this damnation, will be likewise delivered *out* of it; or, in the vulgar phrase, *be saved*, that is restored.

I. *The* Jews *not believing in* Christ *are in the damnation of gehenna or hell.*

This point will be proved without much trouble; not that we have better evidence for it than for the following, but because this is already generally acknowledged, and people mostly believe with the multitude. So

Mat. xxiii. 15. *Wo unto you Scribes and Pharisees, hypocrites, for ye compass sea and land to make one proselyte, and when he is made, ye make him twofold more the child of gehenna than yourselves:* (verse 32, 33.) *Fill up then the measure of your fathers, ye serpents, ye generation of vipers, how can he escape the damnation of gehenna?* Mat. viii. 11, 12. *I say unto you, that many shall come from the east and west, and shall sit down with Abraham, and Isaac, and Jacob, in the kingdom of heaven; but the children of the kingdom* (i. e. to whom the kingdom belongs) *shall be cast out into outer darkness, there shall be weeping and gnashing of teeth.*

From these and many other like texts, it becomes a matter past doubt, that the unbelieving *Jews* have their portion in gehenna.

SECT.

SECT. II.

II. *Those very Jews who are delivered up to the damnation of Gehenna, will be likewise delivered out of it, or in the vulgar phrase, be saved, that is, restored.*

THIS St. *Paul* expressly asserts, *Rom.* xi. 25, 26. *Blindness is happened to Israel in part, until the fulness of the Gentiles be come in, and so all Israel* (σωθησεται) *shall be restored.* So also says *Micha*, (ii. 12.) *I surely will assemble, O Jacob, all of thee* (כלך) *I will surely gather the residue of Israel*, i. e. all whatsoever remains as yet ungathered; verse 13. *The breaker* (i. e. he who breaketh bonds asunder) *is come up before them, &c.* But *Isaiah* expresses himself in still more decisive terms, xlv. 25. *In Jehovah shall all the seed of Israel be justified,* and (יתהללו hith) *shall boast themselves* (ביהוה יצדקו ויתהללו כל זרע ישראל) this passage when

---

NOTES.

" That this word צדק signifies to justify, or to declare or esteem just, appears from numberless places of the old testament. Let the following here suffice, *Gen.* xliv. 16. *What shall we say unto my Lord, and* (מה נצטדק) *how shall we justify ourselves.* Ex. xxiii. 7. *For I will not justify* (לא אצדיק) *the wicked.* Deut. xxv. 1. *And they shall judge them, and shall justify* (והצדיקו) *the just.* Job. xxxiii. 32. *Speak now for I desire to justify thee* (צדקך). Ps. xix. 9. *The judgments of Jehovah are truth, and they are justified* (צדקו

when we consider the use of the general term
(כל זרע) *the whole seed* in the singular number
with the plural future verbs (יתהללו and יצדקו)
shall (plural) *boast themselves, and shall* (plural)
be justified; we must allow to be as conclusive
and emphatical as the words of language can
make a thing. The whole seed of *Israel* therefore
(who (*Rom.* ix.) are now *children of the flesh, and
not the children of God*, who are as yet only (ver. 6)
(οἱ ἐξ Ισραηλ) the seed *of Israel*; and not (οἱ Ισραηλ) *the
Israel of* GOD) *shall be justified, and shall boast themselves in the Lord*; that (ver. 11.) *the purpose of
God according to the election might stand not of works,
but of him that calleth.*

This however, to the glory of GOD's justice,
shall be after an antecedent suffering, and an antecedent blindness. For saith Jehovah, *Lev.* xxvi.
43, 44. *And they shall accept the punishment of their
iniquity—and yet for all that—I will not cast them
away, neither will I abhor them, to destroy them utterly, to break my covenant with them, because I
Jehovah am their God.* And as to their blindness,
St. *Paul* tells us, speaking of the *Israel* who in

his

N O T E S.

altogether. Pf. li. 4. *That thou mightest be justified*
(תצדק) *when thou speakest, and be clear when thou
judgest.* Pf. cxliii. 2. *In thy sight shall no one living be
justified* (כל חי לא יצדק). Isaiah xliii. 26. *Let us plead
together, declare that thou mayst be justified* (למען תצדק)
Isaiah l. 8. *He is near that justifieth me* (מצדיק) *who
will contend with me.* Isaiah liii. 11. *By his knowledge
shall my righteous servant justify the many* (יצדיק) *for he
shall bear their iniquities.*

his days were unbelievers (2 *Cor.* iii. 15.) *That they had a veil upon their hearts untaken away.* And says he (verse 16.) *When it* (Israel, επιστρεψη προς Κυριον) *shall return unto the Lord, that veil shall be taken away.*

So then we might venture to say to every *Jew* we meet, *Isaiah* lx. 20. *The days of thy mourning shall be ended, thy people also shall all be righteous.* For the LORD hath said, *Ezek.* xx. 40. *In my holy mountain—there shall all the house of Israel serve me, the whole of it in the earth.* Again, 1 *Sam.* xii. 22. *For the Lord will not forsake his people, for his great name sake; because it has pleased the Lord to make you his people.* Again, *Jer.* xxxi. 37. *Thus saith the Lord, if heaven above can be measured, and the foundation of the earth searched out beneath, I will also cast off all the seed of Israel, for all that they have done*; i. e. maugre all the wickedness and perverseness of the *Jews*, the LORD notwithstanding will not cast them off eternally.

And hereto agrees what St. **Paul** says of the *Jews* (1 *Cor.* x. 1—4) *I would not that you should be ignorant, brethren, how that our fathers were all under the cloud, and all passed thro' the sea* (i. e. **were** initiated **a** people of GOD by these events) *and were all baptized unto Moses in the cloud and in the sea; and all eat the same spiritual food* (that is were all nourished in their souls as well as in their bodies by eating **that** spiritual food, this being on the part of GOD given, as well to the unbelievers as to the believers among them; see ver. 5, 7, 8, 9, 10.) *and all drank the same spiritual drink, for they drank out of the spiritual rock*

which

which followed them, and that rock was Chriſt. And in ſo doing, the wicked among them (1 *Cor.* ix. 29) did *eat and drink damnation to themſelves.*

And the jewiſh fathers being hereby made a people in covenant with Jehovah, their feed (i. e. all the *Jews*) are likewiſe ſo. As St. *Paul* upon a like occaſion ſays, 1 *Cor.* vii. 14. *Elſe* (i. e. unleſs the parent be made a covenant member) *were the children unclean, but now are they holy.*

However notwithſtanding this, the jewiſh fathers acceptance by perſonal initiation, and their children's acceptance for the fathers ſake; both the fathers and children, which among them are perverſe, eſcape not the judgments of God. For (1 *Cor.* x. 5.) *with the greater part of them God was not well pleaſed,* i. e. by a meioſis was highly diſpleaſed, not ſparing his own inheritance who wickedly preſumed upon his favour; the account of which things ſays St. *Paul was written* (verſe 11.) *for our admonition, upon whom the ends of the ages have met.*

Again this account of the univerſal reſtoration of *Iſrael,* correſponds alſo with that remarkable Chapter *Rom.* 11th. where we learn that that very perverſe part of *Iſrael, in whom is ungodlineſs, who are in their ſins, enemies to the goſpel, and in blindneſs till the fulneſs of the Gentiles is come in;* are notwithſtanding, the elect of God, the objects of his mercy, *for their fathers ſake, and becauſe the gifts of God are without repentance.*

This whole paſſage avows in terms the moſt unavoidable, that not the chriſtian converted *Iſrael,* not its believing and already reſtored remnant

nant only; but that the very perverse part of *Israel* also, *even they who are shut up together in unbelief*, who are *not circumcised of heart*, neither the true children of *Abraham*, but the *uncircumcised and unbelieving*; that *that* very *Israel* shall be restored; and that this their restoration shall also be no longer delayed than whilst the church of the first fruits of the *Gentiles* shall be in collecting. For says the apostle (*Rom.* xi. 15.) These are they who are *cast away to the reconciling of the world, and their receiving shall be* no less than *life from the dead*; for (verse 24.) *if thou* (namely the Gentile) *wert cut out of the old olive tree, which is wild by nature, and wert grafted contrary to nature into the good olive tree; how much more shall these* (namely the unbelieving perverse part of *Israel*) *which are the natural branches, be grafted into their own olive tree.*

But it is notorious that these passages, collected in proof of our two last points, namely the damnation and restoration of the reprobate *Jews*, are, according to the vulgar acceptation of the words *saved* and *damned*, most glaringly repugnant, expresly contradicting one the other; and yet, since they are both notwithstanding true, as they stand in scripture; that is, since it is true that *the unbelieving Israel shall not escape* (κρισιν της γεεννης) *the damnation of gehenna*, and as true *that the unbelieving Israel* (σωθησεται) *shall be restored*; how else can these two truths be reconciled, but by considering the miseries of gehenna as temporally instrumental to the great designs of an universal redeemer?

This view of things will also render clear and intelligible that remarkable passage which has been the astonishment of christian writers, found in *Rom.* ix. 1, 2, 3. *I say the truth in Christ, I lie not, my conscience also bearing me witness in the Holy Ghost, that I have great heaviness, and continual sorrow in my heart; for I could wish* (or it has been my wish) *that I myself were accursed from Christ, for my brethren, my kinsmen according to the flesh.*

All agree that the apostle must not have meant in this place his eternal damnation from *Christ* his LORD as a thing he could wish himself for his kinsmens sake; because such wish, being not only rash, but an high ingratitude to redeeming love, would have been very impious.

And yet a wish (αναθεμα ειναι απο τε Χριστε υπερ των αδελφων μυ) *to be anathematised from Christ for my brethren,* can be no otherwise understood than a wish, that the damnation of his brethren might be his own for their good; that himself could stand in their place; and have their curse transferred upon his own head; in which acceptation, supposing their miseries to be eternal, we must likewise suppose that St. *Paul* wished himself to be eternally miserable, eternally accursed from *Christ* for their sake.

Some indeed have endeavoured to distinguish between the terms anathematised and damned, intimating that St. *Paul*'s wish was not to be damned, but to be anathematized (*i. e.* say they, sacrificed) only for his brethren: but since the most reasonable of these do however acknowledge that this their distinction is unwarrantable from
scrip-

scripture, or the jewish use of the word *anathematised*,ʷ they thereby sufficiently confess that they are altogether perplexed with this passage.

But here, supposing the apostle's wish, to be a subject of gehenna for his brethrens redemption thence, to have been made in an assurance that his curse there would be only for a time, and to the fulfilling an event which his LORD *Jesus Christ* desired, namely the restoration of his brethren; I say supposing this, the difficulty at once vanishes.

For there had been nothing unreasonable in the apostle's wishing himself accursed from the same

---

NOTES.

ʷ The greek word ἀνάθεμα, is used to express the force of the hebrew word (חרם) hrm; which among the *Jews* imports a devoting to be extirpated, destroyed, and, as far as may be, annihilated.

So those who sacrificed to false gods were by *Moses* (*Exod.* xxii. 20) devoted to be extirpated; as *Achan* (*Jos.* vii. 15) was by the order of GOD exterminated, and himself and all that he had was consumed by fire.

Accordingly we read this very word hrma in this place in the syriac testament ܐܢܐ¹ ܚܪܡܐ² ܐܗܘܐ³ ⁴ܡܢ ⁵ܡܫܝܚܐ; '*That I* ¹ *myself* (hrma acud) ³*should be* **anathematised** ⁴*from* (for ܡܢ answering to the greek word απο determines its meaning to be from) ⁵*Christ.*

By this kind of curse the *Jews*, it seems, always understood an excommunication from all society with the faithful, and from all the blessings which belonged to them, even from the benefit of their prayers, and from receiving so much as their public rites of burial; and in consequence hereof, a condemnation to hell-fire. *Ps.* ix. 17. *The wicked shall be turned into hell, and the nations that forget God.* See also *Ps.* xi. 6.

same motive that had already caused his Lord to be actually and voluntarily so accursed.

There could have been nothing wrong in the wish, that as *Christ* laid aside that glory which he had with his father before the world was, and became a curse for man; so himself might forego that glory which awaited him, thro' a desire of the restoration of his brethren.

Most certainly our Lord both wished and willed himself accursed that he might thereby fulfil his father's desire in the restoration of the creature, at least of man: supposing then in St. *Paul* a charity by his Lord's example, and in the power of his spirit; and it must be allowed that he might easily have willed himself a like fate with his Lord, in view of a like end.

And thus the apostle's wish proves great, reasonable and generous, an high instance of the prevailing love of *Christ* working in him; and that from a motive, not of indifference to his own restoration, but of genuine zeal for, and a longing to bring forth, and realize the known desire of his most beloved master.

Doubtless the predominant desire of St. *Paul*'s heart was, that he might be found in *Christ*, not having his own righteousness, but the righteousness which is of God by faith: and his most joyful confidence was *that neither death nor life, nor angels, nor principalities, nor powers, nor things present, nor things future, nor height, nor depth, nor any other creature, could separate him from the love of God which was in Christ his Lord.*

But there could be nothing contradictory to this his doctrine, or this his confidence in a

wish

wish to be only temporally separated from his LORD, with a view to advance his LORD's work, and in the service of his LORD's known inclinations; because such desire and such confidence was also in the son of GOD towards his father, at the same time that he left his father's glory, and became accursed for the service of his father's purposes in the restoration of man.

It may be observed that our proofs of the above proposition reach no farther than to what is contained in the terms of it, namely accursed *to certain* (by which we mean, *to some* of the) pains due to an accursed creature; for we presume that no instance can be given of any creature being accursed *to all* the pains and penalties due to him, that is *to all* the consequences of this defection, but only *to a certain portion of* such penalties, even to that degree of them which suits the purposes of GOD in him, and which as a redeemed of *Christ* is fit for him. And as no creature ever suffers all those penalties which are his due, a creature's being accursed to certain pains only, can by no means suppose him unransomed; they suppose no more than that his ransom exempts him not from all degrees of suffering.

◊◊◊◊◊◊◊◊◊◊◊◊◊◊◊◊◊◊◊◊◊◊◊◊◊◊◊◊◊◊◊

SECT. III.

CHRIST *a ransom for all.*

THERE can be no doubt but that they who in this life are reconciled to GOD in *Christ* will be thenceforth exempt from every taste of misery;

misery; will pass immediately from death unto life, and will ever afterward be where *Christ* is: this is the restoration of which we have already spoken as that especial privilege of the elect so perpetually promised in the scripture.

Yet the rest, namely the unrestored in this life, who must suffer, will however not suffer as unransomed, but as the ransomed of *Christ*; seeing it is expressly said that *Jesus Christ is the ransom for all.* Upon which words I shall therefore make a few remarks, shewing,—I. How *Christ* is a ransom or redemption price.—II. How comprehensively he is so, for all.

I. *How* CHRIST *is the ransom for us.*

This the following scripture texts will illustrate. Eph. v. 2. *Christ hath loved us, and given himself for us an offering and sacrifice to God, a sweet smelling savour.* 2 Cor. ii. 15. *For we are unto God a sweet favour in Christ.* 2 Cor. v. 19. *God was in Christ reconciling the world unto himself, not imputing their trespasses unto them.* Col. i. 19. *For it pleased the father that in him all fulness should dwell; and by him to reconcile all things to himself (having made peace by him thro' the blood of the cross)* * *whether things on earth or things in heaven.* Rev. v. 8, 9. *And the four beings* (ζωα living ones,

i. e.

NOTES.

* It has been already observed (let. 5th, sect. 3d,) that the body of *Christ*, being somehow wonderfully begotten of the Holy Ghost, was pure and without blemish, a spotless lamb; and upon this its purity is

i. e. cherubims) *and the twenty-four elders sung— thou wast slain and hast redeemed us* (ηγορασας) *to God by thy blood.* ver. 11, 13. *And I heard the voice of many angels—and every creature which is in heaven and on the earth, saying, blessing and honour and glory and power be unto him that sitteth upon the throne* (Acts vii. 56. Rev. v. 7) *and unto the lamb* (εις τας αιωνας των αιωνων) *to the æons of the æons.* From whence we may learn

1st. That *Christ* is our ransom by becoming a sacrifice to GOD. This is represented to us typically in the sacrifice *Noah* made to Jehovah. Gen. viii. 21. *And Jehovah smelt a sweet savour, and Jehovah said in his heart, I will not curse the ground any more for man's sake.* See also *Lev.* i. 9. xxiii. 13. *Numb.* xxix. 2. and many other places.

2dly. That therefore the members of *Christ* are a savour of *Christ* (Χριστε ευωδια εσμεν) that is *Christ* is the sweet savour in our persons, *Christ* in us, as aromatic herbs yield a smell in the breath of them that feed on them.

3dly. That GOD was in *Christ* the sacrifice prepared, reconciling the world (for the world's conviction, conversion, and sanctification, is his present and more immediate concern) to reconcile all things (for a general conversion and sanctification, or the restitution of all will be his after-

---

NOTES.

grounded the value of the sacrifice it afforded; by its value with GOD, far beyond the whole creation, it became in itself a sweet smelling savour, and so we in it. *Col.* i. 21, 22.

after-work) and having already reconciled his members to himself: for he is already in his members a life restored. *Col.* i. 27. *Christ in us the hope of glory. We are new creatures in him.* 1 Cor. iii. 16. *The spirit of God dwelleth in us, we are his holy temple*; and by the power of this his indwelling spirit, *we bring forth fruit to God, the works of true righteousness, acceptable to God in Christ.*

4thly. That the voice of men and angels will be (ηγορασας) *thou hast redeemed*, or *ransomed us unto God*; or we are thy *purchased possession.*

II. How comprehensively *Christ is our ransom*, is imported in the words *for all* (ὑπερ παντων).

If man, that is human nature, only had been intended in the words (ὑπερ παντων) for all, the word (ανθρωπος) man, would have been used with the word (πας) all; that is, we should have read (ὑπερ παντων ανθρωπων) for all men, such being the well known style of the scripture greek.[y] Whereas

---

NOTES.

[y] According to the scripture style, ανθρωπος is used as an expletive to all kind of adjectives where man is intended, so instead of τις we read τις ανθρωπος; *e. g.*

Luke x. 30. Ανθρωπος τις κατεβαινεν.

Mat. vii. 9. Η τις ἐστιν ανθρωπος.

Luke xii. 16. Ανθρωπου τινος πλουσια ευφορησεν ἡ χωρα.

Mat. xviii. 12. Τι ὑμιν δοκει; εαν γενηται τινι ανθρωπω ἑκατον προβατα.

And thus we read ανθρωπος with Εθνος, Ρωμαιος, Ιουδαιος, μηδεις, αυστηρος, δικαιος, αγαθος, πονηρος, εχθρος, εμπορος, οὐδεις, ευγενης, ἁμαρτωλος, πιστος, ἁγιος, εὐσεβης, ψυχικος, πνευματικος, πολλοι, &c.

as the adjective (πάντων) all, being used neutrally without (ἀνθρώπων) men, we may conclude that in it is intended, not all men but, all things; that is, that the all for whom *Christ* is a ransom, comprehends the whole universe, or that *Christ* is a ransom for all that which himself created, and will therefore, in due season, work effectually in all that which himself has created, towards their restitution.

Accordingly we hear the good angels, even like *Abraham*, rejoicing to see his day (*Luke* ii. 14.) *Praising God, and saying, glory to God in the highest,*

NOTES.

And thus ἄνθρωπος is no less constantly used (as we contend it ought to have been in our present text, had not a critical import been intended there) with the adjective πᾶς, e. g:

Rom. xii. 18. Μετα παντων ανθρωπων ειρηνευοντες.

1 *Cor.* vii. 7. Θελω παντας ανθρωπους ειναι ὡς κ᾽ ἐμαυτον.

Rom. v. 18. Εις παντας ανθρωπους εις δικαιωσιν ζωης.

1 *Cor.* xv. 19. Ελεεινοτεροι παντων ανθρωπων εσμεν.

2 *Cor.* iii. 2. Αναγινωσκομενη ὑπο παντων ανθρωπων.

Col. i. 28. Νεθετουντες παντα ανθρωπον, κ᾽ διδασκοντες παντα ανθρωπον εν πασῃ σοφιᾳ, ἵνα παραςησωμεν παντα ανθρωπον τελειον.

Gal. v. 3. Παντι ανθρωπω περιτεμνομενω μαρτυρομαι.

Phil. iv. 5. Τὸ επιεικες ὑμων γνωσθητω πασιν ανθρωποις.

1 *Thes.* ii. 15. Και πασιν ανθρωποις εναντιων.

1 *Tim.* ii. 4. Ὃς παντας ανθρωπους θελει σωθηναι.

1 *Tim.* iv. 10. Ὃς ες σωτηρ παντων ανθρωπων.

Tit. ii. 11. Η χαρις τȣ Θεȣ ἡ σωτηριος πασιν ανθρωποις.

N. B. In confirmation of the justness of this remark I have also produced the above instances mostly out of St. *Paul's* writings.

highest, and on earth peace, good-will towards men (*i. e.* all the human race) and so in the above quoted passage out of the *Revelations* (v. 9) *The four living ones* (or cherubims, *Ezek.* i. 4—) together *with the twenty-four elders sung the new* (i. e. evangelical) *song, saying, thou art worthy, for thou wast slain, and hast redeemed us to God by thy blood;* not that these living ones had so fallen as did satan, for the happy angels (of which these four are presumed to be the highest) fell not thus; yet that their condition however was such as to need (a σωτηρ) a restorer (αγοραζων purchasing or) redeeming them unto GOD by his blood.

Neither is this use of the word (πας) all, peculiar to our present text, we find it applied with the same latitude of intention in many other passages of the new testament. So in *Rom.* xi. 36. 1 *Cor.* xv. 28. *Col.* i. 16, 20. *Eph.* i. 10. (τα παντα the all) *Heb.* ii. 9. (υπερ παντος for all) 1 *Cor.* 15, 22. (παντες all) ver. 28. (εν πασιν in all).

We may therefore presume that the joys and praises of the heavenly hosts, are the free tribute of souls delighted with a view of the genuine essential goodness of the divine dignity, and consequently of his love for all his works. These great and wise beings, inspecting the deliberate delicacy and abundant bounty of GOD's provision for all his creatures in his *Christ*, are charmed with a sense of his lovely attributes, and beneficent nature.

Yet then it being repugnant to the constitution of free creatures to admire a partial mercy, a capricious bounty, an irregular, uncertain, precarious

rious generosity; this their heavenly love will rest upon the same foundation as does our earthly love, namely the love of him (1 *John* iv. 19.) *because he first loved us*; and so the words (ὑπερ παντων) for all, becomes a principle ingredient in the cup of angelic consolations.

Indeed all our affiance in GOD (or which is the same, faith) and love of GOD has its root in an opinion of his natural and intrinsic goodness. We can trust him because we believe him faithful, we can love him because we believe him to be lovely. And when we hear him limiting the number of stripes to be laid upon the wicked man, his very severity recommends itself to us. *Deut.* xxv. 1—3. *The judges shall justify the righteous and condemn the wicked; and if a wicked man be worthy to be beaten—forty stripes he may give him and not exceed,——lest thy brother should seem vile unto thee.*

Wherefore also to confound this our idea of our GOD by supposing in him a partial love, a defeasible mercy, a casual, freakish, passionate, indulgence; is to sap the foundation and all true reliance on, and esteem of, the divine excellence.

For if we can suspect in any degree the genuine goodness of GOD; in that degree we grow shy of him, withdraw our affections from him, or in scripture terms, continue unreconciled to GOD.

We no sooner conceive the divine existence as capable of malice, or revenge, or unmercifulness, but our former filial affiance which softened us towards him, crying within us, abba father, at once extinguishes into a dread of him; and a servile terror of his majesty occupies our hearts.

What thinking foul therefore can endure the fuppofition, that potentates of celeftial magnanimity fhould fing praifes to, and adore a perfonal preference, an exclufive munificence, a liberality contrived for the bleffing of a few only; or in a word any benevolence fhort of univerfal!

The praifes of an unequal LORD become hypocrites and flatterers, but not natives of light, and capacities of true honour.

Truth, love and greatnefs are the fame in heaven as on earth; but it is a conftant obfervation among men, that the meaneft fpirits, that is the proudeft of us, are beft pleafed with abfolute dominion, refpect of perfons, and the prerogatives of power.

And if to *haughty*, that is to *mean* fouls, the idea of a fupreme power, void of goodnefs, love or wifdom, and diftinguifhing his favourites by dint of authority, be not a difagreeable object of worfhip; it is to be fufpected that the exercife of fuch authority, is their natural inclination and delight; and that therefore an idol of like complexion with their own, will comport with their blindnefs and degeneracy.

LETTER XII.

The doctrine of an universal reconcilement to GOD *in* Christ, *excludes not that of the damnation of the wicked.*

TO ——

SIR,

SECT. I.

Redemption and salvation how different.

E find the following sublime account of original nature and triumphant grace, in *Col.* i. 15—20.

Who is the image of the invisible God, the first-begotten of every creature (or the whole creation); *for* (ἐν αὐτῳ) IN *himself were all things created that are in heaven, and that are on earth, visible and invisible, whether they be thrones, or dominions, or principalities, or powers; all things were created*

created (δι αυτȣ) by himself, and (εις αυτον) unto himself: and he is before all things, and (εν αυτω) in him all things stood together; and he is the head of the body, the church, who is the beginning, the first-begotten from the dead; that in all things he might be the first (ινα γενηται εν πασιν αυτος πρωτευων) which compare with the syriac ܢܗܘܐ ܩܕܡܝ ܒܟܠ, that he should be foremost in all, or) *in all things; for it seemed good that in him should all fulness dwell, and by him to reconcile all things unto him; having made peace by the blood of his cross, by him (I say) whether (they be) things on earth, or things in the heavens.*

We will take the following words of this passage for our present scrutiny (verse 20.) *and by him to reconcile all things unto him* (κỳ δι αυτȣ αποκαταλλαξαι τα παντα εις αυτον).

And first as to the true meaning of the word (αποκαταλλαξαι) to reconcile (the curious may see it in the scriptures remark'd in note [z]) there is nothing critical, it universally denotes a restoration from a state of discord to a state of peace, so that without being detained hereby, we will make the following our first article. I. By

---

NOTES.

[z] Αποκαταλλάττω is to be found only in *Eph.* ii. 16. *That he might reconcile both unto God*, and in *Col.* i. 20, 21. as above. Καταλλασσω is found

Rom. v. 10, 11. *When enemies were reconciled.*
1 Cor. vii. 11. *Or be reconciled to her husband.*
2 Cor. v. 18. *Who has reconciled us to himself.*
19. *God in Christ reconciling the world.*
20. *Be ye reconciled to God.*

I. *By Christ to reconcile.*

As the terms reconcilement by *Christ* must import all that work wrought by *Christ* alone, and in his single person for our restitution, or which is the same, our recovery from our spiritual death, this first point becomes a matter of fact, indefesible, fast as the creation of GOD, being already past and accomplished. It is of this separately and distinctly the gospel speaks, when it tells us that by means of the most amazing sacrifice of the body of *Christ*, contrived for that end, man is rendered, of a sinner sunk in guilt and misery, acceptable to GOD, welcome before his holy throne, and in all the charms of a beloved child, pardoned and restored to the nearest access of favour, and reconcilement.

That tho' to his own sense he may seem a poor naked inhabitant of this world, exposed to all its miseries and liable to all the circumstances of distress, poverty and shame; that yet he is now as kindly look'd upon of GOD in the atonement by his *Christ*, as if he had always continued his first estate of innocence, and that he has as much indulgent love and kind treatment to expect from GOD, as tho' he had never sinned, from his first creating till now, but were in himself as good and faithful as any angel in the realms of bliss.

For that (*John* i. 29.) *Christ is the one lamb of God which beareth away the sin of the world.* Who (Is. liii.) *was wounded for our transgressions, and bruised for our iniquities, by whose stripes we were healed; for the transgression of his people was he smitten. Jehovah has laid on him the iniquity of us all.*

And (Heb. i. 3.) *when he had by himself purged our sins, he sat down at the right hand of the majesty on high* (If. liii.) *waiting to see the travail of his soul satisfied* in the saving effects of his passion, content therewith as a full recompence for his labours. But then where we read (*If.* xliv. 22.) *I have blotted out as a thick cloud thy transgressions, and as a cloud thy sins*; we read also, in the same verse, *Return then unto me, since I have redeemed thee.*——Whereby we learn that tho' the blotting out of our sins is absolutely effected, yet is a return to our saviour as absolutely requisite for the desired reconciliation: which brings me to the second point.

II. *To reconcile unto him.*

This second article is the foundation of the apostle's comparison which we read in *Rom.* v. 6, 8—10. *For when we were yet without strength*,[a] *in due*

NOTES.

[a] We find this passage in the syriac worded as follows: *But if Christ* ܒܠܚܘܕ[3] ܟܪܝܗܘܬܢ[2] ܐܠܐ[1]) (ܡܝܬ[4] ܚܠܦ[5] ܪܫܝܥܐ[6] *for* (i. e. moved by) [2] *our debility* [3] *in the very time of it* [4] *died* [5] *for* [6] *the ungodly*; herein GOD demonstrateth his love towards us; because if while we were sinners *Christ* died for us, by how far more the rather shall we be now *justified by his blood*, [7] *and by him* [8] *be delivered* [9] *from* [10] *the wrath* (ܪܘܓܙܐ[10] ܡܢ[9] ܢܬܦܨܐ[8] ܘܒܗ[7]); *for if while we were enemies* ܐܬܪܥܝ[1] ܥܡܢ[2] ܐܠܗܐ[3] ܒܡܘܬܐ[4] ܕܒܪܗ[5] ܟܡܐ[6] ܗܟܝܠ[7] ܝܬܝܪܐܝܬ[8] ܒܬܪܥܘܬܗ[9] ܢܚܐ[10]) [3] *God* [4] *is reconciled* [2] *with us* [4] *by the death* [5] *of his son*, [6] *by how much* [7] *then the rather* [9] *thro' his reconciliation* [9] *shall we live* [10] *in his life.*

LETTER XII. [233] SECT. I.

due time Chrift died for the ungodly; but God com-mendeth his love to us in that while we were yet fin-ners Chrift died for us, much more *then being now juftified in his blood, we fhall be (retrieved or) deliver-ed from the deftined wrath thro' him; for if when we were enemies we were reconciled to God by the death of his fon; much more being reconciled we fhall be re-trieved* (delivered) *in his life.* The apoftle's ar-gument here is a majori, and two degrees of bleffing are fuppofed in it. 1ft. Our being recon-ciled to GOD by *Chrift*. 2dly. (And as founded upon this) the being recovered or faved from wrath prepared.[b] It argues that fince we are al-ready the firft, we may eafily become the fecond; that fince we are already reconciled to GOD by *Chrift*, we may eafily prevail to be (refcued, re-covered or) delivered, from the wrath which the æonian GOD will bring upon his incorrigible peo-ple,

N O T E S.

[b] It cannot be doubted that there is a wrath con-trived and prepared by the fon of GOD for ends wor-thy his good nature, and the purpofes of his æonian power. We read *Luke* iii. 7. *Who hath forewarned you to flee* ¹*from* ²*the wrath* ³*prepared* (מן¹ רגזא² דעתיד³ ܠܡܐܬܐ¹). So *Matt.* xxv. 41. *The æonian fire* (το ήτοι-μασμενον) *prepared for the devil and his angels.* And verily, *Job.* v. 17. *Bleffed is the man whom God cor-recteth, for he maketh fore and bindeth up.* Heb. xii. 7. *If ye endure chaftening, the Lord dealeth with you as with fons;* and *Pf.* cxix. 75. fays *David, Jehovah out of very faithfulnefs has afflicted me, but* (Lam. iii. 33.) *he doth not afflict from his heart* (מלבו) *neither grieve*

ple, who will not have him to reign over them, who renounce subjection to his æonian authority, who set at nought their redemption by his blood.

Altho' we are not saved from the wrath of the lamb merely by our being reconciled to his father (since others equally reconciled with us shall however suffer the wrath prepared) yet our reconcilement, at the expence of so great a sacrifice, so forcibly demonstrates an inclination in *Christ* that we should become even recovered in his life (and be thereby secured even from the wrath prepared) that we cannot doubt of it.[c] The opposition therefore in short runs thus. If, while we were yet in our abandoned state, the love of *Christ* could prompt him to die for us; much more, being now by his death reconciled, and in a state of favour with GOD, may we become rescued, from the wrath prepared for unbelievers.

SECT.

NOTES.

the children of men. But if wrath, which includes death and hell and damnation, be prepared of GOD; we ought to respect it as the gracious work of a good father, as a salutary means to life, as an intermediate measure towards rendering himself the fulness of all things, and towards his perfecting the work of (*Eph.* ii. 15.) *creating in himself the two* (namely the creature and creator) *into one new man.*

[c] This is evident from numberless passages in scripture, such as *Ez.* xviii. 32. *I have no pleasure in the death of him that dieth,* saith Jehovah, *wherefore turn yourselves and live ye* (v. 31.) *for why will ye die, O house of Israel?*

SECT. II.

The state of reconcilement to GOD.

THE distinction I have insisted upon between being reconciled by *Christ*, and the being saved from wrath, is farther evident from a comparison of the following texts, as they contrast each other.

The world damned.	The world reconciled.
1.	1.
Mat. xviii. 7. *Wo unto the world* (τῳ κοσμῳ) *because of offences.* 1 Cor. xi. 32. *When we are judged we are chastened of the Lord that we should not be damned with the world* (συν τῳ κοσμῳ κατακριθωμεν) Rev. iii. 10. *Because thou hast kept the word of my patience, I will keep thee from the hour of trial which shall come* (επι της οικουμενης ὁλης) *upon the inhabited universe, to try* (τες κατοικουντας επι της γης) *the inhabitants of the earth.* John xvii. 9. *I pray not for the world* (περι τε κοσμε)	2 *Cor.* v. ix. *God was in Christ reconciling the world* (κοσμον) *unto himself, not imputing their trespasses unto them.* John i. 29. *Behold the lamb of God which taketh away the sin of the world.* (τε κοσμε) Which world is however to be damn'd, and for which *the Lord will not pray,* as the texts in contrast assure us. According to the wisdom of GOD therefore, altho' sin be taken away in the person of *Christ*; yet shall the sinner by *Christ* be both condemn'd & chasten'd.
2.	2.
2 Pet. iii. 7. *The heavens and the earth—re-*	1 John iv. 14. *We have seen and do testify*

served unto fire at the day of judgment and perdition of ungodly men. Rom. ix. 22. *Vessels of wrath fitted for destruction:* yet who the contrast tells us shall be restored; and this can no otherwise be than after their destruction.

3.
Phil. iii. 19. *Whose end is destruction.* Rev. xiv. 11. *And the smoke of their torment ascendeth up æonianly who worship the beast and his image.* John viii. 24. *If ye believe not that I am he, ye shall die in your sins.*

4.
Rom. i. 18. *For the wrath of God is revealed from heaven against all ungodliness and unrighteousness of men.* 2 Thes. i. 7. *The Lord shall be revealed from heaven with his mighty angels in flaming fire, taking vengeance on them that know not*

that the father hath sent the son to be the restorer of the world (σωτηρα τȣ κοσμȣ) John iii. 16. *God so loved the world that he gave his only begotten---* (ver. 17) *that the world thro' him might be restored* (ἱνα σωθη ὁ κοσμος δι αυτȣ, syr. ⟨syr⟩ *ut vivat.*)

3.
1 John ii. 2. *He is the propitiation for our sins, and not for ours only but also for the sins* (ὁλȣ τȣ κοσμȣ) *of the whole world.* John v. 51. *And the bread that I give is my flesh, which I will give for the life of the world* (ὑπερ της τȣ κοσμȣ ζωης)

4.
1 Tim. ii. 6. *Who gave himself a ransom for all, to be testified in due time*; i. e. when the fit season for this testimony shall come: and then it shall appear that among the all, for whom *Christ* gave himself a ransom, are the ungodly, and un-

The world damned.	The world reconciled.
God, and that obey not the gospel---who shall be punished with æonian destruction from the presence of the Lord and from the glory of his power.	righteous; whose doom it is to be punished with æonian destruction from the presence of the LORD, or Jehovah, who is both their creator & redeemer.

5.

Psal. xxxvii. 18, 20. The Lord knoweth the days of the upright and their inheritance shall be æonian.—But the wicked shall perish, the enemies of Jehovah shall be as the fat of lambs, they shall consume, into smoke shall they consume away. Rom. viii. 13. If ye live after the flesh ye shall die.

5.

1 Cor. xv. 22. As in Adam all die, even so in Christ shall all be made alive; but every man in his own order: Christ the first fruits, afterward they that are Christ's at his coming; and after this, the rest; viz. they that are perished and consumed away by the wrath prepared. (παντες ζωοποιηθησονται) all shall be quickened.

6.

Rom. ii. 8. But unto them that obey unrighteousness indignation and wrath, tribulation and anguish upon every (ψυχὴν ανθρώπε) soul of man that doth evil, of the Jew first, and also of the Greek. Rev. xv. 1. The seven last plagues, for in them (ιτελισθη ὁ θυμος) is finished (or consummated) the wrath of God.

6.

Heb. ii. 9. He tasted death for every one.— John xii. 32. And I, when I am lifted up from the earth, will draw all unto me. (παντα) Can. Lin. Copt. Goth. Lat. Sax. Iren. Ambr. Hierom. Leo. Cyril. August. et alii.

For if the world (as is here proved) tho' reconciled by *Christ* unto himself, and tho' its sin be taken away, shall nevertheless be judged or damned; is nevertheless without the prayer of *Christ* for it; if notwithstanding *Christ* be the restorer of the world, yea sent into the world of the father, that the world thro' him might be saved, that is restored; yet the ungodly in it shall be prepared and fitted for destruction, and reserved to the fire of the judgment day; if *Christ* may be so a propitiation for the sins of the whole world, as he is for their sins who are saved; may be the bread given for the life of the whole world, as for the life of the elect; and yet that same world for its unbelief may die in its sins, may be destroyed and burnt æonianly: then are the state of reconcilement and the state of damnation so far compatible, as that the world may be both the one and the other in varying respects at the same time; reconciled to GOD, and condemned of *Christ:* and so the difference here argued for (viz. between the being reconciled by *Christ*, and the being saved from wrath prepared) must be scriptural.

Tho' *Christ* be a ransom for all, yet will he take vengeance on the most part, and destroy the ungodly æonianly; and tho' all who die in *Adam,* even all men, shall be requickened in *Christ*; yet shall all such of these as lived after the flesh die, and consume away into smoke as the fat of lambs. Because tho' *Christ* tasted death for every man, and draws all men unto him, yet his justice shall also have its perfect work; and no soul of man, unreformed from evil, shall escape the wrath of GOD, or be delivered from the anguish of his damnation.   Lastly

Laſtly then, what mean we by being ſaved from the wrath prepared? I anſwer, we mean the being ſo recovered or reſtored unto GOD in this life, as to be delivered from that wrath which muſt fall upon the unreſtored; and which will be their doom 'till their day of reſtitution ſhall likewiſe come; when a diſpenſation of that life which quickens the now in *Chriſt*, being made to them, will alſo quicken them, and ſo render them reconciled unto GOD in *Chriſt* together with us.

When we are reconciled to GOD his peace lives within us; and the means hereto is our abſolution in *Chriſt*, diſpenſed to us in a ſenſibility of our acceptance thro' *Chriſt*. And becauſe this ſenſibility affects our hearts in a ſpirit of believing, the terms faith in *Chriſt*, and reconcilement by *Chriſt*, become reciprocal, and that juſtly; for the believer ſeeing himſelf to be the redeemed of GOD, the ranſomed of Jehovah, the deſire of his creator, opens his heart to this conception, and receiveth it as his conſolation; and in the charms of this light, he enjoys a peace which in other words is called the being reconciled unto GOD.

So then, reconcilement unto GOD is the reſult of a man's believing that GOD is attached to him in his *Chriſt*, by the ſtrongeſt ties of love and alliance; that GOD is his father in *Chriſt*, and that in this alliance he has nothing to expect but diſpenſations of bounty continually. Moreover, becauſe *Chriſt* is conceived by him as the foundation and cauſe of this his acceptance with GOD; *Chriſt* is the firſt object of all his hope and confidence, and conſequently his reconcilement begins in him.

He who believes that the good will of GOD is the pure fountain of all that is good and desirable, must naturally unite himself to the will of GOD, in proportion to the firmness of such his belief. So again, he who believes that the love of *Christ* towards him is the cause of all his favour with GOD; must as naturally unite himself to *Christ* in a love proportionable to the firmness of such his belief. And such uniting of our affections to *Christ* is called our being reconciled unto *Christ*.

The unbeliever has doubts concerning the dying love of *Jesus*, he suspects it to be pretended, not genuine, not cordial, not from a bottom principle of disinterested tenderness; he therefore fears that this will of *Christ* may have selfish purposes in view, and that in pursuit of these it may lead him into disgrace and poverty and misery; at least that it will withold from him the free use of many of the good creatures.

On the other hand when his faith hath taught the believer that the dying love of *Jesus* is cordial, genuine, unfeigned, even from a central principle of pure affection; he then begins to desire no creature but from the hand of his LORD only, and to will, both for himself and all mankind, all that and that only which he thinks is the will of *Christ* for himself and them: and hence it is that you find him, thro' all his secular dealings and concerns, equitable, upright, affectionate; he is therefore so, because he dares venture on the word of GOD and its testimony of reconciliation as no deceitful presumption.

And herein consisted the strength of those holy men of old, persecuted only for being so, of whom

St.

St. *Paul* tells us in his epistle to the *Hebrews*; (chap. xi) *that they wandered about in sheep skins and goat skins, in desarts and mountains and caves of the earth, being destitute, afflicted, tormented, of whom the world was not worthy.* Their faith told them that they were the LORD's property as much as his holy angels were; and in this confidence, they resigned themselves blindly into their LORD's hands to be either rich or poor, happy or miserable in life, as their LORD pleased for them.

When the sufferings of our LORD can reach a man's heart with a conviction of the sincerity of his dying love; when these have taught a man that he is dear, desirable and precious in the eyes of his GOD; then only can he desire nothing out of the will of GOD, and fear nothing in the will of GOD: then are the goods of life to him only so far good as they come from his GOD, and the misfortunes of life he respects as allotted him in view of his true interest; having in his estimation no casual occurrences, or works of chance.

Hunc neq; pauperies neq; mors neq; vincula terrent;
Responsare cupidinibus, contemnere honores
Fortis: & in Christo *totus, teres, atq; rotundus.—*
In quem manca semper ruit fortuna.

Unterrify'd by want, or chains or death;
Brave to repulse importunate desire;
To all the promisings of honour deaf;
Round and intire in *Christ* his LORD, his all.—
Against him hostile fortune vainly points
Her efforts, always worsted in the charge.

Believing this his Master's unfeigned love of him, he unites himself without reserve to his holy will;

will; and in this attachment prosperity and adversity begin to lose their names with him.

" His Lord's his all, nor finds he in the whole
" Creation ought, but God and his own soul."

His contented heart, receiving all that comes from the hand of God with faith and thankfulness, regards even life and death as alike welcome; for which ever offers itself, this is at once considered by him as the best passage to his truest consolation. And to live in this belief is to be holy, for the will of our God is the measure of true holiness.

This doctrine may appear indeed very unreasonable to the reasoning soul, because the powers of our human understanding being conversant only with sensible objects, we cannot judge reasoningly but by reflections drawn from sensible nature; whereas the word of God (having its foundation in truths that stand upon celestial fitnesses, which are invisible, and incomprehensible to our human judgment) transcends all measures of human reasoning. And hence it is that the scripture sometimes sounds so strange to us, and that its precepts seem to want what we men call common sense.

But altho' the divine fitness of these truths may be beyond the length of our fathom, yet as they are truths conceivable enough by their analogy with worldly things, and are certainly pronounced by the messengers of God; they ought to be satisfactory to us, and gratefully entertained by us, in defiance of human reasoning.

When therefore we are bid *to cleave unto the Lord, to believe only in Jesus, to trust in the living God, not to doubt in our hearts, to ask in faith*
nothing

nothing doubting, for that all things are possible to him that believeth: that *without faith it is impossible to please God;* for that *whatsoever is not of faith is sin:* that *the fearful and unbelieving shall have their part in the lake of fire, which is the second death;* that *the wrath of God abideth on them,* that *they shall not see life;* but that *they shall die in their sins, because they believe* not that *Jesus is the* Christ; and farther, that *God consumes their days in vanity because they believe not on him.*

I say reading these **truths** pronounced by **the** word of GOD, we are to presume that there is a depth of divine wisdom in them; that our LORD's command *believe,* must be founded upon a reality in nature, must rest upon divine proprieties; and that the title which such belief can give us to the blessings of GOD in *Christ* is infallible.

Our LORD assures us that in order to work the work of GOD we have only to believe; for *John* vi. 28. *This* (says he) *is the work of God, that you believe on him whom he hath sent.* We are to believe (*Rom.* iv. 18.) *In hope against hope* (1 Cor. ii. 13.) *not as man's wisdom teacheth, but as the holy ghost teacheth* (2 Cor. i. 9.) *trusting* not in *ourselves, but in God, who raiseth the dead.* And whereas all our right or title, is founded solely on, and is sufficiently in the grant of GOD (for as we have no right to any thing but by his grant, so in it we may have a right to all things, because all things are his) our call and command from GOD to believe, must be our sufficient qualification to the throne of grace: and this qualifying belief is that which the apostle means, when he says (2 *Cor.* v. 20.) *We pray you in Christ's stead be you reconciled to God.*

LETTER XIII.

The efficacy of CHRIST's *sacrifice must extend to all his creatures.*

TO ⸻

SIR,

COL. i. 20.

By him to reconcile **all things** *to himself.*

TREATING on this passage in my last letter I shew'd two things, 1st. that the word to reconcile by *Christ*, respected *Christ*'s personal atchievements as our redeemer, or, in the words of the scripture, *his having made peace* (διὰ τȣ αἱματῷ τȣ ϛαυρȣ αυτȣ) by this blood and cross, or *by the blood of his cross:* and 2dly. that by reconciling the creature (εἰς αυτον) unto *Christ*, was meant his rendering them of enemies believers, by which is meant his producing in them (probably thro' a gradual process) an yielding to him, a being pleased with him, a being delighted in him.

Our

LETTER XIII. [245] SECT. I.

Our terms thus settled the thing taught is (ευδοκητε δι αυτȣ εις αυτον αποκαταλλαξαι τα παντα) it seemed good (i. e. to GOD) by him unto himself to reconcile all things, or as in the syriac ܘܒܐܝܕܗ ܠܡܪܥܝܘ ܠܗ ܟܠܡܕܡ *'and by 'him ² to reconcile ³ to him ⁴ all' things whatever,* i. e. that the decree of GOD is to reconcile the lost affections of all things[a] towards him, (namely *Christ*) to render him (namely *Christ*) the complacency, the pleasure, the delight of all things; for that it is his gracious purpose, the purpose of his good pleasure, that all things may find their comfort, consolation and plenitude of joy in *Christ*.

The four chief points of christian knowledge are

1st. That human nature, or man, having lost his life in GOD, has within him a natural hatred of, and enmity against GOD.

2dly. That in order to his recovering a genuine love of GOD, his lost life in GOD must be recovered.

3dly. That this recovery can no otherwise be made, than by his having the christian nature imparted to him.

4thly. That he can no otherwise have the christian nature imparted to him, than by being regenerated in *Christ*.

But

NOTES.

[a] Tho' τα παντα be literally rendered all *things*, yet with equal propriety in the greek tongue, it also expresses all persons, i. e. all intellectual beings; for the greeks often apply the collective neutral adjective to persons.

But all things shall be reconciled to GOD, therefore all things shall again love GOD, therefore all things shall recover their lost life in GOD, therefore all things shall be regenerated in *Christ*.

Now if this regeneration of all things be the decree of GOD, his good pleasure (as the words of our text *to reconcile all things to himself* do most naturally import) no christian man ought to doubt of its due accomplishment.

But since most of our commentators here object against the comprehensiveness of the term τα παντα, and argue that by all things is only to be understood some things, we shall in the next place examine the expression τα παντα, which we render all things.

SECT. I.

The latitude of the expression τα παντα *all things.*

BEZA and his party[e] contend that by the term all, is intended all the members (i. e. those who in this life become the members) of
Christ's

NOTES.

[e] *Omnia,* τα παντα, *sæpe jam annotavimus* το καθολκ *frequenter apud Paulum ad id de quo agitur esse restringendum, ut* (1 Cor. xv. 28. and vi. 12. and viii. 1.) *et alibi sæpenumero. Sic ergo hoc in loco quum de mediatoris officio disseratur, fit autem mediator solis electis destinatus, appellatione* των παντων *intelligo totum ipsius Ecclesiæ Corpus, quod postea in duas veluti partes dividitur: nempe in ea quæ sunt in cælis (scilicet fideles ante Christi*

Chrift's church, or the whole collected body of the elect or chosen; while on the other hand the arminian party, with all those of like persuasion,' contend that by the words *all things* is indeed intended both men and angels, that is, say they, not the wicked of either sort, but all the good, for that all that are good of both men and angels shall be collected together, and united into one perfect whole in *Chrift*, while the bad, having no part or share in this (ἀνακεφαλαίωσις;) recapitulation, must continue in their state of reprobation as beings lost beyond redemption.

But we cannot judge of these passages with either of these parties; because while the term ALL THINGS is so often repeated in the former part of the context, in the most comprehensive

accep-

NOTES.

adventum mortuos) & ea quæ sunt in terris (scilicet eos quos Chriftus vivos deprehendit, vel qui sunt ejus adventum consequuti. Beza *in* Ephes. i. 10. *Annot.*

Again, τα παντα, *i. e. universam ecclesiam, quomodo jam pluribus exposui* (Eph. i. 10.) Beza *in* Col. i. 20. *Annotat.*

ᶠ So says also *Grotius*, in his annotations on *Ep.* i. 10. *Antea inter angelos factiones erant, & studia pro populis,* vide Dan. x. 13—20. xii. 1. *et adde* Jobum iv. 18. *Ea sustulit Chriftus, Rex factus etiam angelorum, unum ex tot populis sibi populum colligens, cui angeli ministerium nunc debeant.* Heb. i. 14. *vide exempla act* v. 19. xii. 11. xvi. 26. xxvii. 23, 44. *adde* Mat. 18. 10. & 1 Cor. xi. 10. *Ubi de angelis agitur.*——Again, *Ad Chrifti regnum, quod in angelos est adeptus, nonnulli referunt id quod est* (Col. i. 16.) *quia* κτίζειν *creare, sæpe ordinationem novam significat. Certe ut pleraque epistolæ ad Co-*

acceptation of the words, with what shew of probability can we confine its meaning in the latter part of the same paragraph?

We read (verse 16, 17.) *By him were all things created that are in heaven, and that are on earth, visible and invisible, whether they be thrones, dominions, principalities, or powers, all things were created by him and for him, and he is before all things, and by him all things consist.* Now if the ALL THINGS here spoken of must mean universally all, all both good and bad; why must all things in the conclusion of this period mean all the good only, and not the bad? If in the term all things it is declared that both good and bad were equally created by him and for him; if by the all things consisting in him, and by his being before all

---

NOTES.

lossenses cum hac epistola congruunt, ita & locus iste huic lucem adferre & vicissim ab eo lucem mutuari videtur.—Nunc mutata omnia, conciliati et deo et inter se utriusq; generis homines qui vocationi paruere.—Item angeli, a nobis, tanquam peccatoribus & apostatis, avulsi & elienati, jam nobiscum reconciliati, & in unum idemque consortium & corpus, sub Christo capite, nobiscum collecti sunt, ut pariter utrique deo conjuncti, communem Beatitudinem obtineant. Angeli Omnes, infensi gentibus ob idololatricos cultus, favent iisdem ad Christum conversis, iisque propter Christum libenter inserviunt, ut ad angelicam dignitatem vocatis—Judæi alienigenas oderant ut idololatras: gentibus invisi Judæi ob institutorum diversitatem (qua de re diximus libro 2do de jure belli & pacis xv. 9.).—nunc qui ex utroq; genere ad Christum veniunt, amici, imo fratres, inter se, unus simul dei populus. Grotius annotat. on Eph. i. 10.

all things, and by all things being made for him, we are to understand all things *universally*, all things bad as well as good; from what rule or form of speech are we to discover that by the all things reconciled to him, is to be meant only all the good, and not all the bad?

There was an heathenising party of christians in the 2d century who persuaded themselves that the world was not made by the Logos or word of GOD: to these were objected the very words of St. *Paul* above-mention'd; and at that time the words (τα παντα) all things, were so forcible that the adversary knew not how to resist them.

If it be asked why these words (τα παντα) all things will not work a like conviction on another occasion now a-days, the only answer is, that if taken in so comprehensive an acceptation, the scripture term (αιωνιος) æonian, cannot mean eternal.

For if all things are reconciled to GOD, and if GOD shall quicken all things, then will no creature be damned to all eternity; but, say our opponents, some creatures will be damned to all eternity, and therefore the terms all things must not be here understood in their extensive signification, or as meaning all intellectual creatures.

They allow that (τα παντα) all things, are applied without distinction, in the passage quoted, to both the created and reconciled; and yet notwithstanding this, they boldly distinguish between the all things created, and the all things to be quickened, that they may not be forced to quit the point of eternal damnation.

We read therefore as in our text, *That it is the father's good pleasure by Christ to reconcile all things to himself, whether things on earth, or things in heaven.* Eph. i. 10. *That he will gather together in one all things in Christ, both which are in heaven and which are on earth.* 1 Tim. vi. 13. *That he quickeneth* (or is in the actual work of quickening) *all things.* That (Rom. xi. 36.) *of him, and to* (or for) *him are all things.* 1 Cor. xv. 28. *That all things shall be subordinated unto him,* as himself shall also be subordinated to his father; for that (Heb. ii. 8.) *the father hath* (by promise) *put all things in subjection unto him; altho' we hitherto see not all things in subjection unto him*; and that (Heb. ii. 10.) *all things being made by him and for him,* he shall in the end (Eph. iv. 10.) *fill all things.* I say we read in these several passages the words all things, without any meaning, left they should affirm more than we like to believe, the restitution of all things.

We resolve to believe that some things shall never be restored, and then affirm that the words all things must not comprehend all the lost, but only those of them who in this life are restored.

For tho' it be acknowledged that we have no better authority to limit the natural import of the terms, *all things,* than to change them for some other; yet rather than that we should doubt of an eternal damnation, these terms must be limited, even to such a degree, that all things shall not only mean some things, but a few things, yea a very few things, even those only *who are entering into the straight gate and narrow path which leadeth unto the æonian life.* The

LETTER XIII. SECT. I.

The cautious commentator knows that it is easier to soften and extenuate an *expression*, than to reform a *received maxim*; that what people have of old believed, they may easily be continued in the belief of, however absurd: and it suits his inclinations rather to cast a veil over offensive passages, than to shock his readers with novelties.

We cannot but impute it chiefly to this, that the words of him *who spake as no man ever spake*, are so lower'd, and accommodated to the received maxims of a blind professing multitude.

But it should be considered that our good LORD declares warmly against the tradition of the elders; that Protestants upon this account chiefly declare against the church of *Rome*; and that the veil, which now covers the scriptures, and which we pray to be removed, can no otherwise be removed than by a free enquiry into the genuine texts of scripture, and a free detachment from ancient sentiments.

Tho' the primitive writers do highly deserve our honour, and were some of them indeed very enlightened men, yet as they had no apostolick deputation from GOD, they are to be considered, not as apostles, but as brethren.

So then this passage in the *Colossians* being an acknowledged proof that *Christ* made all things universally bad as well as good, is as powerful a proof, that he will reconcile all things to himself, bad as well as good: and to presume otherwise, to presume that all things in a former clause of a text, is not the all things in the latter clause of it, is to render the scripture language doubtful, precarious, deceiving, which is by no means warrantable or serviceable to the truth. So that those worthy men who teach that all things universally were created by the Logos, that all things universally consist in him, but that the all things which he is to reconcile unto himself are not universally so, are but partially all things, namely the good only among all things, are not in this respect to be credited.

We must understand this sublime passage as telling us that all the creatures subsist originally and perpetually in the Logos; that he is the source of all the universe; that life and its body or tabernacle matter, are nothing at all but in him; that as the Logos son of GOD is the one single, integral, compleat offspring or production of the father, so are the number of created individuals, the many or diverse and partial productions of *Christ's* fulness.

That altho' as to his unbeginning nature, *Christ* is what no one knoweth beside the father only; yet as in his angelic nature he is revealed to be the first-begotten and foundation of all created existence: also in his human nature he is appointed to become the collective source of all individuals.

The person of the Logos both contains and comprehends all the excellencies of his father, and that not essentially only, or in posse, but in reality of existence.

Moreover, that he might have a temple befitting himself, his human tabernacle likewise is the offspring, not of man, but of the Holy Ghost.

Ghost. And in this, being man begotten of GOD, and not radically a creature, there emerges, that wonder among all intelligent creatures, an human son of GOD.[g]

This prodigy of heaven is called æonian GOD, and has a capacity, even as man, potentially equal to his father's fulness.

And altho' this man-capacity while upon earth was not filled with all the excellencies of GOD, yet now it is filled with them, that is so far filled with them, as that all the excellencies of the divine nature do indeed dwell in or inhabit it; as says the apostle, *Col.* ii. 9. *In him dwelleth all the fulness* (της θεοτητος σωματικως) '*of the Godhead* ² *bodily.*'

And as the man *Jesus* is already the bodily temple of the **divine plenitude,** or has all the excellencies of the divine nature dwelling in him; so shall men and angels likewise, the complex progeny of the Logos (called in scripture οἱ πολλοι the

---

NOTES.

[g] *N. B.* We speak here even with respect to the human **nature** of our LORD; for it is our firm belief that our LORD, excepting that only which he received from the **virgin** *Mary* as his mother, has not any thing **in** him **but** what also **was** from all eternity. As the **Logos was** not created but begotten of the father; so was the man *Jesus* not created, but begotten of the Holy Ghost: and whereas begetting **is** not a production out of nothing; he must have been eternally in the father, altho' temporally generated. See *John* iii. 13. xvi. 28.

the many, who are his images, in oppofition to himfelf who is fingly the image of God)[h] become, when hereafter (during *Chrift*'s æonian government) they fhall be collected together in one, a body, the temple of *Chrift*'s plenitude.

I fay as the man *Jefus* has now all the excellencies of his father dwelling in him; fo fhall (ὁ πολλοι) the many hereafter, have all the excellencies of *Chrift* dwelling in them. Yea and furthermore, in the end their collective capacities will be fo enlarged as not only to be filled with, but even to comprehend the fulnefs, or all the excellencies of the fon of God. And by this means God at laft will be, *all in all.*

We conclude then, that as furely as that all things univerfally bad as well as good confift in *Chrift,*

NOTES.

[h] As every fingle ray of light is a true image of the fun, and yet is not its plenitude; fo every angelic fpirit is a true image of the Logos, and yet is not his plenitude. But *Chrift* is the plenitude of the father, his entire felf, he in whom alone and fingly the fulnefs of the father dwelleth. And this I underftand by the terms partial and compleat: the father, being compleat in his begotten fon, has no other begotten fon than him fingly, and he muft forever be his only begotten fon: whereas the Logos, having no fuch compleat offspring, is reprefented in a multitude of individuals, each of which is a diftinct, and varying ray of his filial glory. The unity of the divine effence is charactered in the perfonage of the only begotten fon of God; but multiplicability is the character of that perfonage.

Christ, so certainly shall all things bad as well as good be by him reconciled to himself.

※※※※※※※※※※※※※※※※※※※※※

SECT. II.

The Catholic Eulogium.

THE doctrine above insisted upon corresponds with many passages in scripture, as *Eph.* i. 9—14. *Having made known to us the mystery of his own will according to his own good pleasure, which he has purposed in himself,* (namely) *in the dispensation of the fulness of times to gather together in one all things anew* (from the beginning) *in Christ, both which are in the heavens and which are upon earth, even in him* (εν ω και ευληρωθημεν) *in whom we also are become his portion, being predestinated according to the purpose of him who worketh all things after the council of his own will, that we should be to the praise of his glory who first trusted in Christ*;

in

NOTES.

¹ But how otherwise are we to the praise of God's glory than by becoming restored by him, quickened again in his life? Our saviour's glory is in his restoring power, as we read (ver. 5, 6.) *Having predestinated us unto adoption—to the praise of the glory of his grace, wherein he has made us accepted in the beloved.* And as this his office is first shewn forth in us who first trust in him, shewn forth by our being sealed with the holy spirit of promise, which seal, evident in us, is the earnest of our inheritance; so will it in

in whom ye also trusted, after that ye heard the word of truth, the gospel of your salvation; in whom also after that ye believed, ye were sealed with that holy spirit of promise, which is the earnest of our inheritance, unto (or until) *the redemption of the purchased possession, unto the praise of his glory.* Phil. ii. 10, 11. *At the name of Jesus every knee shall bow, of things in heaven, and things on earth, and things under the earth; and every tongue shall loudly celebrate*[k] *that Jesus Christ is Lord, to the glory of God the father.*

But farther and lastly, what this catholic eulogium is, which every tongue shall be employed in, and which shall reflect glory to GOD the father, we read as follows; *Rev.* v. 11—13. *And I saw and heard a voice of many angels round about the throne, and of the living creatures, and of the elders; and the number of them was ten thousand times ten thousand, and thousands of thousands; saying, with a loud voice, worthy is the lamb that was slain, to receive the power, and the riches, and the wisdom, and the strength, and the honour and the glory and the blessing.*

NOTES.

others, in due time to be restored by him, who worketh all things after the counsel of his will, this will being made known to the church, as purposing in the fulness of times, to gather together in one all things in *Christ.*

[k] Εξομολογησονται, i. e. (εξ) loudly (ομε) with one accord; *i. e.* with one voice, altogether, both men and angels, whither they have formerly been good or bad, shall at last cordially sound the praises of their catholic redeemer.

blessing. And every creature which is in the heaven and on the earth, and on the sea and all that are in them; I heard them all saying to him that sitteth on the throne, and to the lamb is the blessing and the honour and the glory and the power, to the æons of the æons.

A doxology unutterable but by spirits both 1st reconciled by *Christ* to GOD, and 2dly reconciled also to *Christ* in one concordant heart of love, adoration, and thankfulness.

The opinion that heavenly spirits which we call holy angels, stand in need of a redeemer or restorer, appears to me far from being unscriptural or unreasonable.

There may be degrees of delinquency very consistent with an heavenly continuance, and a favourable access to the throne of the ($\pi\rho\omega\tau\acute{o}\tau o\kappa o\varsigma$) first-begotten, or son of GOD; for the same reason that we find even satan himself, tho' the most stubborn of all the rebellious angels, to have thus access to his throne.

The certainty of this his access appears from *Job* i. 6. *When the sons of God came to present themselves before Jehovah, satan came among them to present himself.* And ver. 12. *Satan went forth from the presence of Jehovah* (מאת פני יהוה) Zech. iii. 1. *And he shewed me Joshua, the high-priest standing before the face of* (מלאך יהוה) *the angel Jehovah, and satan standing at his right hand to resist him; and Jehovah said unto satan, Jehovah* (to the invisible) *rebuke thee, O satan, even Jehovah who has chosen Jerusalem.* Rev. xii. 9. *And the great dragon, that old serpent called the devil and satan, was* cast out into the earth, who accused the brethren before God (that is *Christ*) day and night.

We acknowledge also that the person whom satan saw as GOD before the incarnation, was the personage called Jehovah the angel; and since the incarnation the man *Christ Jesus*. For that tho' the divine nature always shines in full lustre in the person of the Logos, *even that glory which he had with his father before the world was*; yet this his glory, as son of GOD (*John* xvii. 24.) is visible only to the holy, or those who are *by Christ reconciled to God*;[1] and sanctified in his imparted nature.

I say altho' it be certain that Jehovah Adn in his simple glory is invisible to all that are impure; still it is as certain that an access to him personally as the object of divine presence, is both practicable, and at proper seasons allowable to the worst of creatures; and this granted, it will likewise follow that an angel's continuance in heaven is no proof that he is altogether without guilt.

SECT.

NOTES.

[1] As the *Jews*, refusing the testimony of *Jesus* concerning himself, did at last sincerely believe him to be mere man; so it seems probable that the angels who fell, refusing to acknowledge the Logos as their Jehovah, might at length believe him indeed to be mere angel. And if so, since darkness increases by perverse reasonings, they might soon grow utterly blind, and unable (1 *John* iii. 2.) *to see him as he is*; in which condition, if (as we may suppose) they still remain; their present acknowledgment of *Jesus* as the son of GOD, must result rather from revelation, than any real vision of his glory and dignity. *Jam.* ii. 19. *Mat.* iv. 6.

SECT. III.

Angels delinquent.

ST. *JUDE* speaks of the fall of the rebel angels in the following terms, verse 6. (Αγγελες τε τας μη τηρησαντας την εαυτων αρχην[m] αλλα απολιποντας το ιδιον οικητηριον εις κρισιν μεγαλης ημερας δεσμοις αιδιοις υπο ζοφον τετηρηκεν) *the angels who kept not their own principality,* **but** *left their proper mansion, he has reserved for æonian chains under darkness at the judgment of the great day.*

But since these words declare no more than that the reprobate angels so sinned, as to fall by it from their **own proper** mansions, keeping no longer their **principality,** or that royalty which

Jehovah

NOTES.

[m] Αρχη here signifies imperial dignity or principality; so our LORD is said to be set in heaven, *Eph.* i. 21. (υπερανω πασης αρχης) *far above every principality, and power,* &c. So *Col.* ii. 10. *He is the head* (πασης αρχης κ̀ εξουσιας) *of every principality and power;* so (1 Cor. xv. 24.) *when he shall have invalidated* (πασαν αρχην, κ̀ πασαν εξουσιαν) *every principality and every* **power** (Col. i. 16.) *whither they be thrones or dominions or* (αρχαι) *principalities or powers, all things were created by him and for him.* And hereto, agrees also the Syriac (ܠܐܝܠܝܢ ܕܠܐ ܢܛܪܘ ܪܝܫܢܘܬܗܘܢ ܐܠܐ ܫܒܩܘ,) '*who* ²*kept* ¹*not* ³*their principality* ⁴*but* ⁵*relinquished* ⁷*their own* ⁶*habitation.*

Jehovah had given them; they are no proof of absolute innocence in the cælestial inhabitants.

And till it can be proved that any, the least degree of, guilt in angels must render them incapable of living in heaven; we are at liberty to believe that the holy (ἅγιοι [n]) angels are not absolutely void of guilt, altho' they kept their principalities. Our

NOTES.

[n] Altho' ἅγιος may, as applied to God, denote absolute holiness, yet it may also be applied to subjects not in themselves absolutely holy.

A man may be holy as a man, and an angel may be holy as an angel, and therefore called so, even whilst they are defective in true absolute holiness.

Our Lord says, *Mat.* xix. 17. *Why callest thou me good, there is none good but one, that is God.*

And yet (*Acts* xi. 24.) *Barnabas* is called *a good man*, and (*Luke* xxiii. 50.) *Joseph* of *Aramathea* is called (ανηρ αγαθος κȷ δικαιος) *a good man, and a just*: and the like use we also find of the word ἅγιος.

All believers throughout the new testament are called (ἅγιοι) holy; and so are the prophets called (ἅγιοι προφηται) holy prophets; *John* the *Baptist* is also (*Mark* vi. 20.) declared to be (ανδρα δικαιον κȷ ἅγιον) *a just and holy man*. And so are the zealous preachers of legal righteousness among the *Jews* (2 *Pet.* i. 21. ἅγιοι Θεκ ανθρωποι) *holy men of God*; and the women who of old trusted in God, St. *Peter* styles (1 *Pet.* iii. 5. ἅγιαι γυναικες) *holy women*; all who were yet by no means absolutely holy in themselves.

When therefore the scripture speaks of holy angels, this appellation may be intended only to distinguish from the rebellious angels, who left their principalities and became revolt from their loyalty.

LETTER XIII.   [261]   SECT. III.

Our LORD speaking of the æonian tabernacles and heavenly riches, has these remarkable words, *Luke* xvi. 9—12. *Make yourselves friends of the deceitful mammon, that when ye fail, they* (the children of light thus made your friends) *may receive you into æonian habitations. He that is faithful in that which is least, is faithful also in much; and he that is unjust in the least, is unjust also in much. If therefore ye have not been faithful in the deceitful mammon, who shall commit to your trust the true (mammon)? And if ye have not been faithful in that which is foreign* (εν τω αλλοτριω) *who shall give you* (το ὑμετερον) *that which is your own?*

(Το ὑμετερον scilicet μαμωνα) your own, viz. mammon, such as that (οικητηριον) **mansion**, and other your cælestial goods which were your own original inheritance, and which only can be called (αληθινον μαμωνα) the true riches; and from which being now fallen, the mammon you now possess is (αλλοτριον) strange, foreign, unnatural to you° being that which was not created for you; this, I say, while faithless, you must not be entrusted with.

That mammon which was created for us is specifically suited to our natures; whereas that which

------

NOTES.

° That this is the true meaning of the word (αλλοτριος) foreign, the fair enquirer will be easily convinced of, from its use in scripture; so (*John* x. 3, 5.) *My sheep hear my voice—a stranger* (αλλοτριω) *will they not follow—for they know not the voice of strangers* (των αλλοτριων). Heb. xi. 9. *He sojourned in a strange country.* (γην αλλοτριαν) verse 34. *they turned to flight the armies of the aliens* (των αλλοτριων).

which is now ours, we use only as a maimed man walks upon his wooden leg.

Now that the blessed angels did not, as we, loose their orginal mammon, we grant; and yet it does not thence follow that they always continued and still are, so without blame before GOD, as not to need the great restorer.

It is also true that our LORD speaks of some of the angels (*Mat.* xviii. 10.) *as always beholding the personage of his father which is in heaven.* But in speaking thus, he implies likewise that these angels are distinguished from others by an especial indulgence, and exclusive favour, and that consequently other angels in heaven do not always behold in the father's personage or representative, the signatures of his presence and glory.ᵖ

With these reflections corresponds that passage in *Job* iv. 18. *He puteth* (or will put) *no trust in his servants,* 'even in his angels ²he imputeth (or will impute) ³*transgression* (תהלה³ ישים² ובמלאכיו¹).

הלל Elel certainly imports that transgressive kind of folly which renders men sinners in the sight

---

NOTES.

ᵖ The one only (προσωπον απαυγασμα, or χαρακτηρ) personage, effulgence, or express image of the invisible father is the Logos; for *John* i. 18. *no one hath seen God at any time; the only begotten son, which is in the bosom of the father, he has declared him.* John vi. 46. 1 Tim. i. 17. vi. 16. 1 John iv. 12, 20.

All therefore whatever of the father can be seen by any of the creatures, must appear in this his personage or express image: and whereas the glories, and

sight of God. So *Pf* lxxv. 4. '*I said ²unto the transgressors ³deal not transgressingly* (אמרתי ²להוללים ³אל תהלי) *Pf.* lxxiii. 3. *I was zealous against the transgressors* (קנאתי בהוללים) *Pf.* v. 5. *²The foolish,* (i. e. the transgressing) *'shall not stand ²before thy eyes* (לא יתיצבו ²הוללים ³לנגד עיניך) *that is so long as they are* in this ill frame of mind.

And that **elel** imports sinfulness in this place, its application, and use, and opposition, and the whole thread of *Eliphaz*'s discourses do manifestly evince. And that this passage here quoted out of *Job* contains the words of truth, is evident in that it is spoken by a voice from heaven, and only related by *Eliphaz* on this occasion.

Moreover that the ministers of God here charged with elel, and with being such as that in them God putteth no trust, are the holy angels, appears as follows:

1st. That they are angelic spirits and not men, appears in that they are distinguished from men by the particle אף, which we find in the english bible justly translated *how much less*. See *Job* iv. 19. *He putteth no trust in his servants—how much less in them that dwell in houses of clay* (i. e. in men) *whose foundation is the dust, &c.* Especially as
this

NOTES.

other signatures of the father's presence, eminent thus in the person of the Logos, shew themselves only to the holy; our Lord in declaring, concerning the guardian angels of children, that the father's glories are visible to them in his personating presence, or image, does thereby declare that they are great, *i. e.* holy dignitaries; distinguished from other angels as in holiness, so of consequence in the favour of God.

this distinction refers to an opposition in ver. 17, *Shall mortal man be more pure than his maker?—behold he putteth no trust in his ministers.* i. e. his angels or ministering spirits, who are abundantly better than mortal man, and therefore better to be trusted.

2dly. That these angelic servants of GOD, here complained of as in whom he putteth no trust, are not the wicked, but the holy angels, appears from *Job* xv. 15, where the same man *(i. e. Eliphaz)* speaks the same sentiment, in the same terms, changing only the term *his ministers* into that of (קדשיו⁹) *his holy ones or saints.* Let us compare these places together,

Job iv. 17, 18, 19.	*Job* xv. 14—.
¹האנוש ²מאלוה ³יצדק? ⁴אם ⁵מעשהו ⁶יטהר ⁷גבר *Shall mortal man* ¹*be justified* ²*before God?* ⁴ *shall* ⁷ *a man* ⁶*be more pure* ⁵*than his maker?*	¹מה ²אנוש ³כי ⁴יזכה ⁵וכי ⁶יצדק ⁷ילוד ⁸אשה *What is* ²*man* ³*that* ⁴*he shall be clean?* ⁵*and that* ⁷*one born* ⁸*of a woman* ⁶*shall be just.*
⁸הן ⁹בעבדיו ¹⁰לא ¹¹יאמין ¹²ובמלאכיו ¹³ישים ¹⁴תהלה ⁸*Behold* ⁹*in his servants* ¹⁰*he trusteth* ¹¹*not;* ¹²*and*	⁹הן ¹⁰בקדשיו ¹¹לא ¹²יאמין ¹³ושמים ¹⁴לא ¹⁵זכו ¹⁶בעיניו ⁹*Behold* ¹⁰*in his saints* ¹²*he trusteth* ¹¹*not;* ¹³*and the*

NOTES.

⁹ That the word (קדש) qds, is usually applied to the holy angels is notorious: so *Deut.* xxxiii. 2. *Jehovah came from Sinai.—He came with ten thousand of his* (קדש) *holy ones or angels.* For where the LORD dwelleth there is holiness (1 *Cor.* iii. 17.) holiness by participation (*Heb.* xii. 10. 2 *Pet.* i. 4.) but absolute holiness is in none but GOD. *Rev.* vx. 4. *And they sung, saying—Lord God Almighty—thou only art holy.*

LETTER XIII. [265] SECT. III.

in his angels [13] *he imputeth* [14] *transgression.*

heavens (or, heavenly ones) *are* [14] *not* [15] *clean* [16] *in his eyes.*

[15]אַף [16]שְׂמֵי [17]בָתֵּי [18]חֹמֶר
[19]אֲשֶׁר [20]בֶּעָפָר [21]יְסוֹדָם

[17]אַף [18]כִּי [19]נִתְעָב [20]וְנֶאֱלָח
[21]אִישׁ [22]שֹׁתֶה [23]כַמַּיִם [24]עַוְלָה

[15]*Surely then* (in them) [16]*that inhabit houses* [18]*of clay,* [19]*whose* [21]*foundation* (is) [20]*in the dust.*

[17]*Surely then* [18]*indeed* [19]*a-bominable* [20]*and stinking* [21]*man,* [22]*that drinks* [24]*iniquity* [23]*like water.*

K k   Neither

NOTES.

[11], [12], [13]. *N. B.* The futurum in the hebrew tongue importing continuation as usually as futurity; the rendering of יֹאמַר and יָשִׂים as above, namely as present tenses, is just.

Thus Jehovah, continual being, is given us in the future tense, viz. יהוה in the third person, and אהיה in the first; a practice as frequent also in the apostolic writings. So *Rev.* iv. 9, 10. *And when the living creatures give glory* (δώσωσι δόξαν)—*the twenty-four elders fall down* (πεσουνται)—*and worship* (προσκυνησεσι)—*and cast* (βαλουσι) *their crowns before the throne.*———

It may be expedient likewise to observe on this passage, that (שָׁמַיִם) *smim* may be rendered with equal propriety, either heavens, or heavenly ones; for it is well known that the oriental languages use the same words without alteration for both nouns substantive, and nouns adjective, and verbs: so (טוב) tub, is both *bonus* good, *bonitas* goodness, or *bonum est* it is good: (זָקֵן) zqn, is both *senex* an old man, *senium* old age, or *senuit* he grew old: so (טהר) ter, is both clean, cleanness, or he was clean: (צדק) jdq, just, justice, to justify: so (זכה) zqe (or by apocope זך) pure, purity, to purify: (קדש) qds, holy, holiness, to sanctify: (אמן) amn, faithful, fidelity, he trusted, &c.

Neither is this opinion to be rejected under pretence of its being novel, or the whim of a few enthusiasts; it is as ancient as our LORD's days, and was in his time generally received among the orthodox *Jews*, as appears from their *targum* then in use, which explains this text of *Job* xv. 15. in the following words; ⁵יהמי ⁴לא ⁳עלאי ²בקדישי ¹הא
¹⁰קדמוי ⁹צין .⁸לא ⁷טרומא ⁶אנגלי, '*Behold* ²*in his* ³*supreme* ⁴*holy ones* ⁵*he trusteth* ⁴*not*, ⁶*even his* ⁷*sublime* ⁸*angels are not* ⁹*pure* ¹⁰*before him.*

Moreover the default of angels being a doctrine of the targum, and so of the *Jews* in our LORD's time; this must also have been the belief of our LORD's disciples while he lived among them. But what construction must a people thus taught, put upon our LORD's words to them, when he tells them, *Matt.* xix. 17. *Why callest thou me good?* (Ουδεις αγαθος ει μη εις ὁ Θεος) *none* (no being) *is good but one, that is God.* Must not such a declaration naturally refer them to the doctrine of the targum as just? And confirm them in an assurance that angels were defective beings, and that no being was absolutely good or holy, GOD only excepted?

And when the angels, yea the seraphims, are represented as covering their faces before GOD, (*Is.* vi. 2) what else could the disciples, thus taught, think of this, than that these sublime beings must have veil'd themselves from an humble self-abasement, and shame of their own imperfections? As the targum imports on this passage: (¹בתרין
²טנים ³אפוהי ⁴דלא ⁵חזי ⁶ובתרין ⁷טנים ⁸נויתיה ⁹דלא ¹⁰מרחוי) '*with two* (wings) ²*each covered* ³*his face*
⁴*that*

⁴*that he might not ʼsee;* ⁶*and with two ʼhe covered* ⁸*his body ʼthat he might not ʼ be seen,* &c.

But the christian church has also the testimony of St. *John*, which is no less determinate in this account of the creation. *Rev.* xv. 1—4. *And I saw seven angels—and them that had gotten the victory over the beast—and they sung*—(Κυριε ὁ Θεος ὁ παντοκράτωρ) — **Lord** God, *creator of all* — *who shall not glorify thy name, for thou only art holy* (ὅτι μονος ὁσιος).

The angels therefore must have, as we, an interest in *Christ* the restorer of all his creatures; and their knowledge of this is doubtless that (ευαγγελιον) glad tidings which fills them with christian love of us as their brethren; for so we find they style themselves. *Rev.* xix. 10. *And I fell at his* (the angel's) *feet to worship him, but he said unto me, see, thou do it not, I am thy fellow-servant, and of thy brethren, that have the testimony of Jesus: worship God.*

The ministers therefore of God, who are his angels, and holy in comparison with man, are however not absolutely holy; in that they are chargeable with transgressiveness, and are not (טַ) pure in the eyes of God.

But even christian men you say are holy in the eyes of God: I grant it, yet not personally so. It is certain that the most holy of men are absolutely and personally unholy; and so may also the blessed angels be. On the other hand as the human saints of God are in their Lord holy; in like manner may the blessed angels, who are reconciled to God, be in their Lord holy.

And if it be true that the angels in heaven are also sinners, it is no longer a wonder that they desire (1 *Pet.* i. 12.) (παρακυψαι) *to pry into the mysteries of redeeming love*, it is a mystery in which themselves are interested.

To all this you object that, tho' we should suppose a state of delinquency in angels to consist with their heavenly continuance; yet that we cannot suppose such state of delinquency to consist with their enjoyment of the divine vision.

Why not? It will be allowed that we have no scripture passage against the former, namely that a state of delinquency may consist with an heavenly situation, with a continuance in the possession of an heavenly principality and an heavenly mammon; and as to the latter, namely the possibility of a delinquent being's enjoyment of the divine vision, this must also be allowed me upon the christian scheme; because the saints of *Christ* are all of them delinquent beings, and yet all of them will enjoy the divine vision in heaven.

But these you say enjoy the divine vision in *Christ*; true, and so may the blessed angels, whilst (feeling the reconciling sentiment) their minds become softened with that humble thankful reverence which is in the four beings, and the twenty-four elders, when they (*Rev.* v. 7, 9) *fall down before the lamb, and sing, saying thou art worthy, for thou wast slain and hast redeemed us unto God by thy blood*. When thro' this pardoning sentiment they are clean (*John* xv. 3. xiii. 10. 1 *Pet.* i. 2, 15, 22.) *sanctified in Christ* (1 Cor. i. 2, 30. vi. 11.) *and partakers of his holiness* (*Heb.* xii. 10.

Rev.

Rev. xx. 6.) their capacities of sight are restored them, and nothing further can hinder their enjoyment of the divine vision;' and thus these passages in *Job* cease to be the gordian knot, as the learned *Drusius* calls them, *Si in eis* (i. e. *angelis*) *insania, non sunt perfecti, solvat hunc nodum qui potest, ego nihil definio.* " If a dotage be in them " (*i. e.* the angels) then are they not perfect, lose " this knot who can, I determine nothing."

So then (*Rom.* iii. 23.) *all have sinned and come short of the glory of God:* which could not have been permitted to happen but in view of some issue worthy so strange an event.

LET-

NOTES.

' So *Theophilus Antiocenus* imputes the impotence of seeing God singly to a defect in the eye, from our uncleanness, Επει δειξον βλεποντας τους οφθαλμους της ψυχης σου, κ̀ τα ωτα της καρδιας σου ακουοντα—βλεπεται γαρ Θεος τοις δυναμενοις αυτον οραν, επαν εχωτι τους οφθαλμους ανεωγμενους της ψυχης. Παντες μεν γαρ εχουσι τους οφθαλμους, αλλα ενιοι υποκεχυμενους, κ̀ μη βλεποντας το φως τu ηλιου. Και ου παρα το μη βλεπειν της τυφλους, κ̀η κ̀ ουκ ετι το φως τu ηλιου φαινον; αλλα εαυτους αιτιασθωσαν οι τυφλοι, κ̀ τας εαυτων οφθαλμους; ουτω κ̀ συ, ω ανθρωπε, εχεις υποκεχυμενους τους οφθαλμους της ψυχης σου, &c.

LETTER XIV.

The extent of the promise that death shall be no more.

Rev. xxi. 4.

And there shall be no more death, neither sorrow, nor crying, neither shall there be any more pain.

TO ―――

SIR,

SECT. I.

Of that death which the scripture calls our LORD's *last enemy.*

IN order to decide the true import of these words, we should first examine what is here meant by the word death.

Now it is universally agreed that death is the very opposite to life; and as life is said to consist in an enjoyment of those active powers which result from some peculiar union of our constituent principles; death is supposed to consist

in

in a deprivation of the due use of such powers, occasioned by a loss of that peculiar union of our constituent principles: for doubtless life results not merely from an union, but from some especial kind of union, of our constituent principles, to us unknown.

However as all true physical knowledge of these æonian matters vastly exceed human penetration; at least as our disquisitions are intended to be rather scriptural than philosophical; and as the death intended by the scripture passage we are debating, is the second or latter death, declared in *Rev.* xx. 14. xxi. 8. to be in *the* (λιμνη τȣ πυρὸς the) *lake of fire*, which is the last resource of all evil; we shall speak of death, and the efficacy of this last lake as one and the same thing.

Of this lake it is said, that (*Rev.* xx. 14.) *death and hades were cast into it*: and these two words importing an account of things not so well known in our times, as they seem to have been to the church of St. *John*'s days; a short explanation of them may be here needful to the opening the above passage.

We are all agreed that every man consists of a soul and a body, and that a man's soul will not die till the day of his judgment is come, and his sentence is passed upon him; but that the bodies of men die before the day of their judgment comes, is our daily experience.

Now as the dead bodies of men are deposited in the grave, there to corrupt; their souls are convey'd into invisible regions, of which we can know nothing but by revelation.

Of

Of these regions we have different names in scripture, because they are in place different from each other, being different residences suited to the different conditions of those who possess them.

Wherefore when we read of the prison, the abyss or bottomless pit, *Abraham's* paradise, the paradise of GOD, *Jerusalem* which is above, the temple of GOD, the sanctuary, the presence (or before the throne) of GOD; we understand by these terms places distinct and different from one another.

But since what we call death as applied to the soul will not befall any soul till after the judiciary sentence has been passed upon him (that is, till after his day of judgment) it will be asked where then are the souls of those men who are not as yet called to judgment, during their expectation of it?

To this we answer that the souls of some of these may be in the happy mansions of hades, which the *Jews* called sometimes paradise, and sometimes (that is before our saviour's death, till which time *Abraham* presided there) *Abraham's* bosom; that the souls of the wicked will be, at least some of them, in the prison;[1] but that the

NOTES.

[1] The scriptures suppose that in the regions of hades there is a prison for the souls of some of those whose bodies are in the grave, they having not been as yet raised from the dead, or called to judgment. Compare *Rev.* xx. 3, 7. ix. 11. with *Matt.* v. 25. *Isa.* xiv. 9—16. xxiv. 22. *Ez.* xxxi. 14—18. *Job* xxv. 5.

LETTER XIV.   [273]   SECT. I.

the souls of the saved Christians will be in the paradise of God."

For as we find a great variety of fortunes attending the inhabitants of this our small globe,

L l   with

NOTES.

As therefore there is a paradise and gehenna in hades; so is there also in hades a prison, and an abyss, prepared it seems rather for confinement than painful exercises, altho' not without wretchedness. Accordingly of the abyss we read, *Luke* viii. 31. *And they* (the devils) *besought him that he would not command them to* (leave the chearful aereal regions of this world, and) *go out into the abyss.* For the abyss is their proper abode, being here *(Jude 6.) reserved under darkness* (ܒܐܣܘܪ̈ܐ ܕܠܐ) *by unknown* (ܠܐ) not idioa known, gr. αιδιος from α non (ܝܕܥ) ido novit) *chains, to the judgment of the great day.*

"We read of two paradises in the scriptures, the first the paradise in hades; *Luke* xxiii. 43. *To day shalt thou be with me in paradise*; i. e. in the paradise of *Abraham* which was in hades, whither our saviour's soul went when he died (*Acts* ii. 31.) *and the soul of the thief attended him*: therefore says *Piscator, fuit itaq; dives quidem εν αδη, sed fuit εν αδη etiam* Lazarus, *disterminatis αδα regionibus, nam & paradisus & gehenna sunt εν αδη.*

The second paradise is represented to us as not in hades but in heaven, and is called (*Rev.* ii. 7.) *The paradise of God; in the midst of which is the tree of life* which grows in (Rev. xxii. 2. Gal. iv. 25, 26.) *the Jerusalem which is above, the mother of us all.*

The inhabitants of this city are (*Heb.* xii. 22, 23.) *innumerable angels, and the spirits of just men made perfect, and God the judge of all.*

with regard to their perſons, countries, ſubjecti-
ons, poſſeſſions, poverty, relations, dependencies,
and the multiplying circumſtances of all theſe;
we may believe that there is likewiſe as great a
variety

NOTES.

It is of this our LORD ſpeaks when he ſays (*John*
xii. 26.) *Where I am there ſhall alſo my ſervant be:* and
St. Paul (2 Cor. v. 8.) *We are willing rather to be ab-
ſent from the body, and preſent with the Lord* (Phil. i.
23.) *having a deſire to depart and to be with Chriſt,
which is far better.* So *John* xvii. 24. *Father, I will
that they alſo whom thou haſt given me, be with me
where I am; that they may behold my glory which thou
haſt given me.* And again, *Matt.* viii. 11, 12. *And I
ſay unto you, that many ſhall come from the eaſt and weſt,
and ſhall ſit down with Abraham, and Iſaac, and Jacob*
(who at the reſurrection of our LORD were to be a part
of his retinue, and to go with him into the paradiſe
above, and be with him) *in the kingdom of heaven;
but the children of the kingdom ſhall be caſt out into outer
darkneſs, there ſhall be weeping and gnaſhing of teeth.*

The reality therefore ſeems to be this, viz. In the
heavens is the paradiſe of GOD, which paradiſe is the
celeſtial country; and *Jeruſalem* which is above, is
the city of this country; and in this city there is (in
the preſent ſtate of it) a temple, of which we read,
Rev. iii. 12. *Him that overcometh will I make a pillar
in the temple of my God, and he ſhall go no more out;
and I will write upon him the name of my God, and the
name of the city of my God, which is new Jeruſalem,
which cometh down out of heaven from my God: and I
will write upon him my new name.*

Alſo in this temple there is a ſanctuary (*Heb.* viii. 2.
ix. 8, 12.) in which (*Heb.* ix. 12, xii. 24. xiii. 11.) *is the*

variety diversifying the condition of the departed into other states of existence; and that the blessed are as variously blessed, and the wretched as variously wretched in an after life as in this present.

NOTES.

blood of sprinkling, and (Rev. viii. 3.) *a golden* altar *of incense, and a throne, and a divine presence.*

It was *under,* i. e. at the foot of or attending round about, *this altar* of incense, where St. *John* saw (*Rev.* vi. 9.) *the souls of* the martyrs, crying for vengeance, and afterwards, *cloathed with white robes before the throne,* singing a doxology to God. *Rev.* vii. 14—17. *These* (namely the array'd in white robes) *are they who came out of great tribulation, and have washed their robes, and made them white in the blood of the Lamb. Therefore are they before the throne of God, and serve him day and night in his temple: and he that sitteth on the throne shall dwell among them. They shall hunger no more, neither thirst any more, neither shall the sun light on them, nor any heat; for the Lamb, who is in the midst of the throne, shall feed them, and shall lead them unto living fountains of waters: and God shall wipe away all tears from their eyes.*

This paradise is emphatically called the paradise of God, as being that genuine, natural paradise, which (tho' not open'd 'till after our Lord's resurrection) is that prefigured by *Adam's* paradise.

Its manner and form of life and enjoyment was intended to be typified and exhibited to man, in the manner and form of *Adam's* primitive paradisaical life and enjoyment; where the sensations of body and mind were inseparable; and palpable gratifications (or such as resulted from touch) charm'd the intellectual sensibility with knowledge, love, and delight in God.

It is true having very little from revelation to guide us in these inquiries, besides a few different names above-mention'd, viz. the prison, the abyss, gehenna, the lake of fire, the paradise in hades, the paradise of God, the *Jerusalem* which is above, &c; terms which were probably indeed, among the apostolic christians, significant of real knowledge; yet as they afford us, for want of the apostolic conceptions of divine truths, very few, and precarious notions of our future state, we can say very little of them, or by them of the life they relate to, with certainty.

However we are assured that at the last great day, and after that judgment, which shall conclude the scene of triumphant wickedness, all whoever are not then deemed worthy of the paradise of God, shall (together with their bodies, which death must then deliver up) go away into the lake of fire, prepared for the devil and his angels.ʷ

So

NOTES.

ʷ At the time which the scripture calls the last day, every evil, or every one unreconciled to God, who shall be found remaining in gehenna, shall likewise, together with all other inhabitants of hades, and every body that occupies the grave, from their several places, and receptacles, be cast into the lake, the last doom of all wickedness: which a Roman Catholick writer describes as follows: *Cogita fornacem igneam, flammas conglobantem & ejaculantem quaquaversum: & in eo corpora damnatorum volutari, nuncq; ascendere, nuncq; descendere, nunc gyrari in omnem partem, idq; jugitur, nocte & die, in sæcula sæculorum, &c.* But the following of

LETTER XIV. SECT. I.

So that the expression death and hades shall be cast into the lake, is a metonimy, as *Grotius* has justly commented upon this place,* and imports that the accursed, together with all that belongs to them, whether living or dead, that is whether in hades or in death (namely the death of the grave or otherwise) shall become one aggregate mass of wickedness, doom'd to a like catastrophe in this lake, reserved till now to be the last fate, the ultimate doom of all that is abominable.

It is farther observed of this lake that its fire is charactered as devouring and consuming; so *Heb.* x. 27. xii. 29. 2 *Pet.* iii. 7. which suits with that dissolution, consumption, and destruction, so frequently denounced in scripture upon the incor-

---

NOTES.

Gregory's, on *Matt.* viii, is rather a description of gehenna. *Ejicientur in tenebras exteriores, ubi frigus erit intolerabile, ignis inextinguibilis, vermis immortalis, fætor intolerabilis, tenebræ palpabiles, flagella cædentium, horrida visio dæmonum, confusio peccatorum, nulla spes boni, nulla desperatio mali.*

* *Hic est*, says Grotius, *metonymia subjecti; vel continens pro contento, ut cælum pro cælicolis, terra pro iis qui terram incolunt: ita hoc loco mors,* i. e. *mortui; infernus,* i. e. *ii qui erant in inferno*. And thus says our saviour (*Luke* x. 13.) *Wo unto thee Corazin, and unto thee Bethsaida;* i. e. wo unto ye the inhabitants of Corazin, and *Bethsaida:* so (*Acts* viii. 14.) *Samaria received the word of God*; i. e. the inhabitants of *Samaria;* Zech. xiv. 19. *and this shall be the punishment of Egypt*, i. e. of the people or inhabitants of *Egypt*.

incorrigible as their last end. So *Phil.* iii. 19. *whose end is* (ἀπώλεια) *destruction* (Rom. ix. 22.) *vessels of wrath fitted* (εἰς ἀπώλειαν) *for destruction.* Ps. xxxvii. 20. *The wicked shall perish, the enemies of the Lord shall be as the fat of lambs, they shall consume away, into smoke shall they consume away.*^y For the things of this world are the true patterns of the things of the world to come, as says our Milton:

" Earth is the shadow of heaven, the things therein
" Each other like, more than on earth is thought."   So

NOTES.

^y Let it not here be deem'd an absurdity that the subjects of another life have material bodies: revelation gives us no reason to suppose that there are in nature creatures altogether immaterial; or that any the inhabitants of the upper regions are void of matter. From the scripture accounts of them we gather only that the angels are spirits invisible from within, cloathed with material, tho' very subtle vehicles, visible from without. These vehicles it may be presumed befit their inward nature, and that manifesting in them their hidden life, they become sociable, knowable, relative subsistences. And being thus, doubtless they can enjoy certain bodily pleasures as well as we, and for the same reason, evil spirits can also suffer the miseries of the lake of fire.

Neither will our experience of bodily motion, or rather of bodily tardiness afford (as some pretend) any solid argument against this hypothesis. Because he who has given to the rays of light a speed that can carry them 200,000 miles in a second, or the $\frac{1}{10}$ of a minute, can likewise indue other bodies with a like

LETTER XIV. [279] SECT. I.

So that satan who seems to have been proof against the fires of gehenna, and to have exercised his goverment hitherto without suffering much himself from the elements of his kingdom (for the regions of death are satan's kingdom, he there sustains an imperial dignity and power, Heb. ii. 14. (το κρατος* εχων τε θανατε) *Having the empire of death*) will however find in this lake, a fire equal to his firmest faculties, irresistible by the utmost efforts of corrupted nature, even by all whatsoever is not quickened with the principle of christian life, *Rev.* xx. 6.

SECT.

NOTES.

swiftness by numberless means inconceivable to us: yea, and if he pleases (supposing it even true that the velocity of a body proportions its subtilty) can give them a swiftness many hundred times exceeding that in a ray of light, by giving them a constitution many hundred times more subtile than have the minutest rays of sun or stars. Nor indeed is it at all improbable that this will be the case, since a christian body will be quite pure after it has been sown in the earth, and requickened by the resurrective energies into its native vigour, rareness and liberty; for then shall our bodies shine sublimed in glory, and *renewed in strength*, as says the prophet (*Isa.* xl. 31.) *They shall mount up with wings as eagles, they shall run and not be weary, and they shall walk and not faint*, in the realms of our GOD, regions of unbounded space and light.

*The word κρατος, here is in the syriac testament ܫܘܠܛܢܐ sultna which signifies a monarchical or imperial dignity and power, the same as the turkish word sultan which is derived from the syriac sultna. And thus we find it used in *Rev.* vi. 8. xii. 10. xiii.

SECT. II.

The lake which is the second and most properly named death, will, as our LORD's *last enemy, be ultimately disannull'd.*

ALTHO' the second, emphatical death (whose operations are to be in the lake of fire, the last disgraceful result of rebellion) will destroy horribly all the enemies of our LORD, yet as a destroyer it is itself stiled his enemy. 1 *Cor.* xv. 26. *The last enemy that is to be invalidated is death.* And being our LORD's enemy, that is his last enemy, it must itself likewise lastly cease to be, or as is our text, *be no more :* the force of which terms we shall

---

NOTES.

2, 4, 5, 7, 12. xvii. 12, 13. So that the true meaning of this passage must be as it is exactly in the syriac, ܒܐܘܣܐ, ܠܝܓܢܐ ܐܢܫ, *who holdeth the empire of death*; i. e. reigns as king in those regions, where death is produced whether in the (קבר) grave or in gehenna.

In our countryman *Bede*, so learned in the opinions of the primitive writers, we read concerning devils as follows : *Valde verisimile est in inferno dæmones habituros corpora ignea.* Whereby one would think it to have been the notion of his times either that the wicked angels, being imperishable in gehenna, had their bodies assimulated into the nature of its fire ; or that light, render'd gross by impurity, deforms and thickens into fire ; in which case either way, fire may be deem'd satan's true element, and therefore in a degree supportable and consistent with his life.

shall therefore in the next place investigate by a comparison of simular passages.

This comparison is expedient because the words of our text are directly applied to man only (viz. *Rev.* xxi. 3. *Behold the tabernacle of God with man,* (verse 4.) *and God shall wipe away all tears from* THEIR *eyes)* and conclude, no otherwise than by consequence, a like restitution of all other fallen creatures. The arguing they afford by consequence is as follows :

The death of the lake, which death is the second death (into which all wicked men at the last day of this world, called the great day of judgment, shall be cast)[a] will itself ultimately be no more, or cease to be ;[b] therefore all wicked men shall ultimately be no more (or cease to be) its subjects.

But into the same lake at the same time will all the fallen creatures of GOD, together with fallen

M m

NOTES.

[a] That this lake is the last resort of all wicked men, appears from *Rev.* xx. 13—15. *The sea, and death, and hades delivered up their dead; and whatsoever was not found in the book of life was cast into the lake of fire* (ἔτος ἐϛιν ὁ δεύτερος θάνατος) this (death in the lake) is the second death, *Matt.* xxv. 41. *Depart from me ye cursed into æonian fire, prepared for the devil and his angels.*

[b] That the death in this lake, or the second death, is the death here spoken of as what shall be no more, is certain, because the first or former death, had already for an whole period ceased : see *Rev.* xx. 14, 15. *And death and hades were cast into the lake, &c.* Yea

fallen men, be likewise cast;[c] therefore a like inference is to be presumed for all other fallen creatures that are not men; namely that when the death of the lake shall cease to be, these likewise shall be no longer the subjects of its violence.

That this second death found in the lake, shall be no more, cannot mean less than that its period is determined; and this determination of its period must be for the subsequent new scenes related (*Rev.* xxi. 1—4.) viz. *The new heaven and the new earth, and the new Jerusalem descending from God out of heaven.*

Again, by the following compared texts the final ceasing of this second death, the death in the lake, will be yet farther confirmed.

We have lately mentioned one passage to this effect in 1 *Cor.* xv. 26. *The last enemy that shall be invalidated is death*; so that we shall proceed directly to a like passage which we read in *Hos.* xiii. 14. *O death,*

NOTES.

as this second death had been now for an whole period, ever since the last judgment, the one only death subsisting, unless the death of the lake be intended in the words *There shall be no more death*; these words, tho' issuing from the throne, can mean nothing at all.

[c] The certainty of this will appear from *Matt.* xiii. 41. *The angels shall gather out of his kingdom* (παντα τὰ σκάνδαλα) *all that are offensive, and them* (τες men) *which do iniquity, and shall cast them into the furnace of fire*; which compared with *Matt.* xxv. 41. *Rev.* xx. 11, 15. proves to have been prepared for devils as well as men; and for theirs as well as them.

O *death, I will be thy* (דבר) *dissolution*, or perdition: and this teaches us to understand the word invalidated (καταργῆται) in the foregoing passage, as intending the real perdition and dissolution of, this last enemy of *Christ*, death.

It is true our english translators **render this text** in *Hosea, O death, I will be thy **plagues***; upon which account some have fancied that the words intend that *Christ* will be the plague of the condemned; whereas **the word** (דבר) **dbr** signifies a **pestilence**, or **murrain**, or pining away, as we find (דבר) **dbr** translated in the septuagint by the words (θανατος) death (απολλυμι) **to destroy** (εκτήκω) to melt away.[d] According to which this passage means, O *death, I will be thy dissolution:* that is, by the working efficacy of my **own death** and sacrifice and resurrection, I will **cause both thy** works and thee *to be annihilated,* **to vanish** away, to be no more. **Death**, however, shall be our LORD's **last surviving enemy, because** of the use he has to make **of him in his other enemies.**

Isa. xxv. 7. *And Jehovah will swallow up*—*the veil that is spread over all nations, and will swallow* up

NOTES

[d] So by (θανατος) *Jer.* xxi. 6. *Both man and beast shall die with a* **great** (דבר θανατω) *pestilence.* Ezek. v. 12. *A third* **part of** *thee shall perish with* (דבר θανατω) *wasting* Ezek. vii. 15.) *famine and* (דבר θανατος) *pestilence shall devour.* By (απολλυμι) 2 *Chron.* xxii. 10. *And he destroyed* (דבר απωλεσε) *all the seed of the royal house.* By (εκτήκω) 1 *Sam.* i. 16. *For in* the **multitude of** *my meditations and indignation have I* pined *away* (דבר εκτηκα) *even till now.*

up death in triumphant perpetuity; (בלע המות לנצח) or to a victorious durance; see *Isa.* xxv. 8. lvii. 16. *Amos* viii. 7. *Lam.* v. 20.) *And* (Adni Jehovah or) *the Lord God will wipe away tears from all faces, and the disgrace of his people shall he take away from all the earth.* St. *Paul* renders this passage, 1 *Cor.* xv. 54. *And when this mortal* [i. e. this mortality of both the (ψυχη) soul (compare ver. 43—50. 1 *Cor.* ii. 14. *Rom.* v. 14. viii. 9. *James* iii. 15. *Jude* 19. 1 *Tim.* vi. 16.) and body, even all that is corruptible, or mortal in us] *shall have put on immortality, then shall be brought to pass the saying that is written, Death is swallowed up in victory:* whereby is intended that death, our LORD's last enemy, shall in the end be so abolished, as that no traces of it shall remain, even so much as to evidence its having been, as a thing that is swallowed up or devoured, becomes lost and disappears for ever.

But all this you say proves not my point, because these passages are applicable to the elect only, or those whom no damnation shall affect. So that when I say from *Rev.* xxi. 4, That *there shall be no more death,* you demand, Q. But why must I understand this as spoken of all even the lost as well as the elect? I answer,

A. Because *Christ* is called without restriction (2 *Tim.* i. 10. Ὁ καταργησας του θανατου) *He who invalidates,* or is in the very act of invalidating, *death,*[e] for these words import that he is now

working

N O T E S.

[e] The word καταργεω signifies to invalidate, abolish, render effectless, disannul. So 1 *Cor.* vi. 13. *God shall*

working the utter abolition and annihilation of its power and efficacy. And again, *Hof.* xiii. 14. *O death, I will be thy* (דבר) *confumption*; whereby is denoted that gradual decay, and leffening of death's empire, by delivering his fubjects, one after another, out of his hold and tyranny; as firft the elect in this life, who fhall never tafte death; 2dly. and in an after feafon the *Jews*; 3dly. in a ftill more diftant period the nations, and fo on:

Q. But this is all whim and conjecture; prove that the damned will ever be delivered from their death.

A. The damned are our Lord's enemies; yet they are not called his laft enemies, for death is called

---

NOTES.

invalidate (or difannul, or abolifh) *both the belly and meats*; by putting an end to their prefent offices. (xiii. 8.) *He fhall difannul prophefies, tongues, and knowledge*, or fcience; by caufing them to ceafe, or which is the fame, to be fuperfeded by direct view of the Lord. *Eph.* ii. 15. *He fhall difannul the law* by rendering it ufelefs, &c.

This word is often ufed to anfwer the hebrew word (בלע) to fwallow up. So

The hebrew. בלע	*The greek.* καταργεω
Pf. cvii. 27. *So that all their wifdom* (תתבלע) *is fwallowed up.* ------	1 Cor. ii. 6. *Yet not the wifdom of the princes of this age which is invalidated.*
If. xxv. 7. *He will fwallow up the veil* (ובלע הלוט) *fpread over all nations* - -	2 Cor. iii. 14. *Which veil is abolifhed in Chrift* καταργειται.
Job ii. 3. *Altho' thou movedft me* (לבלעו) *to fwallow him up*, or abolifh him.	Rom. vi. 6. (Ἱ.α καταργηθη) *that he may difannul*, or abolifh the body of fin.

called his laſt enemy. Now all the LORD's enemies *ſhall be ſubordinated unto him* before *death ſhall be invalidated* or diſannulled. But ſuppoſing the damned never to be otherwiſe than the LORD's enemies, how is death diſtinguiſhed from all other enemies by being that enemy who ſhall laſt of all be invalidated or diſannulled? At the time when death ſhall be diſannulled, the LORD will have no other enemy than death to diſannul; but the LORD will have other enemies than death long after his accompliſhment of the number of the elect, therefore the time of death's diſannulling ſhall not be immediately upon the accompliſhing the number of the elect;[f] and therefore neither do the terms *diſannul death* reſpect death's tyranny over the elect, but his tyranny over the damned.

The elect, who are our LORD's firſt enemies to be ſubordinated, ſhall firſt be reſcued and ſafe from the influence of death; afterwards the damned (who are the LORD's next enemies to be ſubordinated) ſhall alſo in the next period be reſcued; and then laſtly death himſelf ſhall be diſannull'd. But death it is ſaid ſhall be diſannulled,

---

NOTES.

[f] That death ſhall not be diſannulled immediately upon the accompliſhment of the number of the elect, is alſo evident, becauſe the damned are ſentenced to death in the lake as their ultimate fate; Rev. xx. 14. *This* (death in the lake) *is the ſecond death*; but this ſentence will not be paſſed till the number of the elect is accompliſhed, and ſecure in thoſe arms from whence no creature can pluck them.

LETTER XIV.   [287]   SECT. II.

led, as the LORD's laſt enemy, i. e. not till (1 *Cor.* xv. 27.) *all* other *things* (i. e. perſons, and conſequently the damned) *ſhall be ſubordinated* to *Chriſt.*

Q. But by death is meant thoſe that are damned, and not any imaginary being to ſucceed them as the final ſubject of reſtitution.

A. Yet ſuppoſing this, the conſequence is ſtill the ſame, for if by death is meant the damned, then are the damned they, who 1 *Cor.* xv. 26. *As our Lord's laſt enemy ſhall be diſannulled.* But theſe (1 *Cor.* xv. 25, 28.) ſhall likewiſe be *ſubordinated*; and thus the word diſannulled and ſubordinated will ſignify the ſame thing.

Their enmity will be diſannulled, and thereby themſelves become ſubordinated; and ſo alſo will they be capable to join party with the univerſal body of whom ſays St. *John* in *Rev.* v. 13. *Every creature which is in heaven, and on earth, and under the earth, and ſuch as are in the ſea, and all that are in them heard I, ſaying, bleſſing, and honour, and glory, and power be unto him that ſits upon the throne, and unto the Lamb to the æons of the æons.*

Whether by death therefore be meant ſatan lord of death, or whether that death which is to be found in the lake, or whether the collected multitude of dead ſouls; ſtill it will follow that, as death ſhall be diſannulled, his efficacy as an enemy *ſhall ceaſe*, or, as the prophet expreſſes it (*Iſa.* xxv. 7.) *Jehovah will ſwallow up in the mountain* (otherwiſe called *Zion* upon which the temple ſtood) *the face of the covering caſt over*

(or

(or the covering film which covers, and so darkens the eyes of) *all people, and the veil that is spread over all nations: he will swallow up death to a prevailing perseverance* (לנצח), i. e. to all perpetuity (compare 1 *Cor.* xv. 25—28. *Heb.* ii. 8.)

So then, until to the words DEATH SHALL BE NO MORE you shall have found some other meaning than that " *death* shall continue to exist no longer;" I think it ought to be a doubt with you that death is immortal, and that the truly dead shall never die.

SECT. III.

Death and misery exists providentially.

FROM what has been above argued, I think we may venture to pronounce as a scripture doctrine, that death, even the æonian death, and which our english bible calls everlasting death, which is our LORD's last enemy, being in the lake of fire, the ultimate resort, and doom of all evil, where satan and his angels will find that perdition, whose distinguishing character is the second or latter death; I say we may pronounce as a bible truth, that this death will hereafter be *invalidated*, or loose its effect; that it will be *dissolved*, or *cease to be*; for that Jehovah will *destroy* it, or make it *to melt away*; will utterly consume it; that it shall be no longer visible either in the soul or body where now it reigns;

reigns; but shall be *absorbed* by the prevailing influence of an incorruptible nature, or as St. *Paul* emphatically expresses it, 2 *Cor.* v. 4. *Mortality* (or all that is mortal both in soul and body) *shall be swallowed up by life.*

Moreover, and as a still farther confirmation of this doctrine (since what is here said of death is also said in the same passage of pain, and sorrow, and crying; we conclude that) *Rev.* xxi. 4. *There shall be no more death, neither sorrow, nor crying, neither shall there be any more pain ; for the former things are passed away ; and* (as we read verse 5.) *he that sat upon the throne, said, behold I make all things new ;* so then both pain, and sorrow, and death, shall finally cease to trouble men any longer.

And thus will be accomplished those words of St. *Paul* (expressed in the aorist participles in order to import thereby indeterminate time, viz.) 2 *Tim.* i. 8—10. *Be thou partaker with me of the afflictions of the gospel, according to the power of God saving us—according to his good purpose and grace, given us in Jesus Christ before his æonian seasons, but now appears by the manifestation of our Saviour Jesus Christ* (χριϛε καταργησαντ@ μεν τον θα-ναξοε) *invalidating* (or who is employed in the work of invalidating) *death* (φωτισαντ@ δε ζωην) *but evidencing* (or who is employed in the work of evidencing) *life and immortality thro' the gospel.*

And in this view of things death, and hell, and pain, and sorrow, appear to be (not as usually looked upon, accidental creatures that stole into

LETTER XIV. [290] SECT. III.

into exiftence by a fort of chance, or fome kind of inadvertency in God, but) the provifionary creatures of God's wifdom, and goodnefs; preordained, by reafon of a fitnefs in their nature, to produce, in the contingent cafualties fore-feen, the great events of his benevolence, and communicative inclinations; which, when they fhall have fully ferved (being creatures of a temporary, and æonian confiftence) they muft vanifh and be no more.

And of this kind are likewife the fufferings of this life, which the apoftle tells us are intended by God as a means to our real good. *Heb.* xii. 6—11. *Whom the Lord loveth he chafteneth, and fcourgeth every fon whom he receiveth; if ye endure chaftening, God dealeth with you as with fons, for what fon is he whom the Lord chafteneth not? But if ye be without chaftening, whereof all are partakers, then are ye baftards, and not fons—and no chaftening for the prefent feems to be joyous but grievous, neverthelefs afterward it yieldeth the peaceable fruits of righteoufnefs unto them that are exercifed thereby.*

It is true, terrible indeed muft be the punifhments of the lake, and as fuch fo far from being agreeable to our Lord, that it, together with all punifhment in general, is ftyled the ftrange work of God; a work which he has an averfion to. *Ifa.* xxviii. 21, 22. *Jehovah fhall rife up as in mount Perazim, he fhall be wrath as in the valley of Gibeon, that he may do his work, his ftrange (* זר *zur,* i. e. odious) *work, and effect his ftrange*
(or

(or עד odious) *operation*—*a consumption* (כלה kle[g]) *determined upon the whole earth.*

And yet, however horrible the sufferings of the lake may prove, and however unequal or different our LORD's dealings with different souls may seem, still (as we have all the reason we can wish to believe, that love and benevolence is at the bottom of all the works of GOD) we may well rest satisfied that he (who must so intimately know every individual that he has made) will be sure to contrive what best suits that specifick difference which, thro' all the creation, distinguishes its individuals from each other; as in constitution, so in the several intermediate ends (but above all in that grand ultimate purpose) which the LORD of all may have in each.

And upon this account we are farther to regard the promises and menaces of GOD (not as the effect of any mere absolute power, decreing what either may or may not be, according to the caprice of an almighty sovereign, but) as pursuant to that nature which he has established in his creatures, and whereby his wisdom produces that grand object of his labours, which, as it was his first purpose in creating, must ever after continue his invariable aim, and be (like his gifts and callings which are without repentance) the steady tendency

---

NOTES.

[g] כלה is usually rendered in the septuagint by the verb ἐξαναλίσκω to consume, ἐξολοθρεύω to abolish utterly, διατελέω to put an end to, κατατρίβω to wear away, σαπρόω to rot away, ἀπολλυμι to destroy.

tendency of both his executive and permissive providence; namely that all men become quickened with the spiritual life of his *Christ*, and that himself may become the all in all creatures.

And in this light we are to understand the passage in 1 *Tim.* iv. 10. *He is the restorer* (or  quickener) *of all men, especially of believers,* yea, and his benevolence extends yet farther, for (*Pf.* cxlv. 9.) *Jehovah is good to all, and his mercy is over all his works.* His mercy however will not prevent his chastising every one according to his wickedness. For (*Luke* xii. 47, 48.) *that servant who knew his Lord's will, and prepared not himself, neither did according to his will, shall be beaten with many stripes: but he that knew not, and did commit things worthy of stripes, shall be beaten with few stripes.*

And yet our LORD's severest dispensations of judgment, are only accessaries to those of his benevolence; and whether he brings evil or good upon us, still it all comes from the bowels of his love, and in his faithful provision for our truest happiness.

LET-

LETTER XV.

In CHRIST *the first fruits, the whole creation is deemed holy before* GOD.

TO ———

SIR,

SECT. I.

ROM. xi. 16.

Now if the first fruits be holy, the lump (or rather mass) *is also holy; and if the root be holy, so are the branches.*

THE terms of this passage which need adjusting are,—1st. The first fruits,—2dly. The mass,—3dly. The word holy.
    I. *The first fruits.*
This term throughout the new testament has only two applications.
    1st. It is applied to *Christ* as the only one, who in the most eminent and strictest propriety may be called the first fruits. So 1 *Cor.* xv. 22, 23. *As in Adam all die, so in Christ shall all be quickened, but every one in his own order, Christ the first fruits, afterward they that are Christ's at his coming.*
2dly.

2dly. It is applied to the 144,000 mentioned in *Rev.* xiv. 4. Thefe however it feems are to be deemed firft fruits only in a fecondary acceptation, upon which account, fays St. *James*, i. 18. (εις το ειναι 'ημας απαρχην τινα των αυτȣ κ]ισματων) *that we fhould be a kind of firft fruits of his creatures:* and therefore I think the (κ]) in the paffage of the Revelations ought to be tranflated *even*, viz. the 144,000 (*Rev.* xiv. 4. απαρχη τω Θεω κ] τω αρνιω) *being the firft fruits unto God*, even *unto the Lamb*.

And according to this acceptation, we may diftinguifh *Chrift* (as the only one who, in ftrict propriety, may be called, the firft fruits unto GOD) from the 144,000, who, in ftrict propriety, are the firft fruits unto *Chrift*.

It being then certain that *Chrift* is truly and properly to be underftood by the firft fruits, we will examine

II. *What is meant by the lump or mafs.*

But as the term mafs is difcoverable in its relative firft fruits, we muft again confider our LORD in two relations, 1ft. As a *Jew*, in which relation the whole body of the *Jews* are the mafs: 2dly. As a fon of *Adam*, or as our fecond *Adam*, in which refpect all mankind is the mafs.

For the mafs is all that remains over and above the firft fruits, not the greater part only, but the whole. And we read agreeably hereto, 1 *Cor.* xi. 3. *The head of every man is Chrift.*

And as all the fruits of *Canaan* belonged to Jehovah in the firft fruits, fo *Chrift* being *the firft fruits unto God* of all the fons of *Adam*, all the fons of *Adam* are claim'd of GOD in his *Chrift* as his property; that all fouls are his, himfelf declares

clares, *Ez.* xviii. 4. *Behold all souls are mine, as the soul of the father, so also the soul of the son is mine, the soul that sinneth it shall die*; that is die by the absolute will of Jehovah; which assurance is again a farther evidence of his sovereign right in the souls of all. And upon this account he is also called, *Rom.* xiv. 9. *The Lord both of the dead and the living*; that is [not that he is the GOD of any thing indeed dead and extinct, since he assures us (*Luke* xx. 38.) *That God is the God of the living, and not of the dead*, but] that all those, whether souls or bodies, which to our eyes appear dead and extinct, are to him visible, and displayed in all their both present realities, and future evolutions; or to use his own words they *all live to him.*

Now as to the latter clause of our text, this is only a short comparison, of the same import with the former, a comparing of the first fruits and its mass with a root and its branches, so that our last term to be inquired into, is

III. *The term holy*, ἅγιος.

And as the first fruits and the root are in our text emphatically styled holy, we shall easily arrive at the meaning of this term, by considering how it relates to *Christ* the first fruits or root; for *Christ* will equal the full import of the term (ἅγιος) holy[h] in the sublimest notion of it; being the perfect excellency and adequate likeness of GOD:

NOTES.

[h] Some people will have it that (ἅγιος) holy in this place signifies, devoted or consecrated; others that it signifies a being like GOD, pure, and without blame,

GOD: or as St. *Paul* describes him, *Heb.* i. 3. *The express image of the father:* agreeably to what also he says of himself (*John* xvi. 9.) *He that hath seen me, hath seen the father also.*

And thus the words explain'd, give us the meaning of our text, viz. *If Christ the first fruits be holy,* i. e. without blemish before the father, being his invariable likeness; *the mass,* that is, 1st. the whole body of the jewish race, and, 2dly. all and every the sons of *Adam* are *also holy,* or regarded as without blame before GOD in his *Christ*. Rom. iii. 23, 24.—iv. 5.—v. 18.

Again, if *Christ* (consider'd as the vine, so *John* xv. 5. *I am the vine, ye are the branches,* or as the olive-tree, or as) *the root be holy, so are the branches,* or all those that are ingrafted into him; insomuch that (*Phil.* iii. 9.) *Winning Christ they are found in him* (as the ingrafted branch in the tree) *not having their own righteousness which is of the law; but that which is thro' the faith of Christ, the righteousness which is of God by faith.* And

---

NOTES.

such as the conscience of all GOD's creatures must approve and admire; in which sense, say they, it is to be understood in *Lev.* xx. 17. *Be ye holy, for I am holy,* (1 Pet. i. 15.) *as he who hath called us is holy, so be ye holy in all manner of conversation.* Eph. i. 4. *He hath chosen us that we should be holy, and without blame before him in love.* Col. i. 22. *To present you holy, unblameable and unreprovable in his sight.* But taken either way, this word holy will be of equal use here, since the holiness of the mass is equally averred, whether it be holy, that is blameless in its first fruits, or holy, that is devoted, or dedicated to GOD in its first fruits.

And thus this text corresponds with the following, 1 *Cor.* xv. 22. *As in Adam all die, so in Christ shall all be* (quickened or) *made alive.* Isa. liii. 11. *He shall see the travail of his soul and be satisfied; by his knowledge shall my righteous servant justify the* many (or multitude), *for he shall bear* (as upon his shoulders) *their iniquities.* Rom. v. 12. *As by one man sin entered into the world, and death by sin; and so death passed upon all men, for all have sinned*—(so far greater things may be said of that free gift which will come thro' *Christ*, the second member of the comparison, to all the race of men; since) v. 15. *If thro' the offence of the one* (τȣ ἑνὸς namely the first *Adam* οἱ πολλοι ἀπο-Θανον) *the* many (that is all his sons) *died; much more the grace of God, and the gift, by the grace* (τȣ ἑνὸς ἀνθρώπȣ) *of the one man Christ* (ἐπερίσσευσε¹)
aboundeth

NOTES.

The true import of the scripture expression (οἱ πολλοι) *the* many, *as opposed to* (ὁ εἷς) *the* one.

¹ΕΠΕΡΙΣΣΕΥΣΕ being the first aorist is indefinite, and may mean either does, or may, or shall abound. The Syriac has it ܢܶܬܝܰܬܰܪ for ܐܶܬܝܰܬܰܪ shall be abundant.

By ἑὶς in the above passage is undoubtedly to be understood *Jesus Christ* singly. But (οἱ πολλοι) the many, has a typical and transferrable meaning. 1st. and in the present state of things it regards all the collected members of *Christ* which form his body the church, of which we read, *Heb.* ii. 13. *Isa.* viii. 18. *Behold I and the children whom Jehovah hath given me are for signs and for wonders, &c.* 2dly. and in a larger sense it regards a future gathering, in a future age, of all mankind. But, 3dly. and last of all, it regards all the universe.

LETTER XV.   [298]   SECT. I.

aboundeth (εις τας πολλας) *unto the many.* 2 Cor. v. 12. *He hath made him who knew no sin, a sin-offering for us, that we might be made the righteousness of God in him.* Rom. x. 4. *Christ is the end of the law for* (unto) *righteousness to every one that believeth;* so that
so

NOTES.

For as the one begotten of GOD is singly the (Απαυγασμα) *effulgence of his father's plenitude;* so are all the creatures destined to be collectively the (Απαυγασμα) effulgence of *Christ*'s plenitude.

GOD is represented by one perfect image of himself his son *Jesus Christ*: but *Christ* will be represented by the many called therefore (οι πολλοι) the many; and who shall be collected together into one, in order to form one full image of himself their alpha or source.

And therefore we read, *Eph.* i. 9, 10. *Having made known unto us the mystery of his own will, according to his own good pleasure, which he has purposed in himself; namely, in the dispensation of the fulness of times to gather together in one all things in Christ, both which are in the heavens, and which are on earth, even in him.* And therefore also is even the church itself called *Christ*. So 1 *Cor.* xii. 12. *As the body is one, and hath many members; and all the members of that one body, being many, are one body; so also is Christ,* i. e. the church.

I say as the logos is the total image of, singly expressing the invisible father; so are the creatures altogether to become the total image of, collectively to express, the divine son, their common æonian visible father.

The creatures as yet being only severally, and as so many individuals, the partial images of *Christ*; *Christ* is as yet without his full image; but the workings of the æonian life in him shall produce him such.

so soon as he believeth, he is holy and righteous in *Christ*, and partakes of his sanctifying nature.

And now the words being understood, we will in the next place view them in the passage where we find them.

SECT. II.

Romans xi. 7, to the end.

Verse

7 *ISRAEL hath not obtained that which he*
8 *seeketh;—As it is written, God hath given*
11 *them the spirit of slumber.—Have they stumbled that they might fall? God forbid; but thro' their fall, salvation is come unto the Gentiles to pro-*
12 *voke them to emulation.—Now if the fall of them be the riches of the world, how much more their fulness—*(or to express it in other terms)
15 *If the casting away of them, be the reconciling of the world, what shall the receiving of them be, but life from the dead?* For (that such receiving of the *Jews* into the favour of God as his people, shall surely happen; is evident from an infallible maxim in the methods of divine
16 love, namely) *if the first fruits be holy, the mass is also holy; and if the root be holy, so are the*
17 *branches. And if some of the branches be broken off, and thou being a wild olive tree, wert grafted in among them, and with them partakest of the root and fatness of the olive tree. Boast not,*
20 *—Because of unbelief they were broken off, and*

O o 2

thou

LETTER XV. [300] SECT. II.
Verse.

thou standest by faith. — Behold therefore the goodness and severity of **God**; towards them which
23 fall, severity; towards thee, goodness:—And they also, if they abide not still in unbelief, shall be grafted in; for God is able to graft them in
24 again. For if thou wert cut out of the olive tree, which is wild by nature, and wert grafted contrary to nature into a good olive tree; how much more shall these, who are the natural branches, be grafted into their own olive tree?
25 For I would not, brethren, that ye should be ignorant of this mystery—that hardness is happened to Israel in part, until the fulness of the Gentiles be
26 come in. And so all Israel shall be restored; as it is written, there shall come out of Sion the deliverer (or restorer) and shall turn away ungodliness
28 from Jacob.—As concerning the gospel,—but as concerning election, they are beloved for the sake of the fathers (to wit. Abraham, Isaac, and Jacob, as is evident from another infallible maxim
29 in the ways of GOD, namely) *The gifts and*
30 *calling of God are without repentance*. For as ye in times past have not believed God, yet have
31 now obtained mercy through their unbelief: even so these also have now not believed, that through
32 your mercy they also may obtain mercy. For God hath shut up altogether in unbelief, that
33 he might have mercy upon all. O the depth!—
36 For out of him (ἐξ αὐτῦ) and through him (δι' αὐτῦ) and unto him (εἰς αὐτὸν) are all things, to whom be glory æonian.

Give me leave to comment upon a few points in the above passage.

R E-

REFLECTIONS ON

Verses ?, 25, 26.

When we compare thefe, may we not prefume that the curfes of GOD, fuch as a fpirit of flumber, and delufion (2 *Thef.* ii. 11.) have their commiffion from him, not becaufe he delights in the mifery of his creatures, but becaufe he has fome remoter work of mercy to produce out of them? *Pfalm* cxix. 71.

Verses 29, 26.

A pofthumous reftitution of loft fouls prefumed from the above paffage of fcripture.

Since *the gifts and calling of God are without repentance* (or fuch as GOD repenteth not the having beftowed) how can we doubt but our faviour's work of reftoration muft be carried on in our pofthumous ftate of being? For we muft either fuppofe thefe gifts and callings of GOD without effect; or elfe we muft fuppofe that thro' all the changes and fortunes of an after life, our good æonian king and fovereign will purfue what he has begun in every foul, till he has finifhed his purpofe of grace in him, and accomplifhed the end of his calling and election.

His prefent concern is more immediately with his firft fruits; thefe he now (*Heb.* xiii. 20.) *thro' the blood of the æonian covenant* (καταρτιζει) *redintegrates—working in them what is pleafing* to him; and the efficacy of the fame blood will in due time be applied to the mafs alfo; for the value of his blood may be prefumed to furvive thro' the utmoft ages of his æonian government cry-

ing

ing, in behalf of those for whom it was shed (i. e. for all, see *Col.* i. 20. *Eph.* ii. 13.) till it be satisfied.

And nothing can satisfy the blood of *Jesus* so crying, till all (even the worst of sinners, even those who, *Heb.* x. 29. *Have accounted the blood of the covenant wherewith they were sanctified, an unholy thing*) be redeem'd by it: since even *their unbelief* (Rom. iii. 3.) *shall not make the faith of God of none effect*, or pervert the blessings of *that blood which speaketh better things than that of Abel.*

That the use and efficacy of this blood must needs extend itself beyond the limits of this life is, one would think, clear enough from (ver. 26.) *and so all Israel shall be restored.* Because that the present circumstances of the far greater part of *Israel* are miserable, cannot but be concluded from those frequent terrible denounciations against them in the gospel; such as, *How can ye escape the judgment of gehenna? Therefore ye shall receive the greater damnation, &c.* For unless this blood were of efficacy in an æonian, and after life, there could be no reserves of mercy still awaiting the *Israelites*; *when* hereafter *the fulness of the Gentiles are come in, and when the times of refreshing shall return*, and the sound of the great trumpet shall publish their year of jubilee: (*Lev.* xxv. 9—55. *Is.* xxvii. 13. 1 *Cor.* xv. 52.) when (*Luke* iv. 18.) *he shall heal the broken hearted, and preach deliverance to the captives, and recovering of sight to the blind, and set at liberty them that are bruised, and preach the acceptable year of the Lord*; in a manner of which what is already done is only a shadow.

Re-

Remarkably to this purpose is what we read in *Heb.* vii. 25. *He is able* (σώζειν) *to restore* (εἰς τὸ παντελὲς)[k] *to all perpetuity them that come unto God by him, being* (πάντοτε ζῶν) *forever living to make intercession for them*; for if our saviour were able to restore a man only during the date of his natural life in this world, it would not be true that this his restoring power would continue (εἰς τὸ παντελὲς) to all perpetuity; because that susceptibility of restitution which is at an end, and must cease with the

---

NOTES.

[k] In the syriac testament we find this passage thus, ܡܚܝܐ ܠܐܝܠܝܢ ܕܡܬܩܪܒܝܢ ܠܐܠܗܐ *and he is able to vivify æonianly those who approach unto God by him.*

The expression (εἰς τὸ παντελὲς) to all perpetuity, i. e. thro' all the ages, is by most people applied not to *Christ*'s power of restoring but, to the state of the restored; in which acceptation this text will mean, that *Christ* is able to restore his saints by a restoration to continue to all perpetuity; a sense which supposes some superlative preference of restoration, or two distinct restorations, the one of which was to last to all perpetuity, the other not. Whereas by the christian doctrine we are taught that every true believer is as such in a state of restoration, which is to last to all perpetuity; as will hereafter appear from many scripture passages.

Yea indeed he is so already; for (*John* v. 24.) *He that believeth hath æonian life—is passed from death unto life*; so 1 Cor. vi. 9—11. *Know ye not that the unrighteous shall not inherit the kingdom of God—and such were some of you, but ye are washed, but ye are sanctified, but ye are justified in the name of the Lord Jesus, and by the*

the term of a man's natural life, cannot be said to last (εἰς τὸ παντελές) to all perpetuity.

Christ as a sin-offering is related to every sinner, 2 *Cor.* v. 18. *He made him a sin-offering for us;* and in this relation the restitution of sinners is his proper part and office; that office which gives him his gospel name and character, *Jesus* or *Restorer.* 1 *Tim.* i. 15. *Christ Jesus came into the world to restore sinners.* Luke xix. 10. *The son of man is come to seek and to restore that which was lost.*

And

NOTES.

spirit of our God: compare also, 1 *Pet.* i. 23. *Tit.* iii. 5. *John* iii. 3.—xiii. 8. 1 *John* iii. 2. But every true believer being already restored to life, washed, sanctified, justified, &c. his after restitution, his restoration (εἰς τὸ παντελές) to all perpetuity must be chimerical.

The clause therefore (εἰς τὸ παντελές) in this passage must presume upon our LORD's being as able to restore men in an after state of existence, as in this life. *Christ ever liveth,* why? By making intercession *to restore*; whom? Those who are already restored? Surely not; whom then? *Them* (ὑπὲρ αὐτῶν) in contradistinction to us (ἡμῶν v. 26.) i. e. them the unrestored, and *who hereafter shall come unto him,* as distinguished from us that are already come to him, and are already restored.

But if *Christ* ever liveth to restore by his intercession the unrestored; it follows, that those who after this life, during his æonian reign, shall need restoring, may well expect the benefit of this his perpetual office.

The translators of the english bible render this phrase to the uttermost, viz. *He is able to restore to the uttermost,* but the context [*he continues æonianly—has a*

LETTER XV.   [305]   SECT. II.

And therefore fits he now in the throne of his father: as says St. *Peter*, *Acts* v. 31. *God has exalted him to his own right-hand a prince and a restorer, to give repentance to Israel, and forgiveness of sins.*

Also in prospect of this his covenanting character *(Rom.* v. 8*) whilst we were yet sinners* (i. e.

P p   mere

NOTES.

priesthood that passeth not away—wherefore also, *he is able to restore* (εις το παντελες) *being for ever alive*] plainly infers his æonian power of restoring (εις το παντελες; from the æonian continuance of his life and priesthood, and so takes (παντελες) in the signification of time. The words are literally in the syriac, or original as follows. *He is able to quicken* (ܡܫܟܚ) *æonianly those who approach unto God by him* (ܒܐܝܕܗ ܠܐܝܠܝܢ ܕܩܪܒܝܢ ܠܐܠܗܐ ܒܐܝܕܗ) ²for ¹he liveth ³thro' all⁴ time ⁴and offers ⁵prayers ⁶instead of them. And besides this, the rendering to restore to the uttermost (since all who are restored must be restored to the uttermost) is also chargeable with the same absurdity, as the acceptation above objected to: whereas the supposition that our LORD is as able to restore lost souls in another life as in this, is by no means repugnant either to common sense, or our experience of our redeemer. Whilst upon earth he claim'd the pretogative of forgiving sins absolutely and without reserve. And since no power of his can have been diminished, either by his rising again from the dead, or by his ascension into heaven, we can make no doubt but his power to forgive sins (i. e. virtually to restore) must still continue as prevailing, as absolute, as depending upon his free choice as ever; and thus the one grand question is always, IF HE WILL.

mere finners, finners only, without any affinity to him, and not as now his kindred, his own flesh and blood, his brethren; I fay whilft we were thus aliens, prompted by his native benevolence) *Chrift died for us* (*John* iii. 5) *was manifefted to take away our fins*, much more then, being now conftituted our fin-offering in a famenefs of nature with ourfelves, fhall we be reclaimed, or fome way or other brought home to himfelf.

Wherefore that a man is a finner in any degree, fituation or place, becomes fo far from being a proof that he fhall be excluded forever the poffibility of reftoration, that it even prefumes the certainty of his reftitution.

Alfo it is with a view to this ftate of things that our Lord is called the æonian prieft. *Pf.* cx. 4. *Heb.* vii. 21. *The Lord fware and will not repent, thou art a prieft* (εις τον αιωνα) *æonianly,* or thro' the ages, *after the order of Melchifedeck.*

Is *Chrift* a prieft æonianly? then is he fo not only till, but after the refurrection of the faints, *i. e.* during the continuance (and fo the faints enjoyment) of the æonian life; and feeing the office of a prieft is (*Heb.* v. 1.) *to offer gifts and facrifice for fin, Chrift's* interceffion, which amounts to this, muft likewife then be a part of his office; that is, after his faints are transformed into his own likenefs, and fo enjoy with him æonian life, he will intercede for them who are condemned to the æonian punifhment.

For when our Lord's faints have no longer any fins for which he is to make his prieftly offering, propitiation, and interceffion; for whom is his prieftly interceffion made æonianly, but for

thofe

those whose sins are æonianly remembered, and æonianly punished?

The sins of the saints will (at least and by the acknowledgment of all) after the day of judgment is passed, be altogether *cleansed, purged, abundantly pardoned, no more to be found by those that seek after them, no more to be remembered, covered,* that is buried, *cast into the depths of the sea, blotted out,* annihilated, *done away,* &c.

And since *(Heb.* x. 18.) *where remission of sins is, there is no more offering for sin,* that intercession which *Christ* shall make æonianly (or thro' all time, and after his saints are glorified) must be for them that shall then not be saints, and therefore not as yet glorified: in like manner as his intercession had before been for those sinners who shall then be his saints, *the first fruits unto God in Christ. Christ* is related to sinners as their sin-offering and priest æonianly, and therefore may sinners have æonianly an access to God by him.

Let us not then presume in our own wisdom, without the word of God, and only because our lexicons teach us that the word αιωνιος may be derived from αει ων,[1] to limit the efficacy of the incomparable blood of *Jesus,* begotten of the Holy Ghost; but be assured that it (1 *Pet.* i. 18, 19.) is still

---

NOTES.

[1] It is vulgarly objected against us that (αιων) aion, is derived from (αει ων) aei on, *ever being,* and therefore it must signify eternity; but this is no consequence at all; as most evidently appears from the scripture use of this word above shewn in many instances; besides that, as most greek primitive words come from the hebrew language, αιων may as well come from אח

still fresh in its salutary vigor, a grateful object before the eyes of GOD, ever pleading, ever ready in the heavenly sanctuary^m for the sprinkling

---

NOTES.

where, or (since adverbs and prepositions of place signify also time in all ancient languages) *when*, or *how long*? And thus αει and αιων may well denote time indefinite the same as does עלם—See p. 5th and 6th.

^m *Heb.* ix. 2—8. *There was a tabernacle made* (consisting of two parts) *the first wherein was the candlestick, and the table, and the shew-bread; which* (first part) *is called the holy. And after* (behind) *the second veil* (was the other or second part of) *the tabernacle, which is called the holy of holies; which had the golden censer, and the ark of the covenant overlaid with gold; wherein was the gold pot which had the manna, and Aaron's rod that budded, and the tables of the covenant, and over it the cherubims of glory shadowing the mercy seat.*————*Now the priests went always* (i. e. every day) *into the first tabernacle accomplishing divine service; but into the second* (tabernacle called the holiest) *went the high-priest only, once every year, not without blood, which he offered for himself, and for the errors of the people; the Holy Ghost this signifying, that the way into the holiest was not yet made manifest, while as the first tabernacle was yet standing.*————*But Christ* (ver. 12.) *by his own blood entered in once into the holiest* (or holy of holies) *having obtained æonian redemption for us*; or that redemption by virtue of which we escape the æonian damnation. (Heb. xiii. 11.) But very remarkable is that passage, Rev. xix. 13. *And he was cloathed with a vesture dipt in blood*; compar'd with *Isa.* lxiii. 2. *Wherefore art thou red in thine apparel, and thy garments like him that treadeth the vine fat? I have trodden the vine press alone, and of the people there was none with me; yea, and I will tread them* (i. e. my enemies) *in my anger, and trample them, &c.*

ling[n] the redeemed of his beloved son εἰς τὸν αἰῶνα, æonianly.

SECT. III.

Posthumous restitution farther presumed from other parts of the scripture passage above cited.

REFLECTIONS on verse 20.

BY *unbelief they were broken off* (τῇ ἀπιςίᾳ, see ἀπιςία in *Mark* ix. 24. xvi. 14. *Rom.* iv. 20. I *Tim.* i. 13.)

Unbelief (as we have already observed) is represented by the scriptures as the greatest sin. Says

---

NOTES.

[n] *Christ* is æonianly a priest, and his blood is æonianly in the sanctuary, to effect the restoration of them that come unto GOD by him. So *Heb.* xii. 22, 24. *But ye are come unto mount Sion, and unto the city of the living God, the heavenly Jerusalem—and to the blood of sprinkling, which speaketh better* (things) *than that of Abel* [καὶ αἵματι ῥαντισμοῦ κρεῖττονα λαλοῦντι παρὰ τὸν (i. e. αἷμα τοῦ) Ἄβελ]. 1 *Pet.* i. 2. *Elect—through sanctification of the spirit unto obedience, and the sprinkling of the blood of Jesus Christ.* Even this incorruptible blood, by which, after his resurrection *Christ* entered the heavenly sanctuary; and which is called his *own* blood, in opposition to that whereby (*Heb.* ix. 12.) the earthly high priest was wont annually to enter the earthly sanctuary, and which is here styled the blood of *others*, ver. 7, 25.

See *Bengelius* in *Heb.* xii. 24. *Christus per sanguinem proprium in sanctuarium introivit; (non modo post effusum sanguinem, & vi effusionis, neque cum sanguine in corpus resumpto, sed* PER *sanguinem) ergo seperatim a corpore*

Says the Psalmist, (lxxviii. 21.) *Anger came up against Israel because they believed not God, and trusted not in his salvation.* Says our LORD to the *Jews, John* viii. 14. *If ye believe not that I am he, ye shall die in your sins.* And again, *John* xvi. 9. *He*, the spirit, *will reprove the world of sin, because they believe not on me.* John iii. 36. *He that believeth not the son shall not see life, but the wrath of God abideth on him.* Ver. 18. *He is condemned already because he has not believed on the name* (i. e. efficacy) *of the only begotten son of God.* Heb. iii. 11. *So I sware in wrath that they should not enter into my rest.* Ver. 18. *And to whom sware he that they should not enter into his rest but unto them that believed*

NOTES.

sanguimen proprium hic ipse sacerdos in sanctuarium intulit.—Ipso introitus tempore sejunctum Christus *a corpore sanguinem habebat: esxangue corpus erat; non tamen exanime, sed vivum*———

Sanguis Jesu *seorsum ab ipsius corpore consideratur* Heb. xiii. 11, 12, 20.—*ut* Dorscheus (a *Lutheran*) in-quit, " 1um *Quia hoc requirit typi ratio. Sanguis enim in*
" *V fœdere, ut extravasatus & effusus, considerabatur,*
" *& hoc ipso adumbrabat profusionem & effusionem san-*
" *guinis in N fœdere futuram.* 2do *Quia hoc fœderis di-*
" *vini indoles requirit, quæ postulat* αματεκχυσιαν. 3um
" *Quia in hac ratione sanguinis exercetur actus obedientiæ*
" *satisfactoriæ* DEO *pro peccacis debitæ, &c.*" So Solomon Deylinguis, (a *Lutheran*) " Christus *in cœlos e-*
" *vectus, sedensq; ad dexteram* DEI *res nostras commendat*
" DEO, *& sanguinem pro nobis effusum ac vulnera osten-*
" *tat patri.*" Iterum Rappoltum (a *Lutheran*) *laudans:* " *Patri suo* (inquit) *sanguinem suum,* ut λυτρον
" *& pretium redemptionis pro nobis offert, ejusq; effusione*
" *justitiæ divinæ satisfactum esse docet.*"

lieved not? Ver. 12. *Take heed therefore least there be in any of you an evil heart of unbelief, in departing from the living God.* For (Heb. xi. 6.) *without faith it is impossible to please God.*

Yea and the refusing to believe in *Jesus* as our redeemer, is worse than the sin of *Sodom*, as appears from the woes our LORD denounces upon *Corazin*, *Bethsaida*, and *Capernaum*. Mat. x. 15. xi. 20.—24. of whom he says, *It shall be more tolerable for the land of Sodom in the day of judgment, than for them.*° And the reason perhaps is that given in 1 *John* v. 10—13. *He that believeth not the son* (τω ὑιω) *hath made him* (i. e. GOD) *a liar,* (ψεύσην) *because he believeth not the witness that God gave of his son. And this is the witness that God hath given unto us eternal life, and this life is in his son, he that hath the son hath life, and he that hath not the son hath not life. These things have I written unto you, that ye may know that, believing in the name of the son of God, ye have æonian life.*

And may we not alas from hence conclude, that the unbelieving *Christian* has still more dreadful shocks to suffer, a greater damnation to fear then even the unbelieving *Jews*; since no unbelief can be more highly aggravated than ours; no

ingra-

NOTES.

° *Bengelius* remarks as follows upon *Mat.* x. 15. *Pejus est non credere evangelio quam Sodomitas imitari.* Ch. xi. 22, 24. *Urbs illa in die judicii graviorem pænam subibit quam terra* Sodomorum *aut pridem pertulit aut in judicio habebit. Si perbrevis repulsa tam graviter punitur, quid fiet iis qui morosius resistunt.*

ingratitude enhanced to our degree of it. *Heb. xii. 25. See that ye refuse not him that speaketh, for if they escaped not who refused* (Moses) *him that spake on earth; much more shall not we escape, if we turn away from him that speaks from heaven.* Heb. ii. 3.   Matt. xxi. 44.—vii. 22.

REFLECTIONS ON ver. 31, 32.

From these we infer as follows:

If unbelief be emphatically the sin of the world, then *Christ* died for unbelievers;[p] then is unbelief atoned for before GOD; then have unbelievers their claim in *Christ*; then are they the object and con-

---

NOTES.

[p] That *Christ* died for the sin of the world, we are assured, *John* i. 29. *Behold the Lamb of God that taketh away the sin* (ὁ αιρων την ἁμαρτιαν, that beareth the sin) *of the world.* So 1 *John* ii. 2. *He is the propitiation for our sins, and not for ours only, but also for the sins of the whole world.* And because the sin for which *Christ* died, is called by an *hebraism* (*Rom.* vi. 6.) *the body of sin* (that is, sin emphatick) it has been the enquiry of some what sin is in its root or first principle, but without success; and probably its real nature will remain a secret unknown to us in this life. However we all see it outwardly in its fruits of falsehood, unrighteousness, and cruelty; and feel it inwardly in a spirit of unbelief and aversion to GOD.

The natural man has within him an enmity against GOD, therefore he hates to converse with him; and because of his forsaking GOD, GOD gives him up to follow his own lusts, which he pursuing as his chiefest good, yields forth all the outward works of wickedness.

concern of his restoring power; and then is such their restoration a part of the business of his æonian kingdom, or of his æonianly-priestly office.

Thus we account for two things.

1st. The future restoration of the unbelieving *Jews*, as promised ver. 20. to whom GOD has hitherto given *a spirit of slumber, eyes that they should not see, and ears that they should not hear:* and whom (ver. 15.) *he has cast away to the* prior *reconciling of the world.* (Ver. 31.) They have hitherto disbelieved, that thro' a previous mercy shewn to the *Gentiles, they* (the Israel) *also may obtain mercy.*

And 2dly, we thus account for the apostle's reasoning (ver. 32) viz. *God hath shut up all together in unbelief, that he might have mercy upon all.* For the having mercy is here the end proposed of GOD; but that faith or believing is the direct mean to this end the mercy of GOD, every part of scripture so loudly proclaims that we need no quotation for its proof: and yet we here learn that not belief only, but also unbelief is a mean provided by GOD to this same end his mercy; since *he who shuts and no man opens, who opens and no man shuts, has shut up all* (πάντας) *together in unbelief; that so he might have mercy upon all;* even all in general and every one in particular, since the two characters believer and unbeliever, leave no individual unexcepted.

And thus the severity or wrath of GOD, in its severest act of shutting up in unbelief, thro' his provident contrivance, becomes a means directing to the same end with love itself; a paradox hidden far from the reach of our ken, in the depths of divine wisdom,

And may we not here venture to suppose that mercy the end must be somehow naturally, and by a sort of divine physics, comprehended in severity the means? And if so, love and severity in GOD, tho' opposites in our estimation, not only tend to one and the same end, but have that end somehow involved in themselves the means; that so the great work of divine love may be practicable in earth, and hell, and heaven; thro' time in all its forms and periods; and succeed gradually and unforced in the connection, tendency and relation of a concordant mean and end.

REFLECTIONS ON ver. 36.

Out of him, and through him, and unto him are all things.

The apostacy of the creatures from GOD has indeed produced a vast variety of wonders, which otherwise would not have been in the creation. It is true again that these cannot be numbered among the things created; because, as hath been elsewhere shewn, they are the mere formalities and phantoms of nature in its deformity; or, if I may so speak, the appearances of nature unnatured; of nature shatter'd by the violencies and clashings of her own energies; so as that nothing remains longer visible in her, but the monstruous issues of defect and disorder, the productions of power separate from love.

However, notwithstanding this, tho' nature, as seen thus in her vizard and contrarities, be no creature of GOD's; yet that her fallen circumstances were foreseen and permitted by him, and with a view to his purposes, cannot be denied; since he

upon

upon whom the being and nature of every thing present and future depends, muſt not only intimately know, but exert a controlling power thro' all and every the concern of his creatures. He muſt have foreſeen what events their powers might produce in what circumſtances; he muſt have ſuperintended tho' inviſibly, thro' the whole train of cauſes and effects; and have alſo prefixed, at leaſt in many caſes (tho' in ſome exalted and perfect way, very different from our manner of knowing things, and conſiſtent with the creatures full enjoyment of his liberty of willing) what ſhould, and what ſhould not determine the freedom of his creature's choice.

This conſidered we cannot but preſume that all thoſe events we call evil, however they may ſeem to croſs, impede or oppoſe the will of God in his creatures, do in reality all conſpire (for generals conſiſt of particulars) to produce one compact ſyſtem, ſome prodigious plan of magnificent love becoming ſo great and ſo provident an author. For as ſays the poet,

" All nature is but art unknown to thee,
" And chance direction which thou can'ſt not ſee.'

Neither does this at all infer a fatality; ſince God can accompliſh the ſame end by means infinitely variable, ſince he can bring forth all and every event he pleaſes, conformably with the creature's full enjoyment of his liberty and free choice.

REFLECTIONS ON ver. 28, 32.

If all *Iſrael* be *beloved of God for the father's ſake*, can we preſume leſs of all mankind for our ſaviour's ſake? Are we not all the price of his blood?

and is not his blood declared the full ransom for all? Neither is it any where said that few or less than all shall receive the benefit of it; how then can it be thought that he who forbids (*Lev.* xix. 13. *Deut.* xxiv. 14, 15) that the wages of the hireling be detained beyond the end of the day, shall deny his son the due purchase of his blood beyond its due season?

Were ten righteous persons acceptable to GOD as a ransom for *Sodom?* how much more shall the blood of the son of GOD be a ransom for all? even for all the darling product of his creative power? For *Christ* is a public person not only as an *Israelite,* but also as man: all creatures have a joint interest in *Christ*; and the life of us all was offered up in *Christ* sacrificed (*Luke* xix. 10. 1 *John* iv. 14. *Rom.* v. 6. *Acts* iii. 21. *Eph.* i. 10. *Col.* i. 20) from hence also is the apostle's reasoning (2 *Cor.* v. 14) *If one* (that is *Christ*) *died for all, then were all dead,* i. e. dead virtually in *Christ* so dying for them. But *Christ* died for all men, (see 1 *John* ii. 2. 1 *Tim.* ii. 6. 1 *Cor.* xv. 22, 49. *Rom.* v. 6. *John* i. 29.) therefore are all men dead virtually in *Christ*.

Since then it is promised that thro' the seed of *Abraham* all the families of the earth shall be blessed; where is the absurdity in presuming that in the seed of *Adam* all the inhabitants of other worlds shall find their restorer? As *Abraham* in the term father represents the whole body of the faithful; and as *Adam* in like character represents, or is the head of all men; thus *Christ* in a far higher manner, being only figured by *Abraham* and *Adam,* is the father, head and representative

LETTER XV.   [317]   SECT. III.

of all spirits, as has been already shewn. But this being so, why may not the fate of them all follow him, as the fate of all the sons of *Adam* followed *Adam?*

We read accordingly, *Rom.* xiv. 9, 11. *To this end Christ both died and rose and revived, that he might be the Lord of both the dead and the living—for it is written, as I live, saith the Lord, every knee shall bow to me, and every tongue shall confess to God.* Ep. i. 9. *Having made known to us the mystery of his will, according to his good pleasure, which he hath purposed in himself; namely, in the dispensation of the fulness of times to gather together in one all things* [but (τὰ πάντα) all things importing the same as (πάντας τοὺς ἐχθροὺς) all intellectual beings as yet *Christ*'s enemies (compare *Col.* i. 20. *Phil.* ii. 10, 11.) this text teaches us that all *Christ*'s enemies shall be collected together] *in Christ, both which are in heaven, and which are on earth, even in him.*

And thus as in the first *Adam* fallen, all his sons became likewise fallen; so in the second *Adam,* dying a sacrifice for sin, all spirits, and so all the sons of the second *Adam,* became likewise dead and *sacrificed,* i. e. virtually, and so as to render them in *Christ* acceptable before GOD.

I say acceptable before GOD, because this they may be by imputation, **even while** at the same time they are sinners in regard to themselves (*Rom.* iv. 4—11.—v. 8—19. *Is.* xl. 2.—liii. 6. *Numb.* xxiii. 21. *John* xv. 3.—xiii. 10. *Zech.* iii. 3, 4.) not yet justified in the redeemer's eyes; but obnoxious to the penalties of his government, and (as many of them as *Christ* shall repudiate) to the discipline and death of the æonian punishment.

LETTER XVI.

A passage in the Epistle to the Hebrews *considered, and the fallen angels compared with fallen men.*

TO ———

SIR,

SECT. I.

I HAVE now to offer only one passage more, respecting my present subject, in proof of an universal restitution; which is as follows:

Hebrews ii. 8, 9.

Now we see not yet all things put under him, but we see Jesus, crowned (i. e. rewarded) *for the suffering of death, with glory and honour, lowered for a little while* (βραχυ τι, see *Acts* v. 34) *lower than the angels. that so he might taste death for all, excepting God.*

The expressions of this passage are so very decisive that we should need no other in proof of our point, if the terms of it were not disputed. But as it is usually read in our editions of the new

testa-

testament, it amounts to no higher a proof than many other texts which I pass by without notice; neither would this have been here insisted on by me, but because of the opinion I have of the genuineness of its reading as above given.

The difference of its readings is as follows,

ὅπως {χωρισ (a) / χαριτι (b)} Θεu ὑπερ παντ☉ γευσηται θανατu

which is in english, *that so he might taste death for all* {*Excepting God* (a) / *By the grace of God* (b)}

The reading (a) is found in many of our most ancient and best manuscripts; and so is likewise the reading (b). The reading (b) is also found in most of the editions of the greek testament; that is, it has been preferred by its editors.

However, little regard is to be had to such preference, because the most part of our greek testaments are printed from the *Complutensian* (i. e. cardinal *Ximenes's*) or *Erasmus's*, or *Beza's* editions of it. For *Colinæus's* and *Aldus's* editions are mostly the same with *Erasmus's*; and *Stephen's* edition is mostly one with *Ximenes's* in the beginning, and with *Erasmus's* afterwards. But these, especially *Erasmus's* and *Beza's* editions, being by them collected from different manuscripts, each following that reading which best suited his own judgment, have most deservedly lost their authority, since the publishing the various readings of the several manuscripts themselves.

So that the present text or vulgar readings of our testaments, tho' still continued according to the old editions, have now no authority at all against the authentic reading of good ancient copies;

copies; but we prefer to the text or vulgar reading, any different readings which we find in good and authentic manuscripts correcting it.

This being premised it will follow, that in the passage under our consideration, the question is, not whether χωρὶς or χάριτι be found in the editor's text or vulgar reading, but which of these two readings can claim the best authority from ancient and good manuscripts.

And here I must refer you for what has been said against, and in favour of these two readings χωρὶς and χάριτι, to *Bengelius's Various Readings,* or to his *Gnomon,* where you will find this difference of readings largely discuss'd.

Bengelius was a *Lutheran,* I shall therefore give you the opinions also of *Grotius* of the *Arminian* party, of *Beza* of the *Calvinist's* party, and of *Cornelius a Lapide,* a *Jesuit,* yet a very learned and good man, of the *Roman* party, concerning this important text. But this in my notes for your more leisure consideration.[q]

This

NOTES.

[q] *Grotius* comments upon this text as follows: *Pro* χάριτι Θεῦ *quidam codices jam olim habuere* χωρὶσ Θεῦ; *quod sequuntur nonnulli codices syriaci, &* Ambrosius *de fide ad Gratianum: unde apparet non debere hujus scripturæ mutatæ culpam in* Nestorianos *conjici.* (For *Ambrose* flourished about the year 370, the *Nestorians* about the year 440.) *Videntur qui id mutarunt, id sensisse, christum etiam pro angelis mortuum, atque adeo pro omnibus extra solum Deum.*

Beza, a *Calvinist,* as follows; *Græcus scholiastes admonet* Nestorianos *olim hunc locum ausos fuisse depravare,*

This passage tells us that *Christ was crowned with glory and honour* (חסד) *for* (or because of) *his suffering death*, which suits with what we are taught, *Phil.* ii. 8, 9. *Heb.* ii. 7, 9. *And he was lower'd, for a little* **while***, lower than the angels* (ὅπως) *that so he* **might taste death** (ὑπὲρ παντὸς) *for all*, that is, not for **man only**, but *for all*; which the following verse **tells us were** *made by him, and for his service*, and the foregoing verse tells us were *to be subordinated unto him.*

NOTES.

& pro χάριτι Θεȣ scribere χωρὶς Θεȣ. *Et tamen hanc scripturam secuti sunt* & *Syrus interpres,* & Ambrosius *de fide ad* Gratianum, *lib.* 2. *cap.* 4, *atque adeo* Vigilius *contra* Eutychen.

Cornelius a Lapide, a very learned and ingenious Jesuit, as follows; *Nota,* pro χωρισ Θεȣ *i. e. Deo excepto* Theodoret, Theophylact, Œcumenius *legunt* χαριτ. Θεȣ, *id est gratia Dei; adduntque, ita corruptum esse hunc locum a* Nestorianis, *hinc enim illi probant in Christo duas fuisse personas,* & *Deum ab homine fuisse seperatum: verum ante* Nestorium, Ambrosius, *lib. de fide, cap.* 4. *legit quoque* τὸ *sine* Deo; *sicque explicat;* " *Christus pro omnibus sine* Deo, *id est excepto Deo, mortem gustavit,* q. d. *Christus pro omnibus omnino, etiam angelis non autem pro Deo ipso* (Deum *enim excipio*) *mortuus est.* And then he subjoins, *Non quasi angelos redemerit Christus, sed quod angelos hominibus reconciliarit, eorumq; lætitiam* & *gloriam auxerit, dum sedes eorum ex quibus collapsi erant dæmones, per homines restauravit* & *replevit."*— Which last words shew that he favours the reading, notwithstanding he would willingly avoid our conclusions from it.

Had *Christ* tasted death for man only, this had been here expressed by (ὑπερ παντων ανθρωπων) for all men. Such being the well known style of the scripture greek [see the note (ʸ) in page 224.] and not by the singular neutral adjective (παντος) as of one, as comprehending the whole creation in one singular term.

And therefore we find the ingenius *Origen* arguing on this text as follows: "Whether, says he, (see the passage at large)ʳ we read that text in *Heb.* ii. 9. *He tasted death for all, God excepted,* or (as some copies have it) he tasted death for all by the grace of God, the sense still amounts to the same; since to die for all excepting God, is to die for more than man, even all intelligent beings; and to die for all by the grace of God, is to die for all, God excepted." But

---

NOTES.

ʳ *Hic igitur qui tot nominibus nuncupatur (scilicet* Jesus*) advocatus, propitiatio, propitiatorium, compassus infirmitatibus nostris, tentatus in omnibus humanis juxta similitudinem sine peccato, magnus est pontifex non modo pro hominibus, sed tiam pro omni, quod rationis est capax, hostiam semel oblatum semetipsum offerens. Sine Deo enim* VEL PER GRATIAM DEI (UT IN QUIBUSDAM EXEMPLARIBUS *Epistolæ ad* Hebræos *ponitur*) PRO OMNI *gustavit mortem: sive sine Deo pro omni gustavit mortem, non solum pro hominibus mortuus est, verum etiam pro cæteris rationis capacibus; sive per gratiam Dei pro omni gustavit mortem; pro omnibus sine Deo mortuus est; per gratiam namque Dei pro omni gustavit mortem.* See *Origen*'s comment upon St. *John*'s gospel, *tom.* 2^{dus.} *de variis nominibus filii Dei,* under the name *Justitia*.

But may we not presume from these words of *Origen* that χωρις must have been the most usual reading in the testaments of *Origen's* time; and that this reading must have been refused by the copists after his time, thro' fear of countenancing the supposed errors of this able father; since he says that (viz. in his time) χαριτι was read only IN QUIBUSDAM EXEMPLARIBUS, in some copies, and consequently that χωρις was found in most of the copies at that time extant? Moreover, *Origen* being catechist at *Alexandria* in the year 203, and the epistle to the *Hebrews* being wrote about the year 63; in saying thus of χωρις, we affirm that for 140 years after the writing this epistle (χωρις Θεȣ) *excepting God*, was the reading of most general credit and countenance.

But the two different readings of this text we find in the syriac as well as in the greek copies. So in the *Paris* and *Tremellius's* edition we read ܣܛܪ ܡܢ (excepting, or setting aside) inserted before ܐܠܗܐ (GOD). And I think every reasonable man will allow it to be from hence highly probable that the notion of universal redemption must have run thro' the whole church in very early times, dividing them into two persuasions, altho' without amounting to a controversy; the one insisting that GOD died for all universally, and so abiding by the text; the other insisting that he died not for all, and accordingly supposing that the greek ω was written for an α, and the σ for τι; or that the syriac words ܣܛܪ ܡܢ had crept from the margin into the text: a supposition much more natural than that χωρις could have been wrote for χαριτι, or that ܠܐ ܣܛܪ not found in the text, might have been added to it. For what prefumtuous hand would have ventured to add two fuch momentous words to an apoftolic copy?

In fhort an alteration in the words of this text moft certainly has been; and that in our beft and moft authentic copies; as early as the time of *Origen :* infomuch that no copy can now reafonably be preferred as a ftandard in this inftance; or as an authority whereby we may afcertain the true tranfcript of the original apoftolic writing. And in this cafe I think the boldeft and moft daring alteration (which the changing of χαριτι into χωρις or the adding of ܠܐ ܣܛܪ to the text moft certainly is) muft be the leaft probable.

But if after due confideration your thoughts on this matter will not be my thoughts on it, I muft content myfelf to argue critically upon the term παντος in our text, by St. *Paul's* way of arguing upon the term σπερματι in *Gal.* iii. 16. *Now to Abraham and his feed were the promifes made; he faith not and to feeds, as of many, but as of one, and to thy feed which is Chrift.* After which reafoning, a comment on our paffage will run thus. Now it was ὑπερ παντος for all that *Chrift* tafted death; he fays not for all men, as of men only, but as of one, *he tafted death for all*, which all is the entire univerfe.

So then fince we believe GOD to be the father of the univerfe, becaufe he is called in fcripture (ὁ πατηρ παντων) *the father of all*, i. e. of all angels as well as men: a like expreffion ought to teach

us

us for whom *Christ* died; namely (ὑπερ παντων) *for all*, that is, for all angels as well as men; and consequently the angels as well as men shall become regenerated by that seed which is *Christ*.

Thus *Tertullian* argues upon another occasion, *Quid est omnis? nisi omnis generis, omnis ordinis, omnis conditionis, omnis dignitatis,* **omnis ætatis**; *siquidem* **omne totum est**, *& integrum, & nulla sui parte defectum.* De Virg. Veland. p. 222. "What "means all, but all of whatever kind, order, "condition, dignity, age? seeing that all is the "whole and integer without defect of any part "of it."

SECT. II.

The condition of fallen man paralleled with that of fallen spirits.

THE difference between men and angels seems to be merely fleshly. Man is an angel in the flesh, and when his flesh is laid in the dust, he will be again what he was before, an angel: as says the learned *Cornelius a Lapide, Distrahe homini corpus; & homo erit angelus,* "exempt a man of his body, and he will be an "angel." And so the ingenious Dr. *Young*,

"Angels are men in lighter habit clad,
"High o'er celestial mountains wing'd in flight;
"And men are angels, loaded for an hour,
"Who wade this miry vale, and climb with pain,
"And slipp'ry step, the bottom of the steep.
"Angels their failings, mortals have their praise."

Agree-

Agreeably with what *Justin Martyr* also says of them, την λογικον ψυχην—ἧς ὁμοουσιους ειναι φαμεν τας τε αγίελους ϗ τας δαιμονας—" the rational soul—whose
" essential likenesses we say are both angels and
" demons." *Quest. & respons ad Græcos.*

And these accounts of the human soul answer to all the experiences we have of it. We find among mankind many who are certainly not less wicked than are many among the evil spirits; and such our LORD scruples not to call devils, as in the case of *Judas, John* vi. 70. *Have not I chosen twelve, and one of you is a devil?* But whence can this wickedness in human nature arise? from the body? certainly not; there can be no more wickedness in an human body, than in the body of any other animal. Our wickedness therefore must be in the soul; the soul must be the principle of our pride and fierceness and sensuality and envy and malice and other malignant passions: and for this reason it is that the soul needs to be saved; that in case of non-renewal it will be lost; that in order to be the spouse of *Christ* it must be requickened; that if it be not requickened by the spirit of *Christ* it must die; (*Ezek.* xviii. 4, 20.) and that its death is prefigured by the death of its tabernacle the body.

But you say GOD made man upright, that is in his own image,[1] and this image is the soul. By no means:

NOTES.

[1] We acknowledge that GOD made man upright; but, that he made him more upright than he now makes every christian man, we deny. The uprightness

means. As the chriſtian ſoul **when** quickened by the ſpirit of *Jeſus Chriſt* becomes the image of *Jeſus Chriſt*; juſt ſo the ſoul of *Adam*, being quickened when he was made man by the ſpirit of the Logos, became the image of the Logos.ˈ And this quickening ſpirit of the Logos being loſt in

Adam

NOTES.

of man is in his will or deſire; but the will and deſire of every chriſtian is as upright as was the will and deſire of *Adam* before he fell. We grant that chriſtian men are ſuffered (and doubtleſs for good reaſons) to feel the weakneſſes and propenſities and other evils of fallen nature, which *Adam* felt not. But that the will and deſire, or (as it is otherwiſe called) the heart of chriſtian men is leſs upright than was the will or deſire or heart of *Adam*, we will not grant 'till we have it well proved; but will rather believe with St. *John*, who aſſures us (1 *John* iii. 9) *whoſoever is begotten of God doth not commit ſin; for his ſeed abideth in him, and he cannot ſin, becauſe he is begotten of God.* 1 John v. 4. *Whoſoever is begotten of God overcometh the world, and this is the victory that overcometh the world, even our faith* (ver. 18) *whoſoever is begotten of God ſinneth not; but he that is begotten of God keepeth himſelf, and the wicked one toucheth him not.*

And as to the infirmities of fallen nature, it is ſo far from being either our diſgrace or real harm to feel theſe, that it is our honour and glory to ſupport them; in that by ſo ſupporting them we bear that croſs which *Chriſt* our ſecond *Adam* has dignified, and given a bleſſing to.

ˈ The image of GOD not as yet made fleſh is the Logos, and in or after his image or likeneſs, was *Adam* made; this ſame glorious image of GOD in

Adam before his children were born, his children had no title at all to it in him, but were born mere (ψυχικοι) foul men, and muft continue fo 'till regenerated by *Chrift* the fecond *Adam*, who begets them πνευματικοι fpiritual men, or new creatures in himfelf.

It

NOTES.

carnate is *Jefus Chrift*, and in or after his image are *Chriftians* regenerated. Let us then only learn what makes the fons of *Adam* the images of *Jefus Chrift*; and we at once learn what made *Adam* the image of the Logos.

Now the fons of *Adam* become the images of *Jefus Chrift* by partaking of the fpirit of *Jefus Chrift*. This will follow from the grand character of *Chriftians*, viz. that they (1 *Cor.* iii. 16) *are the temple of God, in whom the fpirit of God dwelleth:* and from their being diftinguifhed *Chriftians* by the very having of this fpirit; fo *Rom.* viii. 9. *If any man have not the fpirit of Chrift, he is none of his.* Becaufe that fpirit which dwelleth in *Chriftians* and quickeneth them, is alfo the fpirit that transformeth them into the image of GOD. Compare 1 *Cor.* xv. 49, with ver 45.

The transforming energy of the fpirit of *Chrift* dwelling in *Chriftians* we learn from numberlefs paffages of the new teftament, let the following fuffice. *Rom.* xii. 2. *Be not conform'd to this æon, but be ye transformed by the renewing of your mind.* Tranfformed (*Rom.* viii. 29) *by being conformed into the image of his fon*, by being (2 *Cor.* iii. 18) *metamorphofed into the fame image* with him, *by the Lord the fpirit*, even the fpirit called (2 *Cor.* iv. 11) ἡ ζωη τε Ιησε) *the life of Jefus*, namely the Holy Ghoft: for

It is the spirit of GOD that makes the creature like his GOD. As the blessed angels are like GOD by partaking of his spirit; so is man also made like him by partaking of the same spirit.

Yea the blessed angels do many of them participate of the divine nature in so intimate and extraordinary a degree and manner, that they are even called

---

NOTES.

the word ζωη in scripture always denotes that life which is by the spirit of GOD.

Christ is called (*Col.* iii. 4. ἡ ζωη ἡμων) *our life*; and this ἡ ζωη is that spirit in *Christ* of which it is said, (*Rom.* viii. 11) *If the spirit of him that raised up Jesus from the dead dwelleth in you; he that raised up Christ from the dead, will also quicken your mortal bodies by his spirit that dwelleth in you.* And its quickening efficacy is to transform into the image of *Christ*; a work to be begun in this life; so *Col.* iii. 10. *Put on the new man which is renewed in knowledge after the image of him that created him:* and to be perfected when *Christ* shall appear. So *Phil.* iii. 21. *who shall transfigure our vile body that it may be fashioned like unto his glorious body, according to the mighty energy whereby he is able even to subordinate all things to himself.* At which time (the object seen by the eye corresponding with the seed hidden in the heart) we shall be raised into the true likeness of *Christ*. 1 *John* iii. 2. *We shall be like him for we shall see him as he is.*

As therefore (ἡ ζωη) the divine life of *Jesus*, by being imparted to his children transforms them into his image; so the same (ζωη) divine life by being imparted to *Adam* before he fell, transformed him into the image of the Logos, and he became (what *Christians* now become in the inner man) the image of him who is the image of GOD.

called by the divine name itself (אלהים) Gods. So *Pſalm* lxxxii. 1. *God* (אלהים) *ſtanding in the congregation* (אל) *a chief, ſhall judge in the midſt of the Gods* (בקרב אלהים ישפט) that is, amidſt theſe great angels, the offspring of the Logos, appearing like himſelf in brightneſs and dignity, and compoſing an aſſembly of which himſelf is chief.

Again, *Pſ.* cxxxvi. 2. *Do homage unto the God of the Gods* (לאלהי האלהים) *for his mercy is to the ages.* Pſ. xcvii. 7. *Worſhip ye him all gods* (כל אלהים) this laſt verſe St. *Paul* expounds, *Heb.* i. 6. *Let all the angels of God worſhip him.* Again, propheſying of the humiliation of *Chriſt*, ſays the pſalmiſt, *Pſ.* viii. 6. (ותחסרהו מעט מאלהים) *Thou ſhalt leſſen him a little lower than the Gods*; that is, thou ſhalt make him a man, in which condition he will be lower or inferior to the angels, his ſons of glory.

And laſtly to extinguiſh all doubt concerning this obſervation, we have our LORD's own words, *John* x. 34. *Is it not written in your law, I ſaid ye are Gods,* (θεοι εςε) whereby he refers us to *Pſ.* lxxxii. 6. *I ſaid ye are gods, and all of you children of the moſt high.* אני אמרתי אלהים אתם ובני עליון כלכם

How exalted a being then is man, *O ſi ſua nôrint!* But ſince our GOD out of his communicative bounty has made us ſo ſublime a creature; how vile, how inexpreſſibly baſe is our ingratitude to him, or ſhame of him and his! and how juſtly will his threatning be verified. *Mark* viii. 38. *Whoever ſhall be aſhamed of me and of my words in this adulterous and ſinful generation, of him alſo ſhall the ſon of man be aſhamed when he cometh in the glory of his father with the holy angels.* What

What then has man to boast himself in? nothing but his LORD: 'till we are regenerated by the spirit of our LORD, we are poor wretched creatures, the children of the devil like other wicked spirits, and differing from them only by being incarnate.

Are they enemies of GOD? so are we; are they deliberate in their rebellion against GOD? so are we; were we created the offspring of GOD? so were they; are we miserable; so are they.

Yea and when we hear them call *Christ the holy one of God* (*Mark* i. 24) one might almost believe that they have some intrinsic love of holiness in them; some instinct of virtue inclining them to goodness and rendering virtue approvable to them like what we observe in ourselves: and that consequently some gracious principle must be already at work within, inclining them to some great end, worthy the GOD of all goodness, as well as founder of all nature.

There is also a like sameness in the divine treatment of them and us. We are alike in banishment from the divine presence, and yet we continue alike prisoners at large, man in this his sublunary world, the fallen angels in their lower etherial regions, see *Luke* viii. 31. *Eph.* ii. 2. For altho' their doom be the abyss, yet they are not very closely confined there.

Again we have alike our liberties to make use of; alike our occasions to employ that liberty: we have alike our remorse and fears and evil propensities; as well as our desires and consciousness of GOD and his *Christ*. *Mark* i. 24. For evil angels now know as well as we their subjection to *Christ*, and that they are fallen from GOD; and that he is a being holy and good and exorable. *Mat.* viii. 31.

Again, like us they roam about *thro' dry places seeking rest and finding none.* Like us they tremble in the woful expectation of their abolished kingdom, and of their torments amidst its ruins. And as man doubts not but he must one day see this world in flames, so are the unhappy angels also assured that all their heavenly habitations, and systems of worlds, now their dear, tho' deform'd, mansions shall withdraw their glory, and fall from their spheres, with themselves in vast combustion. *James* ii. 19.

SECT. III.

HAVING ventured so far on this strange and mortifying subject, the likeness of men to fallen angels; I may as well venture yet a little farther; and by the light which to me seems given from that remarkable passage in *Isaiah* xxiv. compared with other texts, proceed to shew that the same likeness of circumstances which attends evil men and evil spirits in this present time, will also follow them thro' succeeding ages, as far as we have any account of either them or ourselves, even to the last day of this world.

This passage I think ought to be translated as follows:

Isaiah xxiv. 21. 'And it shall be ² in ³ 'that ⁴ day, ⁵ *Jehovah* ⁶ shall visit ⁷ upon the heavenly ⁸ host, ⁹ in the heavens; ¹⁰ and upon ¹¹ the chiefs ¹² of the earth
(or

LETTER XVI.   [333]   SECT. III.

(or the earthly chiefs) ¹³upon ¹⁴*the earth*; ¹⁵*for they shall be gathered together*, ¹⁷*a captive* ¹⁶*society*, ¹⁸*in* ¹⁹*the pit* (or abyss, prepared somewhere in the realms aerial, as a prison for wicked spirits) ²⁰*and shall be shut up* ²¹*in* ²²*the prison* (namely the place of custody for wicked men, somewhere in the regions of (שאול) seul) ²³*and after many* ²⁴*days* ²⁵*they shall be visited.*

¹יהיה ²ביום ³ההוא ⁴יפקד ⁵יהוה ⁶על ⁷צבא ⁸המרום
⁹במרום (') ¹⁰ועל ¹¹מלכי ¹²האדמה ¹³על ¹⁴האדמה (')
¹⁵ואספו ¹⁶אספה ¹⁷אסיר ¹⁸על ¹⁹בור ²⁰וסגרו ²¹על ²²מסגר
²³ומרב ²⁴ימים ²⁵יפקדו.

So

NOTES.

ᵘ במרום in excelso loco, *i. e.* in the aerial heavens. So verse 18th we read (ארבות ממרום) the cataracts from heaven shall be opened; for wicked spirits have their residence in the heavens or aerial regions; as we read *Eph.* vi. 12.—ii. 2. And are therefore here called heavenly hosts in contradistinction to men who are earthly inhabitants.

ʷ ואספו *colligenter autem*, the preter being put for the future. And ו has the same force here as δὲ among the *Greeks*: for the prisoners are supposed to have been already collected for many days; the mighty men in the (מסגר) *clausurâ*, the angels in the pit; and in the day here spoken of, each shall be visited in their respective places, viz. the angels in their aerial aboads; the men become imbodied, for this visitation, on the earth.

This passage is I think literally translated in latin as follows: *Et erit in die illa visitabit Jehovah super exercitum excelsum* (vel *qui excellens est*) *in excelso, & super reges humi* (vel *terrestres*) *super humo. Colligentur autem collectio vincta in puteo & claudentur in clausura & a ... : : Dierum visitabuntur.*

LETTER XVI.   [334]   SECT. III.

So that as there is (מסגר or φυλακῆ see 1 Pet. iii. 19) a prison for wicked men after this life, there is also (בור) a pit or abyss for wicked spirits, where each will be reserved (Acts i. 25. ἐν τῷ τόπῳ τῷ ἰδίῳ) *in his own proper place*, 'till the day of visitation.ˣ

Last of all there is (Rev. xx. 15. ἁ λίμνη τε πυρος) *a lake of fire*, the ultimate doom of those that shall still be found incorrigible; and here again the wicked

---

NOTES.

ˣ By the word *visiting* the scriptures do not always intend *punishing*; for (Gen. xxi. 1. 1 Sam. ii. 21.) *The Lord visited Sarah, and Hannah, by giving them sons;* and (Gen. l. 24.) *Joseph* promises his brethren that *the Lord will visit them by bringing them out of Egypt;* and *David* prays (Ps. cvi. 4.) *O visit me with thy salvation.* So *Jer.* xv. 15.—xxiii. 2, &c.

Moreover that by the word visit in this passage is to be understood deliverance, appears from the syriac bible, in which we read it as follows:

[Syriac text]

¹ *In that very* ²*day* ³*Jehovah* ⁴*shall visit* ⁵*upon* ⁶*the sublime powers* ⁷*in the sublimity* (or sublime place) ⁸*and upon* ⁹*the earthly kings* ¹⁰*in the earth;* ¹²*and assemblies* ¹¹*shall assemble* ¹³*over the* ¹⁴*bound* ¹⁵*of the pit;* and ¹⁶*shall consider* ¹⁷*over* ¹⁸*the imprisoned.* ¹⁹*And after a multitude* ²⁰*of days* ²¹*they shall be delivered* (enlarged, freed).

As therefore both men and devils shall have alike their prison, their visitation, their judgment; so shall they alike *after a multitude of days* 𝔟𝔢 𝔇𝔢𝔩𝔦𝔟𝔢𝔯𝔢𝔡.

wicked both of men and angels will be treated as brethren; for both will be cast together into this lake; and become consorts in one common misery (*Mat.* xxv. 41.) *Depart from me ye cursed* (εις το πυρ το αιωνιον) *into the æonian fire prepared for the devil and his angels.*

And as it is farther remarkable concerning satan, that before he is consigned to the terrors of

---

NOTES.

But delivery, you say, does not always imply a restitution: I grant it: yet many may be restored at this time of deliverance. And as to others (who still proving incorrigible, shall be consigned to the lake,) one may conjecture consistently with their restitution many ways. For instance,

When satan's hatred of GOD is heightened to so exquisite a degree of it, as that he should hate even his own existence; dissolution may be at last his choice, and that wherein his desires may concenter. And in this situation his disease may possibly be advanced and ripen'd to its true, intended and necessary crisis or point of change.

Desire has a most effective power in it; and will, when become intense and determined, procure any thing. And working now in earnest after dissolution, why may it not acquire it? Especially since such desire seems to accord with the real purpose of GOD; as we gather from that maxim (1 *Cor.* xv. 36. *John* xii. 24. *That which thou sowest is not quickened except it die.*

But *Christ* is so the resurrection of the dead as that nothing can die beyond the reach of his quickening energy. 1 *Sam.* ii. 6. *John* v. 21. 1 *Tim.* vi. 13. 2 *Cor.* v. 14. And in his bestowing hereof, two things are observable, 1st. That he bestows it freely. 2dly. That he bestows it by a regeneration or begetting anew.

According to these reflections the lake of fire may be considered as a feed-foil to the ultimately reprobated.

the lake, his previous doom shall be the (בור i. e. gr. αβυσσ⊙ or) pit;[y] the same thing we also learn of the beast or anti-christ who will be a man; that he shall first have been a prisoner in the abyss;[z] (*Rev.* xi. 7. — xvii. 8.) before he shall have his consignment to the perdition of the lake.

And since the parallel between wicked men and wicked spirits answers thro' all the accounts we have of the LORD's dispensation towards them; what can we conclude, but that one indefatigable love pursues both, and that hades and the abyss, and the lake of fire, exist all by the providence of GOD; and for this divine reason; namely, because GOD will be *all in all*; will have all intellectual creatures collected into himself churchwise; will *quicken all men*; will *restore all things*; will be the head of all; will have *every knee bow to him*, and *every tongue confess him, to the glory of God the father.* L E T-

---

NOTES.

[y] At the next appearance of our LORD, satan will be only cast into the abyss (where is even now his proper place, *Jude* 6.) and confined for 1000 years, that is during the time of the millenium; and at the end of the 1000 years, being released, yet continuing still to exert himself as before against GOD, and to gather the armies of Gog and Magog against the beloved city, he shall thereupon be cast into the lake. See *Rev.* xx. 1, 2, 3, 7, 8, 9, 10.

[z] We are told expresly of the beast or anti-christ, tho' not of the false prophet, whence he is; namely, (*Rev.* xi. 7.) *That he ascendeth out of the abyss* (*Rev.* xvii. 8.) *that he was and is not* (ϰϳ παρεςαι) *and shall be again*; in that he shall ascend out of the abyss, and afterward *go into perdition*, i. e. (*Rev.* xix. 20.) *into the lake.*

LETTER XVII.

The scripture passage objected against us, from 2 Cor. iv. 17. *considered.*

TO ———

SIR,

THO' I have several other scripture passages to exhibit in proof of our point in hand, the final restitution of all things, I shall not discuss them at present because they properly belong to my second part: in which I purpose to give you my sentiments concerning the human soul; and so shall reserve them for this work.

My only remaining business therefore, with regard to this first part, will be to answer the farther objections you make against the temporality of *Christ*'s kingdom, or, which is the same, against the temporal exposition of the word (αιωνι©) æonian.

LETTER XVII.   [338]   SECT. I.

Your first, and I think most specious objection, is that passage in 2 *Cor.* iv. 17. *For the momentary lightness* (το γαρ παραυτικα ελαφρον) *of our tribulation worketh for us a weight of glory* (καθ υπερβολην εις υπερβολην αιωνιον); *exceedingly to an excess* (i. e. far more than) *eternal; while we look not at the things seen, but at the things not seen; for the things seen are* (προσκαιρα) *of short continuance; but the things not seen are* (æonian or αιωνια) *for ages.*

You urge that as καιρος and αιων are here so directly opposed to each other, the latter must import somewhat very far exceeding the former; but the former intends temporal life, therefore the latter must intend eternal life; a conclusion by no means just, since an hour and an age will bear a very strong antithesis, tho' an age be far short of some 1000 ages, and yet still this infinitely short of eternity.

One of our moral writers, in his well-meaning Zeal, has illustrated eternity as follows; suppose says he a mountain of sand, of an enormous size; and that once only in every 1000 years, an eagle were sent to lessen this mountain by carrying away from it one single grain of sand; what a prodigious tract of time would it require thus to remove this whole mountain, and before every single grain of this vast body should be carried off: but, adds he, the time required for all this work 10,000 times repeated bears still no proportion with eternity.

Possibly the æonian kingdom of *Christ* may endure a longer time than would be required thus to remove this gentleman's mountain of sand; but that

LETTER XVII. SECT. I.

that the damn'd shall be in torments, during all the periods of *Christ*'s reign as mediator, I cannot believe, having no revelation to found such belief upon.

I cannot but perswade myself that the universal hymn (of which we read in *Rev.* v.) will be heard shouting thro' the universe from every creature to the glory of *Jesus*, long before the said dilatory eagle would perform his task.

I think too that if this gentleman's mountain of sand were much less than he supposes it, the removal of it at the rate of one single grain every 1000 years, would occupy time enough to form a contrast strong as one could wish, between the continuance of our momentary life, and that comprehensive age which we mean by (ὁ αἰὼν τῶν αἰώνων) the great inclusive age, the age of the ages; without having recourse to eternity, of which we can form no conception.

I have already given you in my fourth letter a computation of the æonian periods, which as it advances one step further than *Bengelius's*, does vastly exceed his.[a] But let us here follow him and take

---

NOTES.

[a] BENGELIUS computes only two articles, viz. αἰὼν αἰώνων, and αἰῶνες αἰώνων, as follows:

Αἰὼν, an æon or age being = $2222\frac{2}{9}$ years.

IId. Article,—Αἰὼν αἰώνων, an age of ages, that is, $2222\frac{2}{9} \times 2222\frac{2}{9}$ is = 4938271.605 years: in which product the rank of the figures (4—3—2—1—0, beginning with the first and skipping over every alternate figure; thus again alternately, 9—8—7—6—5) is pretty remarkable; but much more so that of the

take the lowest of his numbers for the duration of the æonian kingdom, viz. 4938271.605, &c. (=one æon of æons) and divide this by $7777\frac{7}{9}$, (the age of the present world according to this author) and the quotient 634.920 will shew that the æonian kingdom cannot be supposed to last less than about 635 times as long as this world's duration, supposing this to consist of $7777\frac{7}{9}$ years. It may indeed, and probably will, be of a prodigiously greater continuance, but it must be owned that this shorter space, a continuance of about five millions of years, will afford time enough to illustrate a sufficient difference between an æonian and a temporary duration; the usual short transit of human life, and an age by angelic computation:

NOTES.

figures in the product of the IId. Article, viz. Αιωνες αιωνων, i. e. two æons of æons (two being the lowest plural) which is double the former article: for an æon being $2222\frac{2}{9}$ and two of these making $4444\frac{4}{9}$, $4444\frac{4}{9} \times 2222\frac{2}{9} = 9876543\frac{17}{81} = 9876543.21$: the order of the figures here is so conspicuous that it needs not to be pointed out.

Thus far *Bengelius* proceeds in the calculation: and if you will go on farther, and multiply an æon of æons by an æon of æons, as in p. 73 (where is given you the lowest number which such calculation will admit of) the amount will be prodigious.

But *Bengelius* supposes, Οι αιωνες ΤΩΝ αιωνων (i. e. αιων αιωνων an æon of æons rendered plural severally by the addition of the plural articles) to be the scripture expression for endless eternity, and in this case all computation is superfluous; since no product of finite numbers can equal an infinite duration.

tion: and consequently that these words of the apostle will not want sense, when they tell us, that **the** momentary shortness of human life will be incomparably exceeded even by the finite continuance of the æonian life.

Indeed that St. *Paul* intends no such thing as eternity in this passage, seems implied in the hebraism in the former clause of it; namely καθ' ὑπερβολὴν εἰς ὑπερβολὴν αἰώνιον) which, *Beza* says, means, *æternitas ipsâ æternitate magis æterna*, eternity more eternal than is eternity itself. For that, as say others also, the reduplicated word ὑπερβολὴ imports excess, and enhances the word (αἰώνιος) *æonian* beyond its natural force;[b] as does the word

NOTES.

The emphatical expressions are certainly to be understood of an extremely greater number of years than the simple one without the articles: but *how much* greater a number, it must be confessed the articles do not determine; possibly they may import some mystical number, concerning which all that GOD intends at present to reveal is, that it is immensely great; and this one should the rather think because the computation of them made in p. 73 is the shortest, or first number, seven of which must go to the constituting one week of these emphatical numbers.

[b] Καθ' ὑπερβολὴν εἰς ὑπερβολὴν *secundum excellentiam ad excellentiam, id est excellenter excellens*, ait Theoph. *sive mire, & supra modum celsum — Sic enim hebræi per geminationem vocis significant vehementiam & superlativum; ut* מאד מאד *mad mad, id est valde valde, hoc est supra modum, & plurimum: q. d. incomparabiliter majus*, incomparably greater than, or exceedingly more than. See *Cornelius* a *Lapide in locum*.

word (מאד) *valde* among the *Hebrews,* which it is well known forms, by repeating, the highest superlative in that language.

And thus the force of this passage is—*The momentary lightness of our tribulation, worketh for us a glory even more than æonian,* [a glory not only (εις τας αιωνας των αιωνων) to the æons of the æons, but yet still farther to (2 *Tim.* i. 10. ζωην κ; αφθαρσιαν) that life that is even incorruptibility] *wherefore over-looking the things visible, we fix our eyes upon the things invisible, since the things seen are but during this short life; whilst the things not seen are* (καθ' ὑπερβολην εις ὑπερβολην,) *hyperpolically hyperbolically* (i. e. exceeding, beyond hyperbole, that immeasurable season of bliss, the life) *æonian;* where all our sufferings shall be recompensed, and ourselves regaled with abundant consolations.

According to this import of the words, this text of scripture, whilst it directs us seemingly but to the promises, gives us at the same time a hint that shall dilate our thoughts, enlarge our prospect, and extend our expectations still beyond them; a practice very observable in numberless passages where the Jews have their promises given them of their earthly *Canaan.*

And so this observation will admit of the following argument, viz. If (as by the apostle's use of the above hebraism) the word æonian be in his opinion too scanty and confined to express the full continuance of the promised glory; if this promised glory, tho' it be æonian, is yet still more than so; then the word æonian must import less than a real eternity; because what is really eternal

cannot

cannot be exceeded or surmounted by any additional continuance; because an eternal continuance cannot be estimated as less durable than the promised glory and consolations purposed of GOD for us.

But without regard to this **phrase** there may well be, and most probably there is, **a great natural difference between** what **we call time as it subsists in the æonian, and** time as it subsists in our transitory life.

We conceive time in this life as consisting **of** successive momentary points, a perpetual alteration; possibly in the æonian life it may prove to be of a more stable nature; **yea** those transitory **points** of which it now seems to consist, may then appear to have been a succession of generating and corrupting parts, like the **succession of** animals and plants.

All the things in this world bear **the characters of** death, but *in the land of the living* it may be otherwise; then our time may possibly bear the visible characters of eternity; **and afford us a** typical representation of that simultaneous manner of existing, of which we now conceive only **by** its opposite, mutability or transitoriness.

But however this be, certain it is that this text can prove nothing against us; because to say that the word ($\pi\rho o\varsigma\kappa\alpha\iota\rho o\varsigma$ proskairos) *temporal,* is here set in opposition to the word ($\alpha\iota\omega\nu\iota o\varsigma$) *æonian,* therefore the word æonian must **signify** eternal; is to argue at as **high a rate of inconsequence as** to say the prophet *Daniel* compares the eternal continuance of the **throne of the** Messiah to the
duration

duration of the sun and moon; therefore the sun and moon must endure to eternity.

For as the sun and moon may last to an exceeding length of time, which yet shall be short of eternity; so may the word æonian import an exceeding length of time, which yet is short of eternity.

And as the reign of an earthly monarch (to which the reign of *Christ* is opposed) may be incomparably exceeded by the duration of the sun and moon, without such sun and moon's enduring eternally; so may a temporal life (to which the æonian is opposed) be incomparably exceeded by the duration of the æonian life, without such æonian life's enduring eternally.

If I was to say that the aerial height of the pic of *Teneriffe* is incomparably exceeded by that of the orb of *Saturn*'s revolution, therefore the orb of *Saturn*'s revolution is the utmost stretch of all altitude; would this be an inference? Can we conceive no possible medium between the very sublimest extremity of all altitude, and the summit of the pic of *Teneriffe*? And may not the orb of *Saturn*'s revolution be incomparably higher from us than the summit of the pic of *Teneriffe*; and yet at the same time as incomparably short of the very sublimest extremity of all altitude?

Thus honeycombs seem palaces to bees;
And mites imagine all the world a cheese.

LETTER XVIII.

The scripture passage objected against us, from 1 Tim. i. 17. *considered.*

TO ―――

SIR,

SECT. I.

CHRIST *the king of the æons.*

YOUR second objection to our doctrine is, That the word æonian must import eternal, because used as one of the characters or attributes of GOD. So 1 Tim. i. 17. *And to the king eternal, &c.* But here again the fault is in the translation. In the original we read not *king eternal*, but king of the æons or ages; so in the syriac (ܠܥܠܡ; &c. ܗܘ ܠܥܠܡܐ) *to the king therefore of the ages, or æons, who, &c.* as also we read in the greek (τῷ δε βασιλει των αιωνων) *to the king of the æons, immortal, invisible, the only God be glory, &c.* So also we read in Ps. x. 16. 'Jehovah 'is king 'of the æons, 'and beyond (יהוה מלך עולם ועד). xlv. 7. Thy throne, O God, is (עולם ועד) *æonian, and beyond.* And in Rom. xvi. 26. *According to the re-*

velation of the mystery kept secret (χρονοις αιωνιοις) *for æonian seasons; but now is manifest by the prophetic scriptures, according to the commandment of the æonian God* (αιωνιε Θεȣ) ; *made known to all the Gentiles for the obedience of the faith.*

To these texts therefore the answer is obvious; namely, that *Christ* is the very GOD of the æons, and may be called the æonian GOD and King, not on account of his eternal nature, but because he shall reign æonianly, as universal king; and because he is most strictly speaking the GOD of the æonian life; and father of that spirit which is to enjoy the æonian life.[e] And also because the

---

NOTES.

[e] Our LORD is called in *Is.* ix. 6. *æonian father*, in *Heb.* xii. 9. *father of spirits,* in 1 *Cor.* xv. 45, 47. *the second man; the last Adam, a quickening spirit,* [for the first *Adam* was intended to be only (*Rom.* v. 14.) *a figure of him that was to come,* namely of the second father.]

Now by being begotten of this second *Adam*, we receive a spirit by which we enter the æonian life, otherwise called, the kingdom of GOD. See *John* iii. 5, 6. *James* i. 18. 1 *Pet.* i. 23. *John* i. 13.

Without this regenerating spirit *(John* iii. 3.) *we cannot see the kingdom of God;* for it becomes visible only by a being born into it, or made alive in *Christ.* Therefore says St. *John* (1 *John* v. 11, 12.) *God hath given us æonian life, and this life is in his son, he that hath the son of God hath life, and he that hath not the son of God hath not life.*

So then in order to enjoy the æonian life, we must be the begotten spiritual sons of the æonian spirit, or spirit of *Christ*; for he only (ver. 20.) *is true God and æonian life.* *Rom.* viii. 9.

the ages or æons are all under his government and direction.

It has been already observed that the æons or ages are portions of duration, working together the will of GOD temporally; that an age may be considered as that in time which our solar system is in space; that as space may comprehend an unknown number of these systems, so time may comprehend an unknown number of ages.

That therefore we read in scripture of a variety of ages, of ages past, and of ages to come, and of this age, and of the next age, and of after ages; but of all these *Christ* is charactered as the king, ruling and conducting them according to his good pleasure.

Against this acceptation of our present text it is objected, that not *Christ* but satan is called (2 *Cor.* iv. 4.) *the god of this age*, being (*Eph.* ii. 2.) *the spirit that now worketh in the children of unbelief*; seeing that (1 *John* v. 19. Ὁ κοσμῷ ὅλος εν τω πονηρω κειται) *the whole world lieth in the wicked one* (or *devil*)[a] Yea that this is spoken in contradistinction to a future age; when (*Isa.* xi. 9.) *the earth shall be full of the knowledge of the Lord, as the*

NOTES.

[a] There can be no doubt but ὁ πονηρὸς denotes the devil; so it is evidently to be taken in the verse preceding the passage here cited; and ought likewise to be so rendered in the following; therefore is εν τω πονηρω in this verse set in contrast to εν τω αληθινω, εν τω Χριςω in the following. Says verse 19. *The whole*

the waters cover the sea; when the whole world shall be quick and *made alive* (εν τω Χριςω) *in Christ*, as now they lie dead in satan. And that since all the ages are not under the immediate government of *Christ*, neither can it be his true character that he is *the king of the ages*.

To this objection we answer that there may be a divine wisdom in appointing the first ages of the world for the portion of the wicked; that so these, having received their carnal life, and manifested themselves by their works in human nature against the day of wrath, which is to happen at the conclusion of the wicked ages; the ages of christian peace and enjoyment, which are to succeed, may be undisturbed by the intermingling of wicked men among the godly.

Also it may be answered that the wicked themselves by being the first possessors of humanity, and so hastened to their doom, may be the sooner prepared for after purposes of gathering them in, or some of them, among the number of the elect (*Eph.* i. 10.). Moreover that other reasons, to us impenetrable, may occasion the wicked to be the first ordained to human life.

But

NOTES.

world lieth in the wicked one, and says verse 20. *We* (who are not of the world) *are in Christ*.

And hence it comes to pass that the world is full of fraud, and violence, and vanity, and wantonness, and neglect of God, and hypocrisy: whilst the christian shines in truth, and meekness, and chastity, and light, and piety.

LETTER XVIII. SECT. I.

But that however this may be, and however satan may seem to govern the first ages of this world, yet that *Christ* is still the invisible king of all these, presiding in even the worst of the ages as really, altho' not as triumphantly, as in the good and happy ages. For that all the ages are by him ordained, being made (*Heb.* i. 2.) *by him* (*Col.* i. 16.) *and to him, and for him.* And that the words ὁ βασιλεὺς τῶν αἰώνων are truly rendered *the king of the ages*, and not the eternal king.

We may likewise suppose that as the ages are different and distinct members of time, they may afford each their different and distinct modifications of life. That therefore that form of life which man now has in this world is so often called by the LORD *the now age, this present age;* to distinguish it from that form of life which a succeeding age will bring, called by him the next or future age.

In this view of things the measure of time as it exists momentarily in this world, most reasonably deserves some other term than æon, or age to denote it; and which still our english word temporal will not answer; because we understand our word time as comprehensive of the ages; but possibly the word (προσκαιρος) proskairos* as used among the *Greeks* may have better served this purpose. Again,

---

NOTES.

* The *Greeks* had three words in use among them to denote time in its several gradations, καιρος, χρονος and αἰων. By αἰων they meant an age, by χρονος a time of considerable continuance, and by καιρος

Again, whereas all the several states and scenes of things existing in the æonian stages may be called nature; and the Logos, who is the GOD of nature, presides in them all as his father's vice-roy and representative; probably upon this account also he, the Logos, may be called *the king of the æons or ages*, and *the God of the ages*, called so, I say, as a character intended to reveal him to fallen nature.

This is the more probable because our LORD is *visible* as GOD to the elect only; since it is said of them only that they *shall see him as he is*, i. e. in the glory of his divine nature; and if to others his subjects he appears at all, this may be only as their supremest (אדן) or LORD; and only so often and

---

NOTES.

a short inconsiderable time. So (*Eph*. vi. 18.) pray (εν παντι καιρω) every part of time. See also Dr. Robertson's translation of *Bengelius's Introduction to the Apocalypse*: so that καιρος and αιων are two extremes of time, having χρονος for their medium; and by this means καιρος and αιων oppose each other in a very natural antithesis. And beside this, they represent, the former, that fleeting transitoriness of which this life consists, the latter that steadiness and stability of perduration which our time will probably have in a future state of being; wherein we may presume it will bear some resemblance of immutability.

Moreover this same observation holds as good in the syriac, as the greek language; the *Jews* having also three names to express their time by, viz. (ܥܕܢ) odn answered by the greek καιρος; (ܙܒܢ) zbn answered by the greek χρονος; and (ܥܠܡ) olem answered by the greek αιων.

and in what manner he in his wisdom and goodness shall deem proper.'

SECT. II.

Of CHRIST's *æonian kingdom.*

WE believe we have shewn sufficient grounds in our former section for admitting that
(ὁ βα-

NOTES.

CHRIST *visible as the begotten son of* GOD, *whilst invisible in his internal nature.*

'IN proof of this distinction, it should be here observed that our LORD may be invisible in his hidden and immutable nature, at the same time that he is visible in both his angelical and human nature.

Altho' therefore he could converse with *Adam,* and *Noah,* and *Abraham,* and *Jacob,* and *Joshua,* and *Gideon,* and *Manoah,* and the prophets, visibly as man with man; without any violence wrought thereby upon their mortal constitution; yet was he in his unrevealed nature the glorious GOD himself; as says St. *Stephen* to the Sanhedrim (*Acts* vii. 2.) *the God of glory* (*i. e.* the glorious GOD, for the *Syrians* and *Hebrews* use a genitive substantive instead of an adjective) *appeared to our father Abraham in Mesopotamia, &c.* even that same glorious being, who in a different display of himself, namely in that glory in which he conversed with *Moses* upon mount *Sinai,* could not be beheld, as himself then declares, (*Exod.* xxxiii. 20.) *thou canst not see my face, for there shall no man see my face and live* (ver. 23.) *thou shalt see (*אחרי*) my back parts, but my face shall not be seen.*

This passage is remarkable for its intelligence concerning Jehovah, 1st. as importing that at the instant

(ὁ βασιλευς των αιωνων) *the king of the æons*, must be one of the characters of *Christ*, as mediator; but if it should seem to you otherwise, we think it must however be granted that the word æonian cannot, either in our present text or elsewhere, be applied to *Christ*, or to his kingdom as eternal; because in such application they must needs fail of their effect; since the terms age and æonian are so often used in scripture, not only in a finite, limited mean-

---

NOTES.

of time whilst (ver. 22.) he covered *Moses* with his hand in passing by him, the divine nature shone forth only from the fore parts of his personage, leaving his hinder parts visible. And 2dly in that the personage here spoken of, was the same who (ver. 11.) spoke with *Moses* face to face; and whom *Moses* calls (*Exod.* xxxiv. 9.) Adni, *my Lord*, and desires to go amidst them himself instead of sending only an angel (xxiii. 2) and prays to him, *Pardon our iniquity, and our sin, and take us for thy inheritance, &c.* i. e. is the very Jehovah tempted by the *Israelites*, whom St. *Paul* tells us (1 *Cor.* x. 9.) *is the Christ*; *and is* (Heb. xii. 29.) *a consuming fire*; as he is also described, *Ex.* xxiv. 17.

In this view of things it is not difficult to suppose that at our Lord's next appearance, his visible personage may be adorned with a glory wherein the characters of divine dignity are distinguishable to his own people (see *Matt.* v. 8. 1 *Cor.* xiii. 12. 1 *John* iii. 2.); their consolation, which yet, as it begins to shine forth from him in its genuine lustre, may become insufferable to the corrupt beholder, his dismay and confusion.

The primitive christian writers speak with great propriety and assurance on this point, ascribing our power of seeing God to our union with God, by virtue of the incorruptible life regenerated in us. So

meaning, as hath been already shewn in numerous instances: but are sometimes moreover spoken even of inanimate things, such as doors, hills, mountains, &c.

So *Gen.* xlix. 26. *Even unto the utmost bound of the æonian hills.* Hab. iii. 6. *He beheld and the æonian mountains were scattered.* Pſ. xxiv. 7. *Be ye lift up ye æonian doors, and the king of glory shall come in.*

Whereas on the other hand, suppose only that *Christ*'s kingdom is what we, in want of other words to express it, may call temporal; that it began upon earth 1700 years ago; that it will proceed to the end of the world, and long after that, even till to the restitution of all things; and at last be resigned into the hands of the father: suppose this, and scripture language will

be-

N O T E S.

Christus, qui in novissimis temporibus homo, in hominibus factus est, ut finem conjungeret principio, id est hominem Deo—etiam hoc concedit iis qui se diligunt, scilicet videre Deum—Homo etenim a se non videt Deum. Ille autem volens videtur ab hominibus a quibus vult, & quemadmodum vult. Videbitur autem & in regno cælorum paternaliter, spiritu quidem præparante hominem in filium Dei, filio autem adducente ad patrem; patre autem incorruptelam donante in æternam vitam, quæ unicuiq; evenit ex eo quod videat Deum. Quemadmodum enim videntes lumen, intra lumen sunt, & claritatem ejus recipiunt, sic & qui vident Deum intra Deum sunt, percipientes ejus claritatem. Vivificat autem eos claritas; percipiunt ergo vitam qui vident Deum.—Vivere sine vitâ impossibile est: subsistentia autem vitæ, de participatione evenit: parti-

become clear and confiftent; and the terms *æonian* GOD, and *æonian kingdom*, will yield us a pertinent revelation, which they would in no wife do in the vulgar acceptation, fince all men know that the one immortal GOD muft be eternal King, without the lame help of των αιωνων to declare it.

But that there are many æons or periods to come in which GOD will erect to himfelf a peculiar and wonderful kingdom, formed upon a conceivable temporal plan; in which GOD will be, in a vifible familiar form, the King and GOD of us all; GOD like ourfelves, GOD-MAN, GOD acceffible, prepared and anointed by his father, with a direct view to us, to be the fenfible object of our delight, benediction and intereft; and in a manner fo aptly and compleatly anfwering this defign,

---

NOTES.

cipatio autem Dei eft videre Deum, & frui Benignitate ejus. *Homines igitur videbunt Deum, & vivent per vifionem, immortales facti, & pertingentes ufq; in Deum.—* Irenæus lib. 4. cap 37.

Ουκ δια το συγγενες ορα (fcilicet ὁ ανθρωπ☉) τον Θεον, ουδ᾽ ὅτι νους ἐςιν, αλλ᾽ ὅτι σωφρων κ᾽ δικαι☉; ναι, κ᾽ δια το εχειν ὡ ιοει τον Θεον.———*Juftin Martyr Dialog. cum Tryphone Judæo.*

Likewife, *Origen*, in his comment upon St. *John*, calling our faviour the autoptes, the felf-feer of his father, tells us, that GOD is not vifible but by him: wherefore, altho' *every eye fhall behold* the man *Jefus* as their judge (*Rev.* i. 7.) yet they only fhall fee him as GOD who are regenerated by him.

design, as that it shall astonish, and amaze at the same time that it blesses, the greatest and sublimest beings in heaven: this is news as important to man now, as it will be comfortable to him hereafter; a treasure of hopeful tidings to counterpoise his mortifying experience of satan's kingdom; which has for so long a time, harrassed and distressed us, and, like *Pandora*'s fabled box, filled this world with all kinds of evils.

It has been a dispute among Philosophers whether love, and goodness, and justice in GOD, be the same in kind as what we call love, and goodness, and justice in man. But this also, at least the ill inferences intended in those who urge it, is utterly invalidated in the knowledge here proposed of the GOD of ages.

The character of the son of GOD as now become æonian, an angelic, visible, and at length human being, annuls and sets aside all the difficulties of this question: in that we know the love, and mercy, and joy, and grief of *Jesus Christ* to have been the love, and mercy, and joy, and grief of a man; as also that the love, and mercy, and joy, and grief of the Logos, before he became the man *Jesus Christ*, was the love, and mercy, and joy, and grief of an angel.

So that tho' it should be uncertain what is love, benevolence, and the other attributes of GOD, as they exist in his original, and from-eternity divine nature; yet as they were in him the first begotten, or visibly-expressed image of the father, from the beginning of the creation; and as they are now found in the blessed GOD-

be-

begotten man, or humanly-expressed image of the father, since the incarnation; we can form as adequate conceptions of them, as of any thing whatever belonging to human nature.

We can therefore now have no doubt but that the love, and goodness, and mercy, and fidelity, which are the objects of our hope and dependence in GOD, are truly and identically the same as what we experience in our fathers, or friends, or benefactors: and this point discovered must surely prove a most plentiful source of comfort and satisfaction to every discreet and considerate mind.

Thus then the believing heart is able to triumph in hope, and pray with eagerness *thy kingdom come*, not only as for an inconceivable and insensible good; but for a good the object of his thoughts and desires; and for a friend who at the same time that he is GOD, is also a man like himself, even that affable, benevolent, harmless LORD, whose history he reads in the bible; who fed the fainting multitude, was kind to publicans and sinners, gave to every one that asked of him, wept with those that mourned, and bore the contradiction of sinners: I say in these reflections it will also be a considerable circumstance to a man's comfort that the kingdom of *Christ* is *itself* likewise to continue thro' ages and periods numberless, yea vastly beyond all the limits of his scanty comprehension and wishes; and yet then even after all, and after himself is rendered a subject of divine fulness, that it is still to be surrendered up, by the gracious king of it,

securely

securely into the hands of his father, GOD of all, who is (1 *Cor.* xi. 3.) *the head of Christ, even as Christ is the head of every man.*

But criticks and philosophers catch and fasten upon scripture texts of this kind to prove their theological systems of divine attributes; (a purpose which the sacred writers never had in view) and being not served in them to their content, wonder that the holy penmen should express themselves in terms so vague and disatisfactory; while to an unvitiated evangelical taste, scripture terms appear to be most critically chosen and best accommodated to truth and reality.

LETTER XIX.

The scripture passage objected against us, from Matt. xxv. 46, *considered.*

TO ———

SIR,

THE objection against our doctrine, which will be the subject of my present letter, is the most commonly made of all, and I think as inconclusive as any. We find it in *Matt.* xxv. 46. *And these shall go away into æonian punishment, but the righteous into life æonian* (αἰώνιον).

Having shewn at large that the æonian life is not properly termed an eternal life, since it will have its temporary periods; and since the æons themselves, of which that life consists, are creatures; distinct parts or portions of time; as every grain of sand is a distinct part or portion of matter; the meaning of this text is obvious; namely that the *æonian life* will be the joy of the righteous; while the æonian punishment and its consequence *death*, will be the curse of the wicked.

And

And herein is the difference between the righteous and the wicked, that the one shall rejoice in the æonian kingdom of GOD; the other mourn and bewail himself æonianly; the one shall suffer, and be banished the presence of the Theanthropy (εις τον αιωνα) æonianly; the other shall be happy, and with *Christ* in his kingdom (εις τον αιωνα) æonianly, or to the æon.

For says the scripture, *Gal.* v. 21. *The workers of lasciviousness, wrath, envyings,—shall not inherit the kingdom of God.* Mark iii. 29. *He that blasphemeth against the Holy Ghost* (ουκ εχει αφεσιν εις τον αιωνα αλλ᾽ ενοχος εστιν αιωνιε κρισεως) *has not forgiveness to the æon, but is liable to æonian judgment,* even as *Sodom* and its adjacent cities being destroyed by fire, *suffer* (as St. *Jude* tells us, ver. 7.) *the vengeance* (πυρος αιωνιε) *of æonian fire;* whilst those who are in the paradise of GOD, shall be æonianly happy, in whose blessed regions (*Rev.* xxi. 27) *there shall in no wise enter any thing that defileth, neither whatsoever worketh abomination, or maketh a lie.*

But how does any thing here said, prove that the punishment of the wicked shall be eternal? there is nothing of eternity so much as hinted at; the whole spoken of as hereby promised, is an æonian life, a life in the secular kingdom of *Christ*; and the whole spoken of as hereby threatened, is the æonian death, or secular punishment of the damned: *these shall go away into the æonian punishment, the righteous into the æonian life.*

But you say, how then can you prove the eternal happiness of the saints? This is easy to be done,

done (tho' not from the passage before us, no such doctrine being there taught, yet) from the many other scripture passages[s] where the immortal blessedness of christians is expressly declared.

The æonian life of christians arises from a principle of immortality in them, which they derive from *Christ*, and which will also carry them thro' all the æons into eternity: but the wicked, not having this principle in them for the power of their existence in the æonian periods, will be in

a state

NOTES.

[s] Such are the following, 1 *Thes.* iv. 17. *Then we who are alive, who are left, shall be caught up together with them in the clouds to meet the Lord in the air, and so shall we be for ever with the Lord,* (παντοτε, for ever, *i. e.* as long as the LORD lives) according to what our LORD says, *John* xiv. 19. *Because I live, ye shall live also,* οτι εγω ζω (in the present tense) κ̀ υμεις ζησεσθε (in the future tense) for the life of believers is in consequence of the life of *Christ*, their life is not in themselves, but in him its fountain, see *John* vi. 57. Again, 1 *Cor.* xv. 53. *This corruptible must put on incorruption,* (αφθαρτιαν) *and this mortal must put on immortality* (αθανασιαν) 1 Pet. i. 3. *Blessed be God the father of our Lord Jesus Christ, who hath begotten us again—to an inheritance incorruptible* (αφθαρτον) *and undefiled,* (αμιαντον) *and that fadeth not away* (αμαραντον) *reserved in heaven for you.* Luke xx. 34—37. *But they who are accounted worthy to obtain that æon, and the resurrection from the dead, neither marry nor are given in marriage; for neither can they die any more; for they are equal to angels, and are the children of God, being the children of the resurrection.* So 1 *John* iii. 2. *Phil.* iii. 21. and many other places.

LETTER XIX. [361] SECT. I.

a state of misery, whence will insue their corruption, and finally death.

A late writer, not observing this, labours to prove the eternity of hell torments by the following argument.

"The punishment of the wicked will not be-
"gin 'till the last day of this world (gr. αιωνος,
"æon, or age); but at the last day of this world,
"time shall be no more; therefore the punish-
"ment of the wicked will not begin till time shall
"be no more. But punishment which is not in
"time must be in eternity; and what is in eter-
"nity must be eternal."

Before I can give a full and more direct answer to this gentleman's argument, I must first desire him to tell me what he means by the time which is to be no more after the last day of this world, (*i.e.* æon); and what he means by the eternity which will succeed the time to be no more; possibly we differ chiefly in terms. And in the mean while I shall observe,

1st. That the end of this present æon, and the day of judgment thereupon, will conclude our present emphatical age, or æon, of prosperous wickedness.

2dly. That this great age or æon concluded, a succeeding age will ensue wherein dwelleth righteousness.

Now during this second great age, the age of righteousness, the wicked will suffer destruction together with satan and his angels, while the righteous will rejoice in life æonian together with their brethren the holy angels; and therefore is this second æon called the æonian life to the righteous, and the æonian death to the wicked.

But our philosophical notions of time or eternity are in no wise concerned in these events. If by time be meant the portion of duration which is divided and distinguished by a succession of occurrences, as we now measure it by the motion of our sun or moon or earth; it affects our point as little to say that, after the last day, duration will be no longer measured by the revolution of planetary worlds; as to say that it will be no longer measured by the motion of a clock.

And as to eternity, if thereby be meant (as it seems to be by the above said late writer) endless duration; I know not how to distinguish such endless duration from time, otherwise than as a man would distinguish between the middle part of a chain which he holds in his hands, and its invisible length which the utmost stretch of his eye-sight must reach after in vain.

However, without insisting upon the true notion of this word, it happens that eternal life in the forementioned acceptation of it, is not the life intended in the terms of the passage before us; because St. *Paul* declares of *Christ*'s kingdom as mediator that it shall have an end; and so the promise here made to the righteous is their shining forth in a kingdom that is to have an end; but their shining forth therein, is their life therein.

The earth is said by *Solomon* (*Ecclef.* i. 4) *to endure* (לעולם) *æonianly*, which our english bible renders *for ever*, in conformity to the septuagint, which translates this word by εις τον αιωνα; yet not-
with-

LETTER XIX. [363] SECT. I.

withstanding this, we have no doubt but that the earth in due time, shall arrive to its end: and in like manner when the æonian kingdom of the christians glory in *Christ* shall have arrived to its period, then will their life in this kingdom be likewise arrived to its period; and being so, will be changed, together with this kingdom, into a life of divine fulness (*Eph.* iii. 19. 1 *Cor.* xv. 28.) of which we can only say (*Eph.* v. 32. το μυστηριον τᾰτο μεγα ἐστιν) *This is a great mystery.*

But besides even all this, it should be here farther observed, that there is no such scripture text as that on which the above-mentioned gentleman rests his argument, viz. " *there shall be time no longer,*" for (*Rev.* x. 6.) χρονος ουκ ἐσται ἐτι, ought to be rendered, *there shall be not even a chronos* (i. e. the term 1111 years shall not be expired) before the fulfilling of these events predicted. See Dr. *Robertson*'s translation of *Bengelius's preface to the apocalypse.*

And thus the argument above-mentioned looses its force. The last day of this æon will not be the last day of this world: the last day of this world may not be the last day of time: the punishment of the wicked will begin in time: and some things which exist in eternity, may (for all that we know to the contrary) be notwithstanding in themselves temporal.

But it is indeed an important inquiry concerning the kingdom of *Christ*, who shall, and who shall not enjoy that glory which is to be displayed in it; and of this we read (1 *Cor.* vi. 9, 10, 11.) *Neither the unrighteous, nor fornicators, nor adulterers, nor drunkards, nor railers, nor extortioners,*

X x 2   *shall*

shall inherit the kingdom of God: and such were some of you, but ye are washed, but ye are sanctified, but ye are justified, in the name of the Lord Jesus Christ, and by the spirit of our God.

Moreover, because no wicked person can inherit the kingdom of GOD; when a man becomes a believer, he is washed with pure water [*Heb.* x. 23. (ὕδατι καθαρῷ) *Ezek.* xxxvi. 25. (מים טהרים) *John* iii. 5.—xiii. 8.—xix. 34. 1 *John* v. 6.] he is sanctified (*Tit.* iii. 5.) *by the washing of regeneration and renewing of the Holy Ghost.*

But every man unwashed, unsanctified, uncleansed, will most surely find himself an inhabitant of outer darkness, in company with other abandoned creatures, *where shall be weeping and gnashing of teeth.* Where tyrants will domineer cruelly beyond conception, and of whom the tyrants of this world are but faint representatives. There will the gay, the careless, the luxurious, the infidel, be shocked at the multitudes devoted to the power and barbarity of those regal spirits, whom they here deem'd as bugbears. These bugbears will there appear dread authorities; and such as may probably know how to avail themselves of the wretchedness of their vassals. Then will the lost soul experience too late the consequence and importance of his transactions in this world; when his every work will have its natural effect, and he shall find nothing lost or forgotten of all his impieties and and perverseness.

And the thus condemned, who (*John* v. 40.) *would not come unto the Lord that he might have life,* must thus abide also in outer darkness; 'till a tedious

LETTER XIX. [365] SECT. I.

a tedious and woeful experience shall horribly manifest his distress, and the morning of a longsome night shall reveal to him his relief; 'till the lingering day of his visitation draweth near; and (*Acts* iii. 19.) *the time of refreshing shall come from the presence of Jehovah:* 'till (as a shipwrecked and despondent mariner grasps at a projecting rock, which the returning dawn presents him as but just within his reach) he shall gain a sight of that true cleanser who alone has the pure water. For still, the LORD can cleanse him, from all his filthiness, and from all his iniquity, with the washing of water, by the word of the æonian gospel; (1 *Tim.* ii. 6.) *to be testified in due time* (καιροῖς ἰδίοις).

Moreover when a people are cleansed, it imports nothing that they have been filthy; they have the same right to enter into the kingdom of GOD as their elder brethren. *Is.* lxi. 3. *Jehovah will give them beauty for ashes, the oil of joy for mourning, and the garment of praise for the spirit of heaviness; that they may be called the trees of righteousness, the planting of Jehovah.*

And in this regard of them those words of our LORD may have a prophetical prospect, which we read *John* v. 25. *The hour is coming* (that is still to come) *and now is* (that is however in one respect really present) *when the dead shall hear the voice of the son of God, and they that hear shall live:* for (ver. 21) *the son quickeneth whom he will.* So *Eph.* ii. 1, 5, 6. *And you hath he quickened who were dead in trespasses and sins: even when we were dead in sins hath he quickened us together with Christ, and hath raised us up together, and made us sit together in heavenly places in Christ Jesus.* The

LETTER XIX. SECT. I.

The *Jews* are a type of the gentile church, and with regard to their calling most eminently so. When now our LORD's death drew near, we observe him denouncing his judgments upon *these* as follows; *Mat.* xxiii. 37—39. *O Jerusalem, Jerusalem, I would have gathered you—and ye would not. Behold your house is left unto you desolate:* and then closing their doom with those memorable words, *for I say unto you, ye shall not see me henceforth, 'till ye shall say, blessed is he that cometh in the name of the Lord.* But were the *Jews* (*Exod.* xix. 5) *a peculiar treasure unto Jehovah above all people?* So are the *Christians:* Were the *Jews* (*Rom.* xi.) cut off from their olive-tree for unbelief? The *Gentiles* will also be cut off for unbelief, *John* xvii. 2, 6: Will the *Jews* be again ingrafted into their original stock? They will, and that too for the remarkable reason given us *Rom.* xi. 29. *because the gifts and calling of God are without repentance*; because (*Rom.* ix. 6) *the word of God must have effect.* But if for this reason the reprobate *Jews* have their day of visitation and glad tidings to expect; why may not the reprobate *Gentiles* also found upon the same reason a like expectation of some future season in the inconceivable stretch of ages, in the unfathomable depths of time; when, what Jehovah says of his returning *Israel*, may likewise be applied to his returning *Gentiles?* Ezek. xvi. 62. *Then thou shalt remember thy ways and be ashamed.—and I will establish my covenant with thee, and thou shalt know that I am Jehovah, that thou mayst remember and be confounded, and never open thy mouth any more because of thy shame, when I am pacified towards thee for all that thou hast done.*

LETTER XX.

The scripture passage objected against us, from Eph. iii. 10---. *considered.*

TO ———

SIR,

SECT. I.

THE text, the subject of my present to you, will again prove no argument against me, but as it stands in our english testament, where we read it (*Eph.* iii. 10---.) *That now unto the principalities and powers in heavenly places, might be made known by the church the manifold wisdom of God, according to the eternal purpose which he made in Christ our Lord.*

You here object that the word *eternal*, used with the word *purpose*, must signify eternal in the usual meaning of that term, because (as you say) the purpose of GOD must be eternal in such comprehensive meaning of that term.

Now

Now altho' this is by no means to be granted you; and altho' the above passage has its answer from what has been already urged; I shall rather object to it as mis-rendered; not for want of a sufficient reply to what you have advanced, tho' the true rendering had been æonian covenant, but because the giving a just construction to a text is always the preferable work.

In greek we read it κατα προθεσιν των αιωνων ἡν εποιησεν, which is litterally thus, κατα θεσιν 'ην εποιησεν προ των αιωνων, in english, *according to the purpose which he made before the ages or æons began*; agreeable with what we read *Heb.* i. 2. where our saviour is said to have *made the æons*, and in 2 *Tim.* i. 9. προ χρονων αιωνιων) *before the æonian seasons*: the like to which we also read, 1 *Cor.* ii. 7. *We speak the hidden wisdom which God pre-ordained* (προ των αιωνων) *before the ages or æons began.*

This hidden wisdom of GOD is the mystery of his love to sinners in *Christ Jesus*, and has probably been opening and unfolding gradually and in parts, long before the foundation of this world; as it has, since the fall, been also gradually opening to man.

During the antidiluvian æon it became the subject of human speculation in the promise of a redeemer to be revealed in the seed of the woman; a promise which, tho' it may appear dark to us, yet to the spiritual souls of those times, such as were *Job* and *Elisha*, afforded a most desirable and bright prospect of comfort.

In the following æon, the æon of the law, it was farther represented to the chosen people of GOD,

LETTER XX. [369] SECT. I.

GOD or to his then church, by typical ceremonies, rites and sacrifices, and in the persons of holy men, as we read thro' all the old testament.

Again in the following age, the now gospel æon, it is declared to us in a still more circumstantial and sublime manner; the which a succeeding æon will in all likelihood illustrate to the intire satisfaction and joy of all true believers.

This gradual and progressive discovery of *Jesus Christ* is appositely described in the first paragraph of the epistle to the *Hebrews*, chap. i. 1.

[Syriac text]

¹*In all* ²*parts* (or portions, gr. πολυμερως, in several parcels) ³*and in all* ⁴*similitudes* ⁵*God* ⁶*spake* ⁷*in times past* ⁸*with* ⁹*our fathers* ¹⁰*by the prophets*; ¹¹*moreover in these* ¹²*last* ¹³*days* ¹⁴*he spake* ¹⁵*with us* ¹⁶*by his son,* ¹⁷*even him whom* ¹⁸*he has appointed* ¹⁹*heir* ²⁰*of every thing,* ²¹*and by whom also* ²²*he constituted* ²³*the* (olema) *ages or æons.*

Now to the construction here given to this passage in *Eph.* iii. 10, 11. the subject of my present to you, the syriac testament answers still more suitably ([Syriac text])

viz. ¹*That* ²*the wisdom* ³*of God* (⁴*abounding with* ⁵*variety*) ⁶*which he had* ⁷*ordained* (or prepared) ⁸*from* (i. e. before or for) ⁹*ages* ¹⁰*and produced*

Y y (or

LETTER XX. [370] SECT. I.

(or effected) "*in Jesus* '*our Lord*, '*might be known* '*thro*' *the church*, viz. to all intelligent beings.

This wise contrivance therefore of GOD is not called by the apostle eternal; but a wisdom or wise plan, prepared only, for ages or æons before, of GOD, and produced or effected in his son *Jesus Christ*.

And what the apostle intends to tell us in this scripture passage, is only that GOD before the ages began, had formed a plan or purpose in *Christ*, for the discovery of his manifold wisdom to the principalities and powers in heaven; that in pursuance to this plan, such discovery should be made to them by or thro' the church; and that, in order hereto, himself is sent to preach the unsearchable riches of *Christ*; and *Eph.* iii. 9. (φωτίσαι πάντας) *to enlighten all* (intelligent creatures)[h] τις ἡ οικονομια τε μυστηριου so as to see) *what is that mysterious œconomy which till then had been a secret hidden in God* (απο των αιωνων ܒܥܠܡܐ ܡܢ *a seculis*) *from the very beginning of the æons,* or celestial ages.

SECT.

NOTES.

[h] Had man only been here intended in the word (πάντας) all, the reading would had been πάντας ἀνθρώπους, whereas it is only (πάντας) all; *i. e.* all the intelligent creatures of GOD.

SECT. II.

The æonian purposes of God more largely illustrated.

IT seems that without revelation no force of created thought or intellect could have devised the astonishing things of GOD; that angels must learn their LORD by man; that it is thro' us they discover rightly who is the author and what the end of created existence; that we are the secondary offspring of the living GOD; that the unbeginning source of being has a son like himself, whom it is his purpose to honour; a son begotten into a distinction from himself; begotten into that form and nature of which angels and men are the likeness, and just copy; and that **he is charactered** by the name Logos or word.

It is from revelation they learn that by the Logos all the creatures were made, and nothing made without him; that they were made *(Col.* 1. 16. ἐν αὐτῷ) *in him* (δι αὐτῷ) *by him*, and (εἰς αὐτὸν) *for himself*; and that this Logos our common creator can love us his creatures even unto death.

It is by means of us that they see him now both Logos and man, as St. *John* also saw him *Rev.* xix. 13. *man cloathed with a vesture dipt in blood*, yet still retaining his first name Logos or the word of GOD; that they see him as Logos-man the support of all things; for *(Heb.* i. 3.*)* he (who *when he had by himself purged our sins, sat down at the right hand of the high majesty)* is the person also *upholding all things by the word of his power*;

power; and of whom it is said (*Acts* xvii. 28) *He is not far from every one of us, for in him we live, and move, and have our being.* And doubtless they must conceive most delightful speculations from what they read in *Col.* ii. 9. viz. that *in him* (this our common æonian father) *dwelleth the fulness of God* (σωματικως) *bodily*.

And as our Lord is now, so will he continue to be seen, admired, adored, for millions of ages or æons, presiding over his universe of creatures in one constant character of Logos-man; being thro' all his natures the single genuine son, and (μορφη Θεου) *form of God*.

This is that lovely glorious object of all the holy scriptures, the wonder of the universe, whom the father alone can truly know, his only begotten our Jehovah Lord.

As the sun in its firmament has a body, a body locally situated and circumscribed, which notwithstanding can diffuse from its habitation the beams of its presence and energy, thro' all its firmaments; and fill the whole of its domains with its ownself, even beyond saturn's orb, the verge of its empire and influence: so, but in an infinitely transcendent manner, the Logos-man from his throne in the heavens (*Prov.* xv. 3) *has his eyes in every place beholding the evil and the good.* Ps. xxxiii. 13. *He looketh from heaven and beholdeth all the sons of men; from the place of his habitation he looketh upon all the inhabitants of the earth*; also he is (*Heb.* iv. 12) *a discerner of the thoughts and intents of the heart:* as says *Job* (xxxi. 4) *Doth he not see all my ways and count all my steps?*

And

And as he always sees us all, so by some way of effluence, or otherwise inconceivably to us, he moreover from his fulness communicates of his presence, his virtue, his glory, his life, to all the millions of saints received into the extensive plains of paradise; whose happiness is his presence, and who therefore behold his glory continually. And yet at the same time,

"His genial parent rays bestow
"Life and light on us below."

He nourishes no less his people on earth personally and severally with suitable relishes of himself. Nor these alone, seeing his omniscience comprehends, in one illimited, perpetual, simultaneous prospect, every circumstance of every individual being in and thro' every individual world.[i]

Great is the difference between a man (*i. e.* the offspring of a man) and a worm (*i. e.* the off-

---

NOTES.

The divine attributes in CHRIST.

[i] WE acknowledge that the visible person of *Christ* is not in itself omnipresent, but of local and circumscribed presence: its glory is however diffused thro' all his kingdom.

It will be acknowledged also that the spirit with which the person of *Jesus Christ* is most intimately united, whose virtues and excellencies it enjoys, and who is immense, omnipresent and infinite; can communicate to that person the efficacy of its attributes, such as its power, knowledge, &c. as truly and universally, as an human soul can communicate to the inert body which it inhabits, the use of all its several powers and faculties.

offspring of that stupid animal). But the difference here, you say, is in kind, and that a worm differs in kind, is in kind a creature different from a man.

This however observed, may illustrate the personal difference between a man, the son of GOD, and a man, the son of a merely human creature.

Jesus is in kind, as we are, perfect man; *i. e.* as to his natural form and constitution altogether like one of us. But he exceeds us all in the *possibilities*

NOTES.

It is by means of the soul, that the bodily eye discerns (or is capable of any sensations from) distant objects. As says *Anselm*,—*Tota sensatio est in anima; cum enim oculo videmus, aure audimus, manu tangimus: ipsa visio, auditio, & tactus perceptio non est in oculo, aure, manu, sed in anima. Non enim corpus, sed anima est quæ per oculum videt, per aures audit, sentitq; per manum.* But since the divine nature may be easily conceived as that in the person of *Christ*, which the soul is in the bodily organs; we may likewise conceive that by means of this union, *Christ* can know all things, and see and act and do all things every where, as if he were every where personally present.

Yea we find that, even while in his mortal state, our LORD discerns (see *Mat.* ix. 4.—xii. 14, 15. *Mark* ii. 8. *Luke* ix. 46, 47. *John* ii. 24, 25.—vi. 61, 64.) the thoughts and reasonings of all about him: (see *John* iv. 17, 18. *Luke* xiii. 16.—xix. 5.) the names and circumstances of every one he set his eyes upon: and (see *John* i. 48.—xi. 11, 14.—xxi. 6. *Matt.* xvii. 24. —xxi. 2.) every occurrence that happened in distant places.

sibilities of his humanity, and the *excellencies* of his human capacities.

As the body of a man must have a constitution, proportion, and fitness for the soul which is to inhabit it; so the body of *Christ* must have had a constitution, proportion and fitness for the soul inhabiting it; and hence it is easy to conclude that this body must have had (what much farther exceeds ours than a man exceeds a worm) a susceptibility of God. Our Lord's body, as to the *powers and susceptibilities innately given to be unfolded* in it, may have excelled the bodies of his brethren, much farther than theirs exceed the meanest animal.

As his native capabilities as an *angel*, must have have been more than equal to all those of all the millions of angels that are or can live; in like manner his native capabilities as a *man*, must have been more than equal to all and every the endowments of all and every man that can be produced. No creature can have any excellency or specific virtue in him but what must have pre-existed in *Christ*. Psalm xciv. 9.

Being also declared to be in the Bosom of his father, we can have no doubt but our Lord inherits the whole of his father in real life; and thereby shews forth to his creatures in his own person an omniscience, omnipresence, and omnipotence, like to, similar with, the copy of his holy father's. For the father reveals him to the universe as his one genuine image; that so, *John* ver. 23. (παντες) *all should honour the son, even as they honour the father.* Wherefore says St. *Paul,*
(Col.

(Col. ii. 3.) in our LORD *are hid all the treasures of wisdom and knowledge; he is* (1 Cor. i. 24.) *the wisdom of God, and the power of God.*[k]

SECT. III.

WHAT we have advanced concerning *Christ* in the foregoing section, is, I think, very conceivable, but what follows exceeds *indeed*

NOTES.

The omnipresence of CHRIST *defended.*

[k] A sneering philosopher here eagerly opposes us. Says he, " *Anima Christi est finita, nec omnium rerum,* " *nec distinctissime conscia.—Corpus pariter est finitum.* " *Ab aliis atq; aliis substantiis necessario longius distat,* " *nisi corpus finitum ex corpore finito tollas.—Finitum* " *non est capax infiniti—infinitum nequit a finito limi-* " *tari.*" That therefore the doctrine of the universal presence of *Christ*, can be only an enthusiastical fancy.

But these maxims affect not our point. We allow that (*infinitum, qua infinitum, nullos admittit limites*) " infinity as such admits of no limits" that therefore as to a physical capacity, these assertions may be true; yet this argues not but that *Christ* thro' his eternal spirit, a simple uncompounded nature, may be intimately present with all his creatures; and exercise his wisdom, and knowledge, and power upon every individual; as the eye may be said to be present with whatever it can see.

Presence is that relation whereby one person may see and act upon another, without any preparation thereto, and in this sense *Christ* may be said to be every where present.

LETTER XX.   [377]   SECT. III.

deed our wisdom. Our LORD tells us (*John* v. 26.) *As the father hath life in himself, so hath he given the son to have life in himself.* For thus the son of GOD becomes the image of his father even in his independency. Because to have life in himself is to have it without continued derivation of it from another: and since the father is said to have

given

NOTES.

The sun cannot shine thro' a cloud, neither thro' any other opaque body, and hence comes darkness, said to be from the sun's absence: but neither clouds, nor worlds, nor distances can exclude the power of *Christ*'s vision; all things are alike transparent to him Heb. iv. 13. *Neither is there any creature that is not manifest in his sight, but all things are naked and open to the eyes of him* (v. 14. this great high-priest) *with whom we have to do.* As says the *Psalmist* (xc. 80.) *Thou hast set our iniquities before thee, and our secret sins in the light of thy countenance.*

Also as the eye can comprehend the magnitude of the sun, without extending itself to the sun's dimensions; so may the human capacity of *Christ* comprehend the whole of his creation, altho' his visible person be less than that of many of his creatures.

But as to the mere act of vision, we find that even christian men may be enabled to extend this thro' all interpositions. Thus not only the lofts and roof of the *Sanhedrim* chamber were transparent to *Stephen*, when he says (*Acts* vii. 56.) *Behold I see the heavens opened, and the Son-man standing at the right hand of God*; but distance itself (which obscures all things) and in its greatest extent, lost its effect to his eyes now strengthened, by the spirit which was in him, to behold his LORD in the highest heavens.

given him thus to have life in himself, *that other from whom he is possessed of life without continued derivation of it, is the father.*

So that his life in himself is a life which he possesseth without continually deriving it from the father. But to have life in himself without continually deriving it from the father, is to be a living GOD in himself.

So then the Logos-man is a living GOD, the fulness of all what his father is, exhibited even to independency itself; exhibited fully, expressly, visibly, and (σωματικως) bodily, in the presence of *Christ.* And thus we arrive at the true import of the terms æonian GOD, æonian father. And, for the manifesting of him in the man *Jesus*, the text we treat of tells us that *God, before the æons began, had formed his purposes.*

What vast truths are these! and how contemptible is the wisdom of the learned, compared with them; *Cogito ergo sum,* says the philosopher, " I " think therefore I exist:" but to the studious in the scriptures, learning there the great and interesting revelations of the decrees of GOD, and their high value in the realms above, such talk is too trifling to excite their notice.

And as are the mysteries of things above, so are likewise the mysteries of things on earth, discoverable only by what revelation affords us concerning our LORD and his æonian purposes, of which our text speaks.

If you ask the philosopher, Why is the pious man despised and miserable; the vicious man honourable and triumphant? why can the tyrant
torment

torment and oppress, while the innocent man must languish under his oppression and cruelty? or why should an omnipotent and an omnipresent God hear the blasphemer daily insult him with impunity? or afford his avowed enemies the strength to resist, and faculties to countermine his declared will?—With all his wisdom, this your wise man can no more account reasonably for such phœnomena, (altho' his daily experience) than for the time and manner and circumstantials of his existence.

But the gospel rightly understood, at once clears up these difficulties: hereby we find that we are creatures made, not for ourselves but, for the pleasure and designs of the son of God; that the best and devoutest of men are notwithstanding sinners: that they suffer however with design; for that not an hair shall fall from their head but by permission of their heavenly father.

That as to the careless and voluptuous part of mankind, they are happy and prosperous in this life, because their day of trial is reserved for the other; because they have a doom to suffer before the work of divine love will take place with them, or the christian calling to the divine life be heard of by them; for that (*Mat.* xiii. 15) *their heart is waxed gross, and their ears are dull of hearing, and their eyes they have closed, least they should see with their eyes, and hear with their ears, and should understand with their hearts, and should be converted, and I* (says our Lord) *should heal them.*

And that as to the barbarians among mankind, and sons of belial, these can now blaspheme and persecute without controul, because gehenna is provided for them, where every tyrant will be consigned to the fury of the tormentors (*Matt.* xviii. 34) who will gratify their appetites of cruelty, in making each, according as he hath been merciless, a spectacle of torture and wretchedness.

Yea and if even gehenna will not soften the reprobate, there is yet lastly a lake prepared for the devil and his angels, which will however not fail to work due effects upon the subjects of its horrors.

The long-suffering *Jesus* endures wickedness, not thro' want of a principle of resentment, or the consciousness of what we all are doing in this world; but because of certain purposes which he is able to render all wickedness productive of, and subservient to: purposes worthy of his justice as well as his love; and which when accomplished, the whole universe will contemplate with amazement, delight and adoration.

And thus the conduct of God with the unbelieving *Jews*, who are the first fruits unto God of the rest of human race, and a type of his concern for all, will be also his conduct with all reprobates; they are brought to grace by affliction.

So we read *Ez.* xx. 37. *I will cause them to pass under the rod, and then will they remember their ways, and loath themselves.* Hof. v. 12. *I will be unto Ephraim as a moth, and to the house of Judah as rottenness;* (ver. 10) *and I will pour my wrath upon them like water,* (ver. 15) *till they acknowledge their offences and seek my face; in their affliction they will seek me* (יְשַׁחֲרֻנְנִי) *eagerly.*

But

LETTER XX.   [381]   SECT. III.

But in order to judge duly of the severity of Jehovah towards his people, we should first see the end and issue of it; and of this we read (*Ez.* xiv. 22, 23.) *behold, tho' there remain in it* (Jerusalem) *a remnant of the banished, sons and daughters;* (who are not as yet carried away into the babylonish captivity, which is a type of some far more desperate state of captivity that shall come upon the *Jews* for their unbelief) *lo these (shall) come forth unto you* (and shall be companions with you in bondage) *and ye (shall) contemplate* (or inspect studiously) *their way and their doings, and (shall) be comforted penitentially over the evil which I have brought upon Jerusalem, (even) with all things which I have brought upon it: yea they shall* (i. e. in my dealings with them shall be a means to) *comfort you penitentially when ye shall contemplate their way, and their machinations* (or devices) *and* (in this your penitential state of contemplation, and convictive light, and holy shame, and joy and gratitude) *ye shall know that it is not without cause* (and a provisionary care for your good that) *I have done all things which I have done against it,* (my church) *saith Adni Jehovah.*

LETTER XXI.

The scripture passage objected against us, from Heb. xiii. 20, *considered.*

TO ———

SIR,

SECT. I.

YOUR next objected text is that in *Heb.* xiii. 20. *Now the God of peace that brought again from the dead our Lord Jesus Christ, thro' the blood of the æonian covenant, &c.* Our english translation has it *eternal* covenant, and upon this rendering you presume that you have here found a passage where the term αιωνι⊕ must mean eternal.

But upon a due consideration of these two words, you will find them to be repugnant terms in your acceptation of them; for the word covenant implies a distinct temporal transaction, a fact before which time was, and after which time is, and which therefore cannot be eternal.

Neither

Neither will the word eternal confift with a covenant made between two perfonally diftinct, as is GOD and the mediator; the latter of whom too was to perform the conditions of it by means of a material fabrick of body and blood; for the blood was an effential confideration in that covenant between GOD, and the mediator *Chrift*; who was to fpill the blood of that body which his father was to prepare for him; and the blood fo fpilt was to ratify that covenant made with his father: and by virtue of this blood-ratification, *Chrift* became immediately intitled to that divine energy which brought him again from the dead.

And thus the abfurdity, which attends this paffage under the notion of an eternal covenant, vanifhes at once. This covenant is term'd æonian, not from its duration but, from the reference it bears to the æonian fpirit; and to the æonian ftate of things during *Chrift*'s reign.

Chrift as king is this very æonian fpirit, and his kingdom is this very æonian ftate of things which the æonian covenant relates to. By virtue of this æonian covenant our faviour is called the GOD and father of the æonian life; and the æonian life becomes what it is, a fecular œconomy conducted fecularly by him the Mefliah, on account of it, he being, in order to this government, both GOD and man.

Himfelf is the image or fimilitude of GOD, and after his own fimilitude he formed the creatures. This form they (at leaft fome of them) loft, and the bufinefs of his æonian kingdom is to reftore it

to

to them anew: to restore it even by a divine birth, for his children are now even begotten of him into his own similitude. We were originally created after the similitude of the Logos; now are we appointed to become that similitude by a divine begetting, a begetting into a life subsisting by the resurrective energies of the Logos become the man *Jesus Christ*.

These are sublime ideas; and when we consider the ignorance of Christians, we cannot but wonder how they became known to the ancient *Jews*; yet we are by them told, that the Messiah is the shadow of GOD, his copy or exact likeness; but that, of the creatures he is the prototype or original. So says *Philo Judæus*, Σκια Θευ ὁ Λογος κυτα εσιν; αυτη δε ἡ σκια κỳ το ὡσανει απεικονισμα ἑτερον εσιν αρχετυπον; ὡσπερ γαρ ὁ Θεος παραδειγμα της εικονος, οὑτως ἡ εικων αλλων γινεται παραδειγμα. liber secundus *Alegor*.
" The Logos is the shadow of GOD; but this
" shadow, and as it were copy, is likewise another
" prototype (or original); for as GOD is that ori-
" ginal after which his image is a copy; so is
" his image that original after which others
" (viz. the many creatures, and who are not
" GOD) are a copy."

All are the purchase of his blood, and he died for all, because all were predestinated to become the εικονες της εικονȣ,[1] as the primitive christian writers

---

NOTES.

The human soul in its own nature mortal or corruptible.

[1] WE read (*Rom.* viii. 29.) *God has predestinated us to be of one form with the image* (or personal represen-

writers term it) the image of the image, the similitude of *Christ* variously represented, and differing in variety of individuals.

It is true the æonian covenant thus represented as concerted only between GOD and his son; and supposing the creatures virtually and by covenant restored already thro' the atchievements of the son singly, without the concurrent concern of the creatures will, excludes all boasting in the creature; and it ought to do so. Says St. *Paul* (*Rom.* iii. 27.) *where then is boasting? it is excluded; by what law; of works? nay, but by the law of faith.*

But

NOTES.

tation *of his son*, i. e. to become like *Christ*, glorious in our outward persons, by being inwardly begotten of him, and so full of his life and immortality. For this life is to be effected in us by a regeneration; the soul of man being, as his body, a mere mortal in herself, until she derives her spirit or quickening principle by regeneration from *Christ* the second *Adam*, 1 *Cor.* xv. 47. *John* i. 13. *Eph.* ii. 1.

By this derivation (which St. *Peter* calls, 2 *Pet.* i. 4. a *being made a partaker of the divine nature*) she becomes, what her second father is, a living spirit, as says our Lord, *John* iii. 6. *That which is born of the flesh is flesh, and that which is born of the spirit is spirit.* *John* vi. 63. *It is the spirit that quickeneth.* So says St. *Peter* (1 *Pet.* i. 3, 4.) *He* (*Christ*) *hath begotten us again* (Rom. ix. 26. *the children of the living God*, and by so being) *to an inheritance incorruptible*.

St. *Paul* tells us that (1 *Tim.* vi. 16.) *God only hath immortality*; and does not this sufficiently prove that his creatures have it not? and that immortality can no otherwise be had by them than from him? and it is produced in us (1 *Pet.* i. 23. &c) *out of an incorrup-*

But then such exclusion is matter of joy for us in that it confirms the certainty of the event; since God would not enter upon a treaty with his son for the realizing a precarious issue; since a contract established between the son of God and his father, argues a power in the parties equipollent thereto, and altogether secure of effecting it.

On the other hand neither does the present forlorn condition of fallen nature at all invalidate this truth; because, tho' God be already reconciled, by this covenant performed in our behalf, to all his creatures; tho' the father looks upon them

---

NOTES.

tible seed (δ.α) *by the Logos of the living God which abideth æonianly*; as we also abide in him, the sons of his own similitude.

The mortality of the soul was therefore a doctrine universally received by the primitive christian writers, namely *Justin Martyr*, *Tatian*, *Irenæus*, *Athenagoras*, *Theophilus Antiocenus*, *Tertullian*, *Cyprian*, *Arnobius*, *Lactantius*, as well as by the *Jews* of the apostolic age; till about the end of the fourth centry; when the opinion of a natural immortality in the soul first begun to spread itself, with the notorious decay of christian faith and light.

Indeed common sense may teach us that whatsoever is passible (as is the soul) must also be mortal in its own nature, since passion or suffering tends to dissolution, and so to death.

In this view of things we learn how to understand the word ($\pi\nu\epsilon\upsilon\mu\alpha$) spirit, as used with the word body, in *James* ii. 26, viz. *As the body without the spirit* (i. e. soul) *is dead*; *so, &c.*——For the spirit, which *Christ* imparts to us, is that to the soul, which the soul is represented to be to the body.

them all as the purchased possession of, and so as righteous and innocent in his *Christ,* their root and first fruits; it is notwithstanding the will of GOD that the creature himself become *reconciled to Christ,* and so created **anew** in his image, made alive and righteous and **innocent** by his spirit, before he can enjoy immediately the benefits of his merits, and the power of his resurrection.

NOTES.

The soul is naturally (i. e. in her unregenerated state) void of a spirit, and so in a corruptible habit. This we learn from *Acts* iii. 23. *Matt.* x. 28. *James* v. 20. compared with *Jude* 10, where the psychical or soul-man is by a periphrasis called a soul (without, or not having, a spirit.

The soul's present unquickened state of living is the result (not of any **immortalizing** spirit essentially united to her, much less of any power of life in her ownself, but) of a נשמת חיים (or which is the same רוח חיים) breath of lives, called in greek πνοη (see *Acts* xvii. 25.) extrinsically communicated to man in common with all other animals -see *Gen.* ii. 7.—vi. 17.—vii. 15, 22.) and imparting to all creatures a successive **vitality** suitable to their respective natures.

So then **to be predestinated** to become the image of *Christ,* is to be predestinated to become his children or to live in his life, of which we read (*Rom.* viii. 10) *Now if Christ be in you, the body indeed is dead,* thro' the sin-offering, *but the spirit* (derived from *Christ*) *is alive,* thro' the righteous one; *and if the spirit of him that raised up Jesus from the dead dwell in you, he that raised up Christ from the dead will also quicken your mortal bodies, by his spirit that dwelleth in you.*

LETTER XXI.   [388]   SECT. I.

Also tho' this covenant, sufficiently accomplished in *Christ*, has as yet so little effect upon the wicked, as says the apostle, it *profits them nothing* (*Heb.* iii. 18, 19) *because of their unbelief*; yet the time must unavoidably come when it shall profit them; and in order to the due and gradual operation of such their profit to be effected, were the æons created, or the æonian revolutions (and probably differing modes of life) contrived. As we read (*Heb.* i. 2.) δι ὅυ καὶ τὲς αιωνας εποιησεν, *by whom also he made the æons.*[m]

They were contrived, I say, for the good of all; as means for our LORD's universal benevolence to exert itself universally. For his providence is as diffusive as his works; he superintends the whole creation as if that whole were one individual; he superintends every individual as if that single one were his whole creation: as numbers cannot exhaust his attention, neither will singularity diminish it.   SECT.

NOTES.

[m] Our english testament often renders the greek word αιων by the word *world*, as tho' it were a substitute or succedaneum for the word κοσμος, world. The absurdity of this practice has been already exposed in the notes of page 7. But that the words (τὲς αιωνας) the ages, should in this place be render'd worlds as a general name for sun, and moon, and stars, is still more unreasonable.

The *Jews* and *Syrians*, being altogether strangers to our modern notions of astronomy, had proper names for the earth, and sun, and moon, as creatures without their equals; the two last they therefore called the king and queen of heaven, and as to all other the

SECT. II.

THE torments which the æonian ages will bring upon the ungodly found indeed frightfully to flesh and blood; and when related, awaken in us a dread of divine majesty, and uneasy jealousies concerning his intrinsic goodness: but this dread and jealousy are the effects, not of right compassion, but of our ignorance of the nature of true love.

When we know the Logos as his holy angels know him, *and see him as he is*; we shall be fully satisfied that he is altogether lovely, that in his heart is pure goodness, that no wrath can dwell there but what love alone must generate, that our

---

NOTES.

cæleſtial appearances they called them their hoſt or militia, and lumped them together under one common appellation (ܟܘܟܒܐ) ſtars or ſparklers: but having no conception of more than one world in the univerſe, and not dreaming that the ſtars were habitable, they no more thought of calling them worlds than of calling them moons or ſuns. So that for our tranſlators of the teſtament to conjecture, 1ſt. that the term αιων may ſignify (κοσμος) the world, and then 2dly. to proceed to apply the term æon ſo render'd as a common name given here by the apoſtle to denote all the celeſtial bodies (*i. e.* αιων, *quaſi* κοσμος, *quaſi* σεληνη, *quaſi* ηλιος, *quaſi* αστηρ; and ſo οι αιωνες, *quaſi* οι αστερες) is an unprecedented preſumption.

our interest is his perpetual concern, that it is the pleasure of his good-will to bless us even in defiance of our own perverseness, that his absolute authority is conducted by a most perfect wisdom, and a most bountiful disposition towards all his creatures, and that his benevolence is so adequate to, as if it were the very reason of his power and prerogatives.

When we know the Logos *as he is*, we shall rather think how desirable an effort is the wrath prepared under the administration of such a power, a power that cannot but have the happiness and recovery of his creatures at heart; that cannot but have a feeling of our infirmities; and perhaps who, in *all our* conflicts and *afflictions*, *is himself afflicted*; as was *Darius* in the doom of *Daniel* which himself commanded. *Dan.* vi. 16, 18.

Our own experiences do constantly teach us that the design of misery is to awaken us, to seperate our affections from a state of slavery and wretchedness, and to kindle in us desires that may give us a free access to what is truly great, and good, and glorious.

We must also have observed that altho' the blessings of heaven are brought down to us, and set within our reach, and altho' our faithful Lord so often stands at our door and knocks; yet are we strangers to him, and insensible of his presence, so long as we withold our hearts from him, *i. e.* in other words, so long as we refuse to believe him our truest good.

Altho' the gospel, were it rightly believed, and conceived in the evidence of gracious light, would

be

be irresistible tidings to us; like that of vision to the blind, health to the wretched, and liberty to the imprisoned: and altho' it is thro' a stupidity to, and ignorance of its privileges and blessings, that it is ever despised or neglected by us; yet by daily experiment we learn that it will be neglected by us, 'till distress, and poverty, and want, and the being heavy laden and labouring, or what is equivalent to these, have made us in *earnest*, to hunger and thirst after a restorer, *as the hart panteth after the water streams*. And these considerations may convince us of the use and necessity of the æonian sufferings.

All true goodness (*i. e.* sincere, genuine virtue, holiness, or purity) is derived from GOD the one fountain of it. As man has only so much goodness as he derives from GOD, so have the angels only so much goodness as they derive from GOD. Therefore says our LORD, *there is none good but one, that is God*; not that there are none among men or angels good, but that no one is absolutely and in himself good besides GOD alone. Thus a ball of glass has only so much light in itself, as it receives from a luminous body; becoming a picture of the sun by his light existing in it, and penetrating thro' it.

The communicable nature of GOD is a most inestimable account of him. To enjoy this were all intelligent creatures made; made therefore the temples of the living GOD, bright in his light, full of his holiness. But this their original beauty and holiness having been obscured in all, must be again recovered in all in its primitive lustre:

and

and such recovery, and so display of the divine likeness in us, is the true motive and principle of Jehovah's being an avenging Judge, a wrathful Lamb, a consuming fire, a quickening spirit.

Wherefore, altho' the LORD may seem to them that suffer to be an angry GOD, and a devouring fire; yet the blessed (whose eyes are clear and strong to see thro' the vail of wrath, into his real character) perceive with all joy and complacency that such anger and such fire are emergent from love only, and that it can only burn up what is heterogenial to true life, can only consume what ought to die; namely, that spirit in us which lives to the ruin of ourselves and others: and this done, all will be well again.

We no sooner affront an earthly friend but we thereby cancel the worth of many years services, and alter his gracious purposes towards us at a stroke; but the genuine love of *Christ* is invincible, indefesible; we may by our perversenefs alter his *conduct* towards us, but not his *heart*: his love must still remain inviolable; insomuch that when he can no longer blefs us with the joy of his countenance, his contrivance will nevertheless be continually at work to blefs us imperceptibly, and in the disguise of a chastiser; for all the while of his anger is our LORD, in his true unveiled reality, that humble, compassionate, harmless being, whom we behold in the gospels, pitying the afflicted, giving to every one what he asks, weeping with the sorrowful, the friend of publicans and sinners, returning blessings for curses, prayers for indignities, good for evil. But

LETTER XXI.   SECT. II.

But is a divine benevolence the source of all our sufferings? Is it the arm of a divine benevolence that chastises us? And does it chastise us that (*Heb.* xii. 10.) *we may become partakers of his holiness?* Let us then believe him to be what St. *John* defines him, and rest satisfied that the expressions of his wrath, are the energies only of a salutary influence, wrought within us to the subordinating all to himself, that so he may accomplish in us his own life, and joy, and plenitude, and render us susceptive of divine happiness.

Blessed vocation! if we knew our true good, how eagerly should we pursue it, in contempt of all the gay scenes of pleasure and interest, and the false friendships of this world; notwithstanding it should lead us thro' that *narrow path*, and that *straight gate*, into which our LORD's bigots and devotees have abandoned themselves, in the renouncing of their own will, in an honourable fellowship of his cross, and persecutions, and shame, and with a resolute attachment to whatever he, their only master, recommends to them, or chooses for them.

LETTER XXII.

The scripture passage objected against us, from Matt. xxvi. 24, *considered.*

TO ———

SIR,

SECT. I.

Matt. xxvi. 24. *Wo unto the man by whom the son of man is betray'd, it had been good for him, if that man had not been born* (καλον ην αυτω, ει ουκ εγγεννηθη ο ανθρωπος εκεινος).

IT is generally acknowledged that these words of our LORD allude to the several exclamations which we meet with from many instances of the distressed in scripture;[n] also that they were proverbial, and of common use as such in men under calamitous circumstances among the *Jews*. Thus

---

NOTES.

[n] *Nam quod viris piis* Jobo & Jeremiæ *impatientia ut dicerent expressit, id hic vere ac serio de juda Christus affirmat.* Grotius.

LETTER XXII. [395] SECT. I.

Thus *David* prays (*Pf.* lviii. 8.) *Let them pafs away like the untimely birth of a woman, that they may never fee the fun.* Jer. xx. 14. *Curfed be the day wherein I was born* (ver. 17) *becaufe he flew me not from the womb, that my mother might have been my grave.*—————*Wherefore came I out of the womb to fee labour and forrow, &c.* Job. x. 18, 19. *Wherefore then haft thou brought me forth out of the womb? Oh, that I had given up the ghoft, and no eye had feen me! I fhould have been carried from the womb to the grave, &c.*

Some have indeed underftood the word εγυνηθη in this paffage as fignifying begotten, in which fenfe it will be affirmed that it had been better for *Judas* never to have been a man, a begotten fon of *Adam*, than to have been the betrayer of the LORD: but our beft critics rejecting this acceptation, agree that his being *born* and not his being *begotten* muft have been intended in this term; becaufe, 1ft. The proverbial ufe of thefe words in our LORD's time cannot well be doubted of. 2dly. Becaufe their allufion to the circumftances of *Job* and *Jeremiah* feems fo very probable; but moft of all becaufe, 3dly. the emphatical ufe of the word ανθρωπος can no otherwife be accounted for, fince a man cannot be called ανθρωπος or man till after he is begotten. And 4thly. Becaufe, as the greek verb γενναω, when applied to a father, fignifies to beget, fo when applied to a child it as conftantly fignifies to be born.ᵃ But

NOTES.

ᵃ γενναω applied to a father fignifies to beget (*Matt.* i. 2.) *and Abraham* (εγεννησε) *begat Ifaac, and Ifaac* (εγεννησε) *begat Jacob, &c.* (John i. 13.) *which were begot-*

But these words of our LORD, thus understood, import no more than that it had been better for (ἀνθρωπῳ ἐκείνῳ) that man that he had died in his mother's womb; that he had proved an abortive birth; that he had been carried from the womb to the grave; that he had never seen the sun; had never been duly born: and in this meaning of them, which I presume every unprejudiced reader will admit of, they contain nothing repugnant to the Doctrine which we are concerned in, and cannot be forced to conclude any thing against our principles.

If *Judas* had died in his mother's womb, he still would have been a man, and so have had all the advantages of a son of *Adam*; and at the same

---

NOTES.

ten *not of blood, nor of the will of the flesh, nor of the will of man, but of God* (ἐκ Θεȣ ἐγεννήθησαν). Acts vii. 29. *And Moses begat* (ἐγεννησεν) *two sons.*

γεννάω applied to a child signifies to be born. So Matt. ii. 1. *Now when Jesus was born in Bethlehem* (γεννηθέντος δὲ τȣ Ἰησȣ) ver. 4. *he demanded where Christ should be born* (πȣ γεννᾶται). Matt. xix. 12. *And some were born Eunuchs* (ἐγεννήθησαν). John ix. 20. *We know that this our son was born blind* (ἐγεννήθη).

But because our LORD talked to his Disciples in the syriac language; and consequently the acceptation of the syriac word, in which he in this place expresses himself of *Judas*, is most to our purpose, I shall here shew (and that by the passages already quoted) that the word (ܝܠܕ) ild, in which our LORD threatens *Judas*, signifies, as γεννάω, when applied to children, to be born, or to come into the world.

same time he would not have been the betrayer of his LORD and redeemer, and so would have escaped that curse which was the horrible issue of his treachery.

The less share a bad man has in this life, and the shorter it is, the more sufferable will be its consequences when ill-spent. This is a truth evident to every man's conscience; for every man's conscience tells him that the longer a wicked person enjoys his state of liberty to do evil, and the more multiplied and complicated that evil grows, the more envenomed will be also his portion of bitterness.

In

NOTES.

So *Matt.* ii. 1. *When therefore Jesus was born at Bethlehem* (ܟܕ ܕܝܢ ܐܬܝܠܕ ܝܫܘܥ ܒܒܝܬܠܚܡ). Ver. 4. *And he demanded of them where Christ should be born* (ܐܝܟܐ ܡܬܝܠܕ ܡܫܝܚܐ,). Mat. xix. 12. *There are eunuchs who are born so from the womb of their mother* (ܡܢ ܟܪܣܐ ܕܐܡܗܘܢ, ܐܬܝܠܕܘ ܗܟܢܐ,). John ix. 20. *We know that this is our son, and that he was born blind* (ܘܟܕ ܣܡܐ ܐܬܝܠܕ,).

We may therefore, I think, fairly conclude, that since (ܝܠܕ) ild, denotes to be born when applied to a child, it may also signify to be born when applied, as in our text, to *Judas*; and that the following words ought to be translated as follows: *Mat.* xxvi. 24. (ܦܩܚ ܗܘܐ ܠܗ ܠܓܒܪܐ ܗܘ ܐܠܘ ܠܐ ܐܬܝܠܕ,) *It had been expedient for that man if he had not been born,* i. e. that he had died in his mother's womb, and had not been a living member of the present age.

In this view of events it might be good not only for *Judas*, but for a great part of mankind, that they had died in their mother's womb.

Again, the oftner a man refists the inward callings of GOD upon his conscience inviting him to repentance, the more ungracious he grows, hardening under indulgences; for sin begets sin; and in this view of *Judas*, it may have been happy for him that he survived not his master till to the day of penticost.

Again, when the time of GOD's chastisements is come upon us, if we meet these with a front of self-righteousness, and with an heart unbruised; our enmity soon faces itself with impudence, and our despair is transformed into insolence.

Thus when hereafter the conscience-seared followers of antichrist (*Rev.* xvi. 19.) shall be scorched with the intense heat of the sun, occasioned by the 4th vial of wrath poured upon it; instead of repenting under their calamities, they will retort upon them in blasphemies: and when (ver. 10.) the 5th angel shall proceed to pour a fresh vial of wrath upon the kingdom of the beast; a greater chastisement will be answered with a greater effrontery; for *they will blaspheme the God of heaven, because of their pains and sores, repenting not of their deeds*.

But *Judas* was not thus abandoned; altho' he was born to the calamity of a traitor, yet was he not spared in his wickedness to the becoming a blasphemer; but, being arrested for sin in this act of treachery (*Mat.* xxvii. 3, 4.) *he repented himself, and went and* confessed his guilt. He confessed

fessed it too before the parties concerned with him; and parties who were well able to refute his confession, as an accusation recoiling upon themselves, with severity; yet in the face of their power, and in defiance of their dignity, he brought the pieces of silver to the chief priests and elders, and cast them down before them, and declared to them all, *I have sinned in that I have betrayed innocent blood.*

However his awakened conscience was not relieved hereby; his guilt was left to prey upon him to the accomplishing its full effect: *Acts* i. 20. (ἡ ἐπαυλις αυτε ἐρημος ἐγενετο) *his estate* or mansion *became desolate, and without inhabitant*; *his office* as apostle, *became Mathias*'s; and his soul [unfit for the ἐπαυλις or μονη (*John* xiv. 2, 3.) *i. e.* that mansion of grace which his master had provided him, *æonian in the heavens*] *went to its own place,* the resort of disembodied souls diseased. *John* xii. 40. *Acts* iv. 12.

※※※※※※※※※※※※※※※※※※※-※※※※※※ ※※※※※※※※

SECT. II.

A few moral reflections on Judas.

THE abuse of our grace is the measure of our guilt; and wicked men will therefore be more miserable than wicked spirits, because they have abused that grace which has never yet been indulged to wicked spirits.

But the sin of *Judas* had an aggravation beyond the degrees of sin usual at that time; in that the grace which he abused was his call to GOD in *Christ.*

As the sin of man exceeds that of evil spirits, so the sin of one called to GOD in *Christ*, exceeds that of man knowing no such call.

It is upon this account, as has been already hinted, that the LORD denounces a more intolerable judgment upon *Corasin, Bethsaida,* and *Capernaum (Matt.* xi. 21—24.) *than upon Tyre and Sidon, Sodom and Gomorrah.* And again (chap. xxiii.) a greater damnation upon the *Scribes* and *Pharisees,* than upon other *Jews*; and (chap. xii.) upon the *Jewish* nation than upon *Nineveh:* comparing them (ver. 43.) to a man dispossessed of a devil, who being *cast out, and walking thro' dry places, seeking rest and finding none,* he resolves to return to his possession, and takes (ver. 45.) *with him seven other spirits, more wicked than himself, and they enter in and dwell there, and the last state of that man is worse than the first.*

The condemnation of the *Jews* was (*Luke* xix. 44.) *because they knew not* (*i. e.* refused to distinguish the day of grace, or) *the time of their visitation.* They refused to observe this their day; and so refusing, their eyes were soon judicially blind to it. *Luke* xix. 42. *If thou hadst known, even thou, at least in this thy day, the things which belong to thy peace*; *but now are they hid from thine eyes.*

A most important hour is life; its occurrences are all a crowd of interesting events that deserve well our observation, being big with purposes of divine love for us. GOD *is not far from every one of us, we are his workmanship,* and he is ever at work upon us. This is so universally true,

true, and so absolutely the condition of human life; that every man living may say of himself, *jam mea res agitur*, now is my fortune at stake.[p]

But *Judas* discovered the use of life too late; had he reflected thus during his first parley with satan, and before the consolation he promised himself from the thirty pieces of silver had determined his resolution, this might have been an happy thought for him.

As it happened, his christian call became a snare to him; and he proved the father of those (*Matt.* vii. 15. ἁρπαγες λυκοι) plundering wolves in the christian church, who have ever since constantly attended every true work of christian grace. *John* xii. 6. Inwardly *he was a thief*; and therefore perverted his holy office into an opportunity to steal, making it a cloak, or *sheeps cloathing,*

NOTES.

[p] The justness of these reflections even an heathen eye could discern, says *Persius* in his third satyr;

Est aliquid quo tendis, & in quod dirigis arcum?
An passim sequeris corvos, testâq; lutoq;
Securus quo pes ferat, atq; ex tempore vivis?
Helleborum frustra, cum jam cutis ægra tumebit,
Poscentes videas *: venienti occurrite morbo—*
Discite O miseri, & causas cognoscite rerum,
Quid sumus, *& quidnam victuri gignimur, ordo*
Quis datus, *aut metæ qua mollis flexus, & undæ:*
Quis modus argento, quid fas optare, quid asper
Utile nummus habet; patriæ, carisq; propinquis
Quantum elargiri deceat: quem te Deus esse
Jussit, & humaná qua parte locatus es in ré,
Disce; nec invideas quod multa fidelia putet
In locuplete penu, defensis pinguibus Umbris, *&c.*

ing, to his designs of *robbery.* And being by this means accomplished (*John* xvii. 12.) *a son of perdition* (*Heb.* xii. 17. *Matt.* xxvii. 3, 4, 5.) *he found no place of repentance,* and died (tho' probably not altogether obdurate, yet) *without hope.*

When the day of mercy is past, and the execution of divine justice begins; then also repentance begins to seem in vain. For the stroke falls upon the offender with that repeated, unrebating violence which proves it to be in earnest.

The dispensations of sorrow Jehovah calls in *Ezekiel* his unrelenting justice, the accomplishing anger; and describes as multiplying troubles. *Rev.* xviii. 8. *Her plagues shall come upon her in one day, death, mourning and famine, and she shall be utterly burnt with fire.*

And thus the restless passion of *Judas's* despair related in the gospel, was but the beginning of his distresses. For when his fleshly tabernacle was laid in the dust, and its refreshments could no longer relieve or ease him; when by his bodily death the faculties of his soul became alive, and thereby his soul's original instincts and desires began to be revealed and awakened within him; revealed in their native strength and urgency; then must he have understood the want of that grace which he had neglected, and the value of that redeemer whom he had sold.

The souls appetites give the true hunger, bodily hunger is but a type or shadow of this; and the fierce impatience of these appetites unsatiated seems to be the condition of hell: as *Tantalus* is fabulously described under the violences of this passion,

passion, making efforts vain and impracticable of fruition.

And as the soul's hunger is that very appetite which *Christ* became man to allay with his grace, and saturate with his own fulness; *Judas* dying under the guilt of grace neglected, and the preference of a pecuniary trifle to his LORD from heaven; was undoubtedly suffered to feel in earnest what it is to exist in an after life without this LORD for a redeemer.

Jehovah complains of his people the *Jews* (*Jer.* ii. 13.) *My people have committed two evils; they have forsaken me the fountain of living waters, and hew'd themselves out cisterns, broken cisterns that will hold no water.* On the other hand of the blessed we read (*Pf.* xxxvi. 8.) *Thou shalt make them to drink of the river of thy pleasures, for with thee is the fountain of life.* Pf. xvi. 11. *The saturating joy is from thy presence, and at thy right hand are pleasures for evermore.*

But when the eager cravings of the soul's life shall be our experience; shall again revive and kindle in us in their primitive vigour (cravings which not the whole universe can satisfy, which can be gratified only by the enjoyment and vision of the GOD of glory denied) what must be that man's despair who sees all his hopes of interest in him, and favour from him, sold, forfeited, or lost!

Judas wanted that eye of faith which should have shewed him his master's true value: here was his misfortune. And this will hereafter prove to be the case not only of *Judas* the *Iscariot*; but

but many *Judases* will the christian world disclose at that day, when the dignity of the crucified person shall be manifested; when the despised *Jesus* shall appear to *have been* the Logos; the first fountain of all life; the beginning of the creation of GOD: and *to be then* and for ever afterward the one source of all glory, that supreme divinity, in whose presence visible is the one true delight and blessedness, for all intellectual beings of every degree of happiness.

However as in the love of the *Jehovah-Jesus* there is a keenness of severity, which has very salutary effects; this account of the ancient or modern *Judases* can in no wise defeat my point; since it will by no means argue their endless damnation, or any unwillingness in GOD to restore even those who have denied him. So far from it that 'could we but clearly see his love of his enemies we should discover every event pointing towards the restitution of all, and every emergent revolution opening into the fulness of him who is about to fill all in all.

S E C T. III.

Farther reflections on the foregoing subject.

WE have already acknowledged a retributive justice in GOD, and in consequence thereof, a damnation of the wicked; a damnation correspondent with all the forms of equity and realities of truth; and verily such as is not only

only confiftent with the higheft notions of univerfal fatisfaction, but feems to be even implied in them; as fays St. *Paul* (*Rom.* iii. 31.) *Do we then make void the law thro' faith? God forbid;* yea, **we** *eftablifh the law.*

In order to judge rightly of the creature it muft be confidered in two relations, viz. its relation to the divine immutible effence, from the which it is afunder and feparate; and its relation to the firft-begotten or Logos, in and by whom it exifts and lives and moves.

With regard to the firft of thefe relations, nothing can be more certain than that the utmoft a finner can do or fuffer for himfelf, or that any creature can do or fuffer for him, will avail him nothing towards expiating the guilt of fin, and reftoring him to the notices of divine favour. This event can be effected only by the invaluable death and humiliation of the only begotten uncreated fon of the holy eternal GOD. But by him it has therefore *been* fo effected, and that too in the moft accomplifhed manner. As we read (*Rom.* iv. 25.) *He was delivered for our fins*; (2 Cor. v. 21.) *he was made fin for us* (Eph. v. 2.) *a facrifice to God of a fweet-fmelling favour* (Col. ii. 14.) *blotting out, by his decree, the hand writing againft us, that was contrary to us, taking it out of the way, nailing it to his crofs.*

And that this great work was finifhed whilft he lived a man on this earth we are alfo taught: for (1 *Pet.* ii. 24.) *he himfelf bare our fins in his own body on the tree—by his ftripes we are healed.*

Heb.

Heb. i. 3.—ix. 12. *Who, when he had by himself purged our sins he sat down at the right hand of God.*

And that this great sacrifice was for all we also learn (1 *Tim.* ii. 6.) *for he gave himself a ransom for all.* Heb. ix. 27. *He has abolished sin by the sacrifice of himself; being once offered to bear the sins of the multitude.* 1 John ii. 2. *He is the propitiation for our sins, and not for ours only, but for the sins of the whole world.* Heb. x. 14. *By one (single) oblation he has perfected for ever the sanctified by him.*

And of the effect of this great sacrifice we read (*Rom.* v. 10.) *we are reconciled to God by his death.* 2 Cor. v. 19. *God was in Christ reconciling the world unto himself, not imputing their trespasses unto them.* Col. i. 20. *And by him to reconcile all things unto him (having made peace by the blood of his cross; by him, I say,) whether they be things on earth or things in heaven.*

But notwithstanding all this, and altho' all creatures are justified already, in the man *Jesus* before his holy father, yet are they not thereby justified before him their justifier; or exempted from the bar of his sovereignty, and the prevailing operativeness of what is called in scripture his wrath.

The usual character of this our justifier in the old testament, where he is also called (דבר יהוה מלאך יהוה) the word Jehovah, the angel Jehovah; is *that he will visit iniquity, transgression and sin; that he will visit both the hosts of angels and the sons of men,* both *Jews* and *Gentiles,* both those who know him and those that know him not. And
there-

therefore are his own people cautioned by Jehovah himself against offending him; as we read (*Exod.* xx. 22.) *And Jehovah said unto Moses* (xxiii. 20.) *behold I send* (מלאך) *the angel before thee, beware of thyself before him; be* **not** *rebellious against him; for he will not spare your perverseness; for my name* (or that which denominates me GOD) *is within him* (בקרבו in his interior or inmost being).

So that as it **is the** prerogative of Jehovah to forgive **sins;** this is also the prerogative **of his** angel (יהוה מלאך the angel Jehovah) in that the fulness of Jehovah dwells **in** him; in whose power also, he will exert himself against his enemies, altho' they **are** his **redeemed** ones, and demonstrate himself an avenging, as well as a redeeming GOD.

To this character **of** our LORD answer numberless accounts of him in the new testament; where he all along assures us that we shall be accepted of him according to our conduct as men; for that (*Matt.* vii. 21.) *Not every one that saith unto me, Lord, Lord, shall enter into the kingdom of heaven,* **but** *he that doth the will of my father who is in heaven.* That (*Matt.* xii. 37.) *by thy words* **thou** *shalt be justified,* **and** *by thy words thou shalt be condemned.* In short, as has been by us so often urged, that *he will bring tribulation and anguish upon every soul that doth evil*, and that in proportion **to** that evil; **for** the difference in degrees of suffering, **is as** the distance between heaven and earth.

And yet we moreover doubt not but that, as the arm which afflicts is directed by the heart
which

which redeemed us, and as our chastiser is our very sin-offering; the utmost misery may, under the conduct of our God, be rendered productive of equal happiness. And surely it is less absurd to believe thus, than to presume that God can be nonplussed by contingencies unforeseen; or that evil coeval with God, is the destined plan of the pure benevolent nature.

What stores of mercies, what a provision for beneficence is disclosed to us from the desperate circumstances of fallen *Adam!* We learn too that the imagined defeat and death of him who was born to be our restorer; was so far from ruining the purposes of his birth, that it proved the very means of finishing it; therefore before he bowed his head and gave up the ghost, he declared (*John* xix. 30. τετελεσται) *it is finished*; by which we are to understand that the great work of redemption is now accomplished, consummated, and the restoration of the lost insured.

And as it pleases God continually to produce good out of mischief, light out of darkness, beauty out of deformity, harmony out of discord, a paradise out of a chaos, and resurrection out of corruption; why may we not also believe him both able and willing to bring happiness out of misery, heaven out of hell, and eternal life out of æonian death and perdition?

And thus when the hated *Judas* shall make one among the twelve apostles (*Matt.* xix. 28.) *sitting upon twelve thrones, judging the twelve tribes of Israel*; this promise of sitting as judge of *Israel* was made to *Judas* as absolutely as to the rest of
the

the apostles, he being one of the twelve. And altho' his office as an apostle in this world was filled by *Mathias* (*Acts* i. 26.) yet his (επαυλις) mansion or estate provided by his master for him (see *John* xiv. 2, 3.) was to lay desolate, *i. e.* was not to be filled by any other. *Acts* i. 20. (γενηθητω ἡ επαυλις αυτου ερημος, κ̣ μη εςω ὁ κατοικων εν αυτη) *Let his mansion become desolate, and let there not be an inhabitant in it*; i. e. it was to lay waste like the principalities of the fallen angels (see *Jude* 6.)— But why? and for how long? for ever? by no means. When the number of the first-fruits shall be accomplished, there will be no desolate mansions within the enclosures of paradise (where *Judas*'s was provided him) each will be surely occupied, and that by its proper owner, even by him *for whom it had been prepared of the father*, Matt. xx. 23. Then will it be his exultation and song of praise, that the blessings of GOD predestined *without repentance* to be his, have been, by the wisdom and bounty of his divine providence, wrapped up securely for him in all his perverseness and unbelief; and that his GOD knows how to unfold to man such treasures of love, and reserves of mercies from the hell opened in his soul, as shall abundantly recompence all his sorrows; and make him to regret his sufferings, chiefly as marks of his ingratitude to injured innocence, and neglected love divine. *Hos.* xiii. 9. *O Israel thou hast destroyed thyself* (*i. e.* without the concurrence of my will) *but in me is thy help.*

So then we cannot escape our ultimate restitution; but we can escape those dark horrible conceptions the GOD of nature which may make us rue in our blindness, not only that we had ever been born, but that we had ever existed at all his creatures.

To prevent this, that is to obviate the dire effects of the now natural stupidity of the human soul, is the gospel published; proposing to us the GOD of all for our true good, pointing out his love and faithfulness and righteousness and plenitude, for our sure dependance, hope, fortune, estate, inheritance, and all-sufficiency for evermore; that so possessing him, and thereby partaking of his holy nature, we may be *delivered out of the hands of them that hate us, and may serve him without fear, in holiness and righteousness before him all the days of our life.*

But if we refuse the GOD of glory thus exhibited to us as our reconciled LORD and Redeemer; and set at nought *his righteousness, sanctification and redemption*; then shall we be left to the workings and progress of our own blindness, which, containing in its issues the elements and principles of misery, will teach us by dreadful experiment, to what extremities of anguish an active, reflecting, darkened, and hungry soul, grown desperate in error and impatience, can arrive.

[411]

LETTER XXIII.

The scripture passage objected against us, from Heb. ii. 16. *considered.*

TO ———

SIR,

SECT. I.

Heb. ii. 16. (Ου γαρ δηπου αγγελων επιλαμβανεται, αλλα σπερματος Αβρααμ επιλαμβανεται) *For verily he catcheth not hold of angels, but he* **catcheth** *hold of the seed of Abraham.*

OUR opponents can no otherwise forge an argument against us out of this text, than by having recourse to a false translation of it in our english testament, where we read it as follows:

For verily he took not on him the nature of angels, but he took on him the seed of Abraham.

Say they, our LORD took not on him the nature of angels, therefore angels will not be restored.

The falsehood of the antecedent proposition here appears from *Gen.* xxii. 15, 16.—xlviii. 16.

Judges

Judges vi. 22.—xiii. 21, 22. *Isa.* lxiii. 9. *Zech.* iii. 1. *Mal.* iii. 1. *Acts* vii. 38. but neither will the consequent serve them, for we hereby retort against them from their own principle as follows:

Our LORD took upon him the nature of all men, therefore will all men be restored; which is as much as to say, that all men are of the seed of *Abraham*, which is not true.

Yea farther, our LORD being as much an angel as he is a man, we might argue with them again as follows:

They whose nature the LORD beareth will be restored; but he beareth the nature of the angels, therefore the angels will be restored.

But because I have no inclination to cavil, I shall only observe that the word ἐπιλαμβανομαι does by no means signify *to take upon him the nature of*, but that it signifies *to catch hold on with ones hands*, or *to grasp fast in ones arms*, as is evident from very many places in scripture, of which I give you some in my notes.[q]

So that this passage declares no more than that he suffers the angels to sink into perdition; he lays no hold on them as they are falling, it is only of the seed of *Abraham* that he catches hold.

He

NOTES.

[q] *Heb.* viii. 9. *In the day of my taking them by the hand* (εν ημερα επιλαβομενα με της χειρος αυτων) *to lead them out of the land of Egypt.* Acts xxiii. 19. *The chief captain took the young man by the hand and went aside* (επιλαβομενος δε της χειρος αυτον). Acts xvi. 19. *They caught Paul and Silas* (επιλαβομενοι τον παυλον) *and drew*

He suffers angels to fall, he suffers also men to fall, all but the faithful among them, who are otherwise called the seed of *Abraham*.

For, as before man was created GOD permitted those rebel angels who forsook their principalities to fall, whilst others their **fellows were** graciously supported by him that they should not fall; in like manner he now catches hold on those among men, who are called the seed of *Abraham*, and suffers them **not to** fall into **that** perdition, **which is** reserved for satan and his followers, and which shall be revealed in proper time on all abusers of preventing grace.

As among the angels those who hearkened to preventing grace fell not, neither shall those among men fall who hearken to preventing grace; but they shall escape the wrath prepared, and pass immediately from death into life; they shall not even taste that death which consists in the soul's separation from *Christ*, the one true life of all spiritual subsistence.

Accordingly they who have their eyes open, observe clearly that whilst all condemned nature is going down the tide together towards one common vortex of misery and death; these, the children

---

NOTES.

them to the rulers. Luke ix. 47. *And Jesus taking up a little boy* (ἐπιλαβόμενος παιδίου) *sat him in the midst.* Matt. xiv. 31. *And Jesus stretched forth his hand and caught him* (ἐπελάβετο αὐτοῦ) *namely Peter sinking in the waves.* See also *Gen.* xxv. 26. *Exod.* iv. 4. *Judg.* xvi. 3, 21, &c. in the septuagint.

dren of *Abraham*, are here and there gather'd out from among the devoted crowd, as *firebrands plucked out of the fire.*

And yet notwithstanding this we may not doubt but that unbounded mercy follows all both loft and saved to their utmost destiny.

The central motive of divine power is love or goodness; for as divine power is ever excited by divine will, and divine will is ever benevolent; the same benevolence which we rejoice in, and which attends every divine effort, must be the one incitement of that we call divine omnipotence, thro' all its exertions; and so it will amount to the same thing whether we say divine benevolence, or divine power, or divine justice, or divine wisdom permitted death to the sons of perdition.

It was permitted by GOD, therefore by love, therefore with a provisionary purpose of good out of evil continually.

We may create evil to ourselves, and this evil when created shall be our portion; but since Jehovah knows how to control all evils in the event, they are all made to subserve a good end; and hence it happens that misery itself becomes instrumental to high designs of grace, and the sublimest projects of mercy.

Saith Jehovah (*If.* xlv. 7.) *I form light and create darkness, I make peace and create evil* (Heb. iv. 13.) *neither is there any creature that is not manifest in his fight.*

All things are naked and open to his eyes, and they are said to be so because he concerns himself in all things; he is also said to be *the Lord both of quick and dead*; because he acts as a LORD whose property are all things; as a LORD presiding over all whether they be quickened or dying souls; as a LORD conducting all things in heaven and earth and hell, among the **lost and among** the recovered.

All must **be restored**, all must be requickened; life is our destiny **we** cannot escape it; we may withstand it and kick against the pricks; **we** may delay it and taste the condition of devils; but to diminish the *efficacy* of the divine sacrifice is impossible; and blessed are they that enjoy it in this life,

SECT. II.

THE CONCLUSION.

I HAVE now answered every objection produced from scripture testimony which, respecting the kingdom of GOD, is usually alledged against the doctrine of universal restitution.

I intend hereafter in the course of my succeeding letters to examine the several scripture testimonies respecting the human soul, usually alledged against this doctrine: among which is that remarkable passage in *Mark* ix. 43—50.

But **before** I conclude indulge **me** in a few familiar reflections with you.

You say that notwithstanding all which has been advanced, you dare not give your credit to this strange doctrine.

Never-

Nevertheless you must acknowledge it to be, if true, (ευαγγελιον) good news, glad tidings; yea, he has not the heart of a man who can abhor it.

It is a pregnant argument of a bad mind to love prerogative, exclusive privileges, and preference above others. *The angels rejoice in heaven over one sinner that repenteth.*

But perhaps the readiest way to the discovery of this great point is the knowledge of *Jesus Christ,* and of our acceptance in him the beloved; at least without this, without the knowledge of our acceptance in *Jesus Christ* the beloved there is no true knowledge of God, and so no true happiness to be found. Let it then be our first business to know *Jesus Christ,* so, by the light resulting from this knowledge, it will be clearly seen, whether this notion of universal redemption be a mote in my eye or not.

My dear friend this is no ill advice, the happiness of angels consists in their knowledge, that is, vision of God; and they who see him most are the most sublimely happy.

And as the vision and therefore knowledge of God is appointed for the enjoyment of angels, so is it no less for the enjoyment of men. We are all both angels and men called alike to this vision of God; as the one fountain of happiness for all intellectual creatures; as that only which is adequate to all our capacities.

Again as it is this knowledge of God which makes the difference between good and bad angels, so it is this same knowledge which makes the difference between good and bad men. This
power

power of vision is grace, distinguishing grace, good spirits have this grace, bad spirits have it not.

Therefore says our good *Justin* the Martyr in his epistle to *Diognetus* [ἀνθρώπων δε ουδεις ουτε ειδεν ουτε εγνωρισεν (scilicet τον Θεον); αυτος δε εαυτον επεδειξεν; επεδειξε δε δια πιστεως; ἡ μονη Θεον ιδειν συγκεχωρηται.] " No man " hath either seen or known GOD; but he has " manifested himself; and this manifestation is " made by faith, to which (virtue) alone it is " indulged to behold GOD."

To this idea of things relates the first commandment which *Christ* gives us as the greatest of all others (*Matt.* xxii. 37.) *Thou shalt love the Lord thy God with all thy heart, with all thy soul, with all thy mind, and with all thy strength.*

For since we cannot be commanded by GOD to love whom we know not; a command to love GOD with the utmost force of all our faculties, must be as sure a command to know or learn GOD with the utmost force of all our faculties. And because it is our highest glory and privilege and duty and blessing to love GOD, it is likewise all this to know him.

And possibly sin originally began by an aversion of the eye from GOD to the fond admiration of creature excellence; seeing it is the testimony of constant experience, that the darkness of the inner man results from the neglect of intercourse with our GOD.

Now suppose a creature to be a sinner, and consequently in darkness, and not seeing GOD, and therefore not knowing him; and you will soon apprehend that in these circumstances his first knowledge of GOD must be that described (*Exod.* xxxiv. 6.) *that he is merciful, and gracious, abundant in goodness, forgiving iniquity, transgression and sin.*

But sin is a strange unnatural thing, and what the creature as he first came pure out of the hands of GOD could have no notion of; and for the same reason we may presume that divine forgiveness must be as strange a thing, and that of which the darkened creature could naturally form no notion, nor discover any fitness in.

This strange idea of forgiveness in GOD the pure essence, must therefore require a fresh revelation from GOD to render it credible to our reason, the object of our hopes: and the now delinquent creature darkened by his delinquency, so darkened as no longer to see GOD in his purity, must be much less able to see his love in the unnatural relation of a sinning creature and a forgiving GOD.

So then a preternatural revelation from GOD being now needful in our state of delinquency, namely a revelation of GOD's pardoning love; we find it made as described in the evangelical writers. Says *Isaiah* (liii. 4—6.) *Surely he hath born our griefs, and carried our sorrows, yet we did esteem him smitten of God and afflicted. He was wounded for our transgressions, he was bruised for our iniquities; the chastisement of our peace was upon him, and with his stripes we are healed. All we like sheep have gone astray, we have turned every one to his own way, and Jehovah hath laid on him the iniquity of us all.*

And

And thus here becomes again opened to us the view, and so the knowledge of GOD in a fresh account of him, namely our vision of him in the person of *Jesus Christ*; a vision for all delinquent creatures whether angels or men, a vision (as **St.** *Paul* expresses it, 2 **Cor.** iv. 6.) *of the glory of God in the face of Jesus Christ.* And whatever this vision of GOD may be in angels, it is called in man his faith; for faith is vision internal.

As there was no entrance into the sanctuary but thro' the veil, and with the blood of the sin-offering; so there can be now no entrance into that knowledge of GOD which *sheds abroad the love of God in our hearts*, but thro' a previous knowledge of *Christ* the Lamb of GOD who beareth away the sin of the world.

The knowledge of our salvation by the remission of our sins thro' the tender mercies of our GOD, this is our only perspective thro' which we can behold GOD in his real nature, love.

Thus much we learn from our LORD's own words to *Simon* the Pharisee (*Luke* vii. 41—47.) *There was a certain creditor who had two debtors, the one owed five hundred pence, the other fifty; and when they had nothing to pay, he frankly forgave them both; tell me therefore which of them will love most?* Simon *answered* and *said, I suppose he to whom he forgave most; and he said unto him, thou hast rightly judged. And he turned unto the woman, and said unto* Simon, *seest thou this woman; I entered into thy house, thou gavest me no water for my feet—thou gavest me no kiss—mine head with oil thou didst not anoint—wherefore I say unto thee, her sins, which are many, are forgiven, therefore she loved much; but to whom little is forgiven, the same loveth little.* So that the degree of our forgiveness is the measure of our love.

We are apt to think that if we were only in a state of perfect innocence, we should address our heavenly father with a confidence that he would hear us graciously. The *Jews* also thought thus. Says the blind man, whose eyes *Jesus* opened with clay, to the Pharisees (*John* ix. 31.) *we know that God heareth not sinners; but if any man be a worshiper of God, him he heareth.*

But a dependance upon being thus accepted of GOD on account of our own innocence would at best be very precarious, because, as says the *Psalmist, who can tell how often he offendeth;* yea who can at any time say, " Now I offend not;" for (*Ps.* cxxx. 3.) *when the Lord marketh iniquities, who shall stand.*

But we know that the only begotten son of GOD is dearer to him than any creature can conceive, (*Prov.* viii. 30. אצלי אמון ישעשועים יום יום משחקת לפניו בכל עת) *his very truth, his daily delight, rejoicing always before him,* or rather whose operations are his perpetual pleasure,ʳ and (*Matt.* xix. 28. *Heb.* viii. 1.) *setting in the throne of his*

NOTES.

ʳ That the *Jews* understood this passage in the *Proverbs* as spoken of the Logos, appears from *Philo Judæus, lib.* 1. *legis allegoriarum.* Ἡ τȣ Θεȣ σοφια ες̓ιν ὁ τȣ Θεȣ Λογος---ἡ τȣ Θεȣ σοφια χαιρει κ̓ γαννυται κ̓ τροφα επι μονω τω πατρι αυτης αγαλλομενη κ̓ σεμνυνομενη Θεω.

his glory: now could we but find means to become dear to GOD in his son; could we but be presented to GOD as holy and unblamable in the righteousness of this his Son, called (2 *Cor.* v. 2.) *the righteousness of God:* could we but become thus accepted in the beloved; we might proclaim with St. *Paul* (Rom. viii. 31.) *If God be for us, who shall be against us! he that spared not his own son but delivered him up for us all; how shall he not with him also freely give us all things. Who shall lay any thing to the charge of God's elect? Shall God that justifieth? Who shall be he that condemneth? Shall Christ that died? Yea rather that is also risen again? Who is at the right hand of God, who also maketh intercession for us?*

David long before our saviour's time foresaw such gratuitous acceptance in the imputed worth of *Christ,* when he said, *Blessed is the man whose iniquities are forgiven, and whose sin is covered; blessed is the man to whom the Lord will not impute sin.*

And if our love of GOD depend upon our knowledge of him, and our knowledge of GOD is revealed to us in the vision of his atonement and pardoning love, then is this vision of GOD atoning our most important business.

It is our highest interest to love GOD, therefore to know GOD, therefore to know *Jesus Christ* and ourselves in him crucified. That seeing

---

NOTES.

" The wisdom of GOD is the word of GOD—the wis-
" dom of GOD glories and exults and has his enjoy-
" ments in GOD, being delighted, and dignified by
" him his only father."

ing our acceptance in *Chrift* the beloved, our eyes may open into the miftery of divine love, and may be able *to love God becaufe he firft loved us*; or to love him in contemplation of that facrifice which he had predeftin'd for us *Jefus Chrift* the innocent.

Till the divine light has difperfed our foul's darknefs, and, by awakening the feeing powers of the inward man, has fhewn us our finful felves; the exhibiting of *Chrift* crucified proves a fruitlefs work: whilft a man has nothing within him that anfwers that great object, it can yield him no more enjoyment than the light of the fun, fhining upon a darkened eye, can delight it with its glory.

Hence is the doctrine of a crucified GOD ftale, taftlefs, impertinent, and void of all excellence to an heart dead in its natural felf righteoufnefs, and In-defire of mercy.

A man may indeed contemplate the Logos as a GOD of all power and perfection, but this is not to know him as a GOD of all confolation and comfort. Yea, and the view of him as an all perfect GOD is fo far from rendering him our happinefs, that it has a contrary effect. Says *Peter* unconverted, *depart from me, for I am a finful man, O Lord*; fay the evil fpirits to him, *let us alone, what have we to do with thee Jefus thou holy one of God? art thou come to torment us even before our time?* They complain of his holinefs, and at the fame time dread him as their enemy. But fays *Thomas* when the converting light of grace and acceptance operated upon him, " *my Lord and my God;*" that is, he appropriated GOD to himfelf. The

LETTER XXIII. SECT. II.

The christian calling is to a life of blessedness; of blessedness thro' the person of *Jesus Christ*; a blessedness given and shed abroad in our hearts, by his enlightning and cheering spirit; who therefore is called the teacher and comforter, and whose part it is to represent *Jesus* to us during his seeming absence, as a present, pardoning, loving GOD and father.

By the light of this comforter our blindness to all that which is lovely in *Jesus* vanishes, as the scales fell from the eyes of *Paul*, turned to his GOD; and then what we hear of him becomes musick in our ears, like the voice of a mother returning to her child for some time witheld from the breasts of her consolation.

What food is to the hungry, and drink is to the thirsty, even that is an intercourse and commerce with *Jesus* opened in the unhappy heart. *Christ* revealed fills it with peace, and joy, and thanksgiving, and godly sorrow, and holy shame, and those sighs of gratitude, whose pleasures none can taste till after he has resolved, as the returning prodigal, *I will arise and go to my father, and will say unto him, father, I have sinned against thee, and am no more worthy to be called thy son.*

Says our LORD, *God is a spirit, and they who worship him, must worship him in spirit and in truth*; or in spirit even in truth, inasmuch as the spiritual worship is the only true worship, and the bodily worship of little use.

But of the spiritual or soul worship the penitent soul only is capable, since it is the penitent soul only that can exert its faculties of admiration,

tion, love, desire, gratitude, humility, resignation, faithfulness, complacency, a single eye, a self contempt, and a confident dependence in the sacrifice of *Christ*; these all being the result of looking upon *Jesus* whom we have pierced.

And since the spiritual or soul worship is intended to be our heaven and perfection and glory; the study of our suffering LORD of glory must certainly be intended for our highest and greatest concern in life.

Neither may we suppose that our knowledge of GOD in *Christ* belongs to this life only; yea, but it yields that very spirit of gratitude which rules, as has been already observed in the four living beings and the twenty-four elders, and the many angels round about the throne of GOD (*Rev.* v. 9, 12.) whose numbers are ten thousand times ten thousand, and thousands of thousands; for these all proclaim aloud with one voice, *worthy is the Lamb for he was slain, and hath redeemed us to God by his blood.*

And since redemption thro' the blood of the Lamb is as truly the topic of joy amidst the hosts of angels in heaven, as in the church of GOD upon earth; we can devise no other reason for its being so, than that the view of *Christ* crucified opens to the eyes of the creature that joyful knowledge of GOD, which alone can ravish the creatures affections with its true delight in him.

I must observe farther, that as the vision of GOD in the face of *Christ* is the fountain of all the creature's enjoyment; so is it the fountain of
all

all the creature's holiness. Our vision of GOD in the face of *Christ* fills us with joy and peace in believing; and this our inward joy and inward peace brings down all heavenly tempers into our hearts, and transforms us into the likeness of *Christ* whom we behold.

The christian is like *Christ* because he sees him, and so long as he sees him, his own natural lust and pride and wrath are stanched, superseded, precluded. His calm joy within, the antepast of celestial bliss, replenishing his heart with a spirit of thankfulness, he becomes dead indeed unto sin, and alive unto righteousness.

All those abominations which we see abroad in the world, the reproach and misery of the sons of *Adam*, owe their origin to a departing from the face of GOD; to a living without GOD in this world. For the now natural tendency of the fallen soul is from GOD.

Indeed, if there were no innate disgust and enmity in the human soul against GOD, she would certainly rejoice in the invitations of friendship, made her by the word of GOD, as her inestimable honour, as a blessing transcending, beyond all comparison, every creature imaginable as an object of her wishes.

But instead of this, it is the character of most men that (*Rom.* i. 28.) *they like not to retain God in their knowledge*; their souls, regarding him not as their highest good, turn away from him; and seek their happiness in vanities which the principal evil spirit has contrived for their fatal amusements.

Vanities which, tho' imbellished with all the beauty this world can afford, are still so much below the excellencies of the human soul, that they could have no charms for her but by means of this aversion which we speak of.

And since our aversion to God appears to be the root of our misery, that great sin from whence all other sins follow as effects, the source of all those evils which disgrace, torment and infest human nature (*Rom.* i. 21—24.—28); wickedness may not unfitly be considered as our shame and punishment for forsaking *Christ*, whose spirit is the fountain head of all true virtue.

In like manner virtue may be considered as the result of a soul's drawing near to her God; her honour and reward of seeking after him.

Man would not willingly be wicked, if by bare wishing he could escape the being so: preventive grace within him, is his hearty approbation of virtue.

So then, according to this way of thinking, to be delivered from our enmity against God and his *Christ*, is to be delivered from every other vice: and on the other hand to love God in the spirit of *Jesus Christ*, is to be possessed of every virtue.

Experience likewise exactly answers to this account; for bring any one, the worst of men, to behold his crucified *Jesus*; and the source of sin within him is stay'd at once, as the flowings of a river by the dropping down of its flood-gate; and he at once proves a wonder to himself, and to his former associates in wickedness.

On

LETTER XXIII. [427] SECT. II.

On the other hand no sooner does the believer ceafe to behold his acceptance in *Jefus*, but the body of fin roufes itfelf again within him; and its inward workings become, as before his converfion, reftlefs like the troubled fea, continually cafting up mire and dirt.

Says Jehovah prophetically, that is, of what fhall hereafter happen, (*If.* xlv. 22.) *All the ends of the earth* (אפסי ארץ) *look unto me* (והושיעו) *and are caufed to be delivered* (or enlarged);[f] *i. e.* they are caufed

---

NOTES.

[f] Having frequently and in many of thefe my letters infifted that the greek word σωζω in our new teftament ought no where to be rendered *to fave, or preferve*; but always *to fet at liberty, to deliver, to reftore* (viz. to our primitive ftate of enlargement, life and happinefs): it may be to your entertainment, as well as to my purpofe, to give you the criticifm of that moft accurate and fagacious linguift *Albertus Schultens* upon the hebrew word ישע; whofe force and import we know the facred writers of the greek teftament have always intended in the ufe of their word σωζω, and which the fyriac teftament moftly renders by the word ܚܝܐ *he lived or revived*, in Aphel ܐܚܝ *he quickened or made alive*, &c.

This author, after fhewing in general the neceffity of knowing the proper or radical fenfe of a word in order to have a juft idea of the many various figurative fignifications of it, metaphorical, metonymical, &c. in which moft words in all languages are much more frequently ufed than in the proper (a principle eftablifhed, and a fact well known to all judicious critics) gives feveral examples of the ufefulnefs of difcovering this original or radical fenfe, in he-

caused to be delivered by looking; and till they look they are not caused to be delivered.

For in consequence of this look there springs forth within us that truly divine influence, in the power of which alone we are able *to serve* GOD *without fear in holiness and righteousness before him, all the days of our life*. But to serve him without fear is to serve him voluntarily, as his children and not as his slaves; in the restored liberty of our wills, by dint of that life in which the new creature,

---

NOTES.

brew words, and first in a word of the highest importance, viz. ישׁע from which root the name of our Lord and Restorer, JESUS, is derived: the proper import of which he shews both *Jews* and *Christians* have been at a loss for. Its proper and original sense is *roominess, spaciousness, wide extention,* in opposition to צרה implying, *narrowness, confinement, straitness,* as the two words are joined together in *Psalm* xxxiv. 6. *Jehovah* (הושׁיעו ³ צרותי ² מכל ¹) ³ *has set him at large* ¹ *from all* ² *his streights.* Ps. xliv. 7. *Thou hast caused me to stand enlarged* (חושׁעתנו מצרינו) *from all my streightners or distressers.* Jer. xiv. 8. *Jehovah the expectation of Israel,* ¹ *his enlarger* ² *in the time* ³ *of confinement* (צרה ³ בעת ² מושׁיעו ¹). This neutral signification in the first conjugation kal, becomes active in hiphel, and signifies to bring another out of straits and confinement into full room and free space. This being set at large is by a metaphor extended to signify being set free from distresses, oppression, troubles and sufferings, whether temporal or æonian, and enjoying without restraint all the advantages of that freedom and deliverance.

ture, our inward man, lives: but this lives and grows thro' his beholding the face of *Jesus*, and, by the vision of him, spontaneously produces in us all the blessed works of humanity and godliness.

Again, says the apostle (*Heb.* xii. 2) *Let us run with patience, looking unto Jesus the beginner and perfecter of our faith*, i. e. we are first to look unto *Jesus* because in this vision he is the *beginner*; we are afterwards to continue to look upon him, because in this vision he is also the *perfecter* of our faith.

By

NOTES.

The method the author uses to find out these radical senses of words, and the spring from whence he draws the necessary informations, will be best learned from his own writings; and the application of them to יש״ע may be found in p. 15—20, of his *Origines Hebrææ*, Vol. I, and a curious specimen of the same critical art applied to latin words may be read in the beginning of Cap. iii. of Vol. 2.

However as this excellent author is not in your study, nor to be bought in *England*, I here send you a large part of what he writes on this word: " יש״ע
" spatiosus, laxus, amplus fuit.———Valde quidem
" liberales vulgo sunt lexicographi, & sex septem
" plura vocabula latina, pro uno hebraico largiuntur
" —quæ si omnia omni ex parte colligerem, atq; ad
" radicem hebraicum cumularem, tanto majoribus
" eam tenebris implicuisse videri deberem, quanto
" ampliorem lucem, ex verborum ubertate, præ me
" tulissem.—Sed id laboratur, quidnam illud sit quod
" a primo sui ortu יש״ע complectatur, & cui max-
" ime cogitationi, tanquam propriæ suæ formæ,
" hebræi verbum hoc alligarint, unde velut ex capite

By our first looking upon *Jesus*, that principle of sinning convey'd into us from our conception and nativity, and wrap'd up in our mortal nature, becomes stunn'd and inactive; and by our continuing to look, it languishes apace towards death. The vision of *Jesus* as it delivers us from the bond of sin and satan by its first exercise; so by our persevering in it, it preserves us from all defilement.

Many indeed have believed that holiness or virtue is the purchase of human labour, the acquirement of our own will and good purposes; but

---

N O T E S.

" alter ille usus decurrerit—Ea est hujus verbi in
" sacris ratio, ut primitiva ejus significatio, cujus
" genuinam virtutem & vim perveftigamus, ne unico
" quidem in loco compareat; cum alter ille tran-
" sumptus & a prima stirpe deflexus usus, loca ter-
" centa. & quadraginta admodum obtineat, ex quo
" efficitur, a nemine unquam veram ejus indolem
" vel indagari vel saltem finiri & certa ratione ac via
" constabiliri posse, nisi uberiori abundet ope & luce,
" atq; ea est quam una sola sacri textus lectio &
" meditatio suppeditare valet.

" Quis enim, ut re ipsa, verborum velitatione
" omissa, in aciem prodeam, unquam assequi se po-
" tuisse, sibi sumere ausit, verbi nostri naturam sitam
" antiquitus fuisse, *in amplitudine, laxitate, & spacio*;
" primamq; radicis ישע ut conjugationem, sic signi-
" ficationem dixisse, *amplus spatiosus & late patens*
" *fuit*, unde cum הרשיע facili & perquam proclivi
" via, gradus factus sit in servare & salutem ferre
" (i. e. *nostro sensu, restituere, expedire, libertate do-*
" *nare, &c.*) quod est, *aliquem qui angustiis pressus*
" *erat & circumseptus, in spatium & libertatem, cum*

but that this is a mistake both scripture and constant experience will convince the awakened heart.

That righteousness which will exceed the righteousness of the Scribes and Pharisees, is altogether an imparted grace, the effects singly of our correspondence and communion with *Christ*; and is therefore *ours* only so long as our intercourse with our GOD is continued; for its influences are easily lost, altho' on our humiliation, they as soon return again.

While

NOTES.

" *amplitudine & abundantia* conjunctam, *traducere*.—
" Hæc vera hebrææ radicis vis est hæc dignitas,
" hæc majestas, ad quam amplificandam si vel unum
" faciam verbum, putidus sim : quemadmodum
" nec animus est, in locum communem excurrere,
" qui omnibus hic patet, ad divinam nominis *Jesu*
" gravitatem ex fonte hoc deducendam, atq; supra
" astra evehendam. Illud tamen monuisse, fortasse
" non plane de nihilo fuerit, frequentari a spiritu
" sancto oppositionem inter צרה *angustiam* & ישע *five*
" ישׁעה quod proinde *laxitatem & amplitudinem* proprie, dein *omnis felicitatis omniumq; copiarum magnam*
" *quandam abundantiam* sonare nemo est qui ultra dubitare possit.—Quàm vibrare,—quàm fortiter intorquere esset, has consimilesq; phrases? מכל צרותיו
" הושׁיעי *ex omnibus ejus angustiis* הושׁיעי *ad spatium*,
" *lucem, liberum spiritum eum revocavit, &, in uberrima*
" *omnium rerum copia, in amplissimo beatitudinis gradu*
" *collocavit.* Ps. xxxiv. 7.—xliv. 8. הושׁעתנו מצרינו &
" *Jer*. xiv. 8. מושׁיעו בעת צרה quorum locorum radii
" ut neminem prætervolare possunt, ita non est quod

While we breath in his spirit, while we live in him as a branch liveth in its vine, and so partakes of its substance and virtue; so long only are we holy, and able to produce fruit answerable in nature and excellence with the vine whose we are: but immediately when our correspondence and connection with our LORD fails us, our power of virtue likewise at once ceases with it.

And that this doctrine may not be blasted with the stale unmeaning reproach of new, chimerical, enthusiastic, let it be considered that this again is as old as *Abraham* the father of believers, to whom Jehovah himself prescribes it as the true mean of god-

---

NOTES.

" pluribus notionem a me positam adurgeam — ex
" Arabum lingua — hic primum vidi ישע sua in ori-
" gine dicere, *spatiosus, & late patens fuit,* & actionem
" verbi ישע esse *contrarium angustiæ*: & in pihel sive
" 2da conjugatione dagessata, ישע *contrarium esse pre-*
" *mendi & arctandi,* ut docet Gjeuhari æterni nominis
" lexicographus quum ait, " dicis in secunda ישעת
" spacium & amplitudem feci, & in octava אתשע
" spatiosus factus est, similiter in decima, factus est
" amplus: & in quinta, inconcessibus הישיע spatium
" & locum habuere: & vir ושאע qui amplo incedit
" passu; de quo etiam in prima dicitur ושע plenum
" gradum fecit."

" Hoc de prima radicis indole nemini dubium re-
" linquunt; inde immensum sibi sumit campum, in
" quo decurrat, & linguam permittat. Præsertim
" sedem fixit in *beatissima rerum omnium copia, inq; eo*
" *fortunarum statu, qui omnibus undiq; bonis tam corpo-*
" *ris quam animi circumfluit.*"

LETTER XXIII. [433] SECT. II.

godliness. *Gen.* i. 17. *And Jehovah appeared unto Abraham and said* (לפני ׳התהלך ׳שדי ׳אל ׳אני) (׳היהוהים) (*i. e.* והיה תמים) *¹I am ²God ³Almighty, ⁴cause thyself to walk ⁵in my presence ⁶and thou shalt be upright* (or innocent, simple, without guilt or wickedness.)

He who lives in this vision may expect indeed to be the hated spectacle of evil men and evil spirits; and therefore hated of the former, because the latter dare not come near him; as the *Israelites* could not behold the face of *Moses* for the glory of his countenance.

Because the wicked one cannot without harm touch the Christian himself, he sets his emissaries at work upon him; satan can both see and feel the brightness of the believers light, tho' man cannot: therefore says this evil spirit to the sons of *Sceva* the *Jew* (*Acts* xix. 15.) *Jesus I know and Paul I know, but who are ye* that presume in your own strength to oppose my kingdom? but to suffer for *Christ* is the Christian's glory and not his discouragement.

So then christianity is faith, and faith is vision, and vision is happiness, and happiness is love and holiness.

The evidences of this important truth to the observant scripture-reader will be continually presenting themselves. What an unintelligible passage is that in the *Psalms*, without light thrown upon it by this conception of divine vision, *viz.* (*Ps.* civ. 4.) *who maketh his angels spirits, and his ministers a flaming fire.*

But when we are taught that *Jesus* (ζωοποιει) *quickeneth all things*, that he (1 *Cor.* xv. 45) *the last Adam is made a quickening spirit*; and that (2 *Cor.* iii. 18) the christian *beholding as in a glass, with face unveiled, the glory of Jehovah Christ, is changed into the same image from glory to glory*: I say reading this we can easily conceive that angels like men become quickened spirits by beholding the face of *Jesus*; and that *those who minister before him* are rendered (אש להט) *a flagrant flame*[s] (even like himself, as described in *Rev.* i. 14, and elsewhere) by being perpetually familiar with his glory.

It was also this vision, tho' in a less seraphick, that is, in a faith-degree of it, which gave St. *Stephen*, the first martyr, all that wisdom and spirit by which he spake; and which the *Jews* were not able to resist. It was this vision that made his face to shine before the grand sanhedrim as if it had been the face of an angel: and this also made him to pray with his last breath, LORD *lay not this sin to their charge*.

Nor

NOTES.

[s] Some by transposing the terms of this passage render it as follows: "Who maketh the winds his an-"gels, and fire his ministers." But that this construction is false appears from *Heb.* i. 7. where the apostle quoting this very verse, assures us, that it is spoken of the angels; and consequently not of the winds or fire. Και προς μεν τας αγγελυς λεγει; ὁ ποιων τας αγγιλυς αυτυ πνευματα, ᾗ τυς λειτυργυς αυτυ πυρὸς φλογα.

LETTER XXIII. SECT. II.

Nor is it in its operation less powerful now. The sweetest offers of sin lose their inchantment; the most importunate cravings of appetite their energy; the sudden efforts of innate corruption their success; and the trifling subtleties of the learned their authority, before the prevailing ascendency of an eye attentive to his GOD; his GOD becomes a plentitude of pardoning love.

Christianity consists not in a set of pious rules instructing us to deal scientifically with corrupted nature, or to escape the snares of satan, and pollutions of this world, by a slight and artifice learnt in devout books: but it consists in a power and life, which, being derived from *Jesus* and having him for its parent, supersedes the ill propensities of the fallen soul with a prevailing victorious efficacy. Therefore, says St. *Paul (Rom.* 14. 17.) *the kingdom of God is not meat and drink, but righteousness, and peace, and joy in the Holy Ghost;* importing hereby that the christian righteousness results spontaneously from a divine knowledge of *Jesus Christ* filling the heart with joy and peace in believing: and that the same spirit which is joy in the heart, is at the same time a power of righteousness in the will. And thus we clearly understand the apostle's words (*Rom.* viii. 2.) *The law of the living spirit in Jesus Christ hath made me free from the law of sin and death:* that so, (Rom. vi. 22.) *being made free from sin, and become the servants of* GOD, *we have our fruit unto holiness and the end æonian life.*

I well know the usual objections advanced against this great truth; and to obviate them I grant that not every elevating sally of a self-excited hope is from a genuine love of GOD in the soul, or that it bespeaks a true victorious faith there. We grant that the force of believing is contained, not in every fond weening of a presumptuous mind, but, in a confidence founded upon sure grounds, and confirmed by as sure an experience.

We allow also that faith is of a progressive augmenting efficacy, that it encreases from degree to degree, from strength to strength, is nurtured by grace upon grace; and has an inexhaustible abundance and fountain of good to feed upon, even that **righteousness of GOD for us, which** (*Rom.* i. 17.) *is revealed from faith to faith.*

Yea angelick ages and capacities are too short and too weak to exhaust the wisdom and riches of this righteousness; much less is the human life equal to its mysterious energies. Like a vegetive seed it may be improved, every hour of it, to the effecting our nearer conversion to GOD, and a more intimate closing with him in dependence, resignation, and fœderal attachments.

Says the Apostle (1 *John* iv. 18.) *There is no fear in love, but perfect love casteth out fear, because fear has torment; he that feareth is not made perfect in love.* But so to know the heart of *Jesus* as to be void of all fear, is not the lot of those who slightly know him.

Fear notwithstanding its repugnancy to, is usually the first motive of our approaches towards GOD; for we usually fly to our restoring LORD in terrors, and begin the work of our restitution with trembling

And

LETTER XXIII. [437] SECT. II.

And even after the windows of heaven have been opened upon us; and we perceive ourselves adopted the sons of GOD, and heirs of his glory; our fears are still too apt to continue the servile motives, the feeble pillars of our infant obedience: and the sensibility of our personal vileness, and guilt, and worldliness, and dryness, and want of all things; instead of bringing us home to him who can content and relieve us; too often confuses the powers of our souls; indeed sometimes imbitters it with relishes even of dispair itself; repelling and witholding many, for years together, from the arms of his security: so unnatural is it to man to believe!

However the issue of this wavering is mostly good, because, GOD in his faithfulness leaves not the warmed heart without applying his shapening hand to it; by repeating again and again the peaceful testimonies of his love, and so reconciling it more and more to himself; till by a second and a third, and many fresh manifestations and assurances, we are at last convinced that the sense of our own vileness is our best qualification; that a weariness of our own righteousness, and of the performances of an evil nature, are the highest evidences of our LORD's drawings; and that sinners self-condemned are the prepared subjects of his triumph.

Says the Apostle *(Rom.* v. 3.) *Tribulation worketh patience, and patience experience, and experience hope, and hope maketh* not *ashamed.* That hope therefore which gives us a firmness in our christian calling, and hardens our face like a flint against

gainst every soothing and afflicting enemy; springs from a steady experience of, and a mature acquaintance with our God; such as a well cultivated correspondence, and frequent intercourses can give; establishing the reposed soul in the knowledge of him as our (1 *Cor.* i. 30.) *righteousness, sanctification and redemption*,[h] as our all absolutely and independantly of all besides him.

As the plant unwatered drops and withers, so will the strong faith unexercised become weak and languishing. On the other hand the feeblest drawings of grace duly cultivated, and kept in exercise, will soon become, of a grain of mustard-seed, a flourishing tree, which all the violences of the elements cannot injure.

It is the exercise of the body which makes it robust and athletic; it is the exercise of the mind that gives its faculties a vigour and penetration; and the like effect will attend the exercise of our christian belief. Wherefore St. *Peter* advises that *by crowding every effort* (2 Peter i. 5. σπουδὴν πᾶσαν παρεισενεγκαντες) we *add to our faith courage, and to courage prudence, and to prudence temperance*, &c.

abound-

NOTES.

[h] The Christian man (existing in *Christ* as the branch in the vine into which it is ingrafted) partakes of the fulness, and thereby of all the virtue which belongs to our Lord, as says St. *Paul*, speaking of himself (*Phil.* iii. 9.) *For him I have suffered the loss of all things, and do account them but dung that I may gain* Christ *and be found in him, not having my own righteousness which is of the law, but that which is thro' faith in* Christ,

abounding in the knowledge of our LORD Jesus Christ.

The power of believing is in the least degree of it, a true talent, a gift of GOD, an invaluable depositum; which we may not bury in a napkin, but improve by every means that offers: and in our studious improvement of it the daylight will break gradually upon us; we shall thrive in the knowledge of his love; we shall see ourselves as his *pleasant children*; we shall live secure in his care and wise provisions for us; we shall begin to reduce our desires to him alone; to be his without reserve; to want nothing which he does not give us; to deposite all we have and all we are into his hands as our benevolent father; and firmly to fix our feet upon his word, as on a rock of stedfastness, losing our fears and sin and guilt, even in proportion as we lose also our unbelief.

Then shall we " behold (as says the excellent *Justin*, whom we have so often quoted) " tho' " ourselves are on earth, GOD in the heavens ruling

---

NOTES.

the righteousness which is from GOD *by faith.* So (*Rom.* xi. 16.) for the Christian is reputed as (*Col.* ii. 20.) *dead with Christ*, and (*Gal.* ii. 20. *Rom.* vi. 6) *crucified with Christ*, because (*Gal.* iii. 27.) they who are *baptized into Christ, have put on Christ*, which also is the foundation of that blessing (*Rom.* iv. 7.) *Blessed is the man whose iniquities are forgiven, and whose sins are covered; blessed is the man to whom the* LORD *will not impute sin.* Rom. vi. 8. *John* xvii. 19. *Jer.* xxiii. 5, 6.

" ruling here as supreme magistrate; then shall
" we begin to speak the mysteries of GOD; then
" shall we love and admire those who suffer
" because they will not deny GOD; then shall
" we condemn the cheat and mistake of the
" world; when we have learnt indeed to live as
" denizons with saints of heaven:"

Τοτε θεαση τυγχανων επι της γης οτι Θεος εν ουρανοις πολιτευεται, τοῖς μυστηρια Θεȣ λαλειν αρξη, τοῖς τους κολαζομενους, επι τω μη θελειν αρνησασθαι Θεον, ϰ᾽ αγαπησεις ϰ᾽ θαυμασεις, τότε της απατης τȣ κοσμȣ ϰ᾽ της πλανης καταγνωση; οταν τω αληθως εν ουρανω ζην επιγνωση.

To believe is to live in light, and light inflames the heart with a love, and reliance, and gratitude, which nothing can withstand. It is by walking with GOD in light, and with our eyes open, that we discover his faithfulness manifested in all dispensations; that we adore and rest upon him with confidence in all distresses; that we bless his bounty and goodness in all difficulties; that we find him ready and near us in all extremities, and perplexities; and read his mercies in the book of occurrences thro' all the emergencies of life, to the extinguishing of every terror, to the suppressing of every distrust; and to the quickening and prosperity of the divine life and thankfulness in our souls.

Regarding then the christian life as a life of knowledge, and Jehovah GOD, as the object of it; let us begin to improve ourselves in this our knowlegde of Jehovah GOD, by exercising the eye of our inward man upon him continually: let us

observe

observe and trace him in his severity, in his indulgence, in his justice, in his humility, in his reproofs, in his fidelity, and in the inviolableness of his love; so shall we learn to live, rejoice and glory in his good pleasure only.

We shall learn to justify *his severity* in experience of the sweets accompanying it: to be modest with *his indulgencies* in a filial resigned enjoyment of them: to bless *his justice* in confidence that his heart and hands can design and produce good only: to admire *his humility* in the abasing consciousness of our own presumption: to loath ourselves under *his reproofs* in the sense of a cordial softening hallowing shame: to adore *his faithfulness* in the pleasing emotions and mixture of grief and joy and gratitude; and to draw our motives of obedience from the indefeasibleness of our master's love.

Let us cultivate a continual intercourse of peace with him, and refuse to live but in an uninterrupted sense of his friendship and absolution. And when upon any occasion our peace with him is weakened, let prayer be ever our resource as soon as may be: *Christ* alone can help us here; *there is no other name under heaven given among men whereby we can be restored.*

Let us consider him as always opening the arms of his mercy towards us; as always the same gracious father ready to receive his returning prodigal.

Our greatest injury from sin is, that it withdraws our heart from our redeemer, and separates between him and us. But as his voice always is, *My son give me thine heart,* let us not in unbelief protract our darkness, but rather incessantly plead with him before his throne of grace, till we have found our pardon returning upon our hearts afresh, and till our sense of acceptance is again our consolation.

This is a devotion I must again call old, for it is old as the days of *Solomon,* who advises *(Prov.* iv. 23.) *Keep thy heart with all diligence, for out of it are the issues of life:* and he who pursues it will find it so; for by an intercourse thus persisted in he will thrive apace; and will soon be brought home to that rest in GOD, which is the true end of Christianity.

The true end of Christianity, we learn in our LORD's discourse with his disciples *(John* xiv.) Judas *saith* (v. 22.) *Lord, how is it that thou wilt manifest thyself unto us, and not unto the world?* (v. 23) *Jesus answered, If any man will love me he will keep my words, and my father will love him, and we will come unto him, and make our abode with him.* (v. 20.) *At that day ye shall know that I am in my father, and you in me, and I in you.* (v. 16, 17.) *I will pray the father and he will give you another comforter, that he may abide with you forever, even the spirit of truth, whom the world cannot receive because it seeth him not, neither knoweth him, but ye know him, for ye dwelleth* WITH *you and shall be* IN *you.*

When the LORD has so manifested himself to a soul as to be no longer only *with him,* but *in him;* that soul will converse with his GOD in a ready and close correspondence, in an unveiled fellow-

fellowship and communion not 'till then known; he will live in his presence, so as to be *(Rom.* xv. 13.) *filled with all joy and peace in believing.*

Being *(Eph.* ii. 21.) *an holy temple in the* Lord, (2 *Cor.* vi. 16.) **God will** *dwell in him and walk in him*; and *(Rom.* v. 5.) *will shed abroad his love in his heart by the Holy Ghost.* For these **are the bles**-sings of which we read as distinguishing **the first** churches of GOD from **other** men. Says *Peter* **of them** (1 *Pet.* i. 8.) *whom having not seen the love, in whom tho' now ye see him* **not,** *yet believing ye rejoice with joy unspeakable and full of glory.*

Happy is the man to whom the LORD is *a God at hand, and not a God afar off:* but when *(Heb.* vi. 4.) *we shall have tasted the heavenly* **gift,** *and have been made* **partakers** *of the Holy Ghost,* **and have** *tasted the good word of God,* **and the powers of** *the æon to come,* when (1 *Cor.* xv. 22) *we are made alive in Christ*; and *(Phil.* iii. 10) *experience the power of his resurrection*; when *(Gal.* iv. 19) *Christ* (μορφωθη) *is fashioned in us*; when *(Eph.* iii. 17) *Christ dwelleth in our hearts by faith*; when *(Col.* i. 27) *Christ is in us the hope of* **glory:** then shall we *taste* indeed that *the Lord is gracious*; and experience what it means to love GOD; that high, sacred privilege and prerogative of saints, which is singly **all** what an human soul can need, her strength, **her** transformation, **her** glory, her holiness, her righteousness. See *Mat.* xxii. 36—40.

Then will the divine stranger, the spirit of our GOD, now become our comforter, (1 *Cor.* ii. 10, 12) *reveal to us the things that are freely given to us of God* (2 *Cor.* i. 5.) with *abundant consolations,*
such

such as *no one knoweth but he that receiveth them.* Pf. xciv. 19. תנחומים) *confolations* that will *delight the foul* with things which (1 *Cor.* ii. 9) *eye hath not seen, nor ear heard, neither have they entered into the heart of man* to conceive.

This heavenly gueft is called by St. *Paul* (2 *Cor.* iv. 7.) *a treafure in earthen veffels*; and it proves to be fo, in that it not only abolifhes the power of fin in us, and clears our confciences of (*Rom.* viii. 1) *all condemnation*; and *(Eph.* i. 13) *feals us with the holy fpirit of promife, the earneft of our inheritance:* but is moreover within us (1 *John* ii. 20*) an unction from the holy one* (1 *Cor.* ii. 19.) *difclofing to us the deep things of* GOD (*John* xvi. 13.) *guiding us into all truth*; enlarging our hearts with a capacity of (1 *Cor.* ii. 15.) *difcerning all things* (that is all perfons) *tho' ourfelves be difcerned of none*; and blefling us with comforts which neither poffeffion will rifle or abate, nor familiarity render cheap or contemptible.

But St. *Peter* calls it a *marvellous light*; becaufe the difference between feeing the fame divine truths by the common light of the underftanding, and by the evidences given by the Holy Ghoft; is as the difference between the firft glimmerings of the morning dawn, and the bright fhining and glory of the fun at noon day.

However you will at leaft acknowlege, that he who has (*Rom.* viii. 9) *the fpirit of* GOD *dwelling in him*, has therewith (1 *Cor.* ii. 16.) *the mind of Chrift*; and that having the mind of *Chrift* (1 *John* ii. 27.) *he needeth not that any man teach him*; but is (1 *Thef.* iv. 9. Θεοδίδακλ۞ 1 *John* ii. 27.) *taught*

LETTER XXIII. [445] SECT. II.

of GOD (περι παντων) *concerning all things* which the occasions and occurrences of life shall make requisite for him to know: and being assured of this, you have at once an expedient pointed out to you, whereby you may escape the being deceived, either by the well-meaning mistakes of the *religionist*; or the artificial sanctity of the *wolves and robbers*; or the warm remonstrances of the learned *zealot*.

THE
QUOTATIONS
IN THE NOTES
Translated into ENGLISH.

Page 45.—*Hic locus est partes &c.*

'TIS here, in different paths, the way divides:
    The right to *Pluto's* golden palace guides:
The left to that unhappy region tends,
Which to the depth of *Tartarus* descends;
The seat of night profound, and punish'd fiends.

Dryden's Virgil.

N. B. We have all along used in the Greek and other quotations, the same stops (or points) which are used in the Latin, English, and all our modern languages; by which means the eye may at once distinguish the paragraphs in the translation answering to those in the original.

Page 46.—Καὶ γὰρ καθ' &c.

Two are the paths to *Hades*; one the juſt
To life, the other to perdition takes
The wicked.—In the end however all
That are deſtroy'd ſhall be reſtor'd again.

Page 46.—*Ante adventum Chriſti &c.*

Before the coming of *Chriſt* (when he had not yet open'd the gate of paradiſe, neither had his blood extinguiſhed that flaming ſword and brandiſhing of the cherubim that kept it) all in like manner were conducted down into hades, and hence *Jacob* ſays that he likewiſe ſhould deſcend into hades; and *Job* complains that in hades both the godly and ungodly were detain'd; and the goſpel teſtifies, that in hades is a great interpoſing gulph; and that *Abraham* was there with *Lazarus*; and that the rich man was there in a ſtate of puniſhment.

Page 48.—*Si quis tamen &c.*

If one might venture to make a modeſt conjecture, one would choſe to ſuppoſe this (abyſs) as alſo the regions of bleſſed ſpirits, to be ſituated without the limits of this our viſible world, rather than, as ſome do, in the center of the earth. Indeed the word *abyſs* imports a kind of vaſtneſs; and the expreſſion *outer darkneſs* ſeems uſed purpoſely to imply a ſituation without the limits of the orb which is deſtined for our uſe. Nor perhaps is that paſſage in St. *John* unfitly referred to on this occaſion, viz. (*John* xii. 31.) *The prince of this world ſhall be caſt out.*

Page 54.—*Ut autem Hebraiſmos &c.*

But the reaſon why they made uſe of hebraiſms, was, not only becauſe they were *Hebrews* (for the ſpirit of God could have amended any thing in them that he had diſapproved of) but becauſe ſeeing they treated of things delivered in hebrew, it was necessary to retain many expressions, least they should seem to propound any new doctrine. And indeed I do not wonder that so many hebraisms were preserved by them, seeing many of these are of that nature as not to be so happily expressible in any other language, nay sometimes as not to be express'd at all: so that if they had not retain'd these forms, they must have sometimes invented new words and new phrases which no one could have understood. Lastly, to say no more, seeing God has chosen these only, by which he would have the several things written which are necessary for us, we ought also to be satisfied that the same God had so limited their language that not a word might rashly drop from them, nay that they might speak all so plainly, properly, and to the purpose, that nothing could be express'd concerning these things, more fully and better by any one.

Page 61.—*Solus enim (Christus) fuit &c.*
For *Christ* alone was at liberty among **the dead**, and being so, having subdued him who has the empire of death, he led captive the captives that were detained in death; and raised up not only himself from among the dead, but those likewise who were in the custody of death, and quickened them together, and caused them to sit together in the celestial habitations.

Ascending up on high, he lead them captive, not only bringing forth their souls, but also awakening their bodies, as the gospel testifies; *for many dead bodies of the saints were awakened, and appeared unto many, and entered Jerusalem the holy city of the living God.*

Page 61.—*Ea propter Dominum &c.*
That therefore he *(Christ)* descended into the places that are beneath the earth, and preached his advent,

and

and the remission of sins to them who believe in him. But all the just, and the prophets and patriarchs believed in him; whose sins he remitted in like manner as ours. For all men have need of the glory of GOD: and are justified, whoever apply to his light, not of themselves, but by the advent of the LORD.

Page 62.—ΕΜΝΗΣΘΗ δε &c.

The LORD GOD was mindful of his deceased *Israel*, which slept in the land of graves, and went down to them, to preach his restitution to them.

Page 62.—*Quum dicit*; *excitata* &c.

When he says, many bodies of the saints who slept, arose: he denotes a perfect resurrection. The resurrection of those saints was effected, as a demonstration that the death of *Christ* was the abolishing of the death of us all, which death he endured for the restitution and life of all mortals. In very deed he exhibited his quickening power in an amazing manner, in the present condition of things, raising up the dead, and delivering all the pious souls of the deceased that were in hades. For this reason they died not again, but abide in immortality, even as *Enoch* and *Elias*, and are with them (εν τω παραδεισω, αναμενοντες) in the paradise (*viz.* of GOD) awaiting the as yet æonian energy of the resurrection of *Christ*, according to that order, by which, as says the divine apostle, *we shall all be changed:* for to that immortal and incorruptible life there has been hitherto no resurrection of any one, excepting of *Christ* alone the restorer; wherefore he is pronounced the first-begotten of the dead, and the first fruits of them that sleep.

Page 62.—Ο ΚΥΡΙΟΣ ευηγ[γ]ελισατο &c.

The LORD preached to them in hades———whose appointment was in hades, and who had devoted themselves to destruction, like men that had cast themselves

out

out of some ship into the sea; even these are they who have hearkened to the divine power and calling.

Page 62 and 63.—*INFERNUM petit &c.*
He visited in hell the woful souls
For crimes, done in their days of nature, bound,
An helpless croud, beneath the legal weight
Oppressive, fast: long had their cries implor'd
The tardy promises, a ceaseless suit.
Quick in the light of life he lifts them, rais'd
To be co-habitants with saints in rest.
'Twas his third day of Death; when to th' shades
Expectant, their embodied GOD, he came
Descending, character'd as conqueror
Supreme, and in his father's virtue fraught,
Effulgent; GOD in man imperson'd one.
Up to the heavens, sublim'd in *Christ*, arose
The wretched, with him chang'd to sons of day;
First-fruits triumphant of redeeming power,
Retinue, prize, and image, of our LORD.
This done, he sat him in his father's throne
In state divine; array'd in ornaments
Victorious; partner in his father's life;
Yet linked with us in human ties of love.
Him, LORD and CHRIST and King and GOD, his GOD
Shall send the future judge and despot of this world.

Page 63.—ΑΛΗΘΩΣ δε, κỳ ε δοκησει &c.
He verily, and not in appearance (only) was crucified and died, a spectacle to the *heavenly* and *earthly* and *subterranean* inhabitants: to the *heavenly* as are the natures unimbodied; to the *earthly* as are the *Jews* and *Romans* and such men as were present at the time of his crucifixion; to the *subterranean* as the multitude who arose together with him. For it is said, that, *the graves being opened, he raised up many bodies*

bodies of the saints that slept. He descended into hades *alone*, but he returned *with a multitude.*

Page 68.—*Esse quoq; in fatis &c.*

It stands recorded in the book of fate,
That the dire time shall come, when earth and sea,
Yea *Lucifer's* high palace in the skies
Shall burn; and the world's labour'd mass shall prove
A wreck in flames.

Tunc ardens fluvius &c.

The burning torrent shall descend from heaven,
A bickering flood; and spread it's desolation.
The earth and mighty waters of the main
With all its rivers, lakes, and seas and depths,
Shall this consume, exhale, reduce to fire.
Thine empire, *Pluto*, shall it's rage devour:
Yea all the stars of heaven, convuls'd, shall fall,
'Fus'd in one confluent flaming mass;
Their beauty, place, foundation, lost and gone.

Page 68.—Εςαι γαρ ιςαι &c.

That time of the prolapsing æons must arrive,
When golden æther shall resolve her stores
Full fraught with fire; a fierce devouring flame
Raging o'er all things, earthly and sublime,
In furious conflagration.

Page 72.—*Ævi quadratum &c.*

The square of an æon (to say nothing of its cube) is an æon of æons, of $4938271\frac{22}{37}$ years reaching far beyond the age of the world: the double of the square, æons (two) of æons, of $9876543\frac{17}{12}$ years This I have therefore noted only because a figur'd number appears more plainly. In the age of ages the skip is notable from 9 to 8, to 7, and from 4 to 3,

to

to 2, to 1. And the fraction (into decimals) being resolved in the same proportion the numerator supplies 6, 5. In the ages of the ages the gradations are remarkable from 9 to 3, and so on in the fraction, by resolving it in the same proportion, the numerator supplies 2, 1, &c. But this will appear more clearly in the numbers extended as follows:

$$\begin{array}{r}\frac{2}{3}\\3\\40\\500\\6000\\70000\\800000\\9000000\end{array}$$

In the one the fraction $\frac{49}{3}$ is nearly equal to $\frac{1}{6} + \frac{1}{100}$ &c. In the other the fraction $\frac{1}{3}$ is nearly equal to $\frac{1}{3} + \frac{1}{100}$ &c. In each fraction the numerators 6, 5, and 2, 1, fill the series from 1 to 9 (thus 4938271.605 and 9876543.21.)

But if you proceed, to what an immense sum will 3, 4, 100, 1000, &c. æons of æons amount? O the depth! and yet all this is not so much as the shallows of the sea of absolute eternity denoted by the emphatical æons of æons. The scriptures sometimes hint by small strictures, and as it were *en passant*, matters of immense moment. He that can receive this, let him.

They who speak of the restitution after this life, should beware not to imagine that this matter is exhausted in a millenary jubilee (or 50,000 or 49,000 years); far wider is the measure of the æons. This we have here touched upon, not to provoke curiosity, but to dilate the mind; let us receive it as candidates of eternity. We are in time.

Page 76.

Εις τας αιωνας	To the ages.
εις αιωνα αιωνος	to the age of the ages (or to the æonian age)
εις αιωνα αιωνων	to the age of the ages.
εως της συντελειας τȣ αιωνος	to the common boundary of the emphatical æon.
εις ους τα τελη των αιωνων κατηυτησεν	in whom the ends of the ages are met.
εις τας αιωνας των αιωνων	to the ages of the ages.
εις πασας τας γινιας τȣ αιωνος των αιωνων.	to all the generations of the age (emphatical) of the ages.

עלמה	The æon. *Heb.*
עלמא	the æon. *Syr.*
לעלמין	the ages.
לעלמיא ועד	to the ages and beyond
עד עולמי ועד	even ages and beyond.

Page 84.—*Non enim (ut quidem putant) natura &c.*

For the nature of GOD is not (as some imagine) invisible to some, and visible to others; for the apostle says not *that the appearance of God is invisible to men, or invisible to sinners*; but most constantly pronounces of the nature of GOD, saying, *the appearance of the invisible God.* Yea and St. *John* says in his gospel, *no one has seen God at any time,* plainly declaring to all that are capable of understanding, that there is no nature to which GOD is visible. Not as tho' he was visible in his nature but as it were escapes and transcends the sight of a frail creature; but because it is naturally impossible he should be seen.

Page 90.—ὥσπερ ὑμων οἱ διδασκαλοι &c.

As your rabbies deem, fancying that the father of all, even the ungenerated GOD, has hands, and feet, and

and fingers, and a foul, like a compound animal; and who therefore teach that the father himself appeared to *Abraham* and *Jacob*, &c.

Juſtin Mar. dial. with Trypho *the Jew.*

Page 93.—ιρεις εν μοι &c.

But you object to me; " You aſſert that GOD is not contained in place, how then ſay you that he walks in paradiſe? Hear what I reply; the GOD and father of all is incomprehenſible, **neither is he found in place;** for the place of his abode is not: yet his Logos, by whom he made all things, being his power and wiſdom, aſſuming the perſonage (in that he became *the expreſs image*) of the father and LORD of all, even he went to paradiſe in (this) the perſonage (i. e. *apparent in the expreſs image*) of GOD, and converſed with *Adam*.

Theophilus to Autolycus, 2d book.

Page 94.—Ουτε ουν Αβρααμ &c.

Neither *Abraham,* neither any other man hath ſeen the father and ineffable LORD of all univerſally, and even of *Chriſt* himſelf; but *(they have ſeen)* him *(who is)* according to his *(viz. the father's)* own council both GOD his ſon, and alſo angel for the adminiſtering his purpoſe; and whom he *(the father)* will'd alſo to become a man of the virgin; *(and)* who alſo formerly became a fire for the talking to *Moſes* at the buſh: *(This muſt be granted)* becauſe, unleſs we thus underſtand holy writ, it will follow that the father and LORD of all was not then in the heavens, when it is ſaid by *Moſes (as follows) and the Lord rained upon Sodom fire and brimſtone from the Lord out of heaven,* and again when by *David* it is thus ſaid, *take away your gates ye princes, be ye lifted up ye æonian gates, and the king of glory ſhall enter in.* Moreover, that the *Chriſt* is alſo GOD the ſon of GOD, who alſo appeared of old as a man and angel, and was ſeen in a glory of fire as in the buſh, and

Justin Martyr's dialogue with Trypho the Jew.

Page 100.—ευθεν εμωρχινοτο &c.

Hereby is worldly wisdom befool'd, the darkness of ignorance dispersed, and the tyrannical empire abolished, *(namely)* God appearing as a man, and man operating as God. But neither is the former a *seemingness* only *(since God became true man)* nor is the latter *mere human energy (since the man operating is very God)*; yea the former is a reality, and the latter is (a step of his) œconomy.¶

Page 101.—*Quod ex carne natum &c.*

That which is born of the flesh is flesh, because it is born of the flesh; and that which is born of the spirit is spirit, because God is a spirit, and it is born of God.

Page 113.—*Edocuit autem Dominus &c.*

But the Lord has taught us, that no one can know God, unless God himself teaches him, that is, without God, God cannot be known. But that the very knowledge of him is the will of the father; for they know him to whom the son shall have revealed him: and to this end the son has revealed the father, that thro' him he may be manifested to all, and may receive those that are justified by faith in him to the incorruptible state and eternal refreshment. To believe is to do his will, but he will justly shut up those that believe not, and for this reason shun the light, in the darkness which they have chosen for themselves.—

And

¶ The antient christians understood by the term œconomy the whole process of our redemption towards which God saw it expedient to assume humanity.

And therefore the judgment of God is (just **on**) *them who did not so believe on* **him** *as they had seen him.*—And that **by** the very word made visible and palpable the father might be shewn; **altho'** all did not accordingly believe **on him,** yet all have seen the father in **the son;** seeing that the father of the son is invisible, while the son of the father is visible.———As says *Irenæus,* his ineffable production **or** generation **who** has **known?** neither angels **nor** archangels, but only the father who begot and **the son** who **was** begotten.

Page 115.—ὅταν γὰρ ὡς υἱὸν *&c.*

But when *Daniel* speaks **of** him as **the son of man** receiving the æonian kingdom, does not this import **thus much?** for the expression *as* **the son of** *man,* indicates **that he** indeed appeared as and was a man; tho' certainly **not of** human feed. Also the expression *this stone was cut* **out** *without hands,* proclaims **the same** thing in a mystery; in that the saying that *he was* **cut out without hands** *(proclaims* **the** *cutting out)* to have been no human work, but *(a work)* **of** the will of the father, GOD of all who produced him. The same may appear from that passage in *Isaiah, who hath declared his generation?* which manifests that he has a generation ineffable. But **no man** *(begotten)* of man *(can be said to)* have **an ineffable generation.**

Page 246.—*Omnia* τὰ πάντα *sæpe, &c.*

We have often observed already, that the words τὰ πάντα, *all things,* universally spoken are frequently intended by St. *Paul* as restrictively relative to those things of which he speaks, in 1 *Cor.* xv. 28, and vi. 12, and viii. 1, and **in numberless other** places. Thus then in this place **when he treats of the** office of a mediator, **but the mediator is destin'd such only** to the elect; by the appellation (τῶν πάντων,) *of all,* I understand the whole body of the church itself, which afterwards is divided as it were into two parts; namely that in heaven (*viz.* the faithful who were dead before

K k k the

the coming of *Christ*) and that on earth (*viz.* those whom *Christ* shall find alive, or who have obtained his advent.)* *Beza* in *Eph.* i. 10.

Page 247.—τα παντα &c.

All things, that is the whole church, as I have already expounded in at large, *viz. Eph.* i. 10.

See *Beza* in *Col.* i. 20.

Page 247.—*Antea inter angelos &c.*

Heretofore there were factions among the angels, and they were interested for their respective people. See *Dan.* x. 13—20. xii. 1. and also *Job.* iv. 11.— *Christ* removed this, being also made king of the angels, by chosing one out of so many people to himself, to whom the angels now owe their service, *Heb.* i. 14. See examples also in *Acts* v. 9. xii. 11. xvi. 26, 27. xxiii. 44. in *Matt.* xviii. 10. and 1 *Cor.* xi. 10. where angels are treated of (Again) To the kingdom of

---

* N. B. *Beza* by this note of his confutes himself; for if, as he allows, St. *Paul* always intends by the expression (τα παντα) all things, the whole universally of (*id de quo agitur*) that concerning which he is treating; he must in the place before us intend the whole of the creation, and not the whole of the elect only; because the things created, and not the things elect are by this apostle here spoken of. The *all things* here (ver. 16) spoken of, are all things that were created in heaven and on earth, visible and invisible, whether thrones, dominions, principalities or powers; therefore the *all things* intended here as to be reconciled to GOD, must be all things in heaven and earth, visible and invisible, even all things that were by *Christ* created.

GOD is in *Christ* reconciled to all, and being so he will have that all be reconciled to himself in *Christ*; but the all hitherto reconciled to GOD are only the Christians truly so called, and the heavenly inhabitants, as we read (*Col.* i. 21. 2 *Cor.* v. 20.) *You that were enemies has he now reconciled to God*: so (1 *Pet.* iii. 22.) *angels, authorities and powers* (ὑποταγεντων αυτω) *being subordinated* (and consequently reconciled) *unto him*.

So then unchristian men and evil spirits are the future subjects of reconcilement and subordination; agreeably to what we read (*Heb.* ii. 8) *But now we see not as yet all things subordinated unto him*, their subordination then is a work to come; see also *Phil.* ii. 10, 11. *John* v. 23. *Rev.* v. 13.

of *Christ* which he gain'd over the angels, some refer that which is spoken in *Col.* i. 16. because (Κτίζω) *to create*, often signifies a new administration. Certainly as several parts of the epistle to the *Colossians* agree with this epistle, even so that passage seems to throw light upon this, and alternately to borrow light from it— Now all things are changed, the men of every kind who have obeyed the calling (*of God*) are reconciled both to GOD, and to each other.—Also the angels who were torn away and alienated from us, as being sinners and apostates, are now reconciled to us, and gathered with us into one company and body under *Christ* our head, that both being in like manner united to GOD, may obtain the blessing, *now* common to both. All the angels being displeased with the *Gentiles* on account of their idolatrous worship, are reconciled to them when converted to *Christ*, and serve them willingly for *Christ*'s sake, as a people call'd to angelic dignity.———The *Jews* hated those of other nations as being idolaters: and they themselves were hated by the *Gentiles* on account of their different forms of religion (of which we have spoken in our treatise on war and peace xv. 9) Now of both kinds those who come to *Christ*, being both friends and brethren, are together one people of GOD.‡

Page 269.—Ἐπεὶ ὀυξὸν βλεποίας &c.

Approve the eyes of thy soul seeing (*eyes*) and ears of thy heart hearing (*ears*)——for GOD is seen by them that

---

‡ *N. B. Grotius* by interpreting the expression τα παντα all things, as intending only things of all sorts, *i. e.* men and angels, *Jews* and *Gentiles*, or all that are good of these, would insinuate that *Christ* did not make all things, and accordingly he tells us roundly, that κτίζω, to create, in *Col* i. 16. may mean no more than that *Christ* put all things into (ordinationem novam, or novum quendam statum) a new order, state or administration. But I presume this exposition of the expression τα παντα, is too contrary to our text to be admitted of by any but those of the Socinian persuasion, and such as wou'd at any rate escape the force of the apostolic language.

that have power to behold him, after that they have the eyes of the foul opened. All indeed have eyes, but fome fuffufed *(eyes)* and which difcern not the light of the fun; but that the blind do not fee, is no proof that the light of the fun does not fhine. Let then the blind blame themfelves and their own eyes. In like manner thou alfo, O man, haft the eyes of thy foul fuffufed, &c..

Page 273.—*Fuit itaq; Dives &c.*

Therefore, fays *Pifcator*, the rich man then was indeed in hades, but *Lazarus* alfo was in hades, the regions of hades being divided into diftinct appartments. For both paradife and gehenna are in hades.

Page 276.—*Cogita fornacem igneam &c.*

Imagine a fiery furnace convolving, and cafting about it's flames; and in the midft of thefe the bodies of the damned toffed to and fro, afcending now, now plunging in its waves; then whirl'd to diftant parts; and this inceffantly, day and night, to ages of ages.

Page 277.—*Ejicientur &c.*

They fhall be caft into outer darknefs, where the cold fhall be intollerable, the fire unquenchable, the worm immortal, the ftench intolerable, darknefs which may be felt, the fcourges of the tormentors, the ghaftly appearances of devils, the confufion of finners, no hope of good, no defpair of evil.

Page 277.—*Hic eft*, fays *Grotius &c.*

Here, fays *Grotius*, is a metonimy of the fubject; or the containing for the contained, as heaven for its inhabitants, the earth for thofe that live in it. So in this place death is put for the dead; hades for its inhabitants.

Page 309.—*Chriftus per fanguinem &c.*

Chrift entered by his own blood into the fanctuary (not only after he had fhed his blood, and by the efficacy

efficacy of the effusion, neither with his blood resumed into his body, but by blood) therefore even this highpriest himself brought his blood separate from his body into the sanctuary. At the very time of his entrance *Christ* had his blood separate from his body, his body was bloodless; yet not inanimate but living.

Sanguinis Jesu seorsum, &c.

The blood of *Jesus* is considered apart from his body (*Heb.* xiii. 11, 12, 20.) as *Dorschæus* (a *Lutheran*) says, " 1st. Because the nature of the type
" requires this. For the blood in the old covenant
" was considered, as extravasated and poured out,
" and by this very thing it shadowed the pouring out
" and effusion of blood that was to be under the new
" covenant. 2dly, Because the nature of the divine
" covenant requires this, for it requires a shedding
" of blood (αἱματεκχυσιαν) 3dly, Because by this
" condition of the blood is exercised the act of sa-
" tisfactory obedience to GOD due for sins, &c."
So *Solomon Deylingius* (a *Lutheran*) " *Christ* being taken
" up into heaven, and sitting at the right hand of
" the father, commends our affairs to GOD, and ex-
" hibits his wounds and blood poured out to his fa-
" ther for us." Again, citing *Rappoltus* (a *Lutheran*) he says, " He offers (*i. e.* shews) his blood to his
" father as a ransom and the price of redemption for
" us, and teaches us that by it's shedding, the divine
" justice was satisfied."

Page 311.

Bengelius remarks as follows upon *Matt.* x. 15. Not to believe the gospel is worse than to act as the *Sodomites.* Col. xi. 22, 24. *That city in the day of judgment shall endure severer punishment than the land of the Sodomites has either already suffered, or will in the day of judgment.* If so slight a neglect shall be so grievously punished, what will be done to those who obstinately resist!

Page 320.—*Pro χαριτι Θεῦ quidam codices &c.*

Instead of *by the grace of God*, some copies of great antiquity have, *God excepted:* which last reading is also in some of the syriac copies, and in St. *Ambrose* in his book de *Fide ad Gratianum:* from whence it is evident that the *Nestorians* are not to be blamed as having altered this text (*for* Ambrose *flourished about the year* 370, *and the* Nestorians *after him about the year* 440) It seems to have been the opinion of those who altered this text that *Christ* died even for angels, and so for all excepting God.   *Grotius.*

Beza, a *Calvinist*, as follows; (*Græcus Scholiastes, &c.*) the greek commentator admonishes us that the *Nestorians* had formerly presumed to corrupt this passage and write *God excepted*, instead of *by the grace of God.* And yet this reading (i. e. God excepted) is found both in the syriac testament, and in St. *Ambrose* in his *de fide ad Gratianum*, lib. 2. cap. 4; and moreover in *Vigilius* against *Eutyches.*†

Cornelius à Lapide, a very learned and ingenious *Jesuit* as follows; (*Nota, pro χωρις Θευ id est*)—Note, instead of *God excepted*, both *Theodoret Theophilact* and *Œcumenius* read *by the grace of God*, and add that this passage was thus corrupted by the *Nestorians*, who from its testimony prove that in *Christ* were two personages, and that the Godhead was distinct from the manhood: but before the *Nestorians*, *Ambrose* in his book *de fide*, cap. 4, reads also the expression *God excepted*; and expounds it as follows: " *Christ* tasted " death for all excepting God, which is as much as " to say, *Christ* died for all altogether (even for an- " gels) only not for God, God I except." And *then he subjoins*, not that *Christ* REDEEMED angels, but

---

† *i. e.* The reading *God excepted* is acknowledged to be the true reading both by *Eutyches* and *Vigilius*, (viz. *Tapsensis*) who, tho' of contrary opinions, were both alike condemners of the *Nestorians*.

but because he reconciled them to men and enhanced their joy and glory in that he restored and filled again those mansions from which the Demons were fallen with men.§

Page 322.—*Hic igitur qui tot nominibus &c.*

This man therefore even *Jesus* called by so many names, advocate, propitiation, propitiatory, compassionating our infirmities, tempted as men are in all things,

---

§ *N. B.* The closing paragraph here of this Author is surely both incredible and unscriptural. The scripture tells us, That *Christ appeared to put away sin by the sacrifice of himself.* That *he was once offered to bear the sins of the many*, or multitude. That *he bare our sins in his body on the tree.* That *he was wounded for transgression, and bruised for iniquities.* That *the iniquity of us all was laid upon him;* and that *he was manifested to take away sin*.

If therefore *Christ* died for angels, he died to bear the sins of, and consequently to redeem angels; and not merely to reconcile them to man, and much less to increase their joy in seeing the mansions of the wicked spirits filled up by a substitution of wicked men redeemed in their stead. Why should wicked men be redeemed to fill up the mansions of wicked angels? At least, from what authority are we to believe that this was so?

Moreover, redemption is so inseparably connected with the death of *Jesus* as not to admit of the above distinction, see 1 *Tim.* ii. 6. *Mat.* xx. 28. *Col.* i. 14. *Tit.* ii. 14. to redeem is to buy again by paying a price for; see *Lev.* xxvii. 20.—xxv. 24. so that if *Christ* died for angels, he paid a price for them (See 1 *Pet.* i. 18.) and by this Price they became his redeemed property, the reward of his sacrifice.

All things are redeemed by *Jesus*, and therefore are all things (*John* xiii. 3. *Mat.* xi. 27) *delivered of the father into his hands;* even (1 *Cor.* xv. 27. *Heb.* ii. 8) *all things excepting God:* delivered to him in pursuance to his death, whereby he purchased them; and as (*Eph.* i. 14) *his purchased possession.* For (*Rom.* xiv 9.) *to this end Christ both died and revived, that he might be the Lord both of the dead* (i. e. the as yet unquickened) *and the living* (i. e. the really quickened, since these two terms comprehend the universe).

Ambrose's notion therefore of our Lord's dying for angels, and yet not redeeming angels is without foundation. And the only Question is, what our Lord will decree concerning his redeemed rebels, and as to this we have great reason to hope favourably, because (*Ps.* cxlv 9) *Jehovah is good to all, and his tender mercies are over all his works.*

things, yet without sin; is the great High-Priest not only for men but for all, whatever is intellectual, offering himself a victom once sacrificed. For he tasted death for all *excepting God,* or (as certain Copies have it) *by the grace of God.* (But) whether (we say) he tasted death for all GOD excepted, he died (however) not only for man, but for all intellectual beings; or whether (we say) he tasted death for all by the grace of GOD, he died (however) for all excepting GOD; because it was by the grace of GOD that he tasted death for all. *Origin on St. John's gospel.*

Page 341.—Καθ' ὑπερβολὴν εἰς &c.

By hyperbole upon hyperbole, *i. e.* excellently excellent, says *Theophrastus,* or wonderfully, and above measure exalted,—for thus the *Hebrews* by doubling a word express a vehemence, and superlativeness; as *mad, mad, i. e.* very, very, or above measure, and extremely much; as much as to say, incomparably more. *Cornelius a Lapide.*

Page 353.—*Christus, qui in novissimis &c.*

Christ in the latter times became man among men that he might join the end to the beginning, that is man to GOD—also this privilege of seeing him he gives to them that love him—for man of himself sees not GOD. But GOD likes to be seen of those whom he wills to see him, and in the manner he so wills. And he will be seen in the kingdom of the heavens as father, the spirit preparing man into a son of GOD, and the son *(i. e.* of GOD) presenting him to the father; while the father gives him incorruptibility for the enjoyment of the eternal life; this happens to each by his seeing GOD. As they who see light are in that light, and receive of its brightness; so also they who see GOD are in GOD, and partake of his brightness. For the brightness quickens them; so then they who see GOD possess life.———To live without

without life is impossible; but life springs from the participation as its source, and to partake of GOD is to see GOD, and enjoy his bounty. Men therefore shall see GOD, and shall live by seeing him, becoming immortal, and arriving even into GOD. *Irænæus.*

Page 354.—Ουκ διὰ τὸ συγγενὲς &c.
He (*i. e.* man) seeth GOD not by virtue of his consanguinity, neither because he is an intelligent creature, but because of his probity and uprightness; yea, and because he has wherewith he apprehendeth GOD. *Justin Martyr.*

Page 374.—*Tota sensatio est in anima* &c.
All sensation is in the soul; for when we see with the eye, hear with the ear, touch with the hand; the real vision, hearing, and feeling are not in the eye, ear, or hand, but in the soul: for it is not the body but the soul which sees by the eye, hears by the ears, and feels by the hand.

Page 376.—*Anima Christi est finita* &c.
The soul of *Christ* is finite, conscious neither of all things, nor with absolute distinction——Also his body is finite, necessarily and proportionably distant from objects variously so, unless you exempt a finite body of its finiteness.——A finite is not capable of an infinite——an infinite cannot be limited by a finite.

Page 401.—*Est aliquid quo tendis* &c.
Hast thou not yet propos'd some certain end,
To which thy life, thy ev'ry act may tend?
Hast thou no mark at which to bend thy bow?
Or like a boy pursu'st th' carrion crow
With pellets, and with stones, from tree to tree:
A fruitless toil, and liv'st *extempore?*
Watch the disease in time: for when within
The dropsy rages and extends the skin,

In vain for *Hellebore* the patient cries,
And fees the Doctor; but too late is wife:
Too late, for cure, he proffers half his wealth;
Conquest and *Guibbons* cannot give him health.
Learn, wretches, learn the motions of the mind,
Why you are made, for what you were defign'd;
And the great moral end of human kind.
Study thy-felf: what rank or what degree
The wife creator has ordain'd for thee:
And all the offices of that eftate
Perform; and with thy prudence guide thy fate.
   Pray juftly, to be heard: nor more defire
Than what the decencies of life require.
Learn what thou ow'ft thy country and thy friend;
What's requifite to fpare, and what to fpend:
Learn this; and after envy not the ftore
Of the greaz'd advocate, that grinds the poor:
Fat fees from the defended *Umbrian* draws;
And only gains the wealthy client's caufe:
To whom the *Marfians* more provifion fend,
Than he and all his family can fpend.
Gammons, that give a relifh to the tafte,
And potted foul and fifh come in fo faft,
That e'er the firft is out, the fecond ftinks:
And mouldy mother gathers on the brinks.
Dryden's Perfius.

F I N I S.

ERRATA.

[*f.* for, *d.* dele, *n.* notes.]

Page.	Line.	Read.	Page.	Line.	Read.
5.	n. 2.	זה *f.* וה	107.	n. 10.	the first-begotten
	n. 4.	maid *f.* **woman**	164.	n. 25.	ܠܐܐܐ ܚܐܚܐ
	n. 5.	(העלמה whom thou hast appointed for אשה a wife to my master's son. See v. 40.)	224.	n. 2.	expletive with
			225.	n. 3.	**critical** difference
			239.	16.	to *Christ f* by *Christ*
7.	n. 4.	Succedaneum	240.	13.	bottom-principle
8.	n. 21.	(æon age)	248.	n. 5.	*tanquam*
	n. 22.	(Κοσμ☉ wor!d)		n. 5.	*alienati*
12.	7.	(or common boundary) of the æons		n. 11.	*libenter*
	11.	æons have met *f.* are come	257.	30.	Jehovah (the invisible) i. e. *d.* t●
25.	17.	to be the æonian GOD	261.	15.	οικητηριον
			269.	n. 7.	ηλιου;
26.	7.	superseded	276.	n. 11.	*jupiter*
59.	24.	stigmatized *f.* signalized	304.	n. 6.	εις το παντελες;
			308.	n. 30.	wine fat? wine press alone
62.	2.	Κατιδη	310.	n. 1.	*sanguinem*
	17.	παραδισω, αναμενοντες		n. 11.	ανατεταγμεναι
			310.	n. 10.	*separatum.*
63.	20.	καταχθονιων	333.	9.	ההוא
80.	14.	only begotten son	334.	6.	*Rev.* XX. 15. λιμνη του πυρ☉, i. e. *d. a*
	33.	only begotten son			
94.	n. 18.	γεννηθηναι			
96.	n. 5.	אתוה		n. 13.	ܠܒܒܐ i. e. *d.*;
98.	17.	increases upon			
99.	8.	*Theophilact*	435.	8.	become *f.* becomes
103.	n. 9.	bear a	456.	4.	εμιζαντο.
104.	n. 3.	*Mat.* xi. 27.			

Advertisement.

THE Author of the foregoing Work intends to publish a SYRIAC GRAMMAR, which will be prefaced with a Treatife in Defence of the Syriac Teftaments, old and new: fhewing their authenticity, antiquity, and great authority; and anfwering the Objections ufually made againft them, to the leffening that high credit and veneration among us (who rely altogether on the greek) which they fo juftly find in the Eaftern churches.

This work will be concluded with the original fyriac epiftle to the Hebrews tranflated, as is *Montanus*'s hebrew bible, with the literal latin over each word; together with a lexicon of all the fyriac words in that epiftle englifhed.

But as this work will be expenfive, the Author, before he begins to print it, will require 600 Subfcribers, who by applying to Mr. DODSLEY, or Mr. CADELL, may know the Terms on which it will be executed.

www.ingramcontent.com/pod-product-compliance
Lightning Source LLC
Chambersburg PA
CBHW022113300426
44117CB00007B/694